The health of the schoolchild

A history of the school medical service in England and Wales

BERNARD HARRIS

Open University Press
Buckingham · Philadelphia

For my parents

Open University Press
Celtic Court
22 Ballmoor
Buckingham
MK18 1XW

and
1900 Frost Road, Suite 101
Bristol, PA 19007, USA

First Published 1995

A catalogue record of this book is available from the British Library

ISBN 0 335 09995 5 (hb) 0 335 09994 7 (pb)

Library of Congress Cataloging-in-Publication Data

Harris, Bernard, 1961–
The health of the schoolchild: a history of the school medical service in England and Wales, 1908–74 / Bernard Harris.
p. cm.
Includes bibliographical references and index.
ISBN 0-335-09995-5 – ISBN 0-335-09994-7 (pbk.)
1. School health services – England – History – 20th century.
2. School health services – Wales – History – 20th century. I. Title.
II. Title: Health of the school child.
LB3409.G7H38 1995
371.7 – dc20 94-48785
CIP

Typeset by Best-set Typesetter Ltd., Hong Kong
Printed in Great Britain by St Edmundsbury Press, Bury St Edmunds, Suffolk

The health of the schoolchild

Contents

Tables

Figures

Preface

I first began to carry out research into the history of the school medical service as part of the process of writing my Ph.D. thesis. The original thesis was largely concerned with the history of school medical inspection, the assessment of children's 'nutrition', and the analysis of changes in the average value of children's heights. The present work builds on the thesis to present a more general picture of the development of both medical inspection and treatment during the first seventy-five years of the twentieth century. The book has undergone a long period of gestation, and I have incurred a large number of debts. I am particularly grateful to Roderick Floud, who supervised the thesis and first introduced me to the study of anthropometric history, and to Annabel Gregory, who wrote the computer program which enabled me to convert the original height data into centiles of the Tanner–Whitehouse distribution. I should also like to acknowledge the help and support which I have received over a number of years from the thesis examiners, Pat Thane and Charles Webster. I am particularly grateful to Pat Thane, who commissioned the book, and to my colleague Tony Rees, who read the entire manuscript and made a vast number of helpful and erudite comments.

My second set of debts is to the various individuals, institutions and organisations who have supported my research in various ways over the last eleven years. The original Ph.D. thesis was supported by the Social Science Research Council, which subsequently changed its name to the Economic and Social Research Council, and further support has been provided by the University of Bristol Research Fund and the History of Medicine Committee of the

Wellcome Trust. I should also like to acknowledge the intellectual and moral support I have received from colleagues in the Department of Economic and Social History at the University of Bristol and the Department of Sociology and Social Policy at the University of Southampton. I should also like to thank the librarians of both universities, as well as a large number of other librarians and archivists, for their help in tracking down a wide range of school medical reports and other publications.

My third set of acknowledgements is both academic and personal. I began my own research into the history of the school medical service shortly after the completion of David Hirst's Ph.D. thesis on the origins and development of the school medical service between 1870 and 1919, and a year before the commencement of John Welshman's D.Phil. thesis on the development of the school medical service between 1907 and 1939. I should like to thank both these scholars for allowing me to read their work and for helping me to understand the history of the school medical service in these periods. My greatest debts are, however, more personal. I am particularly grateful to my parents, who have been a constant source of help and encouragement over a period which extends well beyond that covered by the writing of this book. I am deeply indebted to my wife, who has borne the frustrations and obsessions of academic life for more than a decade, and who may or may not be looking forward to seeing more of me now that this book is completed. I also owe an indefinable debt to our son, whose own schooldays have yet to begin.

one

Introduction

In recent years, historians have begun to pay a growing amount of attention to the history of public health provision in England and Wales in the twentieth century. In addition to such general studies as Jane Lewis's *What price community medicine?* (1986) and Helen Jones's *Health and society in twentieth-century Britain* (1994), there have been a number of more specialised studies of the maternity and child welfare service (Lewis 1980; Dwork 1987) and the tuberculosis service (Bryder 1987; Smith 1988). The history of public health provision has also been discussed, albeit more briefly, by historians of the National Health Service after 1948 (see, for example, Webster 1988: 5–9; Ham 1992: 6–9). However, although a number of recent Ph.D. theses have focused on different aspects of the school medical service (Hirst 1983; Welshman 1988; Harris 1989), there has been no published full-length account of this aspect of public health provision since 1959 (Leff and Leff 1959). This book is first and foremost an attempt to fill this gap, and, in addition, to bring the history of the school medical service up to the point at which it surrendered its 'independent' status in 1974 (Henderson 1975: 1).

The book is also intended to make a more general contribution to the history of British social policy. Taken together with the introduction of the school meals service in 1906, the establishment of the school medical service in August 1907 was one of the first examples of the Liberal welfare reforms of 1906–11, and it has often been described as a major step towards the creation of the welfare state (Gilbert 1966: 102; Hirst 1983: 488–9). This book examines the different factors which lay behind the establishment of the school medical service, including the campaign for national efficiency and the alarm over 'physical deterioration', as well as the economic and administrative constraints which inhibited its subsequent development. It also examines the debates surrounding the practice of routine medical inspection, and uses some of the statistics generated by the school medical service to discuss the history of child health in Britain during the first seventy-five years of the twentieth century. Finally, it examines the role played by the school medical service in the creation of the National Health Service, and assesses the impact of the new service on the development of school medical provision after 1945.

The book is also designed to contribute to the growing sub-discipline of the social history of medicine. In their seminal essay, 'Towards a social history of medicine', John Woodward and David Richards highlighted a number of issues which were central to the social history of medicine, including the history of medicine in society, and the impact of economic and social factors on health and disease (Woodward and Richards 1977; Pelling 1983; Webster 1983a). This study addresses both of these issues by examining the role played by economic and social factors in the development of the school medical service, and the impact of war, poverty and unemployment on the health of the schoolchild. Woodward and Richards also drew attention to a third area which has attracted increasing attention in recent years, namely the history of the patient (Porter 1985a; 1985b). It is one of the regrettable limitations of this study that it is able to offer very few insights into the way in which both parents and children responded to the invasion of the school medical service into their lives (see Hirst 1983: 290–93, 441–2).[1]

The school medical service was formally established in England and Wales by the Education (Administrative Provisions) Act of 1907, and came into being on 1 January 1908. The Act gave local education authorities the duty 'to provide for the medical inspection of children immediately before or at the time of or as soon as possible after their admission to a public elementary school, and on such other occasions as the Board of Education direct', and the power 'to make such arrangements as may be sanctioned by the Board of Education for attending to the health and physical condition of the children educated in public elementary schools' (7 Edw. VII Ch. 43, section 13 (1) (b)). The Fisher Education Act of 1918 gave local authorities the duty to make arrangements for the medical inspection of children in elementary and secondary schools, and the power to attend to the health and physical condition of children in secondary schools. It also converted the power to attend to the health and physical condition of children in elementary schools into a duty (8 & 9 Geo. V Ch. 39, sections 2 and 18).[2] The Butler Education Act of 1944 gave local authorities the duty to make arrangements for the medical inspection and treatment of children attending both primary and secondary schools, and the Handicapped Pupils and School Health Service Regulations of 1945 caused the school medical service to be renamed the school health service (7 & 8 Geo. VI Ch. 31, section 48; Ministry of Education 1945b: para. 42). The National Health Service Reorganisation Act of 1973 transferred the statutory responsibility for providing school health services from the Department of Education and Science to the Department of Health and Social Security, and the school health service became part of the National Health Service on 1 April 1974 (1973 Ch. 32, section 3; Henderson 1975: 1).

The establishment of the school medical service marked an important step forward in the history of public health provision for at least three reasons. In the first place, the school medical service represented an important departure from the traditional pattern of public health work. During the nineteenth century, the public health service had concentrated almost entirely on the improvement of the environment and the control of infectious diseases, and this meant that the school medical service was the first branch of the public health service to be directly concerned with the individual (Frazer 1950: 257). It also marked a radical redefinition of the role of preventive medicine, and represented a significant stage in the gradual erosion of the boundaries between preventive and curative medicine (Lewis 1986: 8–10). In 1913 one anonymous school medical officer wrote:

> The public health service is still mainly, if not exclusively, a defensive organisation content, as it were, to remain entrenched against the onslaughts of periodic epidemics. But the school medical service is militant. It carries the battle into the camp of the enemy and attacks disease among its hereditary stronghold in the camp of the young (One of them 1913: 249–50).

The establishment of the school medical service also represented an important stage in the development of the government's statistical services (Szreter 1991). During the nineteenth century the government had compiled an enormous mass of mortality data, but it possessed very little direct information about the health of those who were living (Oddy 1982: 121). In 1904 the Interdepartmental Committee on Physical Deterioration urged the government to establish 'a permanent anthropometric survey', and said that 'in the first instance, this survey should have for its object the periodic taking of measurements of children and young persons in schools and factories' (PP 1904 Cd. 2175 xxxii: 84). The government rejected the Committee's proposal on grounds of cost, but the desire to obtain information about child health played a powerful role in the decision to establish the school medical service (PRO ED24/590, W. Anson, [Notes on a meeting on Wednesday, 7 December, 1904]: 1). In 1939 Sir George Newman recalled that:

> What the English public, as well as the Government of 1906, really wanted to know were the facts about these children; and when they had obtained the facts they were in the mood to deal with them as competent official committees had advised. This humanistic curiosity was steadily growing in the nineteenth and twentieth centuries, and the emergence of the school medical service was one of its fruits (Newman 1939: 194).

Finally, the establishment of the school medical service marked a radical redefinition of the role of education authorities and an important stage in the development of state welfare provision. In 1911 the Education Officer of the London County Council remarked that

> the State has now come to see that it is not enough to impart knowledge, but that it must also see that the child is capable of assimilating that knowledge, and that his environment is not such that it will entirely undo the effect of the school training (Webb and Webb 1929: 603).

When the school medical service was set up, it soon became apparent that an enormous number of children were suffering from 'defects' which interfered with their education and impeded their development, and this forced many local authorities to provide their own medical treatment schemes. By the end of the 1930s, virtually every local education authority provided treatment for minor ailments, dental defects and defective vision, 292 authorities provided treatment for enlarged tonsils and adenoids, 270 provided orthopaedic services, 200 provided X-ray treatment for ringworm, and 118 used artificial light in the treatment of rickets and other 'bony defects' (Board of Education 1940: 65).

Although this book is designed to provide a general introduction to the history of the school medical service after 1908, it is important to consider its limitations. In the first place, it is mainly (though not exclusively) concerned with the history of medical inspection and treatment, and with the development of the school meals service. It has relatively little to say about the history of the other 'special services' which were administered by the Medical Department of the Board of Education, such as the provision of special schools and the organisation of physical training. Its second major limitation is that it is largely concerned with the provision of medical services in elementary schools, at least until 1945. Although the Fisher Education Act gave local education authorities the duty to make arrangements for the medical inspection of secondary schoolchildren, this section of the Act was never enforced, and the majority of Local Education Authorities continued to concentrate on the elementary school population (Welshman 1988: 13). The book also suffers from a familiar geographical limitation. Although the school medical services of Scotland and Northern Ireland developed for many of the same reasons as the school medical service of England and Wales, they were organised along rather different lines, and their story must be told elsewhere.[3]

The book includes nine further chapters in addition to the present chapter. Chapter 2 'sets the scene' by examining the debate over physical deterioration and the background to the development of the 'personal health services'. Chapter 3 looks at the development of school medical provision in Britain and abroad between 1870 and 1907. Chapter 4 examines the history of the school medical service between 1908 and 1914, and Chapter 5 focuses on developments during the First World War. Chapters 6 and 7 consider different aspects of the school medical service between 1918 and 1939.

Chapter 6 looks at the financial and administrative history of the service and the development of medical inspection and treatment. Chapter 7 examines the efforts made by the school medical service to monitor children's 'nutrition', and includes an examination of the impact of unemployment on children's stature. Chapter 8 concentrates on the development of the school medical service during the Second World War, and Chapter 9 presents an overview of developments between 1945 and 1974. The concluding chapter discusses the impact of the reorganisation of the National Health Service on the development of the school health service from 1974 to the present day.

Notes

1 Although the Administrative Provisions Act compelled local education authorities to make arrangements for the provision of medical inspection, it did not compel parents to allow their children to be submitted to it. School medical inspection was only made compulsory for individuals in 1944 (7 & 8 Geo. VI Ch. 31, section 48 [2]). The majority of parents (and children) appear to have welcomed the introduction of medical inspection, but some parents refused to allow their children to be inspected, and other children 'resisted passively' by staying at home when inspections occurred (Hirst 1983: 290–93, 441–2).

2 Although the 1918 Education Act said that local education authorities should be compelled to carry out medical inspections in secondary schools, the Board of Education declined to bring this section of the Act into operation. See PP 1919 Cmd. 420 xxi: 32.

3 In Scotland, school boards acquired the power to make arrangements for medical inspection under the Education (Scotland) Act, 1908 (8 Edw. VII Ch. 63, section 4) and the power to make arrangements for medical treatment under the Education (Scotland) Act, 1913 (3–4 Geo. V Ch. 12, section 3). In Ireland, the government set aside the sum of £7500 for the establishment of school dental clinics in 1912/13 (PP 1913 Cd. 6986 xxii: 11–12).

two

The Physical Deterioration Committee and the origins of the personal health services

The early years of the twentieth century witnessed a fundamental change in the nature of public health work in Britain. Following the Public Health Act of 1848, the public health service had concentrated almost entirely on the improvement of the environment and the protection of the community against the spread of infectious diseases. Towards the end of the nineteenth century, public health officers began to pay more attention to the role played by infected individuals in the dissemination of disease, and this led to the introduction of such measures as the Infectious Diseases (Notification) Act of 1889 and the Isolation Hospitals Acts of 1893 and 1901 (Wohl 1983: 136–7; Frazer 1950: 288). However, the public health service only really began to focus on the health of the individual *per se* at the beginning of the twentieth century. The 'new era' was initiated by the establishment of the school medical service on 1 January 1908 (Frazer 1950: 257). The establishment of this service was followed by the establishment of other 'personal health services' such as the tuberculosis service in 1912 and the maternity and child welfare service in 1918 (Bryder 1988: 31–45; Frazer 1950: 411–18).

Many writers have argued that the foundations of the new era were laid by the Interdepartmental Committee on Physical Deterioration, whose report on the physical condition of the British population was published in 1904 (see for example, Gilbert 1966: 81–101; Dwork 1987: 3–21). The Committee was appointed in September 1903, and was instructed to carry out a preliminary inquiry with a view to the appointment of a Royal Commission, but its own terms of reference were later amended, and it went on to produce a full report of its own. The report contained a wealth of information about contemporary health conditions, and it provided a blueprint for public health reform for many years to come. In 1953 Professor J.M. Mackintosh wrote: 'In the scattered recommendations of the Committee we can pick out enough material in relation to personal health to last more than two generations of legislators. The aspect of personal health is remarkably well-represented' (Mackintosh 1953: 16).

Although the debate over physical deterioration has been joined by a large number of historians, the history of the Physical Deterioration Committee has only rarely been studied in any detail. The fullest account of its deliberations is to be found in Gilbert (1966), and this account has been followed closely in subsequent work by such authors as Richard Soloway (1982) and Deborah Dwork (1987). The first part of this chapter discusses the way in which different sections of the medical profession responded to the allegation that the average level of public health was deteriorating, despite the improvements which had taken place in public health administration over the previous fifty years. Many doctors believed that the standard of public health had deteriorated because of the disproportionate increase in the number of people who lived in towns, but the public health service rejected this view. Its members argued that the average level of public health had improved, but they also claimed that the rate of improvement would only be maintained if new measures were introduced. They argued that the public health service would have to pay far more attention to the individual if further progress was to be secured.

The second half of the chapter looks at the formation of the Physical Deterioration Committee and the contents of its report. Gilbert (1966) argued that the Committee was appointed in response to the alarm generated by the medical examination of British Army recruits during the Boer War of 1899–1902. He claimed that the government was fiercely opposed to any inquiry into the state of the nation's health and that it only agreed to appoint the Committee as a way of heading off demands for a Royal Commission. He also argued that the government only agreed to amend the Committee's terms of reference when it became clear that it would have to appoint a Royal Commission if the Committee failed to conduct a full inquiry of its own. However, this account is misleading in at least three respects. First, it fails to take sufficient account of the political circumstances of the time, or of the degree of internal dissension within the Conservative government. Second, it minimises the role which the Committee itself played in transforming its own terms of reference. Finally, it exaggerates the importance of the part played by the Army recruiting statistics in ensuring that an enquiry into 'physical deterioration' actually occurred.

Physical deterioration and the doctors

The origins of the debate about physical deterioration must be sought initially in the broader context of the campaign for national efficiency. In his book *The quest for national efficiency*, Geoffrey Searle (1971) showed how this 'campaign' came to dominate political discussion in Britain during the early years of the twentieth century. The campaign developed out of a set of fears about the decline of Britain's international supremacy which had been growing since the mid-nineteenth century. These fears were brought to a head by the military humiliations which were inflicted on the British Army during the Boer War of 1899–1902. In 1901 the Imperialist writer Leo Amery observed:

> The War has not only shaken our military organisation. It has profoundly affected the whole nation in many ways. The Mournful Monday of Nicholson's Nek, the Black Week of Stormberg, Magersfontein and Colenso, the alternate hope and disappointment of six weeks' fighting on the banks of the Tugela, the long anxiety for the fate of Ladysmith, Kimberley and Mafeking, have taught lessons that nothing else could have taught so well. . . . [The War] has set on foot a movement for administrative reform which, one may confidently hope, will not be confined to the War Office alone, but extend to every other department of the national life, and not least to the constitutional framework of the Empire (Amery 1900: 11; see also Searle 1971: 39).

As this quote implies, the efficiency campaigners were concerned with a wide range of issues, but their primary concern was with the nation's human capital – its population. Searle wrote that:

> in the view of the 'Efficiency Group' men and women formed the basic raw material out of which national greatness was constructed: hence, they argued, the statesman had a duty to see that these priceless resources were not squandered through indifference and slackness (Searle 1971: 60).

This attitude was reflected in Sidney Webb's article on 'Twentieth century politics: a policy of national efficiency', which was originally written in 1901. Webb argued that 'twentieth century politics for this country will certainly assume the maintenance, as against all external aggression, of that great commonwealth of peoples styled the British Empire'. However, he insisted that the security of the Empire depended not on military expenditure overseas, but on the health of the people at home. He wrote:

> Even more than in the factory, the Empire is founded in the home. How can we build up an effective commonwealth – how, even, can we get an efficient army – out of the stunted, anaemic, demoralised denizens of the slum tenements of our great cities? Can we, even as a mere matter of business, any longer afford to allow the eight millions of whom I have already spoken – the 'submerged fifth' of our nation – to be housed, washed, watered worse than our horses? (Webb 1909: 80–85).

Although the death rate had declined dramatically since the mid-nineteenth century, many people believed that the health of the population was deteriorating. The most important cause of this alleged deterioration was urbanisation. The nineteenth century had witnessed a dramatic increase in the number of people who lived in towns and in the size of the towns in which they lived. In 1801 only 20 per cent of the population of England and Wales lived in towns containing more than 5000 inhabitants, and only London contained more than 100,000 inhabitants. However, by 1901 the proportion of the population classed as urban had risen to 77 per cent, and 44 per cent of the population lived in towns with more than 100,000 inhabitants. There were 760,000 people living in Birmingham, 685,000 in Liverpool, and 654,000 in Manchester. The population of Greater London was 6.6 million (Wohl 1983: 3–4; Waller 1983: 6–9).

The nature and pace of urban growth alarmed contemporaries for three reasons. Some observers believed that the unhealthy effects of town life were transmitted from one generation to the next, and that the population was therefore *degenerating*. A second group rejected this hypothesis on the grounds that each generation 'started afresh'. They believed that the average level of public health was deteriorating because of the disproportionate increase in the number of people who lived in towns, but they did not believe that each generation began life weaker than the last. A third group believed that the population was deteriorating as a result of rural depopulation. They argued that it was vital for the healthiest members of the rural population to remain in the countryside and rear healthy children. However, they feared that these people were leaving the countryside for the towns, and forcing their children to grow up under less healthy conditions (PP 1904 Cd. 2175 xxxii: 34).

The most important question was whether physical deterioration was essentially hereditary, or whether it was principally the result of environmental causes (Winter 1986: 10–15). It is clear that many writers thought that the unhealthy effects of town life were transmitted from one generation to the next (Jones 1984: 127–8). In 1890 Dr J.P. Williams-Freeman observed that

> the child of the townsman is bred too fine, is too great an exaggeration of himself, excitable and painfully precocious in its childhood, neurotic, dyspeptic and undersized in its adult state . . . If it be not crossed with fresh blood, this town type in the third and fourth generations becomes more and more exaggerated . . . it has been maintained with considerable show of probability that a pure Londoner of the fourth generation is not capable of existing (Williams-Freeman 1890: 5).

In 1902 Professor James Cantlie told the Royal Commission on Physical Training (Scotland) that it was 'impossible to find anybody whose grandfather and grandmother had been born in London'; he claimed that the offspring of native-born Londoners were so weak and debilitated that 'nature steps in and denies the continuance of such, and weakness of brainpower gives such a being but little chance in this struggling world' (PP 1903 Cd. 1508 xxx: 210; see also Cantlie 1885: 19–23).

However, despite the alarm generated by the degenerationist case, most medical observers rejected the view that the health of the population was actually degenerating. The orthodox case was expressed very strongly by the Medical Officer of the Local Government Board in Scotland, Dr William Leslie Mackenzie, in his evidence to the Royal Commission on Physical Training. He told the Commissioners that

> what is particularly regarded as the degeneration of the slums . . . is largely . . . confined to the particular generation concerned, and is capable of removal by the improvement of . . . housing and nurture. It is also capable of arrest by the transplantation of the individuals (PP 1903 Cd. 1508 xxx: 263).

In 1903 Dr Alfred Eichholz, a medical inspector at the Board of Education, told the Physical Deterioration Committee that

> it is not possible to obtain any satisfactory or conclusive evidence of hereditary physical deterioration – that is to say, retrogression of a gradual retrogressive permanent nature, affecting one generation more acutely than the previous. There is little, if anything, in fact, to justify the view that neglect, poverty and parental ignorance . . . possess any marked hereditary effect, or that heredity plays any significant part in establishing the physical degeneracy of the poorer population (PP 1904 Cd. 2210 xxxii: 20).

However, the argument that neglect, poverty and ignorance did not possess any hereditary effect did not invalidate the view that the health of the population was deteriorating. In July 1903 the Earl of Meath told the House of Lords that the urban population was healthier than it had ever been, but the overwhelming increase in the number of people who lived in towns had 'completely altered the physical condition of England, and turned a negligible national defect into one of the most serious gravity' (Parliamentary Debates 1903: cols 1325–6). This view was shared by Amelia Watt Smyth, the *British Medical Journal*'s 'Commissioner on Physical Deterioration'. In 1904 she wrote:

> If, then, we have to admit that town influences are injurious, we must also admit that they are affecting a larger share of the population. The ratio of town to country, which was 212 to 100 in 1881, and 258 to 100 in 1891, was found at the last census [in 1901] to have risen to 335 to 100. . . . It follows of necessity that there is increasing physical deterioration of the population as a whole, although, to the shame of those responsible, there are no statistics to prove it in black and white (Smyth 1904: 51–2).

These views were also underlined by the editor of the *Lancet*. In April 1904 he wrote:

> that the physical condition or fitness of those who spend their lives under rural conditions is *ceteris paribus* better than that of those who live in the din and dirt of our large cities must, it seems to us, be accepted

> as a fact, and if this be conceded the rapidly increasing tendency to forsake the country for the town must be making for deterioration rather than improvement.

He continued:

> the fact that the death rate is diminishing and that the average duration of life is increasing cannot be regarded as negativing a view that the physical condition of the people is deteriorating. By tending plants in greenhouses during the winter months we can reduce the death rate almost to zero, but it would be altogether erroneous from this to assume that the plants were more hardy (*Lancet* 1904a: 1003).

However, the arguments which were put forward in the *Lancet* and the *British Medical Journal* were rejected emphatically by members of the Society of Medical Officers of Health. For over half a century medical officers of health had used mortality statistics to measure the health of the population. They argued that the conditions which produced a high death rate also impeded physical development, and they associated a fall in the death rate with improvements in physique (Dearden 1905: 238–9). They also argued that any 'diminution in the elimination of the unfit' was outweighed by a reduction in the amount of sickness generally (PP 1904 Cd. 2210 xxxii: 346). In 1903 Dr Arthur Newsholme told the University Extension Club in Brighton that

> the weeding out of weakly lives, caused by the greater mortality among weakly children suffering from an infectious disease, is in my opinion counterbalanced by the greater number of children made weakly in former times by non-fatal attacks of an infectious disease (Newsholme 1905: 298).

The Society of Medical Officers of Health recognised that the health of the urban population was central to the whole debate, and its members agreed that urban conditions were often prejudicial to health. In 1904 Dr Henry Armstrong, the Medical Officer of Health for Newcastle upon Tyne, said that 'life in the country should be encouraged, and the urbanisation of the population discouraged, in every possible way' (Armstrong 1905: 302). Arthur Newsholme also believed that town life increased the risks of infection. He said that 'although domiciliary overcrowding may be as great in a country village or remote hamlet as in a densely populated town, the chances of acquiring the infection of the acute infectious diseases, and probably also of tuberculosis, are much greater in the latter'. He added that 'the atmosphere of towns is more dusty, more contaminated with organic matter and less invigorating than that of rural districts; and the sun is prevented from exercising its beneficent effects in crowded streets and houses' (Newsholme 1905: 295).

However, it was also clear that the standard of health in towns was improving. In Newcastle, the general death rate fell by over 30 per cent between

1870 and 1903, and the death rate from zymotic diseases fell by over 70 per cent (Armstrong 1905: 302).[1] In central Manchester, the death rate fell from 35.8 per thousand living at the end of the 1830s to 29.6 in the 1890s. In 1904 Dr W.F. Dearden told the North-Western branch of the Society of Medical Officers of Health that these improvements were particularly remarkable because the social character of the area had changed, and it was now inhabited by the poorest sections of the population (Dearden 1905: 238–9). In London improvements in health were reflected in the statistics of average life expectancy. In the 1860s the average five-year-old boy had a life expectancy of 47.5 years; thirty years later this figure had risen to 51.6 years (PP 1904 Cd. 2186 xxxii: 50). In Glasgow, the death rate among children under the age of five was almost halved between 1871 and 1902 (PP 1904 Cd. 2210 xxxii: 240).

Medical officers of health used the mortality statistics to refute allegations that the level of public health had deteriorated. In his speech to the University Extension Club, Arthur Newsholme pointed out that the urban death rate had improved steadily throughout the nineteenth century, and that the urban death rate in 1901 was lower than the rural death rate had been ten years earlier. He said that if the urban death rate had been higher than the preceding rural death rate 'it would have been probable that deterioration was going on', but 'under present circumstances the *onus probandi* lies with those who believe that there is degeneration' (Newsholme 1905: 296).

However, despite the overall decline in mortality, substantial inequalities remained. In 1904 Dr H. Beale Collins compared the death rates from different diseases in the London borough of Hampstead and the parish of St Luke's. He found that the death rate from pulmonary tuberculosis in St Luke's was 3.11 per thousand, whereas the figure for Hampstead was only 0.74 per thousand. The overall death rate in St Luke's was 42 per cent greater than the death rate for the whole of London, and twice as great as the Hampstead death rate. Collins also examined the incidence of infant mortality in different parts of the country. He found that the highest death rates were recorded in industrial counties such as Lancashire, East Yorkshire, Staffordshire and Warwickshire, and the lowest in counties such as Sussex and Surrey. The infant mortality rate in Lancashire was 180 per thousand live births, 50 per cent greater than in Surrey, where it was 120 per thousand (Collins 1904: 403).[2]

The existence of substantial disparities in the health of different sections of the population was confirmed by the Medical Officers of Health for London and Glasgow in their evidence to the Physical Deterioration Committee. In London Sir Shirley Foster Murphy showed that the level of infant mortality in seven different districts was directly related to the level of overcrowding. He also showed that the life expectancy of a new-born baby in Hampstead was 50.8 years, whereas that of a new-born baby in Lewisham was only 36.5 years (PP 1904 Cd. 2186 xxxii: 50). In Glasgow Dr Archibald Chalmers found that the death rate from pulmonary tuberculosis was 2.4 per thousand in one-roomed tenements, 1.8 in two-roomed tenements, and 0.7 in houses with four rooms or more. The overall death rate in one-roomed tenements was nearly three times greater than the rate for houses with four rooms or more, and 50 per cent greater than the rate for the whole city (PP 1904 Cd. 2186 xxxii: 25). In Manchester in 1902 the following death rates were recorded in different parts of the city: central Manchester, 26.74; Ancoats, 25.28; St George's, 24.24; and Northern Cheetham, 12.74. The average for the city as a whole was 20.00 (PP 1904 Cd. 2210 xxxii: 220–21).

The Society of Medical Officers of Health argued that these statistics demonstrated the strengths and weaknesses of traditional public health work. Its members had little doubt that the sanitary improvements of the previous fifty years had made an important contribution to the decline in mortality, but they also argued that the state would have to pay far more attention to the promotion of personal health if it wanted these improvements to be maintained. In 1905 Dr J.C. McVail told a meeting of the Society's London branch that

> they were just at the beginning of a great advance movement in public health. Up to the present they had been occupied with the environment, with the improvement of the environment of the individual. They had made great progress in that direction, and now they were beginning to attack the individual himself (Brunton 1905: 286).

This theme was echoed by Shirley Murphy in a memorandum which he submitted to the Education Committee of the London County Council at the end of 1907:

> Enquiries into the causes of mortality brought the Medical Officer of Health into touch with the personal factor in relation to disease. The destitution of the poor, the intimate association of their diseases with want of cleanliness [and] the part played by ignorance and neglect in fostering ill-health necessarily impressed upon him the knowledge that it was not external environment alone which determined . . . the health of the community, and hence . . . he has allied himself with movements which have had as their aim the improvement of the personal hygiene of the people (London County Council 1908: 55).

The concept of personal hygiene had two important implications for the development of school medicine. First, it helped to focus the attention of the medical profession on the whole question of education. This was reflected in the evidence which was presented to the Physical Deterioration Committee in 1903 and 1904. Dr Henry Ashby thought that the best way to improve the health of young children was to employ health visitors to visit the homes of the poor and 'instruct' the mothers in the rudiments of child care (PP 1904 Cd. 2210 xxxii: 331). Dr Eichholz said that

> another very necessary step is the instruction of men and women by every possible agency in the laws of health – and women and girls especially as, how to feed, clothe and tend their children; how to cook and how to mend, as well as to do needlework, and how to look after the house (PP 1904 Cd. 2210 xxxii: 28).

Dr James Niven thought that it was vital for girls to receive 'a prolonged practical course' on domestic economy and hygiene 'even at the expense of some of their bookwork' (PP 1904 Cd. 2210 xxxii: 255). Shirley Murphy argued that girls between the ages of fourteen and sixteen should be compelled to attend evening classes on subjects such as domestic hygiene, the care of infants, household management and cookery (PP 1904 Cd. 2210 xxxii: 348).

Second, the new emphasis on personal hygiene also helped to focus attention on the care of the child. This point emerges very clearly in the writings and speeches of doctors such as Beale Collins and Leslie Mackenzie. In 1902 Collins told the Thames Valley branch of the Society of Medical Officers of Health that

> we must show the world, and our own country in particular, that the greater part of our troubles and miseries are of our own making, that disease is not a dispensation of Providence any more than the plague is the scourge of God. We know it is due to the dirty habits of the people. The doctor, by stepping in between the child and the State, can impress that kind of knowledge on the child at the most impressionable age. The child who is taught to recognise that the doctor can prevent illness better than he can cure it is on the first rung of a ladder that will lead him into a state where contentment, health and happiness are the common lot (Collins 1902: 606–7).

The same points were also made by Leslie Mackenzie in a speech to the Royal Society of Edinburgh in March 1905:

> The present universal ferment of social ideas is not without a meaning. If any clear issue has yet emerged it is that we are entering on an era of personal hygiene. As the beginning of the last century witnessed the great movement towards an improved environment, so the beginning of this century is witnessing a movement towards the improvement of the organism. It has taken a century to persuade the ordinary citizen that his environment of home and street and atmosphere is . . . in some measure his own creation, a thing plastic and manageable, a form answering to his will. Perhaps, with the greater pace of today, it may take less than a century to fit himself to live in it. The vastness of the problem need not appal us. Time is on our side, and many little things point the way to practice. One truth we have already realised – if we would fit the man for his environment, we must begin with the child. 'The child is father of the man' (Mackenzie 1906: 50).

The Physical Deterioration Report

The debate which took place within the medical profession over the question of physical deterioration was amply reflected in the deliberations of the Interdepartmental Committee on Physical Deterioration, which was appointed by the Government in September 1903. Many historians have argued that the establishment of the Committee symbolised the alarm which many people felt about the alleged deterioration in the health of the British population (e.g. Gilbert 1966: 87–8; Dwork 1987: 11). However, although the Committee canvassed a wide range of opinions, the general tenor of its report was closely related to the optimistic views of the Society of Medical Officers of Health. The report provided a powerful platform for the Society's efforts to extend the boundaries of social intervention and establish new forms of public health provision.

It is generally agreed that the campaign to appoint the Physical Deterioration Committee was initiated by a series of revelations regarding the poor physical condition of British Army recruits. In 1899 the journalist, Arnold White, claimed that over 40 per cent of those who volunteered to join the Army in Manchester had to be rejected on grounds of physical fitness (White 1899: 239–41). In 1901 Seebohm Rowntree suggested that 21.1 per cent of the volunteers in Leeds, Sheffield and York were rejected unconditionally, and that 26.4 per cent were accepted in the hope that they could be brought up to the required standards of health and fitness after a few months of Army life (Rowntree 1902: 216–17). In 1902 Major-General Sir John Frederick Maurice alleged that 'out of every five men who are willing to serve [in the Army], only two are fit to become effective soldiers' (Maurice 1902: 79; see also 1903: 42).

Maurice published a second article on the health of Army recruits in January 1903. On this occasion he argued that the health of the population from which the bulk of the recruits were drawn was not only poor but also deteriorating. He thought that there were many factors which might tend in that direction, including

> the continuous rush of the people from the country districts into the towns, the disappearance of the class of yeomen, the general depression of the agricultural districts, the fact . . . that it is capacity or skill alone which in some form or other commands or can command an adequate wage in the towns, and . . . the enormously strong presumption that neither the unskilled labourer who has been tempted into the towns, nor the hereditary townsman who after two or three generations has deteriorated in physical vigour, will be able to rear a healthy family (Maurice 1903: 49–50).

He concluded by asking the Royal Colleges of Physicians and Surgeons to lead a national inquiry into the facts he had uncovered:

> I have set forth here the aspect which this question presents to me as a soldier. My object is to call upon the great professions whose immediate concern is health to give us the guidance and leading we need, and primarily it seems to me that we ought to call upon the Councils of the Colleges of Physicians and Surgeons, as *ex officio* the great National Boards of Health, to help and guide us. I should suppose they have not at this moment, despite the census, sufficiently comprehensive data on

> which to pronounce, but if that be so no Government could or would wish to resist an appeal from them for assistance in getting at the truth on the tremendous question which has been raised by the investigations of Mr Rowntree: 'is it or is it not true that the whole labouring population of the land are at present living under conditions which make it impossible that they should rear the next generation to be sufficiently virile to supply more than two out of five men effective for the purposes of either peace or war?' We want the truth . . . (Maurice 1903: 55).[3]

These allegations played a very important role in the background to the formation of the Physical Deterioration Committee. On 2 April 1903 the Director-General of the Army Medical Service, Sir William Taylor, circulated a memorandum in which he said that

> a deep interest has been aroused, both in the lay and medical press, by the writings of Sir Frederick Maurice and others, who have brought into prominence certain observations pointing to the fact that there is an alarming proportion of the young men of this country, more especially among the urban population, who are unfit for military service on account of defective physique (PP 1904 Cd. 2175 xxxii: 95).

On 1 July the Home Secretary wrote to the Councils of the Royal Colleges of Physicians and Surgeons, and invited them to submit observations

> on a proposed enquiry into the causes which have led, during recent years, to the rejection, on the grounds of physical fitness, of so large a number of recruits for the Army, and as to the possible measures by which this state of affairs may be remedied (Royal College of Physicians 1903: 92–4).

However, although the recruiting statistics provided the initial impetus behind the enquiry, there was no clear consensus on the significance of the facts they disclosed. Both the Royal College of Physicians and the Royal College of Surgeons said that they saw little point in an inquiry which dealt with the physical condition of Army recruits. They argued that the recruiting statistics were a misleading guide to the health of the population because the recruits were drawn from 'the poorest portion of the population among whom the lowest standard of physique would be found' (PP 1904 Cd. 2175 xxxii: 98). The editor of the *Lancet* also claimed that:

> The candidates for enlistment in the Army are usually those who have shown no great aptitude for any of the trades or mechanical pursuits; in some cases they have found out for themselves that their physique and powers of work do not qualify them for the more coveted of civil occupations. We are not suggesting that every lad who desires to take the king's shilling has failed in other walks of life . . . but at the same time it cannot be denied that a certain proportion of shiftless folk regard the Army as a possible haven when other resources have failed them. These are for the most part ignorant and self-indulgent lads, and

> their health suffers on both accounts. . . . The presence of a large quantity of this shiftless class among those who offer themselves for enlistment makes the would-be soldier's health not representative of the public health of this country (Lancet 1903: 316).[4]

In view of the doubts expressed by the medical profession, it is important to consider other factors which may also have played a part in the Committee's appointment. On the day that the Home Secretary invited the Royal Colleges of Physicians and Surgeons to submit their observations on a proposed inquiry into the physical condition of Army recruits, the President of the Board of Education convened a special meeting to discuss the alleged 'physical inferiority' of certain classes of children attending public elementary schools (PRO PC8/584, Campagnac to Morant, 5/7/03; Eichholz to Morant, 25/7/03). On 14 August 1903 the minutes of this meeting were passed to the Clerk of the Privy Council, Sir Almeric Fitzroy, who had been asked to chair the Committee and to 'complete the dispositions for [its] sitting' (PRO PC 8/584: 'Enquiries as to physical deterioration', nos 1, 3; Fitzroy 1925, i: 147). At the meeting the Board's own medical inspector, Dr Alfred Eichholz, presented a short paper on the physical condition of London children in poorer districts. He said that there were at least 60,000 children in the whole of London who were unable to keep pace with the ordinary elementary school curriculum because they were 'imperfect in physical development to an extent well over fifty per cent', and that the principal causes of this 'retardation' were hunger, overcrowding, want of clothing and sleep, lack of cleanliness, parental drunkenness and poor heredity. He argued that although conditions had recently improved, 'want of food, air, light and cleanliness are factors which must be met in order to effect a tangible change' (PRO PC 8/584: Note on physical condition of London children in poorer districts).

This meeting also considered a series of four letters which Dr William Hall had recently published in the *Yorkshire Post* (PRO PC 8/584, Evidence submitted by certain inspectors as to physical inferiority amongst certain classes of children in elementary schools; see also Hall 1903a, b, c and d). The letters were based on an investigation which Hall himself had carried out in Leeds during the previous year. In his first letter Hall compared the health of fifty children from a poor part of the city with the health of fifty similar children 'from a district inhabited by working men of the "well-to-do" class'. He found that the poor-class children were much less healthy than the well-to-do children, but even the well-to-do children showed signs of ill health, and 'there was a general tendency to bow-legs, especially amongst the boys' (Hall 1903a). Hall thought that the main reason for the poor standard of physique was the absence of proper food. In his second letter he compared children from both schools with a group of Jewish children of the same age, and although the Jewish children came from poor families, they were considerably healthier. He attributed their apparent superiority to the domestic training of the Jewish mother. He wrote:

> The Jewish mother is giving us an object lesson in the art of feeding children. Today, the poor Jewish children in this city are much superior in physical well-being to the poor Gentile. Proper food and plenty of it is the secret of Jewish success (Hall 1903b).

The impact of this meeting on the subsequent development of the inquiry is reflected in the fact that more than a third of the Physical Deterioration Report was devoted to the question of 'conditions affecting the condition of the juvenile population' (PP 1904 Cd. 2175 xxxii: 44–76). It is also reflected in the prominence which was given to Dr Eichholz's evidence. On 18 December 1903 Almeric Fitzroy noted in his diary that

> we spent three hours and a half in the examination of Dr Eichholz, an M.D. on the Inspectorate of the Board of Education, and were favoured with a wealth of information conveyed with a resolute air of self-assured confidence that carried great weight (Fitzroy 1925a, i: 175; 1925b, iii: 165–7).

Dr Eichholz's remarks were cited on numerous occasions throughout the Report, and his suggestions formed the basis of many of the Committee's recommendations. On the question of physical deterioration itself, the Committee observed:

> The evidence of Dr Eichholz contains a summary of his conclusions on this point, so admirably epitomising the results of a comprehensive survey of the whole subject, that the Committee cannot do better than reproduce it in full at this stage of their Report (PP 1904 Cd. 2175 xxxii: 13; see also ibid.: 5–6, 13–15, 30–31, 33, 40, 46, 51, 59–68, 73, 81; PP 1904 Cd. 2210 xxxii: 19–39; PP 1904 Cd. 2186 xxxii: 73–80).

The Physical Deterioration Committee was appointed formally on 2 September 1903. It was chaired by Almeric Fitzroy, and the other members were H.M. Lindsell, John Struthers, J.G. Legge, G.M. Fox, J.F.W. Tatham and George T. Onslow. According to Gilbert (1966: 89), Fitzroy was 'a sincere social reformer, but one who was also a gentleman of unimpeachable Unionist connections'. His wife's uncle was Lord Hampden, and his brother-in-law was the Unionist MP for Woodbury between 1886 and 1892, Colonel Lloyd-Anstruther. Fitzroy began his professional career as an inspector of schools with the Department of Education in 1875, and he was promoted to the post of junior examiner in February 1884. Between 1885 and 1892 he served as Private Secretary to three Privy Council vice-presidents, and he was appointed Clerk to the Council, 'on the introduction of my wife's uncle', in 1895 (Fitzroy 1925a, i: i, ix, xvi). When he died in June 1935, the *Times* obituarist wrote: 'he was Chairman of the Departmental Committee [*sic*] on Physical Deterioration in 1903, and was largely responsible for the report, which has proved a mine of information to students of physiology and social conditions' (*Times* 1935).

The Physical Deterioration Committee included two official representatives of education departments. H.M. Lindsell was the official representative of the Board of Education. He joined the Privy Council Department of Education in 1876, and he was appointed Principal Assistant Secretary to the Board of Education in 1903. His main area of responsibility was in legal affairs (*Who Was Who* 1947a: 633; *Times* 1925a). John Struthers represented the Scottish Education Department. He was appointed Principal Assistant Secretary to the Department in 1898, and he became Permanent Secretary in 1904. When he died in 1925 his obituarist wrote that 'it would be impossible within the limits of this notice to do justice to Struthers' career in education in the true sense of the word' (*Who Was Who* 1947a: 1009; *Times* 1925b).

In addition, there were two other members of the Physical Deterioration Committee who had strong links with the educational world. These were Colonel G.M. Fox and Mr J.G. Legge. Colonel Fox was the War Office representative. He was described officially as the former head of the Army's Gymnastic School, but he was also Inspector of Physical Training at the Board of Education, and he had been closely involved with the organisation of physical training by the London School Board. Both he and John Struthers were members of the Board of Education's Committee on the Model Course of Physical Exercises (PP 1904 Cd. 2032 xix: v; *British Medical Journal* 1904d: 1091). J.G. Legge was the Home Office representative. He had previously worked as Private Secretary to Herbert Gladstone and G.W.E. Russell, and in 1894–5 he was Secretary to the Departmental Committee on Prisons. However, in 1895 he was appointed Inspector of Reformatories and Industrial Schools, and in 1906 he left the Home Office to become Director of Education in Liverpool. In 1919 he was invited to join the Prime Minister's Committee on the Classics in Education (*Who Was Who* 1947b: 797; *Times* 1940).

The remaining members of the Physical Deterioration Committee were Dr J.F.W. Tatham and Colonel George T. Onslow. Dr John Tatham was the official representative of the General Register Office. He was Medical Officer of Health in Salford between 1873 and 1888, and Medical Officer of Health in Manchester between 1888 and 1893. He joined the General Register Office as Superintendent of Statistics in 1893. He was also a member of the Council of the Royal College of Physicians, and he helped to draft the College's reply to the Home Secretary's initial request for observations on an inquiry into the health of Army recruits (Pickstone 1985: 227; Royal College of Physicians 1903: 119). Colonel George T. Onslow represented the Admiralty. He joined the Royal Marines in 1875, and saw active service in Sudan and later in South Africa. He became a full colonel in 1902. At the time the Physical Deterioration Committee was conducting its inquiry he was Inspector of Marine Recruiting (PRO PC 8/584: 'Privy Council Office – Internal Circular'; *Who Was Who* 1947a: 797; *Times* 1921).

When the Physical Deterioration Committee was originally appointed, it was instructed

> to make a preliminary enquiry into the allegations concerning the deterioration of certain classes of the population, as shown by the large

> number of rejections for physical causes of recruits for the Army and by other evidence, especially the Report of the Royal Commission on Physical Training (Scotland), and to consider in what manner the medical profession can best be consulted on the subject with a view to the appointment of a Royal Commission, and the terms of reference to such a Commission, if appointed.

These instructions were later 'explained and enlarged' in the following way:

1. to determine, with the aid of such counsel as the medical profession are able to give, the steps that should be taken to furnish the Government and the nation at large with periodical data for an accurate comparative estimate of the health and physique of the people.
2. to indicate generally the causes of such physical deterioration as does exist in certain classes.
3. to point out the means by which it can be most efficiently diminished (PP 1904 Cd. 2175 xxxii: v).

In his account of the history of the Physical Deterioration Committee, Bentley Gilbert argued that:

> By the end of the Parliamentary session of 1903, it had become clear that even an interdepartmental committee of docile civil servants would be bound to find a Royal Commission necessary. A Government that had no desire for investigation at all wished still less to see its works, or the lack of them, criticised by a body of non-political, independent experts. The original terms of reference, therefore, were enlarged, and the decision to investigate the need for an investigation became an enquiry into the question of physical deterioration itself (Gilbert 1965: 146; 1966: 88).

However, it is important to remember that the government was preoccupied with the question of tariff reform at this time, and it was the Committee, rather than its political masters, which initiated the changes (see Holland 1911, ii: 285–371). In 1905 Fitzroy wrote:

> When I began to scrutinise the terms, and to confer with those with whom I was to work, the expediency of making [their] meaning clear became apparent, and a conference I had with George Murray [Treasury Secretary] on the necessary financial arrangements, when he declared himself quite unable to determine what we were asked to do, decided me to submit to the Duke [of Devonshire] a draft from which the real intention of the Government might be gathered. I explained, in [my] letter to Gerald Balfour [President of the Local Government Board], my view of what the changes amounted to, and that the Duke had no hesitation in agreeing to the amendment, to which Londonderry [President of the Board of Education] and Walter Long [Home Secretary] were also parties (Fitzroy 1925a, i: 260; 1925b, v).

The decision to amend the terms of reference caused considerable controversy after the report had been published. Both the Home Office and the

Local Government Board claimed that 'the alteration in the original terms of reference had been made without consulting them, and that . . . their representation on the Committee [was] . . . inadequate for the protection of their interests' (Fitzroy 1925a; 1925b, v: 47–52, i: 258). Fitzroy argued that they had been aware of the changes, and that they were taking advantage of the opportunity presented by this issue to conceal the real reasons for their hostility to the Report.[5] He thought that the Home Office would have preferred a Royal Commission because this would have led to 'an inquisition into the question which they would have controlled and shaped to their own ends'. The Local Government Board disliked the Report because 'there are elements in the office of a most obstructive and do-nothing character, and the upholders of these views had manipulated certain passages of the Report to make it appear that the Board's competence had been impugned' (Fitzroy 1925a, i: 259; 1925b, v: 47–52).

Between September 1903 and July 1904 the Physical Deterioration Committee interviewed a total of sixty-eight witnesses. Many of these witnesses were invited to give evidence on behalf of particular medical bodies. The Royal College of Physicians was represented by Dr Henry Ashby, Dr Robert Hutchison, Dr Eustace Smith and Dr Joseph Wigglesworth, and the Royal College of Surgeons was represented by Sir Alfred Cooper and Mr John Tweedy. Mr W. MacAdam Eccles and Dr Robert Jones were nominated by 'a specially convened conference of medical men and others'; and Sir Victor Horsley and Dr F.W. Mott represented the views of 'a private committee' on the subject of syphilis. A number of non-medical bodies also nominated their own representatives. The Manchester and Salford Sanitary Association was represented by Mr T.C. Horsfall, the Manchester and Salford Ladies' Health Society was represented by Mrs Worthington, and the Salford Education Committee was represented by the Reverend W.E. Edwards-Rees. Mr W.H. Dolamore gave evidence on behalf of the British Dental Association.

The Physical Deterioration Committee also interviewed a number of official witnesses who gave evidence in their own right. This list was headed by Sir William Taylor, the Director-General of the Army Medical Service, and Dr Leslie Mackenzie, the Medical Officer of the Scottish Local Government Board. It also included the Medical Officers of Health for London, Glasgow, Manchester, Dublin and Worcestershire. Three witnesses had direct experience of medical work in schools. Dr Eichholz gave evidence on behalf of the Board of Education, and Drs Kerr and Collie worked for the Medical Department of the London School Board. It is also likely that the medical officers of health who were interviewed by the Physical Deterioration Committee would have had some experience of school work. Dr Osmund Airy gave evidence about school feeding in Birmingham, and Dr T.M. Legge, a medical inspector of factories at the Home Office, discussed conditions in factories and workshops.

The Physical Deterioration Committee also interviewed a number of other witnesses who had special knowledge of factors which were thought to be associated with the question of physical deterioration. Sir Frederick Maurice gave evidence about the physical condition of Army recruits, and Charles

Booth and Seebohm Rowntree discussed the results of their inquiries into the standard of living in London and York. The Secretary of the Charity Organisation Society gave evidence about urban conditions generally. The Committee also heard evidence about the educational value of boys' and girls' clubs, and about the importance of teaching domestic management in schools. A number of witnesses spoke about the extent of underfeeding among schoolchildren and infants (PP 1904 Cd. 2175 xxxii: iii–v).

The Physical Deterioration Report was published on 28 July 1904. The Committee found that 'while there are, unfortunately, very abundant signs of physical defect traceable to neglect, poverty and ignorance', there was no evidence that these possessed any marked hereditary effect, and therefore 'there is every reason to anticipate rapid amelioration of physique so soon as improvement occurs in external conditions' (ibid.: para. 69). In order to bring this improvement about, the Committee said that an advisory council should be formed 'whose duty it should be . . . to advise the Government on all legislative and administrative points in respect of which State interference might be expedient' (ibid.: para. 423/3). It also suggested that county councils 'should be empowered when necessary . . . to act in default of urban and rural sanitary authorities within the area of their administration' (ibid.: para. 423/10). Another very important recommendation included the suggestion that whole-time medical officers of health should be appointed in all areas above a certain population, with full security of tenure (ibid.: para. 423/9).[6]

The Committee's second set of proposals concerned the need for more accurate arrangements for monitoring standards of health and sickness. Although it stated that 'the impressions gathered from the great majority of witnesses do not support the belief that there is any general progressive physical deterioration' (ibid.: para. 68), the Committee was unable to obtain any firm statistical evidence which would enable it to make an accurate assessment of changes in the average standard of health over time, and this led to the recommendation that 'a permanent anthropometric survey should be organised as speedily as possible' (ibid.: para. 423/1). The Committee said that 'in the first instance this survey should have for its object the periodic taking of measurements of children and young persons in schools and factories', and that this should be supplemented, in the future, by 'a more comprehensive and specialised survey, spread over a longer period, of the population of the country at large' (ibid.). In addition to this, the Committee also called for the establishment of a national sickness register, which would provide information about all types of disease, and not simply infectious diseases. It thought that such a register could be compiled without too much difficulty with the aid of the Poor Law medical officers and the voluntary hospitals (ibid.: para. 423/2).

The third set of proposals concerned the need for changes in the general field of environmental health provision. The Committee thought that local authorities should fix a standard of overcrowding and that after a certain date 'no crowing in excess of such a standard should be permitted'. It even suggested that those who were 'incapable of independent existence up to the standard of decency which [the State] imposes' should be housed in labour colonies such as the Salvation Army colony at Hadleigh (ibid.: paras 423/4–423/5). It thought that local authorities should be compelled to introduce satisfactory building regulations, and that efforts should be made to improve the arrangements for urban planning (ibid.: para. 423/6).[7] It said that greater attention should be paid to the medical inspection of factories and workshops (ibid.: paras 423/13, 423/16), and that provisions for the medical inspection of young people should be extended to cover those employed in coal-mines (ibid.: para. 423/15). It attached particular importance to the provision of clean milk, and in order to achieve this it said that milk depots should be established in every town (ibid.: paras 423/28, 423/30).

The fourth set of proposals was concerned with the need for improvements in personal hygiene. The Committee said that even though there had been significant improvements in the quality of the urban environment, 'in large classes of the community there has not been developed a desire for improvement commensurate with the opportunities offered to them', and in order to rectify this it advocated a wide range of measures of 'social education' (ibid.: paras 70–73). The majority of these measures were concerned with the instruction of mothers and older girls in methods of infant care and management, cookery, hygiene and domestic economy (ibid.: paras 423/20, 423/29, 423/33, 423/37). The Committee also urged local authorities to provide facilities for physical training (for both sexes), and it said that local education authorities should pay greater attention to the organisation of children's games (ibid.: paras 423/43, 423/45, 423/46, 423/47). It thought that local authorities should do their utmost to ensure that physical exercises were performed in the open air (ibid.: paras 423/36, 423/45).

The final set of proposals focused directly on the health of the schoolchildren, and in particular on the need for the introduction of limited schemes of school feeding and school medical inspection. The Committee said that local authorities should have the power to provide school meals in those areas 'where the extent or the concentration of poverty might be too great for the resources of local charity', and that 'a systematised medical inspection of schoolchildren should be imposed as a public duty on every school authority' (ibid.: paras 362, 423/41). It thought that a medical inspector should be appointed to supervise the arrangements for medical inspection and to provide advice 'in respect of all matters where the advice of a person skilled in the hygiene of child life may be wanted' (ibid.: para. 325). However, it did not think that it would be necessary for the medical inspector to examine all the children personally. It said that 'with teachers properly trained in the various branches of hygiene, the system could be so far based on their observation and record that no large and expensive medical staff would be necessary'. The doctor would only have to examine every child 'in that class of school which from its character and surroundings affords clear evidence of the type of which its scholars are composed', and in other schools the examination could be limited to those children whom the teachers considered in need of attention (ibid.: para. 324).

These recommendations were welcomed by all sections of the medical profession. The founder of the National League for Physical Education and Improvement, Sir Lauder Brunton, told a meeting of the Society of Medical Officers of Health that 'all the recommendations of the Committee . . . must have the approbation of all medical men' (Brunton 1905: 277). The *British Medical Journal* said that the Committee should be congratulated 'upon the intelligent and conscientious manner in which it has tackled the social problems placed before it' (*British Medical Journal* 1904e). The *Lancet* said that:

> After careful study of the report before us . . . we think that the public will approve of the Committee's conclusions, although the body arriving at them may be destitute of the authority, independence and prestige which the King's mandate implies. Whether or not the recommendations are carried into effect by the Government or by the several minor authorities concerned, we have no hesitation in saying that the Committee has done most useful work (*Lancet* 1904c: 391).

The Physical Deterioration Report also attracted support from powerful sections of the lay public. Many newspapers welcomed the conclusion that the case for progressive physical deterioration remained 'unproven', because this meant that there was every reason to expect a rapid improvement in health standards once appropriate measures had been taken. The *Westminster Gazette* said that 'the fact that the case for national physical deterioration is "not proven" is the most interesting feature of the Report' (*Westminster Gazette* 1904), and the *Manchester Guardian* said that 'there could hardly be a more cheering reason' for hastening on with reform measures (*Manchester Guardian* 1904). The editor of *The Times* also greeted the Report enthusiastically. He described the main body of the Report as 'an emphatic recognition of the supreme importance of health, and the absolute necessity of taking active legislative, educational and social measures for its preservation and improvement, and for the removal of all circumstances by which it is imperilled' (*Times* 1904: 12b).

The Physical Deterioration Report marked a turning point in the history of public health policy because it paved the way for the development of a new kind of public health service. Its most important contribution to the contemporary debate was to demonstrate the overriding importance of public health issues and to lay the foundations for a wide-ranging campaign of health service reform. Over the course of the next few years, the Report became associated with the introduction of a large number of public health measures, including the Open Spaces Act (1906), the Education (Provision of Meals) Act (1906), the Education (Administrative Provisions) Act (1907), the Notification of Births Act (1907), the Public Health (Regulations as to Food) Act (1907), the Public Health Amendment Act (1907) and the Maternity and Child Welfare Act (1918) (Newman 1935: 168; Stevenson 1984: 207–8). However, despite the wide-ranging nature of its proposals, the Report has been most closely associated with the introduction of measures to improve the health of children, and in particular with the introduction of school meals and school medical inspection (PP 1918 Cd. 9206 ix: 160–1; Fraser 1973: 138–9; 1984: 148–9). Even though the Report failed to anticipate the precise form which the school medical service would take, it focused attention on the need for medical inspection, and played a very important role in generating the political momentum which was necessary to bring it about.

Notes

1 The term 'zymotic' or 'specific febrile' diseases was used for the last time by the Registrar-General in his annual report for 1899. It included the following disease classifications: smallpox, measles, scarlet fever, enteric fever, diphtheria, diphtheria and croup, whooping cough, epidemic influenza, diarrhoeal diseases, hydrophobia and puerperal fever. See PP 1900 Cd. 323 xv, 1: xviii–xxix.

2 It is salutary to compare these figures with those for the more recent past. Even the comparatively health county of Surrey had an infant mortality rate which was more than ten times greater than the average for the whole of England and Wales in 1981. See McPherson and Coleman (1988: 427).

3 Maurice drew a sharp distinction between the poverty surveys conducted by Charles Booth and Seebohm Rowntree: 'The ditch, with falling into which we are . . . threatened by Mr Rowntree, is a very deep one. On the other hand, I do not think that anyone who has studied Mr Booth's book can doubt that what he presents to us is a hopeful and encouraging picture of our modern life' (Maurice 1903: 49; see also Fraser 1984: 137).

4 For a more positive view of the value and potential uses of the Army recruiting statistics, see Floud *et al.* (1985: 18).

5 Fitzroy thought that the Duke of Devonshire had discussed the changes with his colleagues, but the Duke subsequently confessed that he may have forgotten to do so. The Duke resigned from the government shortly after the alterations were made. See Parliamentary Debates 1905: col. 1352; Holland 1911, ii: 360–71.

6 The majority of Medical Officers of Health were appointed for fixed periods of between one and five years, and they had to apply to the local authority for reappointment at the end of each period. See Wohl (1983: 187–91).

7 In 1907 Dr J. Middleton Martin reported that, out of 595 rural sanitary districts in England and Wales, 210 had no building bye-laws. See Martin (1907: 117).

three

The development of medical inspection before 1907

Gilbert (1966) argued that 'systematic medical inspection originated as a humanitarian measure in Bradford and grew as a means of combating, or investigating, the frightening problem of racial physical deterioration after the outbreak of the Boer War'. The need for a national system of medical inspection was highlighted by a series of government reports, including those of the Royal Commission on Physical Training (Scotland), the Interdepartmental Committee on Physical Deterioration, and the Interdepartmental Committee on Medical Inspection and Feeding of Children Attending Public Elementary Schools. However, despite this pressure, the clause which formally established the school medical service had to be smuggled on to the statute book by Sir Robert Louis Morant, the Permanent Secretary of the Board of Education, and was never properly discussed (Gilbert 1966: 117–31).

This account of the origins of the school medical service has been repeated on a number of occasions (Searle 1971: 236; Fraser 1973: 138–9; 1984: 148–9; Hay 1983: 44; Thane 1982: 76–7; Peden 1985: 12; Dwork 1987: 184–94), but it raises a number of questions. First, Gilbert ignores the extent to which the development of school medical inspection systems was an international phenomenon, in which doctors repeatedly used the experience gained from other countries to reinforce the case for policy innovations in their own. Second, he makes little reference to any existing arrangements for safeguarding the health of children in British schools, and as a result of this he fails to explain how medical officers of health used this experience to support their claims for the establishment of a school medical service in the country as a whole (Hirst 1983: 5–96). Third, and most importantly, he fails to explain why a measure which was apparently regarded as central to the preservation of national life should have to be smuggled on to the statute book before anyone could realise what was happening. In fact, as we shall see, this aspect of Gilbert's argument is simply misleading.

School medical provision abroad

In 1910, in his first annual report as Chief Medical Officer of the Board of Education, Sir George Newman said that

> the growth of practical interest in the health of schoolchildren is, both in England and on the Continent, of comparatively recent date. It is indeed only in the nineteenth century that the question has received systematic study and attention even from the medical profession, and the work, both theoretical and practical, was for a long time limited in scope and somewhat spasmodic in character (PP 1910 Cd. 4986 xxiii: 2).

A number of writers, including George Newman, have identified the 'father' of school medicine as Johann Peter Frank (1745–1821). Between 1779 and 1819 Frank published a nine-volume study of public health work, entitled *System einer vollständigen medizinischen Polizey* (Frank 1779–1827). He argued that the state had a duty to itself to promote the health and welfare of its citizens, and he believed that the various branches of public health work should be administered by the local community as part of an integrated public health system. The second volume of his study was devoted to 'the hygiene of childhood'. In 1939 Newman said that this book constituted 'the first authentic and comprehensive outline of the statecraft of school hygiene in the modern sense' (Newman 1939: 185–6; Leff and Leff 1959: 27; Hogarth 1909: 13; see also Sigerist 1956: 47–63; PP 1910 Cd. 4986 xxiii: 2).

Three other pioneers of school medicine were Per Henrik Ling, Carl Lorinser and Edouard (Edward) Seguin (Hogarth 1909: 13–14; PP 1910 Cd. 4986 xxiii: 2; Newman 1939: 187). Per Henrik Ling (1776–1839) was the originator of the Swedish system of free-standing physical exercises. He was appointed Director of the newly-created Royal Gymnastic Central Institute in Stockholm in 1813, and published a book on gymnastic training in 1836 (Ling 1836; Hogarth 1909: 13; Hyamson 1951: 371). Carl Lorinser (1796–1853) wrote a controversial pamphlet on the care of health in schools in the same year. He claimed that the health of schoolchildren was deteriorating because the lessons were too long and because the curriculum was badly designed, and called for a number of improvements in the way schools were managed (Lorinser 1861; Hogarth 1909: 14; Hyamson 1951: 377). Edouard Seguin (1812–80) wrote a very influential book on 'the moral, hygienic and educational treatment of idiots' in 1846. He became the first superintendent of the Massachusetts School for Idiots and Feeble-Minded Youths in 1848, and played a major role in the development of special education on both sides of the Atlantic during the rest of the century (Seguin 1846; Hogarth 1909: 14; Pritchard 1963: 53–4, 177–9; Steedman 1992: 25–31).

However, although a small number of pioneers made strenuous efforts to stimulate interest in the general problems of school hygiene, the work only really began to bear fruit in the 1860s. In 1910 George Newman wrote that

> in the period between 1840 and 1865 there is little or no sign that the movement was gaining ground, but in the latter year the report of the Schools Commission in Norway did something to bring the importance of school hygiene once more before the general public, and in 1866 Hermann Cohn undertook his classic researches into the eyesight of over 10,000 children at Breslau.

He argued that

> these researches form both the beginning and the inspiration of the systematic and extensive enquiry into the physical conditions of school life which, in the writings of many experts of various countries, has been one of the marked features of modern educational progress (PP 1910 Cd. 4986 xxiii: 2; Kommission for forandret af det høiere skolevæsen 1867; Cohn 1867).

Two things particularly impressed Newman about Hermann Cohn's contribution to the development of medical inspection. First, Cohn's work was especially important because it was far more thorough than anything which had preceded it. Second, Cohn used his findings to formulate definite theories on the subject of school hygiene (PP 1910 Cd. 4986 xxiii: 2–3). Cohn discussed some of these ideas in a paper which he wrote for the Fourth International Congress of Hygiene and Demography in Geneva in 1882. He said that every country ought to appoint a chief medical officer to advise its Ministry of Education; that every local authority ought to have its own district medical officer; and that every school should have its own school doctor. The school doctor would be expected to advise the school authorities on medical and sanitary issues; to measure the children and to ensure that they were seated comfortably; to examine the children's eyes; to ensure that all the rooms were well lit; and to make arrangements for schools to be closed during outbreaks of infectious and contagious disease. At the end of every year the school doctor would be expected to submit a report to the district medical officer, the district medical officer would submit a report to the chief medical officer, and the chief medical officer would compile an annual report on the sanitary condition of the country's schools (Cohn 1883: 433–4).

During the 1860s and 1870s, a growing number of doctors and educationists argued that the health of children was being undermined by parental pressure and intellectual overexertion (see also Robertson 1972a; 1972b). In 1879 Dr Treichler told an audience at Baden-Baden that one-third of the children attending schools in Darmstadt, Paris and Neuenburg were suffering from 'habitual headache' which 'destroys much of the happiness and cheerfulness of life, produces anaemia and want of intellectual tone and . . . reduces many a highly-gifted and poetic soul to the level of a discontented drudge' (*Times* 1880; see also PP 1884 (293) lxi: 21). In 1884 Herr Menno Huizinga of Harlingen highlighted 'the dangers to which the nervous system of pupils and students was exposed by overwork in study and examination' (*British Medical Journal* 1884b: 485), and in 1885 Dr Hertel concluded that 'it must therefore . . . be regarded as an established fact that school . . . exercises a pernicious influence upon the health of the child' (Hertel 1885: 31–3). In 1887 Dr Lagneau of Paris said that 'over-pressure was making its baneful effects felt in a perceptible degree in most schools' as a result of 'bad, or too elastic regulations' (Medical Press 1887: 595). M. Peter argued that large numbers of children suffered from 'involuntary fatigue', and that the symptoms ceased when the overpressure was removed (ibid.: 596).

The question of educational overpressure aroused considerable controversy, both in Britain and abroad. In Britain, Dr James Crichton-Browne claimed that 46.1 per cent of the schoolchildren in London were suffering from 'habitual headache', but one of the Department of Education's Chief Inspectors of Schools, J.G. Fitch, said that Crichton-Browne's methods of investigation were 'neither judicious nor trustworthy' (PP 1884 (293) lxi: 23, 56). The majority of observers believed that the claims made by the supporters of 'overpressure' were highly exaggerated, but there was growing evidence that a large proportion of schoolchildren were in a poor state of health. In 1882 a Danish Commission examined more than 28,000 children in Copenhagen, and found that 29 per cent of the boys and 41 per cent of the girls showed signs of ill-health. The most common complaints were anaemia, scrofula and headaches, but many of the older children were also suffering from myopia (Hertel 1885; 147; British Medical Journal 1884a: 477). In 1884 Professor Axel Key collected evidence from surveys of the health of the 18,000 children in a number of different countries. He also found that more than a third of the children were suffering from some form of physical defect (Burgerstein 1889: 134–57; Hogarth 1909: 14).

These inquiries had an important effect on the development of medical inspection in the latter part of the nineteenth century. There are reports of the existence of school medical officers in Poland in the 1780s and in Sweden in the 1830s, and France introduced a law regulating the conduct of school medical officers in 1833, but the first effective system of medical inspection for primary schoolchildren was only introduced in Brussels in 1874. However, between 1874 and 1906 school medical officers were appointed in at least twenty different countries, including Finland, Norway, Sweden, Russia, Germany, Austria, Hungary, Switzerland, France, Holland, Belgium, Romania, Czechoslovakia, Serbia, Portugal, Spain, Argentina, Chile, the United States and Japan (*British Medical Journal* 1906d; Kerr and Wallis 1908, ii: 490; Royal Swedish Committee 1908: 54; Hogarth 1909: 25–32; Gulick and Ayres 1908: 18–28). The areas which appointed school medical officers were usually large urban centres, and the range of tasks which they performed was often very limited, but many areas had made elaborate and sophisticated arrangements for medical inspection, and these had a major influence on the campaign for medical inspection in Britain (see Dawson 1906: 30).

The most elaborate system of medical inspection was introduced in the German city of Wiesbaden in 1896. In 1910 George Newman wrote:

> the Wiesbaden system marks the introduction of a new conception and understanding of the problem [of school hygiene]. This system, which has been widely adopted in Germany, treats the child as the centre of interest and his well-being as the end of reform (PP 1910 Cd. 4986 xxiii: 3–4).

Archibald Hogarth said that Wiesbaden

> was the first municipality in the world to establish a model system of medical inspection – a system which took account not only of the health but also of the educational requirements of the children on admission, and at the same time made provision for the re-examination and supervision of all children (Hogarth 1909: 29).

This system had an extremely strong influence on the development of medical inspection in Britain. In 1908 Dr C.J. Thomas argued:

> the Wiesbaden experience has had an immense influence on the development of medical inspection, and its system is seen reflected, to some extent, in the Schedule which the Board of Education has issued, and which is to form the pattern for work all over England and Wales (Thomas 1908: 189).

The Wiesbaden system was described in minute detail by the Medical Officer of the Local Government Board in Scotland, Dr William Leslie Mackenzie, and by William Harbutt Dawson (Mackenzie 1906; Dawson 1906). The regulations stated that all new entrants should be examined thoroughly within six weeks of the start of the school year, in order to see whether they should be placed under permanent medical supervision, or whether they ought to be excused from certain activities. School doctors were expected to say whether the constitution of each child was 'good', 'medium' or 'bad'. Children whose general constitution was marked down as 'bad' were placed under continuous medical supervision until their health improved. The doctors were also expected to give all the entrants a superficial examination within two to three days of the start of the school year. This examination was designed to detect vermin and infectious and contagious diseases.

The Wiesbaden authorities also made arrangements for the continuous medical supervision of schoolchildren throughout their school career. Doctors were expected to examine each child thoroughly during the third, fifth and eighth school years. The details of every examination were recorded on a special 'health certificate', which was kept by the school in a 'durable portfolio'. At the end of the final examination the doctor was expected to complete a report on the child's 'entire physical development during school life'. Doctors were also expected to visit the schools once every fortnight, in order to give each child a superficial examination, and to inspect the school buildings. The regulations stated that 'on pedagogic grounds it is expected that the doctor will tactfully avoid any deprecation of a teacher before his class'.

School doctors were not allowed to provide medical treatment, but on certain occasions they were expected to examine children at home, if the children were absent from school without a proper medical certificate. They were also expected to make a thorough inspection of the school buildings on at least two occasions in the school year, once in the summer and once in the winter. Although they did not have the power to force the school managers to make improvements, they were entitled to make recommendations, and if they thought that these were being ignored they could appeal to the municipal health committee. In urgent cases, they were advised to notify the municipal school inspector or the district medical officer of health (Mackenzie 1906: 88–101; Dawson 1906: 4–6, 36–9)

A very different system of medical inspection was introduced in a number of American towns. Under the Wiesbaden system, the school doctor was expected to visit each school every two weeks, but in New York the doctor was expected to visit the schools every day. The main aim of medical inspection in New York and elsewhere in America was to prevent the spread of infectious and contagious diseases. The procedure was as follows: the children were examined by a teacher when they arrived at school, and if they appeared to be unwell they were placed in a special room; they were then given a detailed examination by the school doctor. The doctor also conducted a periodic examination of all the children in the class. This examination took the form of a 'march-past': the doctor stood with his or her back to the window, the children marched past, and any child who appeared to be unwell was then examined more thoroughly. There were no arrangements for the doctor to conduct a detailed personal examination of all the children in the school (*Lancet* 1905: *British Medical Journal* 1905d; Hogarth 1909: 29–30; Gulick and Ayres 1908: 29).

This selective system of medical inspection was also introduced in a number of other American cities, including Boston, Orange, Chicago and Philadelphia. Amelia Watt Smyth included the following account of medical inspection in Boston in her book, *Physical deterioration: its causes and the cure*:

> The medical inspector visits the school each morning soon after it opens. The first duty of the teacher, as soon as the class assembles, is to pick out any child who appears to be ill, who complains of any symptoms, or whose parents wish for an examination. These children are sent to a special room where they are seen by the medical inspector, who decides whether they are fit to attend school; if a child is found to be ill, it is sent home with a note stating the reason why it is dismissed, and

> advising the parent as to the steps which should be taken. He keeps a record of all cases declared to be unfit to attend school, and sends reports in respect of all infectious cases to the Health Authorities, but never undertakes the treatment of the child; his duty ends with the recognition of illness, and the advice to the parents to have it treated. Before a child is permitted to return to school after illness it is again examined by the medical inspector (Smyth 1904: 121; see also *British Medical Journal* 1901; 1904b; 1904c).

Many other towns and cities also made arrangements for medical inspection. In Stockholm the school medical officers were expected to examine every child during the first, fourth and sixth school years; they were also expected to examine any 'delicate' children who had been recommended for a place on a vacation colony, as well as any other children who had been reported for examination by the head teacher (Royal Swedish Committee 1907: 59). In Nice each child was given a special booklet, or *livret scolaire de santé*, which included details of the child's age, domicile, place and date of birth, vaccination record, weight, height, chest girth and aptitude for sport. The booklet also contained a special card, which had to be handed to the medical inspector whenever the child was examined (Kerr and Wallis 1908, ii: 536–7; *British Medical Journal* 1906b). In Prague the school medical officers were expected to examine every school entrant, and to maintain a regular supervision over the health of the children throughout their school careers (Kerr and Wallis 1908, ii: 546). In Hobart the medical inspectors had the following duties: they had to examine every new entrant, and to record both the details of the examination and the child's medical history on a special record card; they also had to visit each school at least once a week in order to examine any child whose health had given teachers cause for concern (Elkington 1908: 5; *British Medical Journal* 1907d: 531).

A number of areas also made special arrangements for dental inspection. Dental inspection was introduced in Brussels in 1875, and a dental clinic was opened in Strasbourg in 1902. Attendance at the clinic was compulsory and treatment was free. In 1904 10,664 children were examined and 6282 children were treated; 7985 teeth were extracted and 7065 teeth were filled. The dentist also instructed the children in the use of a toothbrush; free brushes were handed out, and the children were told to use them three times daily. The introduction of dental inspection in Strasbourg led to a considerable improvement in the teeth of the children, and similar schemes were introduced in many other cities. In February 1907 the *British Medical Journal* reported that school dental services were now being offered in New York, Brussels, Darmstadt, Wiesbaden, Mühlhausen, Strasbourg, Ulm and Prague (*British Medical Journal* 1906c; 1907a).

The early development of medical inspection in Britain

The campaign for school medical inspection in Britain was initially concerned with the sanitary control of school buildings and the prevention of the spread of infectious diseases, and the question of individual medical inspection only really came to the fore in the early years of the twentieth century. The most important single piece of legislation was the Public Health Act of 1875. Although the Act did not include any specific references to schools, it did refer to the sanitary control of houses, and the preamble to the Act stated that the term 'house' included 'schools, [and] also factories and other buildings in which more than twenty persons are employed at the time' (38 & 39 Vict. Ch. 55, Preamble). The Act obliged local authorities to carry out periodic surveys in each district, and if they found any properties which were insanitary or overcrowded, they were expected to take steps to improve them. Section 92 stated that

> it shall be the duty of every Local Authority to cause to be made from time to time inspection of their district, with a view to ascertain what nuisances exist calling for abatement under the powers of this Act, and to enforce the provisions of this Act in order to abate the same.

The Act included eight different definitions of the term 'nuisance': the first definition was 'any premises in such a state as to be a nuisance or injurious to health' and the fifth definition was 'any house or part of a house so overcrowded as to be dangerous to the health of the inmates, whether or not members of the same family' (38 & 39 Vict. Ch. 55, section 91).[1]

The Public Health Act also included a number of other sections which affected the sanitary control of schools. Section 23 of the Act stated that

> where any house within the district of a Local Authority is without a drain sufficient for effectual drainage, the Local Authority shall by written notice require the owner or occupier of such house . . . to make a covered drain or drains emptying into any sewer which the Local Authority are entitled to use, and which is not more than one hundred feet from the site of such house; but if no such means of drainage are within that distance, then emptying into such covered cesspool or other place . . . as the Local Authority direct.

Section 36 of the Act stated that

> if a house within the district of a Local Authority appears to such Local Authority . . . to be without a sufficient water closet, earth closet or privy and an ashpit furnished with proper doors and coverings, the Local Authority shall, by written notice, require the owner or occupier of the house . . . to provide a sufficient water closet, earth closet or privy, and ashpit furnished as aforesaid, or either of them, as the case may require.

Section 120 stated that

> where any Local Authority are of opinion . . . that the cleansing or disinfecting of a house or part thereof, and of any articles therein likely to retain infection, would tend to prevent or check infectious disease, it shall be the duty of such Authority to give notice in writing to the owner or occupier of such house or part thereof requiring him to cleanse and

> disinfect such house or part thereof and articles within a time specified in such notice.

The Public Health Act was reinforced by the sanitary provisions of the Education Code (see also Hirst 1983: 19–20). When the Government passed the Forster Education Act of 1870, it said

> before any grant is made to a school the Education Department must be satisfied that the school premises are healthy, well-lighted, drained and ventilated, properly-furnished, supplied with suitable offices [i.e. latrines] and contain in the principal school-room and classrooms at least eighty cubical feet of internal space, and in the school-room and classrooms at least eight square feet of area, for each child in average attendance (PP 1871 C. 252 lv: para. 17 [c]).

This regulation was subsequently amended, but the Department (and later the Board) of Education continued to insist on a minimum of eighty cubic feet of internal space and eight square feet of area for all new schools until the end of the century (PP 1878–9 C. 2287 lvii: para. 17 [c]; Richards 1902: 124–6).[2] The Department introduced an additional clause, which was designed to strengthen the power of Local Authorities to prevent the spread of infectious diseases, in 1882. It said that

> the school managers must comply with any notice of the Sanitary Authority of the district . . . requiring them for a specified time with a view to preventing the spread of disease either to close the schools or to exclude any scholars from attendance, subject to an appeal to the Department if the managers consider the notice to be unreasonable (PP 1882 C. 3152 l: para. 98; see also *British Medical Journal* 1882).

However, although the Public Health Act conferred a number of powers on the local sanitary authority, and although the Education Code incorporated a number of sanitary provisions, the value of these powers was limited by at least three factors. First, the medical officer of health had no automatic right of entry into school premises. Second, the Department's regulations only applied to schools which received grants from it, and could only be enforced if they had been incorporated into building bye-laws. Third, the regulations themselves were hopelessly inadequate. In 1902 Dr Meredith Richards told his medical officers that

> most of us would agree that even the ten feet of floor space and 120 cubic feet required in new schools need safeguarding by special attention to ventilation, and there can be no . . . justification for continuing the still smaller minimum of 8 square feet of floor space . . . in . . . older schools, a minimum which is not infrequently further reduced by overcrowding in special rooms and departments (Martin 1907: 117; Richards 1902: 126).

The local authorities' powers of entry were defined by Section 102 of the Public Health Act 1875. This section stated that

> the Local Authority, or any of their officers, shall be admitted into any premises for the purpose of examining as to the existence of any nuisance thereon, or of enforcing the provisions of any Act in force within the district requiring fireplaces and furnaces to consume their own smoke, at any time between the hours of nine in the forenoon and six in the afternoon, or, in the case of a nuisance arising in respect of any business, then at any hour when such business is in progress or is usually carried on.

However, the section conferred no automatic right of entry, because it also stated that if the officers of the local authority were refused permission to enter the property, then they had to appeal to the magistrates court, and the court would have to adjudicate between the rival claims of the officers of the local authority and the owners of the property in question. It is easy to see how this section militated against an effective system of sanitary supervision, because it meant that the officers of the local authority had to prove that a nuisance already existed, before they had a chance to investigate (38 & 39 Vict. Ch. 55, section 102).

The problems which this clause presented to medical officers of health were illustrated by the case of Dr Edward Jepson, the Medical Officer of Health for the Rural District of Durham. At the beginning of 1907 Jepson decided to carry out an investigation into 'the insanitary condition of the premises and building of a certain Board School' in the district. The investigation had been prompted by two serious outbreaks of an infectious disease, but although he had every reason to investigate conditions in the school, Jepson's actions sparked a storm of protest. Matters came to a head when the District Clerk remarked that

> the Medical Officer of Health had nothing to do with the sanitary defects of the school referred to. All he had to do in the case of an epidemic was to see that the school was closed, and there his duties ended. If the sanitary conditions were defective, it was for the educational authorities to make complaint.

On 20 February Jepson wrote to the Local Government Board. He pointed out that the Board had recently issued a Circular instructing medical officers of health to pay more attention to the sanitary condition of schools, and asked the Board to support him in the pursuit of his duties. However the Board's reply confirmed that the medical officer of health did not have any automatic right of entry under the 1875 Act:

> Sir – I am directed by the Local Government Board to advert to your letters of the 20th ultimo and the 1st inst., as to your right to enter Public Elementary Schools in your capacity as Medical Officer of Health, and in reply to state that in the case of non-provided schools you should apply to the managers for permission to enter, when such is required, and in the case of provided schools your application should be to the Local Education Authority – i.e. to the Education Committee of the

> Durham County Council. I am to state, however, that as the Board are advised, the position of a Medical Officer of Health as regards right of entry is the same in the case of a school as of any other premises (e.g. a dwelling house) to which Section 102 of the Public Health Act 1875 applies, and a Medical Officer of Health has no right, with or without an order from a sanitary authority, to insist, in virtue of his office, on admission to a school for the purpose of inspecting the school premises (signed: John Lithiby, Assistant Secretary; reprinted in *British Medical Journal* 1907e).

By the end of the nineteenth century, the sanitary condition of the nation's elementary schools had already begun to attract a great deal of criticism. In 1904 Sir George Kekewich told the Annual Congress of the Royal Institute of Public Health that 'the Board of Education had not done and was not now doing its duty in regard to seeing that suitable buildings were provided' and that 'tenderness for the pockets of the owners meant cruelty to the children' (*Lancet* 1904b). In 1905 Mr J. Osborne Smith, a Fellow of the Royal Institute of British Architects, complained that both old and new schools suffered from inefficiency of adapted buildings; insufficient floor space, excessive size of classes, absence of direct sunlight in classrooms, insufficient size of cloakrooms, unsuitable floor spaces, inconvenient access to and faulty construction of sanitary conveniences, unintelligent use of open windows, defective arrangements for admitting and warming fresh air, and inadequate extent of covered playgrounds (*British Medical Journal* 1905a: 380).

The sanitary condition of Irish schools was reviewed by Professor Anthony Roche in 1900. Roche surveyed a total of 8452 schools, with a combined average attendance of approximately 800,000. He found that 2411 schools were housed in buildings which were either 'middling' or 'bad'; that 2690 schools contained defective furniture and apparatus; and that 2068 schools possessed inadequate lavatory facilities. Moreover, 823 schools had no lavatory facilities at all (*British Medical Journal* 1900: 530). In Scotland the Royal Commission on Physical Training found that even in the best schools 'the atmosphere in which teachers and scholars spend so many hours each day is not such as can be considered consistent with healthy conditions'. The Commissioners also found that the offices and latrines of the schools were often neglected, and that too many teachers 'seem to regard extra-mural decency as beyond their province' (PP 1903 Cd. 1507 xxx: para. 154).

Many of the worst sanitary conditions in England and Wales were found in the voluntary or non-provided schools which were still responsible for the education of nearly half the elementary school population at the start of the twentieth century (see Fraser 1984: 87). In 1904 Dr G. Arbour Stephens argued that the sanitary condition of the voluntary schools in Carmarthenshire was a factor which might have a considerable bearing on the alleged physical deterioration of the British population. Many of these schools were old and dilapidated, and many of the roofs had given way. The cloakrooms were small and uncovered, and the children's coats were often exposed to the rain. Most of the schools were ill lit and poorly ventilated, and some schools were three-quarters of a mile from the nearest tap. Only a few schools had lavatories, and the privies were often difficult to clean. In one school, the privies were washed out in the local stream, while further down the stream the water was used for drinking purposes (*British Medical Journal* 1904a; see also *British Medical Journal* 1905b; 1905c).

In addition to commenting on the insanitary state of the school buildings, many medical officers were becoming increasingly concerned by the role played by school attendance in the dissemination of infectious disease (see also Hirst 1983: 8–11; 1991). In 1871 Edwin Chadwick told a meeting of the Social Science Association in Leeds that 'schools, as at present constructed, were the centres of children's epidemics', and the *British Medical Journal* argued that 'the facilities afforded for the spread of infectious diseases . . . through the agency of schools have often resulted in epidemics of considerable magnitude' (*British Medical Journal* 1871: 482; 1874a). In November 1874 the *British Medical Journal* put forward a scheme for the compulsory inspection and exclusion of any scholars who were suspected of spreading disease (*British Medical Journal* 1874b). In 1878 the Liverpool Medical Institution addressed a memorandum on the subject to George Sclater-Booth, the President of the Local Government Board, pointing out that similar measures were already being taken in factories and on emigration ships (*British Medical Journal* 1878c; see also *British Medical Journal* 1876; 1878a; 1878b).

So far as schoolchildren were concerned, the diseases which attracted the greatest attention in the second half of the nineteenth century were diphtheria, scarlet fever and measles. Both diphtheria and scarlet fever (or scarlatina) are droplet infections which can be spread by coughing or sneezing, in dust, or by touching infected clothing. The diphtheria bacillus causes its victims to suffer from sore throats, fevers, headaches and vomiting, and in more serious cases patches of dirty grey or yellow membrane form in the victims' throats, leading to difficulties in breathing or swallowing. The majority of fatalities are caused by a toxin which enters the bloodstream through the bacillus and attacks the central nervous system, but some victims die as a result of suffocation. Scarlet fever produces many of the same symptoms as diphtheria, but is usually accompanied by a malignant skin rash which lasts for up to a week before fading. Between 1891 and 1900, these two diseases were responsible for nearly 130,000 deaths, the vast majority of which occurred up to the age of fourteen (PP 1905 Cd. 2618 xviii: 3; Smith 1990: 136–50).

Following the passing of the Education Act of 1870, a number of investigations were carried out which showed that school attendance was a primary factor in the spread of infection. In 1876 Sir Richard Thorne Thorne conducted an investigation into an outbreak of diphtheria at Great Coggeshall in Essex, and discovered that children between the ages of three and twelve were almost twice as likely to catch the disease as children under the age of three or between thirteen and fifteen (Thorne 1888: 43). In 1882 W.H. Power investigated a series of outbreaks in the village of Pirbright. He found that 'on four successive occasions when the village school was open, well-marked diphtheria occurred among the schoolchildren', despite the fact that the school had been carefully disinfected after each outbreak (ibid.). In 1897 the Medical Officer of Health for London, Dr Shirley Murphy, found that there was 'a notable decrease in the prevalence of [diphtheria] . . . at all ages, and . . . especially . . . among persons of the school age' when the schools were closed during the summer months (London County Council 1898: 1).

The influence of school attendance was also apparent in the case of scarlet fever and measles. In 1882 Dr Edward Ballard conducted an investigation into an outbreak of scarlet fever in Potton in Bedfordshire, and found that in the majority of the households which were affected by the disease, the first person to fall victim was a child of school age. He concluded that 'the attendance at school of children in an infected condition . . . has been the principal means by which the infection has been spread' (*British Medical Journal* 1883). In 1895 the Medical Officer of Health for Coventry, Dr Mark Fenton, reached a similar conclusion following an outbreak of measles. He found that the numbers of cases reported in four successive weeks when the schools were open were 162, 213, 275 and 492, respectively. The schools were then closed, and figures fell steadily (*British Medical Journal* 1895; *Public Health* 1895: 264).[3]

Although it was widely agreed that school attendance did play a part in the dissemination of disease, it was not entirely clear why this was so. Some observers, such as Sir Richard Thorne Thorne, believed that in the case of diphtheria it was the school environment itself which was to blame. In 1878 he told the Epidemiological Society of London that

> this is not at all a question of the development of a living organism independently of antecedent life, but merely the production, by means of a process of evolution, of that which gives to an already existing organism that property by which it becomes infective – a property which it may lose directly it is deprived of the circumstances which favoured its development, in much the same way as special characteristics may be artificially developed in higher plant life and be as easily lost again (Thorne 1878: 245–6; 1888: 41).

However this interpretation was fiercely challenged by the School Medical Officer for Bradford, James Kerr, in 1897. Kerr argued that 'there is no evidence for England and Wales that school attendance is any considerable factor in disseminating diphtheria', and even though there was some evidence of a 'holiday effect' in London, this was 'small compared with home influences in the poorest parts of London, and more evident in the better class districts' (Kerr 1897: 626–31).

Kerr's arguments received a significant boost from an investigation carried out by C.J. Thomas into the incidence of diphtheria in London in 1903 and

1904. Between September 1903 and March 1904 Thomas carried out an investigation into a total of twenty-nine outbreaks of diphtheria in the city's elementary schools. He found that four out of every five cases were caused by children who were only mildly affected, and that when these scholars were excluded the outbreaks ceased. He concluded that it was not the school buildings but the individuals inside them who were primarily responsible for the spread of the disease (Thomas 1904: 432). In 1905 Thomas carried out a similar investigation into the incidence of measles. He found that measles only spread in classes of children under the age of five years, because 75 per cent of the older children had already acquired an immunity to the disease from a previous attack. However, this did not mean that the incidence of measles in schools would fall if the under-fives were excluded. On the contrary, the disease would then spread more rapidly among older children, because the number of 'unprotected' children would increase dramatically (*British Medical Journal* 1906a).

These investigations had important implications for the way in which public health officers tried to tackle the spread of infectious diseases in schools. The view that the schools themselves were responsible for the spread of infection implied that the best way to stop an epidemic was by closing the school, as occurred in Pirbright in 1882. However, if the children themselves were the source of infection, then school closure would be of limited value, because there was no guarantee that they would be free from infection when the schools reopened. In 1904 Thomas described the closure of schools in cases of diphtheria as 'a confession of impotence and defeat'. His work played a very important role in demonstrating to medical officers of health that if they wished to prevent the spread of infection in schools, they would have to devote much more attention to the children themselves (Thomas 1904: 432; Wilkinson 1905: 228).

The presuppositions of compelled attendance

Although the government had introduced a number of measures which were designed to protect the health of children in school, it made little effort to encourage school boards to appoint their own school medical officers (Hirst 1983: 46–50). The first school board to appoint its own medical officer was that of London, which appointed Dr W.R. Smith in 1890. Smith was appointed on a part-time basis, and his primary duty was to make arrangements for the medical examination of applicants for teaching posts, but he was also responsible for coordinating the efforts of London's medical officers of health to combat the spread of infectious disease in schools (Hirst 1981: 282; *British Medical Journal* 1890). The first full-time school medical officer was Dr James Kerr, who was appointed by the School Board of Bradford in 1893. In 1909 Archibald Hogarth described Kerr as 'the first medical man to enter the schools daily in the role of a School Doctor, and to study all problems of school hygiene . . . in the interests of the children' (Hogarth 1909: 20). In

1901 Kerr became School Medical Officer for London, and the capital's school medical service grew rapidly. In 1905 it employed two full-time doctors, twenty-three part-time doctors and twelve nurses (PP 1906 Cd. 2784 xlvii: 235).

During the 1890s the development of medical inspection was closely associated with the introduction of a series of measures for the education of children with special needs (Pritchard 1963: 95–150; Hirst 1983: 64–71). In 1893 the Elementary Education (Blind and Deaf Children) Act compelled local authorities to maintain special schools for blind and deaf children, and to appoint medical officers to supervise their operation (56 & 57 Vict. Ch. 42). Three years later the Department of Education appointed a Committee 'to enquire into the existing systems for the education of feeble-minded and defective children not under the charge of Guardians, and not idiots or imbeciles, and to advise as to any changes . . . that might seem desirable'. The Committee concluded that every school authority should make arrangements to decide '(a) what children, resident in their district, not being imbecile, are, by reason of mental or physical defect, incapable of receiving proper benefit from the instruction in ordinary schools', and '(b) what children are unfit by reason of epilepsy to attend the ordinary schools'. It also said that each authority should be required to make special arrangements for these children, either by means of special day classes, or by boarding out, or by establishing special homes for defective and epileptic children (PP1898 C.8746 xxvi: iii, 36). These recommendations were incorporated in the Elementary Education (Defective and Epileptic Children) Act of 1899, and although this Act was not compulsory, it did lead to the appointment of school medical officers in a number of different areas (PP 1898 C. 8746 xxvi: iii, 36; PP 1910 Cd. 4986 xxiii: 5).

However, although the introduction of special measures for 'defective' children undoubtedly played an important part in the development of medical inspection in certain areas, the most important factor to influence the development of medical inspection before 1907 was the (Balfour) Education Act of 1902 (2 Edw. VII, Ch. 42). This Act abolished the school boards and transferred their powers to the county councils and the councils of the larger boroughs and urban districts (Martin 1907: 116; Simon 1965: 219). The Act led to a greater degree of coordination in the administration of public health and education and enabled many areas to appoint school medical officers for the first time, while other areas made fundamental changes to their existing services (Martin 1907: 116; Simon 1965: 219; *Lancet* 1904a: 1003; London County Council 1908: 55). In 1906 the Interdepartmental Committee on Medical Inspection and Feeding commented that:

> In the majority of areas . . . the system of medical inspection has been established for the first time by the new Authority. Not infrequently the Medical Officer of Health has been appointed Medical Officer to the Education Authority. This arrangement has many conveniences, and has often been the outcome of the work done by the Medical Officer of

Health in visiting the schools for the prevention of the spread of infectious disease. More than one such officer had previously been accustomed on the occasion of his visits to give informal advice on subjects, such as eyesight, when appealed to by the teachers (PP 1906 Cd. 2779 xlvii: 2).

The 1902 Act also helped to bring about a more general change in public health thinking. During the latter part of the nineteenth century, the campaign to extend school medical inspection had been largely if not entirely concerned with the sanitary control of school buildings and the prevention of infectious and contagious diseases, but as more medical officers became involved in school work, they began to focus much more attention on the children themselves. The 'Inspectress of Physical Welfare' in West Sussex, Mildred Moseley, said that the introduction of medical inspection had enabled a number of children to receive spectacles, and that other children had received treatment for defects of the eyes, nose and ears (PP 1906 Cd. 2784 xlvii: 239). The Medical Officer of Health for Swansea, Dr Rhys Davies, wrote:

> From my evidence and from this memorandum, it is clear that the medical inspection of schools in Swansea, though in existence for some years, has been . . . very limited in scope. It is therefore too soon to expect many results. Enough work however has been done to show that a large number of children are physically defective – so defective as to be very seriously handicapped in their school work. It is only just to add that this grave condition is chiefly due, not to any neglect or indifference, but to the lack of knowledge, in the past, of the actual state of affairs, on the part of the school authority and the parents. But there are undoubted signs that the medical inspection has already done much good. I have, in my evidence, referred briefly to this good effect on the child, the teacher and the parent (PP 1906 Cd. 2784 xlvii: 264).

The development of a more wide-ranging conception of the role of medical inspection was closely associated with the work of Dr William Leslie Mackenzie, the Medical Officer for the Local Government Board in Scotland. In his book *The medical inspection of schoolchildren*, published in 1904, Mackenzie argued that the case for medical inspection rested on 'the presuppositions of compelled attendance'. He argued that 'compulsion in education presupposes two things – first, that the child is mentally and physically fit to be educated; [and] second, that after his state education is completed he is capable of remaining fit for the duties of civil life'. The most important question was whether the children attending school were sufficiently fit to derive the maximum benefit from school life. Mackenzie argued that even though the majority of children were sufficiently fit to attend school, 'the second standard has not even been approximately realised'. This fact 'gives to every serious proposal of medical inspection its extreme cogency' (Mackenzie 1904: 6–8).

Mackenzie's analysis of the reasons for medical inspection was based to a considerable extent on his own experience as a medical examiner for the Royal Commission on Physical Training in Scotland. In 1902 the Commission had invited Mackenzie and Matthew Hay to conduct a detailed survey of the health and physical condition of 1200 children in Aberdeen and Edinburgh. Mackenzie claimed that over 92 per cent of the children whom he had examined in Edinburgh were suffering from defects of the nose or throat, more than 30 per cent were suffering from defects of the eye, and 18.5 per cent had diseased glands. The Royal Commission itself estimated that at least 700 Edinburgh children were suffering from unrecognised pulmonary tuberculosis and that 1300 children were suffering from 'unrecognised heart disease of a serious nature'. It also claimed that 15,000 children were suffering from diseases of the throat and that 12,000 children were suffering some form of ear disease (PP 1903 Cd. 1507 xxx: 26–7).

This was not the only inquiry to show that large numbers of children were suffering from some form of hitherto undetected disease. Between 1898 and 1902 Leslie Thorne Thorne examined 1890 boys between the ages of nine and sixteen who had been awarded scholarships by the London Technical Education Board. He found that ninety boys showed definite signs of cardiac disease, and that 330 had defective hearing. One-third of the boys had enlarged tonsils or adenoids, and two-thirds had defective vision (Thorne 1904: 829–30; see also Berry 1904). In 1906 Dr William Robertson examined 806 children in Leith, and found that nearly one child in seven had rickets, and one in twelve had curvature of the spine. Twenty per cent of the children had enlarged glands, 45 per cent had some form of visual defect, and more than 50 per cent had 'affections of the ears or throat'. Forty-one children had bronchitis, seventy-eight had weak hearts, thirty-six had abdominal defects, and 103 showed clear signs of malnutrition (*British Medical Journal* 1907b).

The development of medical inspection was also closely bound up with the question of physical training. In 1902 the Board of Education issued *A model course of physical training for use in the upper departments of public elementary schools*, and a revised *Syllabus of physical exercises* was introduced three years later. In 1903 the Royal Commission on Physical Training said that 'even weakly or ill-formed children may receive the greatest possible benefit from physical training carefully devised', and in 1904 the Physical Deterioration Committee said that 'methodical physical training' would improve the health and physique of the nation (Newman 1939: 269–71; PP 1903 Cd. 1507 xxx: 31; PP 1904 Cd. 2175 xxxii: 90). However, it was widely recognised that there was little point in introducing an elaborate system of physical exercises if the children were too unhealthy to take advantage of them. In 1906 Lauder Brunton told the President of the Board of Education that 'the basis on which all physical training must be founded is acknowledged in all the Blue Books issued on the subject to be medical inspection' (PRO ED24/279: National League for Physical Education and Improvement).

If it was necessary to have a system of medical inspection in order to ensure that the education system helped the development of the adult, it was also important to make sure that the education system did not hinder the development of the adult. Dr Mackenzie claimed that

> although a few ophthalmic surgeons have recently expressed a contrary opinion, yet they cannot get rid of the fact, established by an examination of hundreds of thousands of schoolchildren, that the cause of myopia is near-work and that schools make children myopic (Mackenzie 1904: 307).

Also in 1904 Ettie Sayer discovered that

> at six years of age three per cent [of children] have seriously bad vision, and 88 per cent can see 6/6 with each eye; at eleven years of age 11 per cent have seriously bad vision, and only 58 per cent can see 6/6 with each eye (Sayer 1904: 1419).

In 1906 Hugh Thompson showed that myopia accounted for 23.4 per cent of all visual defects between the ages of seven and ten, and for 31.3 per cent of visual defects between the ages of twelve and fourteen. Although Thompson's main conclusion was that 'in very young children myopia exists to a greater extent than has hitherto been . . . realised', his work also showed that large numbers of children developed the condition during their school years (Thompson 1906: 193).

In addition to the monitoring of routine defects, it was also important to have a system of medical inspection to detect developmental diseases. Mackenzie found that thirteen of the children he examined in Edinburgh were suffering from some form of organic or acquired heart disease: two of the children were under the age of seven, three were aged between seven and nine, three from nine to eleven, and five were aged eleven or over (Mackenzie 1904: 325–6). Of the 806 children examined in Leith in 1906, fourteen showed signs of pulmonary tuberculosis. In 1907 the editor of the *British Medical Journal* said that it was difficult to imagine a more serious argument for medical inspection. Here, if anywhere, 'medical inspection is imperatively called for, to ensure the active treatment of all cases of lung weakness, whether of bronchitis or of those cases of consumption in the earliest stage which is usually unrecognised' (*British Medical Journal* 1907c).

The Administrative Provisions Act

Bentley Gilbert argued that 'the establishment of the school medical service excited little of the public controversy that surrounded the provision of [school] meals'. The school medical service attracted little attention because the clause which brought it into being 'was buried among more than a dozen other clauses dealing with uninteresting . . . details of . . . school administration', and because the Permanent Secretary of the Board of Education, Sir Robert Louis Morant, devised a form of words which left the door open for medical treatment, while only referring specifically to medical inspection.

Morant was assisted in his endeavours by the fact that 'medical inspection had already built some tradition as a public service', and no new issues of principle were involved (Gilbert 1966: 117–31).

The thesis that the school medical service 'came peacefully because it came secretly' (Gilbert 1966: 117) has found its way into a number of textbooks. Derek Fraser wrote that 'R.L. Morant . . . drew up the 1907 Bill and in effect smuggled medical inspection through by surrounding it with other, much less significant administrative proposals' (Fraser 1973: 138; 1984: 149). Roy Hay said that 'medical inspection of schoolchildren owed something to backbench . . . pressure, but Sir Robert Morant . . . was responsible for its introduction, hidden among the clauses of the Education (Administrative Provisions) Act of 1907' (Hay 1983: 44). Pat Thane claimed that the clauses which established the school medical service were 'buried among a number of routine administrative changes in the education service' (Thane 1982: 77) and Deborah Dwork said that they were 'buried in the Bill with such consummate skill that they hardly raised a ripple in the House' (Dwork 1987: 184). However, Gilbert's thesis has been questioned on a number of occasions, and it is now clear that his account is almost wholly misleading (see Hirst 1982; 1983: 154–91; 1989; 1991; Daglish 1990).

Gilbert's account rested on five major assertions. First, he claimed that when the government introduced the Education (England and Wales) Bill in 1906, it contained no clauses dealing with medical inspection. Second, he argued that the government subsequently agreed to insert a rather limited clause which would have given local authorities the power to make arrangements for medical inspection, without enabling them to provide medical treatment. Third, the clause which led to the establishment of the school medical service was drafted by Sir Robert Morant at the beginning of 1907. Fourth, Morant's 'concern was increased by the appearance on 1 March [1907] of a Private Member's Bill' which 'simply used the inspection clause of the 1906 Bill' and 'would have excluded any provision for treatment'. Finally, this Bill was a source of political embarrassment to the government, which was therefore obliged to provide 'a substitute of its own'.

The statutory provision of school medical inspection was first raised in Parliament by the Labour MP, Will Thorne, when he presented the State Education Bill to the House of Commons on 2 April 1906 (Parliamentary Debates 1906a: col. 191). Clause 7 of the Bill would have required local education authorities to record the height, weight and chest measurements of children entering public elementary schools and to furnish returns to the Board of Education at the end of each year. Clause 8 required each local education authority to appoint a medical officer or officers 'whose duty it shall be to medical examine and to test such children as the teachers may consider in need of medical advice' (PP 1906 (143) ii, clauses 7–8; see also Simon 1965: 257–8). This Bill was withdrawn following the introduction of the government's Bill on 9 April, but the new Bill included a proposal to give local education authorities the power 'to make such arrangements as may be sanctioned by the Board of Education for attending to the health and physical condition of the children educated in public elementary schools' (PP 1906 (160) i: 20; see also PP 1906 (317) i: 16). On 16 July the Liberal MP for Berwickshire, H.J. Tennant, suggested that this power should be converted into a duty, but the President of the Board of Education, Augustine Birrell, said that he would prefer to put down his own amendment when the Bill reached the Report stage. He suggested that the text of such an amendment might read as follows:

> It shall be the duty of every Local Authority to provide for the medical inspection of every child on its application for admission to a Public Elementary School, and on such other occasion as the Board of Education or the Local Education Authority may think fit (Parliamentary Debates 1906c: col. 1398).

If the government had introduced this amendment as an alternative to the original clause, Gilbert would have been correct to say that the amended Bill failed to make any allowance for medical treatment (Gilbert 1966: 127–8). However, when the government presented the revised version of the Bill to Parliament on 25 July, it became clear that Birrell's amendment was an addition to, rather than a substitute for, the original clause. The full text read as follows:

> The powers and duties of a Local Education Authority . . . shall include . . . the duty to provide for the medical inspection of children before or at the time of their admission to a Public Elementary School, and on such other occasions as the Board of Education direct, and the power to make such arrangements as may be sanctioned by the Board of Education for attending to the health and physical condition of the children educated in Public Elementary Schools (PP 1906 (327) i: 18).

Although the main aim of the Education (England and Wales) Bill was to amend the status of religious education in grant-aided schools, the revised medical inspection clause received a considerable amount of attention. On 30 July the Chancellor of the Exchequer, Herbert Asquith, said that the new clause gave

> much-needed powers and duties to all these Local Authorities which will make a great difference not only to the happiness but [also to] the intelligence of the children, and the duty which is imposed upon them of providing for medical inspection, and the power given to them to attend to the health and physical condition, is an even more necessary supplement for the statutory equipment of these local bodies (Parliamentary Debates 1906d: col. 490).

During the same debate Thomas Macnamara said that the medical inspection of children 'was worth the whole of the rest of the Bill put together' (ibid.: col. 544). On 12 December Charles Masterman pleaded with the President of the Board of Education to ensure that 'even if no agreement could be come to in regard to the religious controversy . . . this charter for the physical welfare of the children should by some truce of God become law' (Parliamentary Debates 1906f: cols 413–14).

The introduction of school medical inspection was also debated in the House of Lords on 21 November. Lord Belper said that it was unfair to large agricultural districts to compel them to make arrangements for medical inspection, and although he had no objection to medical inspection in principle, he thought that the introduction of medical inspection in individual areas should be optional (Parliamentary Debates 1906e: cols 741–3). He was supported by Lord Harris, who said that medical inspection was bound to become increasingly expensive, and that it was unreasonable to expect local authorities to bear this expense without any help from the Treasury (ibid.: cols 743–4). However, the Lords doubted whether these objections provided sufficient justification for deleting the government's proposal. Lord Farrer said that 'everybody who had experience of country schools would agree that if this duty were placed on County authorities the health of the nation would be greatly improved' (ibid.: col. 744). The Marquess of Lansdowne said that although the introduction of compulsory medical inspection might well pose problems for rural districts, 'there is a very great weight of authority in favour of inspection of the kind suggested in the Bill' (ibid.: col. 750). Lord Fitzmaurice said that the county authorities had overcome much bigger problems in the past, and the government's clause would strike a real blow 'on behalf of the improvement of the health of the people and the better sanitation of the country' (ibid.: col. 753).

The Bishop of Ripon proposed three further amendments. The first was designed to ensure that every child was examined immediately before leaving school. The second sought to convert the second half of the clause into an obligatory clause which would have forced local authorities 'to make such arrangements as may be sanctioned by the Board of Education for attending to the health and physical condition of the children educated in Public Elementary Schools'. The third sought to limit the scope of this duty by deleting the phrase 'attending to' and putting the word ' supervising' in its place. The Bishop thought that the inclusion of the phrase 'attending to' would prejudice the interests of local general practitioners by allowing Local Education Authorities to treat the children in their schools, but the President of the Privy Council, the Earl of Crewe, rejected the amendment on the grounds that 'medical treatment is not included *as the term is ordinarily understood*' (ibid.: col. 755, emphasis added). The Earl's response raised a number of questions about the precise nature of the government's intentions, but it did not mean that no medical treatment of any kind would be provided. In 1907 the Earl of Crewe told the House of Lords that

> provision is made for the medical care of the minor ailments to which children are subject, and the manner in which it is thought that this can best be carried out is by visits of nurses employed by the local authority to the homes of the children (Parliamentary Debates 1907d: col. 726).

These debates are important because the amended version of the original medical inspection clause was copied into two Bills which were introduced at the start of the following year. The first of these was Walter Russell Rea's Private Member's Bill, which was published on 15 February 1907. The second was the government's own Education (Administrative Provisions) Bill, which was laid before Parliament on 28 February. Gilbert suggested that the government persuaded Rea to drop his Bill so that it could introduce a 'substitute' of its own, but the relevant sections of the two Bills were identical (PP 1907 (22) i: section 1(b); PP 1907 (83) i: section 10(b)). The real reason why the government asked Rea to withdraw his Bill was not because it objected to Bill itself, but because it was afraid that Rea might accept a number of amendments which ministers would be reluctant to countenance (Parliamentary Debates 1907a: cols 1102–3). The clause which established the school medical service received the Royal Assent on 28 August 1907, thirteen months and three days after it was originally presented to Parliament (Parliamentary Debates 1907e: col. 425).[4]

Notes

1 The other definitions of the term 'nuisance' were as follows: (2) any pool, ditch, gutter, watercourse, privy, urinal, cesspool, drain or ashpit so foul or in such a state as to be a nuisance or injurious to health; (3) any animal so kept as to be a nuisance or injurious to health; (4) any accumulation or deposit which is a nuisance or injurious to health; (6) any factory, workshop or workplace (not already under the operation of any general Act for the regulation of factories or bakehouses), not kept in a cleanly state, or not ventilated in such a manner as to render harmless as far as practicable any gases, vapours, dust or other impurities generated in the course of the work carried on therein that are a nuisance or injurious to health, or so overcrowded while work is carried on as to be dangerous or injurious to the health of those employed therein; (7) any fireplace or furnace which does not as far as practicable consume the smoke arising from the combustible used therein, or any mill, factory, dyehouse, brewery, bakehouse or gaswork, or in any manufacturing or trade processes whatsoever; and (8) any chimney (not being the chimney of a private dwelling-house) sending forth black smoke in such quantity as to be a nuisance (38 & 39 Vict. Ch. 55, section 90).

2 In 1901 the minimum requirements for new schools were increased to 120 cubic feet of internal space and 10 square feet of floor space for each child in average attendance, but the previous regulations continued to apply to older schools. See PP 1901 Cd. 513 lv: para. 85 (a); ibid., Schedule VII; Richards 1902: 126.

3 This episode is also discussed by Smith (1990: 147). Smith points out that the number of cases might well have declined independently of the measures which were taken.

4 The government made two minor amendments to the clause during the Bill's Committee stage. The final version of clause 13 (1) (b) read as follows: 'The powers and duties of a local education authority . . . shall include . . . the duty to provide for the medical inspection of children immediately before or at the time of or as soon as possible after their admission to a public elementary school, and on such other occasions as the Board of Education direct, and the power to make such arrangements as may be sanctioned by the Board of Education for attending to the health and physical condition of the children educated in public elementary schools'. See PP 1907 (288) vi; 7 Edw. VII Ch. 43, section 13 (1) (b).

four

The foundation of the school medical service

Although the Administrative Provisions Act did not pass through Parliament without debate, the legislation provided little indication of the form which the school medical service would take. The Act instructed local authorities to make arrangements for the medical inspection of children before or at the time of their admission to a public elementary school, and on such other occasions as the Board of Education might direct, and it gave them the power to make such arrangements as might be sanctioned by the Board for attending to their health and physical condition. However, it said nothing about the procedures which the Board itself must follow in advising local authorities, nor did it specify the arrangements which the local authorities would have to make in order to comply with that advice. As a result of this, it was clear that a great deal of work would have to be done within a relatively short space of time if the Administrative Provisions Act was to have any practical effect.

In addition to these administrative issues, the Act also made no reference to the financial arrangements which local authorities would be required to make in order to pay for medical inspection. When the government issued its first memorandum on medical inspection in November 1907, it said that the effectiveness of an Authority's arrangements for medical inspection 'will . . . be one of the elements to be considered in determining the efficiency of each school as a grant-aided school' (PP 1910 Cd. 4986 xxiii: 146), and this requirement was reiterated in the Code of Regulations issued to local education authorities in 1908 (PP 1908 Cd. 4158 lxxxii: i). However, although the Board was prepared to withhold grants from schools which failed to make satisfactory arrangements for medical inspection, it only began to provide special funds for medical treatment in 1912, and for medical inspection in 1913 (PP 1912 Cd. 6138 lxv; PP 1913 Cd. 7041 l). The absence of any earmarked funds for either inspection or treatment before 1912 was a major source of discontent among local education authorities, and it represented a significant obstacle to the development of the school medical service before the First World War (see e.g. *Times* 1908a; 1908b; 1908c).

The establishment of the Medical Department of the Board of Education

We have already seen that, in addition to imposing new obligations on the local authorities, the Administrative Provisions Act also imposed new obligations on the Board of Education. The Board was now required to draw up suitable schemes of medical inspection and sanction proposals for the provision of medical treatment, but the Act gave no indication as to how the Board was expected to discharge these duties. The Department of Education had appointed Dr Alfred Eichholz as Her Majesty's Inspector of Schools in the education sub-district of West Lambeth in 1898, and after an initial settling-in period Eichholz began to devote more and more of his time to the supervision of schools for the education of children with special needs (PP 1904 Cd. 2210 xxxii: 19; PRO ED24/280, Alfred Eichholz – personal details).[1] However, although the Board appointed a second medical inspector in 1906, neither officer was primarily concerned with the medical condition of schoolchildren as a whole (see *Times* 1907a).[2]

This gap in the Board's access to technical medical advice was highlighted on a number of occasions. On 14 June 1906, when the Birrell Bill was still under consideration, Keir Hardie asked the President of the Board of Education 'whether he contemplates the creation of a special State medical staff to supervise the efforts of local educational authorities for attending to the health and physical condition of the children educated in public elementary schools' (Parliamentary Debates 1906b: cols 1144–5). In response, Birrell said that the Board 'already possess one Medical Inspector of Schools and I am contemplating the appointment of a second', but 'it would be unwise for the Board to embark upon the establishment of a large staff of such officials . . . until there has been time to see to what extent the development of Local Authorities' activities . . . render[s] such a course desirable' (ibid.: col. 1145). However, by the time the medical inspection clause had been reintroduced in 1907, there was a growing recognition on the part of the Board that some form of medical department would have to be established. On 16 May 1907, three-and-a-half months before the Administrative Provisions Bill became law, Birrell's successor, Reginald McKenna, told Ramsay MacDonald that:

> There can be no doubt that when the Administrative Provisions Bill becomes law, some guidance or advice from the Board of Education as to the methods of inspection and classification of results will be necessary. How to secure the maximum of advantage from a general system of medical inspection, consistently with securing the smooth running of the scheme and the cooperation of Local Authorities, is a matter which requires and is receiving careful consideration, but I am not yet in a position to make any statement (Parliamentary Debates 1907b: cols 1101–2).

Much of the existing literature on the foundation of the Medical Department has focused on the role played by Sir Robert Morant in the appointment of George Newman as the Board's first chief medical officer (Gilbert 1966: 131–7; Hirst 1983: 192–202). In 1966 Bentley Gilbert said that this episode illustrated 'the vast power possessed by a truly energetic and imaginative civil servant who is armed with a coherent plan and is supervised by an amateur, inexperienced and transient Minister' (Gilbert 1966: 131). At the time of his appointment, Newman was the Medical Officer of Health in the London Borough of Finsbury, and Consulting County Medical Officer for Bedfordshire. He was the author of a number of important studies, including a standard text on public health and bacteriology, and lecturer in Public Health and Sanitary Administration at St Bartholomew's Hospital (PRO ED24/280, press release). His appointment to the post of Chief Medical Officer marked the latest stage in a career which was to establish him as the most important single figure in the history of British public health administration in the first half of this century. He became the first chief medical officer of the Ministry of Health in 1919, and held both chief medical officerships simultaneously until his retirement fifteen years later (*Who was Who* 1952: 843).[3]

The controversy surrounding Newman's appointment was primarily concerned with the question of how far school medicine should be regarded as a branch of the existing framework of public health provision. Morant was anxious to ensure the greatest possible degree of coordination between the school medical service and the rest of the public health service, and he believed that the appointment of a senior medical officer of health as head of the school medical service would help to achieve this. On 28 August 1907 he told Alfred Eichholz that

> the fight outside has, as you know, turned somewhat on the point of whether the Board will emphasise the trend in the direction of the School Doctor as such, or in the other direction of the Medical Officer of Health. The matter is a large one with many ramifications [, b]ut . . . the Board has . . . decided to emphasise the trend [in favour of the Medical Officer of Health] . . . and ha[s] selected Mr George Newman . . . for the post of Chief Medical Officer (PRO ED24/280, Morant to Eichholz, 28/8/07).

Two months later he wrote again, in similar vein, to Charles Masterman, the Liberal MP and editor of the *Nation* magazine:

> There is a certain comparatively small clique of so-called 'School Doctors', who consider that the predominant, indeed almost exclusive, point to make for is the medical man's work on the school premises. . . . We have definitely taken the line against them . . . by . . . appointing as head of our small staff a man who is not a school doctor as such . . . but . . . who is an especially capable Medical Officer of Health (PRO ED24/280, Morant to Masterman, 4/11/07).

The most prominent opponent of Newman's appointment was Dr James Kerr, the Medical Officer to the Education Committee of the London County Council. Kerr was widely regarded as the leading advocate and practitioner of school medicine in the country, and one of Kerr's assistants (and Newman's former pupils), Archibald Hogarth, claimed that he had in fact been promised the post fourteen months earlier (Hogarth 1907a; 1907b). It is impossible to know how much truth to attribute to these claims (see *British Medical Journal* 1907f: 761), but it is clear that Kerr embodied a very different conception of the form which school medical provision should take. In 1905 he told a conference at the Royal Sanitary Institute that 'nine-tenths of the School Doctor's work had no affinity with the Medical Officer of Health's duties', and that the appointment of medical officers of health as school medical officers would set back the course of school medicine by twenty years (*British Medical Journal* 1905a: 381; Kerr 1905: 59–63). In 1907 he told the Education Committee of the London County Council that

> school hygiene is . . . a highly specialised branch of public health, which the ordinary sanitarian cannot be expected to follow, and which requires officers experienced in the technique and specially trained to do justice to the children and the public interest (London County Council 1907: 3).

The debate over Newman's appointment therefore raised a number of issues which were central to the future of the school medical service, but it also left a certain degree of bitterness in its wake. Newman wrote at least five separate memoranda to Morant alone between 20 and 27 September, complaining bitterly about Hogarth's 'impertinent attack' (PRO ED24/280, Newman to Morant, 20/9/07, 21/9/07, 23/9/07, 25/9/07, 27/9/07), and Kerr himself continued to call for the establishment of an entirely separate school medical service throughout his career (Kerr 1926: 293). However, it would be wrong to regard the differences which were revealed by this episode as being entirely unbridgeable. Even George Newman was obliged to admit that 'we are all . . . greatly indebted . . . to the admirable work which has been done for school hygiene in England by Dr Kerr' (Newman 1909: 160), and on 12 June 1908 a large but informal meeting of medical officers of health passed a unanimous resolution calling on the Council of the

Society 'to form a School Medical Officers' Section' and to ask Dr James Kerr 'to accept office as first chairman of the section' (Public Health 1908b: 188).[4]

Newman's own desire to maintain his links with the 'school doctors' was reflected in his even-handed approach to the recruitment of the remaining members of the Board of Education's Medical Department. Morant had agreed previously that the second post in any medical department should go to Eichholz, and Newman suggested that the remaining posts should be divided between 'a lady doctor' (if necessary), a school doctor (C.J. Thomas of the London County Council), and 'a middle man' (Meredith Richards, the Medical Officer of Health for Croydon) (PRO ED24/280, Newman to Morant, 6/9/07). However Newman's proposals were vetoed by the Treasury, and although there is some evidence that both Thomas and Richards were interviewed by Morant, neither was eventually appointed (Hirst 1983: 210–15; PRO ED24/280, Newman to Morant, 3/10/07, 11/10/07). The Treasury did agree to the appointment of a 'lady doctor', Janet Campbell, in June 1908, and Dr Ralph Crowley joined the Board in 1909 (PP 1910 Cd. 4986 xxiii: 12). Campbell carried out medical inspections for the London County Council, and Crowley succeeded Kerr as Medical Superintendent of Schools in Bradford. In November 1907 he told Morant that although he accepted unreservedly 'that the basis [of the school medical service] should be a public health one', he also believed that the school medical officer 'should be directly responsible to the Education Committee in the same way that the Medical Officer of Health is . . . directly responsible to the Health Committee' (PRO ED50/5, Crowley to Morant, 4/11/07).

The organisation of school medical work

The Medical Department completed the first phase of its growth in June 1909, but many other practical matters had to be resolved before that date. The most important of these concerned the advice which the Board of Education was expected to give with regard to the organisation of school medical provision in individual areas. In giving this advice, the Board was determined to encourage local education authorities to follow the policy which it itself had followed in appointing George Newman – namely, one of seeking to ensure the closest possible degree of coordination between the school medical service and the public health service. This policy raised a number of important questions, not merely about the ideal form of administrative arrangement for the school medical service, but also about the extent to which central government could force local education authorities to implement a policy which some of them might regard as inappropriate (see, for example, PRO ED24/280, Legge to Morant, 14/1/08).

The Board's policy with regard to the organisation of school medical provision was drawn up after consultation with a large number of medical officers of health, and published in Circular 576 on 22 November 1907 (PP 1910 Cd. 4986 xxiii: 141–50). The Circular rehearsed a number of familiar arguments in favour of the association of school medical work with the existing machinery of public health administration. First, it argued that the school medical service was 'not intended to supersede the powers which have long been exercised by sanitary authorities under various Public Health Acts, but is meant to serve rather as an amplification and a natural development of previous legislation' (ibid.: para. 3). Second, the Board argued that the association of school medicine with public health would help to prevent the establishment of new and possibly competing agencies under the education authorities, and thereby facilitate the progressive unification of all the country's health services (ibid., paras 5, 18). Third, the Board insisted that the establishment of the school medical service on a public health basis would lead to greater administrative efficiency. Medical officers of health were already responsible for a wide range of services affecting child health, and the addition of school medical work would enable them to discharge their existing duties more effectively (ibid., para. 6).

In addition to these arguments, the Board also made a number of specific recommendations with regard to the appointment of school medical officers in individual areas. It said that county authorities should appoint the county medical officer as senior school medical officer, and that the inspections themselves should either be carried out by district medical officers of health, or by medical inspectors who had been specially appointed for the purpose. It said that county boroughs, municipal boroughs and urban districts should appoint their medical officer of health as the senior school medical officer, and that the medical officers of health should either carry out the work of medical inspection themselves, or supervise the work of any assistants who may be required to act on their behalf. The Board also said that when local authorities appointed assistants, they should give preference to candidates who had either been trained in state medicine or held diplomas in public health; who had definite experience of school hygiene; and who had special experience in the study of children's diseases (PP 1910 Cd. 4986 xxiii: 144).

The publication of Circular 576 generated a number of different responses. The vast majority of medical officers of health welcomed the Circular and applauded its public health emphasis. The editor of *Public Health*, Arthur Newsholme, argued that the Circular formed a landmark in the history of public health and foreshadowed 'the immense advances in unification and associated completeness and efficiency which are about to be realised in that administration' (Newsholme 1907: 161). Leslie Mackenzie praised the Circular for emphasising 'the primary importance of the home and its hygiene in the school-life of the child, and the absolute necessity for maintaining continuity of inspectorial interest between the home and the school' (*Nature* 1908: 426).[5] However, although the majority of public health officers supported the Board, there were some notes of criticism. Archibald Hogarth said that 'the principle that the work of medical inspection should be under the direct supervision of the Medical Officer of Health' was 'in direct opposition to the experience of foreign countries, to the recommendations of the British Medical Association, of educationists, and of the few medical men . . . who have so far had real practical experience of the necessary routine in the schools' (Hogarth 1907c), and James Kerr claimed that 'the official writer who speaks of establishing this new service "on the broad basis of public health" gives us serious reason for doubting the extent of his knowledge or the value of his judgements in these matters' (PRO ED50/7, James Kerr, 'The medical inspection and treatment of schoolchildren': 3).

The Board's Circular also received a mixed reaction from other sections of the medical profession. The editor of the *Lancet* argued that 'the proposal [that medical inspection should be placed under the jurisdiction of the medical officer of health] should appeal not only to the economically-minded but also to those who desire to see a further development of public health organisation throughout the country', but he was afraid that

> the scientific study of the health of children [may] . . . go to the wall under a cast-iron principle that the Medical Officer of Health, whether he has or has not special claims, should always be the medical inspector of the schools of his district (*Lancet* 1907).

The Medico-Political Sub-Committee of the British Medical Association said that it had not yet decided 'whether the supervision of this work should be carried out by Medical Officers of Health or by Medical Officers specially appointed for the purpose', but 'the general opinion in the Association [is] that [the actual work of inspection] . . . could not . . . be efficiently discharged by Medical Officers of Health personally' (Supplement to the *British Medical Journal* 1907). The editor of the *British Medical Journal* himself argued that the Board had made a serious mistake 'in laying down a definite detailed scheme at the present juncture', and that it would have done better to consult the whole of the medical profession 'before adopting a narrow sectional view of a reform important enough to interest every doctor in the land' (*British Medical Journal* 1907g).

These exchanges provide some indication of the passion which the Board's Circular aroused in some sections of the medical profession, but it was up to the local education authorities to decide how far they intended to comply with its recommendations. In January 1908 the Director of Education for Liverpool, J.G. Legge, told Morant that he was 'not prepared to face the prospect of having another individual giving orders for the routine of medical inspection . . . while the real responsibility will still be mine', but the majority of local education authorities welcomed the Board's recommendations and agreed to follow its advice (PRO ED24/280: Legge to Morant, 24/1/08; see also Hirst 1983: 264–7).[6] In November 1907 the Executive Council of the County Councils Association 'affirmed the principle embodied in paragraph 7 (a) of [the Board's] memorandum with respect to the appointment of a County Medical Officer', and said that 'the County medical inspection staff should in all cases be instructed to maintain close relations with the sanitary officers' (*Times* 1907b). By the end of 1909, forty-four county councils, fifty county boroughs, 104 municipal boroughs and forty-two urban districts had appointed the local county medical officer or medical officer of health as their school medical officer, and only eighty-three local authorities had appointed an independent school medical officer (PP 1910 Cd. 4986 xxiii: 131–40; Table 4.1). By the end of 1910, forty-eight county councils, fifty-six county boroughs, forty-two municipal boroughs and twenty urban districts had appointed at least one assistant, and the total number of doctors employed by the school medical service had risen to 966 (PRO ED50/1, The duties of county medical officers as school medical officers; PP 1910 Cd. 5426 xxiii: 187–97).

Although the Board had repeatedly stated that the main reason for advocating the appointment of medical officers of health as school medical officers was to ensure the effective coordination of the school medical service with the remainder of the public health service, its attitude may also have been influenced by financial considerations. When the government established the school medical service, the British Medical Association said that the minimum starting salary for a full-time school medical inspector ought to be £500 per annum, but it subsequently agreed that local authorities could appoint a junior officer for as little as £250. The Board's decision to encourage local authorities to appoint the medical officer of health as their senior school medical officer enabled many authorities to reduce their salary costs. In 1913 one discontented school medical officer wrote:

> It need not be explained to anyone with a week's experience of the ways of local authorities that the new arrangement was eagerly availed of as a means of evading the payment of the originally-proposed £500. And, in effect, 99 out of every 100 of the men who were to do the actual work . . . were appointed as assistants to someone or other – generally to Medical Officers of Health. The latter were offered, and accepted with alacrity, £30 or £50 in lieu of the £250 mulcted from the assistants under the new arrangement (One of them 1913: 239).

The appointment of so many junior officers may have had an adverse effect on the long-term development of the service as a whole. As the range of public health work expanded, an increasing number of assistant medical officers of health were appointed, but there was no corresponding increase in the number of senior posts. This meant that there was very little incentive for junior officers to concentrate on school work. In 1913 W. Spencer Badger warned readers of the *Medical Officer* that

> until the payment of adequate salaries by Education Authorities is secured by alteration in the conditions of Government grant, many School Medical Officers can hope for adequate remuneration only outside the school medical service. The latter may come to be . . . regarded as affording merely temporary occupation, and as a stepping stone to better-paid appointments (Badger 1913).

In 1915 HCTL told readers of *Public Health* that 'in the few instances where the school medical officership is a separate and distinct post, the salary is not, as a rule, attractive' (HCTL 1915: 279), and the President of the Society of

Table 4.1 Number of medical officers of health acting as principal school medical officers in local authority areas, end of 1909.

	Full-time		*Part-time*		*Other*	*Total*
	Male	*Female*	*Male*	*Female*		
County councils						
MOH	44	0	0	0	0	44
SMO	13	1	2	0	0	16
Other	0	0	0	0	5	5
Total	57	1	2	0	5	65
County boroughs						
MOH	50	0	0	0	0	50
SMO	24	0	0	0	0	24
Other	0	0	0	0	0	0
Total	74	0	0	0	0	74
Municipal boroughs						
MOH	103	0	1	0	0	104
SMO	5	3	22	2	0	32
Other	0	0	0	0	1	1
Total	108	3	23	2	1	137
Urban districts						
MOH	42	0	0	0	0	42
SMO	3	1	7	0	0	11
Other	0	0	0	0	0	0
Total	45	1	7	0	0	53

Abbreviations: MOH = medical officer of health; SMO = school medical officer (SMO figures in these rows refer to areas in which the person designated as school medical officer was not the medical officer of health).

Notes: The description 'full-time' refers to medical officers who devoted the whole of their time to public health or school medical work, even if they did not devote the whole of their time to one particular area.

These figures exclude the Urban District of Gorton in Lancashire, which was regarded as part of Manchester for school medical purposes. The Welsh County of Carnarvonshire was divided into three separate administrative districts (Central, Southern and Northern), each with its own medical officer of health, who also served as school medical officer. Five Welsh counties (Anglesey, Breconshire, Denbighshire, Pembrokeshire and Radnorshire) made arrangements for medical inspection without appointing a school medical officer. The post of school medical officer in the municipal borough of Batley was vacant at the time of the survey. Two counties (Isle of Wight and Carmarthenshire) appointed a district medical officer of health to act as school medical officer for the whole county. Cornwall appointed two separate school medical officers, both of whom gave their whole time to school medical work. Dr S. Childs held a joint appointment as School Medical Officer to West Sussex County and Chichester Municipal Borough Council.

Source: PP 1910 Cd. 4986 xxiii: 131–40.

Medical Officers of Health said that 'unless the appointment [of assistant school medical officer] be associated with that of Assistant Medical Officer of Health the chances of preferment seem to be limited' (Allan 1915).

The introduction of routine medical inspection

The third major issue which the Administrative Provisions Act raised but failed to resolve was the question of medical inspection itself. The Act required local authorities to make arrangements for the medical inspection of children before or at the time of their admission to a public elementary school, and on such other occasions as the Board of Education might direct, but it made no attempt to specify the character of the inspections or the frequency with which they should be carried out. The Board attempted to answer these questions in the Memorandum which it issued to local education authorities on 22 November 1907. It said that every child ought to be inspected at the time of, or as soon as possible after, it first entered the school; during the third and sixth years of its school life (i.e. at ages seven and ten), and before its departure into the world of work. The Board recognised that very few local authorities would be able to comply with these regulations in the first instance, and it said that it would be satisfied if local authorities made arrangements for the inspection of school entrants and leavers in 1908, and for the inspection of children aged five, seven and thirteen in 1909 (PP 1910 Cd. 4986 xxiii: 147).

In addition to defining the ages at which medical inspection should take place, the Board also sought to inform medical officers about the type of conditions which they should seek to investigate. The medical inspector was expected to discover whether the child had suffered from any previous disease; to assess its general condition and circumstances; to examine its nose and throat; to test its eyes, ears and teeth; to assess its mental capacity; and to establish whether it was suffering from any present disease or defect (PP 1910 Cd. 4986 xxiii: 146). In January 1908 the Board issued a further memorandum (Circular 582), setting out in detail the full 'schedule of medical inspection' which the inspectors were expected to complete. This included a check-list of twenty-four separate items which the medical inspector was expected to note in the course of the inspection, with a separate section listing general observations and directions to the child's parent or teacher (PP 1910 Cd. 4986 xxiii: 154).

In the final paragraph of Circular 576, the Board stated that the Circular was of a preliminary nature only, and that it concerned 'almost entirely the work of the new Act at its initiation' (PP 1910 Cd. 4986 xxiii: 150). However, it soon became apparent that many local authorities would be unable to satisfy even the minimum requirements of the Circular without some financial support from the Treasury, and the absence of this meant that the Board was forced to postpone the introduction of the third 'routine age-group' until 1 April 1915 (PRO ED50/3, Memorandum on age-groups for next Code [1909]; Draft circular on medical inspection: postponement of the requirement of inspection of a third group [1909–10]; As to burden of medical inspection work during Code years 1910/11 and 1911/12). The new regulations also incorporated a change in the age at which school-leavers were to be inspected. A number of medical officers argued that school-leavers should be inspected between the ages of twelve and thirteen so that any defects which had been exposed by medical inspection could be 'followed-up' before the children left school (*Medical Officer* 1911; 1913). This change came into effect on 1 April 1914, and remained in force until the school leaving age itself was raised in 1947 (PP 1914 Cd. 7484 lxv: para. 8; Ministry of Education 1945b: para. 49).

We have already seen (in the previous section) that the Board drafted the contents of Circular 576 in consultation with a large number of medical officers of health, and it engaged in a similar process of consultation over Circular 582 (PRO ED50/6). These consultations helped to ensure that the Board's proposals regarding the nature and character of routine medical inspection enjoyed the support of the majority of public health officers. However, a small number of observers, both within and outside the public health service, did express reservations. One of the most controversial statements accompanying the Schedule of Medical Inspection was the observation that 'the inspection of each child should not occupy on the average more than a few minutes, and . . . the child need only, as a rule, have its clothes loosened or be partially undressed' (PP 1910 Cd. 4986 xxiii: 151). This statement led one anonymous medical practitioner to respond:

> The whole tendency of the memorandum is to underestimate the amount of work involved in these routine examinations, and this will result in the understaffing of the schools. If the Medical Officer is to do the whole examination with any pretence to thoroughness it will take close upon a half an hour, and, with all the assistance teachers or clerks can give, at least twenty minutes. It is important that the profession should make this clear, for obviously Local Authorities in their natural and laudable desire to keep down the rates will only engage the minimum amount of medical assistance, and if this is calculated on the basis that a child can be examined in five minutes the result will be that the statistics will be unreliable, many defects overlooked, and the Medical Officer will have no time to think of what he is doing (HH 1908; see also Wilkin 1908).

In addition to the length of time allowed for medical inspection, the Board also faced a more general problem of standardisation. In Circular 576, the Board stated that one of the main aims of school medical inspection was the production of accurate information about the health and physical condition of the children (PP 1910 Cd. 4986 xxiii: 141), and in 1939 George Newman argued that 'what the English public . . . really wanted to know were the *facts* about these schoolchildren; and when they had obtained the facts they were in the mood to deal with them as competent official committees had advised' (Newman 1939: 194). However, it soon became apparent that many of the statistics which were produced by the school medical service were flawed because they had not been compiled on any nationally agreed basis. In 1909 the County Medical Officer for Essex, Dr J.C. Thresh, told a meeting at the Incorporated Institute of Hygiene that 'the reports of school medical examiners were of no value, owing to the varying standards adopted and the different methods of tabulating results'. He produced a table showing that, in a total of twenty different areas, the proportion of children who were returned as showing signs of defective vision varied from 4.1 per cent in one area to 39 per cent in another, while the proportion of children who were found to be 'unclean' ranged from 1 per cent to 60 per cent (*Medical Officer* 1909; see also *Medical Officer* 1910a; 1910b).

The third major complaint which was levelled against the Board's Schedule of Medical Inspection concerned the Board's insistence that every child ought to be medically examined. In 1939, George Newman argued that the reason why '*all* the children had to be examined by a doctor' was that

> this was a rate-aided service for the parents of all the children in the public elementary schools; and its primary objective was not to create a healthy people, but to enable every schoolchild to take full advantage of the education provided for it by the State.

He also argued that every child had to be examined by a doctor because the doctor was the only person who was qualified to decide whether the child was free from disease (Newman 1939: 193–4). However, this line of argument was challenged on a number of occasions, not only by local authorities who were anxious to reduce the cost of medical inspection, but also by doctors who doubted the need to subject every child to a medical examination (see, for example, *British Medical Journal* 1909a, 1909b).

The controversy over the need for a universal system of medical inspection was particularly acute in London, where the School Medical Officer was James Kerr. Kerr believed that it was unnecessary to subject every child to a medical examination, and that there was little point in examining children for whom there was no prospect of obtaining medical treatment. In November 1908 he put forward a modified scheme of medical inspection, which would enable him to test the value of these arguments and the need for the Board's own medical inspection schedule. He proposed that the London County Council should make arrangements for the inspection of all the entrants and all the leavers in two of the schools in each district, and that while the children in one school should be examined according to the Board's schedule, the children in the second school should be examined according to a simpler schedule which he himself had devised. In addition to this, he also proposed that in all the other schools the teachers should conduct a preliminary examination, and that the doctors should only examine those children whom the teachers referred to them (Hirst 1981: 287–90).

In view of the special difficulties associated with the school medical service in London, the Board of Education agreed to endorse these proposals, subject to the proviso that it intended to subject the Council's arrangements to a more searching scrutiny in the following year. During the first six months of 1909 the Council made arrangements for the medical examination of 4552 children in thirty-nine schools according to the Board's schedule, and 5874 children in thirty-one schools using James Kerr's schedule, but it then decided to abandon its original plan in favour of inspecting all the children attending schools within easy reach of London's voluntary hospitals. This meant that by the end of 1909 only 2.4 per cent of the total number of entrants and leavers had been examined in accordance with the Board's schedule, and only 3.8 per cent had been examined in accordance with Kerr's schedule, while the vast majority of entrants and leavers had not been examined by a school doctor at all (Hirst 1981: 290–93).[7]

These arrangements were subjected to a great deal of criticism by the British Medical Association and by the Progressive members of the London County Council, and in June 1910 the Council decided to appoint a further twenty-eight part-time medical inspectors and to make arrangements for the medical inspection of intermediate children (aged eight and nine) as well as entrants and leavers. However, the scheme once again fell short of the Board's expectations: first, the Council proposed to examine the children according to Kerr's schedule rather than the Board's schedule; and second, it decided that the doctors would not be required to inspect all the school entrants personally (Hirst 1981: 295–6). In October 1910 he persuaded the Children's Care (Central) Sub-Committee to agree 'that as from 1st January 1911, a card be prepared by the Head Teacher, in respect of every "entrant" . . . that this card be initialled by the School Doctor, and that the School Doctor should examine the children individually only when he considers a detailed examination necessary' (*British Medical Journal* 1910).

The revised scheme of medical inspection which the London County Council introduced in 1910 provided James Kerr with an opportunity to demonstrate the superiority of his selective system of medical inspection over the routine system favoured by the Board of Education, but the experiment was not a success. In June 1911 the British Medical Association sent a deputation to the President of the Board of Education to discuss 'the medical inspection and treatment of schoolchildren in London'. The Deputation complained 'that the method adopted by the London County Council with regard to the examination of entrants . . . is exceedingly inadequate . . . the children are inspected by a teacher and a nurse and . . . paraded before a school medical officer, who selects certain of them for examination'. The Deputation also objected to the basis on which the examination itself was carried out. It said that Kerr's schedule 'contained nothing like the details which the Board's Medical Officer said were required'.

In their comments to the President, both Dr Christopher Addison and Sir Victor Horsley claimed that large numbers of 'defects' had been ignored because the Council refused to follow the Board's advice. Dr Addison said that so far as the entrants were concerned, 'it is very evident . . . that a large proportion of the defects . . . are overlooked', and Sir Victor claimed that 'if you take one hundred defects . . . as discovered by [the Board's] . . . schedule, you find . . . that the County Council method reveal[s] but fourteen'. He concluded that the Council scheme was 'a definite breach of faith on the part of a public body towards the nation', and he urged the President of the Board of Education to compel the Council 'to carry out medical inspection according to your Code and the Regulations of your Department' (Supplement to the *British Medical Journal* 1911: 24; PRO ED24/282, Minutes of Proceedings from a Deputation of the BMA: 3).

The BMA's intervention in this debate was directly responsible for the reorganisation of the London school medical service and Kerr's replacement as school medical officer (Gilbert 1966: 140–3; Hirst 1981: 297). However the Association failed to prove unequivocally that Kerr's method of inspection was inadequate. In order to provide a more rigorous test of Kerr's system, it would have been necessary to examine the unselected children as well as the selected children, and the same doctor would have needed to examine both groups of children using the Board's schedule and Kerr's schedule. Nevertheless, the episode brought to an end the first stage of the debate about the need for routine medical inspection. After 1912, every local education authority in the country agreed to comply with the Board's regulations, and the possibility of introducing more selective methods of examination only returned to the agenda in the early-1930s (Auden 1935; 1936; Cronk 1935; Herd 1935a; 1935b).

The development of school medical treatment

The relationship between the introduction of medical inspection and the development of medical treatment has been discussed on a number of occasions. In 1966 Bentley Gilbert said that although Sir Robert Morant had recognised that the introduction of medical inspection would lead inevitably to the introduction of medical treatment, he failed to tell his Minister, and sought to conceal his true intentions from Parliament by 'burying' the medical inspection clause in a routine administrative Bill (Gilbert 1966: 128–9). This view has been challenged by David Hirst, who argued that Parliament recognised the inevitability of medical treatment, but gave little thought to the form which it would take (Hirst 1989: 318–23). These debates are important, because the introduction of school medical treatment represented the most important extension of public medical provision outside the Poor Law before the creation of national health insurance in 1911 (Hirst 1983: 488–9).

In order to examine the extent to which Parliament intended to provide medical treatment, it is necessary to return to the debates which accompanied the passage of the medical inspection clause through Parliament. When the House of Lords debated the Birrell Bill in 1906, the Bishop of Ripon sought to amend the second half of the clause because he thought that the words 'attending to the health and physical condition of the children' would harm the interests of local doctors, but the President of the Privy Council insisted that the words complained of did not include 'medical treatment . . . as the term is ordinarily understood' (Parliamentary Debates 1906e: col. 755). However, when the House of Commons debated the same clause in 1907, it was clear that some form of medical treatment would be provided. On 12 August the Conservative MP, Sir William Anson, criticised the 'extreme vagueness' of the clause, and pointed out that the Parliamentary Secretary to the Board of Education, Thomas Lough, had already indicated that treatment might be provided in 'a small hospital outside the school' (Parliamentary Debates 1907c: cols 920–1). On 21 August, the Earl of Crewe said that

> provision is made for the medical care of the minor ailments to which children are subject, and the manner in which it is thought . . . that this can best be carried out is by visits of nurses employed by the local authority to the homes of the children, where they are able to deal with small ailments very often caused . . . as much by . . . ignorance as by . . . neglect or want of care (Parliamentary Debates 1907d: cols 725–6).

During the first few months of the new service, the Board's main priority was to emphasise the need for caution, and it urged local authorities not to introduce any new services until they had established an efficient system of medical inspection and had made a thorough survey of existing medical facilities (PP 1910 Cd. 4986 xxiii: 148–9). However, in August 1908 the Board issued a third Circular on medical inspection, setting out a series of suggestions for measures which local authorities could take to improve the health of their schoolchildren. The majority of these measures involved the use of existing services and existing powers, but two proposals represented a major extension of the scope of school medical work. The first was the suggestion that local authorities should pay fees to local hospitals, dispensaries or nursing associations in return for the treatment of minor ailments. The second suggestion concerned the establishment of school clinics. The Board said that the establishment of such clinics 'gives rise to questions of considerable difficulty', but it would support their establishment if the authorities were unable to make equivalent provision through other means (PP 1910 Cd. 4986 xxiii: 155–62).

In view of the rapid growth of the school clinic after 1908, it is interesting to look more closely at the reasons for its development. In his account of the growth of medical treatment through the school medical service in 1989, David Hirst argued that the Board was actively hostile to the development of school clinics, and that it only agreed to support their introduction when it became clear that all other possibilities had been exhausted (Hirst 1989: 330–31). However, this judgement may seem a little harsh. The Board was concerned that the establishment of school clinics might prejudice the interests of the medical profession, and it was worried that the provision of medical treatment might pauperise the parents of the children who received it (PRO ED50/7, Dr Newman's rough notes on . . . the means of amelioration and the establishment of clinics), but its main concern was that neither it nor the local authorities had any direct experience of the schemes which were under consideration. As Newman himself observed:

> The Board are aware that neither they nor any other body . . . are . . . in a position to make any final pronouncements as to the legitimate scope of schemes of treatment, or the conditions which will ultimately be found to govern their usefulness. This can only come with time and the experience of Local Education Authorities all over the country (PP 1910 Cd. 4986 xxiii: 86).[8]

The first local education authority to submit a proposal for the establishment of a school clinic was Bradford, in June 1908, and the scheme helps to illustrate the considerations which led an authority to propose a school clinic, and the types of condition which could be treated in it. Bradford had been the first school board in the country to introduce a regular system of medical inspection, and it had tried to encourage parents to obtain medical treatment either by consulting their local medical practitioner, or by attending the out-patients' departments of one of the city's three voluntary hospitals. However, despite these efforts, the majority of children had remained untreated, and it was for this reason that the Education Authority had decided to establish a school clinic (PRO ED125/8, Establishment of a school clinic; PP 1910 Cd. 4986 xxiii: 99–100). The clinic itself was widely regarded, both at home and abroad, as a model of good practice. In 1910 the clinic consisted of ten rooms on the ground floor of the Town Hall, including a waiting room, clerk's room, school medical officer's room, bacteriological laboratory, X-ray room, dental room, nurses' room, assistant medical officers' rooms, and a treatment room, which was also used as an eye clinic. The clinic provided treatment for a range of conditions, including defective vision, external eye disease, ringworm, pediculosis, skin diseases, discharging ears, dental treatment and the control of vermin. The total number of children who were treated at the clinic in 1910 was 3520, and the total number of attendances was nearly 16,000 (PP 1911 Cd. 5925 xvii: 159–61).[9]

Between 1908 and 1913 the circumstances which had led to the establishment of a school clinic in Bradford were repeated in local education authorities throughout the country. When the school medical service was formally established, many local authorities either advised parents to consult a private medical practitioner, or to visit the out-patients' department of their local hospital, but neither of these arrangements proved satisfactory. Many parents were unable to afford the fees charged by private practitioners, and the demand for medical services was much greater than the voluntary hospitals could bear. As a result of this, many local authorities sought to reduce the burden on the voluntary hospitals either by paying them for the services they provided, or by establishing provident societies which would enable the children to be treated at reduced rates. However, both of these arrangements proved unpopular with the medical profession, and the voluntary hospitals were only able to provide services to patients who lived within easy reach of them. Under these circumstances, it was hardly surprising that a growing number of local authorities concluded that they would have to establish a school clinic. The number of school clinics grew slowly at first, but by the end of 1913 the Board had sanctioned the establishment of more than 260 clinics in 139 local authority areas (Hirst 1983: 355–65; 1989: 330–34; PP 1914 Cd. 7184 xxv: 129–35).

The rapid growth of the school clinic after 1908 represented a major extension of school medical work, and it marked a further stage in the transformation of the public health service. In 1921 the President of the Society of Medical Officers of Health, Dr W.J. Howarth, said that

> up to a few years ago there was a clear-cut line of demarcation between [the practitioners of preventive medicine and the practitioners of curative medicine] . . . and we, as Medical Officers of Health, concerned ourselves mainly with work in which the general body of practitioners took only passing interest (Howarth 1921: 39–40).

However, the expansion of medical treatment through the school medical service meant that the boundaries between preventive and curative medicine were becoming increasingly blurred, and this meant that medical officers of health and school medical officers devoted an increasing amount of attention to the treatment of disease (One of them 1913: 249–50; Lewis 1986: 8–10). The development of the school clinic also reflected a major change in the role of the local education authority. As the Education Officer of the London County Council commented in 1911:

> Formerly, education was in the main confined to (1) the growth of character, and (2) the growth of the mind. Now education looks increasingly at the social problems that present themselves for solution in the case of the individual child, the problem of physical deterioration, of underfeeding, of impoverished homes and unsuitable employment. The State has come to see that it is not enough to impart knowledge, but that it must also see that the child is capable of assimilating that knowledge, and that his environment is not such that it will entirely undo the effect of . . . school training (qu. Webb and Webb 1929: 602–3).

The cost of school medical services

One of the biggest issues raised by the establishment of the school medical service was the government's failure to provide Treasury assistance for it. This subject was raised on a number of occasions during the Parliamentary debates which accompanied the Administrative Provisions Bill. A number of members argued that it was wrong to impose a duty on local education authorities without ensuring that they had the means to discharge it. The MP for Glasgow and Aberdeen universities, Sir Henry Craik, said that the government should only be allowed to force local authorities to introduce medical inspection if assistance was provided by the central department (Parliamentary Debates 1907c: col. 1107). The MP for Tewkesbury, M. Hicks-Beach, said that although he accepted the principle of medical inspection,

> he could not agree to its being imposed without some assistance . . . from the general finances of the country. He could not conceive [of] anything more likely to put the people of the country against education than continued appeals to pay for it out of the rates (ibid.: col. 1125).

The debate over the financial arrangements for the new service continued after the Administrative Provisions Bill became law. On 27 November 1907 the Executive Council of the County Councils Association said that in view of the 'heavy cost [which] would have to be incurred by the ratepayers . . . the Board should be asked what assistance will be given . . . by the Treasury' (*Times* 1907b). On 18 December the Chair of the Association's Education Committee, Sir Henry Hobhouse, advised Sir Robert Morant that 'if he desired to make efficient arrangements for carrying out the medical inspection order, it was extremely desirable that he should give . . . some definite idea as to the amount of Treasury aid' which might be expected (PRO ED24/280, Hobhouse to Morant, 18/12/07). Two months later he told Reginald McKenna that

> all the County Education Authorities in England and Wales . . . were unanimously of opinion that they had considerable claims on the Exchequer, first, because [medical inspection] . . . was a national object; secondly, in the interests of education itself . . . and thirdly, with a view to the regulations being more efficiently carried out (*Times* 1908a).

The government's response to these claims was spelt out privately by Robert Morant, in a letter to Hobhouse, and publicly by McKenna, in two separate meetings with the Association at the beginning of 1908 (*Times* 1908a; 1908c). Morant said that although he personally believed that in the absence of a separate grant for medical inspection the service 'will hardly get off to a proper start in many places', the government believed that the financing of medical inspection and treatment should only be considered as part of a general review of educational finance (PRO ED24/280, Morant to Hobhouse, 20/12/07; see also Hirst 1981: 285–7). In February 1908 McKenna introduced a new Education Bill – the Education (England and Wales) Bill – which would have resulted in the provision of an additional £1.4 million for educational expenditure (PP 1908 (112) ii, section 2 (2); Parliamentary Debates 1907f: col. 1384). However, the government was eventually forced to withdraw the Bill, and no new funds were made available for medical inspection or treatment before the end of the year (Hirst 1981: 285–7; 1983: 222–31).

Following the defeat of the Education (England and Wales) Bill, the spotlight turned to the question of medical treatment. During the debates on the Administrative Provisions Bill, the MP for Barkston Ash, George Lane-Fox, made two separate attempts to give local authorities the power to charge parents for the provision of medical treatment, but on both occasions his amendments were either withdrawn or defeated (PP 1907 (288) vi: 8; Parliamentary Debates 1907c: cols 917–27). However, in April 1909 the MP for Bury St Edmunds, Walter Guinness, introduced a new Bill to enable local authorities to charge 'the parent of every child in respect of any treatment provided for that child such an amount not exceeding the cost of treatment as may be determined by the Local Education Authority' (PP 1909 (143) iii, section 1). When the Bill was debated in the House of Lords, the Earl of Crewe said that although he had some reservations about the impact of the Bill on parents 'who are really poor if not absolutely indigent', he was willing to believe that it 'may prove to be in some respects a useful measure', and the Bill became law later that year (House of Lords Debates 1909: cols 842–5; 9 Edw. VII Ch. 13; see also Hirst 1989: 340).

The passage of the Local Education Authorities (Medical Treatment) Bill went some way towards meeting the local authorities' complaints, but its effectiveness was limited by at least three different factors. First, it was apparent from the discussions which took place in 1907 that the main reason for supporting the measure was not to raise money, but that 'a great many people . . . objected to having more serious medical treatment . . . thrown on the rates when the parents of the children could afford to pay' (Parliamentary Debates 1907c: col. 922). Second, many authorities found that the cost of administering the scheme was much greater than the revenue it generated (Hirst 1989: 340–41). Finally, although the Act gave local authorities the power to recover the cost of medical treatment from parents who refused to pay, it made no attempt to reimburse them for the treatment of children whose parents were unable to pay (9 Edw. VII, Ch. 13, sections 1–2).

In view of the limited nature of the Medical Treatment Bill, it is hardly surprising that many MPs continued to press the government for more direct forms of support. In March 1909 Ramsay MacDonald drew the President of the Board of Education's attention 'to the dissatisfaction of Local Education Authorities regarding the burden which adequate medical inspection of schoolchildren will put upon rates', and in April 1910 Francis Newdegate described 'the immense expenditure which is being placed on the rates [by] . . . medical inspection' as 'a very great hardship' (House of Commons Debates 1909a: cols 1227–8; 1909b: col. 2488). However, although there was considerable sympathy for these claims, the government was unable to take any further action because of the political and financial crisis which followed the rejection of the 'People's Budget' in 1909 (Murray 1980: 209–35). In February 1910 the Chancellor of the Exchequer, David Lloyd George, told the President of the Board of Education 'that in view of the present financial situation it is quite impossible for me to make the further financial provision which you think is necessary for elementary education', and he only agreed to reopen the question towards the end of the following year (Hirst 1983: 233–4).

The government's attitude to the funding of school medical work also reflected a more general debate about the role of government finance. When the government discussed the problem of the school medical service, Lloyd George argued that it would be wrong to provide an earmarked grant for medical *inspection* because 'this was one of the ordinary burdens of educational expenditure' (Hirst 1983: 234), but the same argument could not be applied to the provision of medical treatment. This distinction was reflected in the government's decision to introduce a grant for treatment alone in the Spring of 1912. The grant was made conditional upon 'the completeness of the arrangements made by the Authority', and local authorities were encouraged to make the maximum use of their powers by the introduction of a sliding scale (PP 1912 Cd. 6138 lxv: para. 5f). The most assiduous authorities were rewarded with grants of 60 or 66 per cent of their recognisable expenditure, while the less assiduous authorities received grants of 50 per cent or less (PRO ED24/1312: Medical treatment grants – rate of assessment).

The introduction of the medical treatment grant was welcomed by the vast majority of local education authorities, but the government's refusal to provide a grant for medical inspection attracted considerable comment. On 1 January 1913 Jesse Collings asked the President of the Board of Education 'what proportion of the medical examination and supervision of children in elementary schools is paid by the Board of Education', and on 13 January Captain Clive pointed out that local authorities were not only liable for the whole cost of medical inspection, but also suffered a loss of grant if children were excluded from school on medical advice (House of Commons Debates 1913a: cols 373, 1335). However, although the government was coming under growing pressure to support the cost of medical inspection, it only agreed to do so following the introduction of the Mental Deficiency and Elementary Education (Defective and Epileptic Children) Bills in 1913. The first of these Bills required local education authorities to make arrangements 'for ascertaining what persons within their area are defective children within the meaning of this Act', and the second required them to make provision for the education of such children in special schools (PP 1912–13 (213) iii: section 13; PP 1913 (60) ii: section 1). In May 1913 the Board of Education's Permanent Secretary, L.A. Selby-Bigge, pointed out that although the government had set aside funds to pay for the special schools, it had failed to take account 'of the extra cost which will be thrown on . . . Part III Local Education Authorities' by the ascertainment of 'mentally-defectives'. He concluded that:

> The only satisfactory way of dealing with the . . . matter is to get rid of the more or less artificial distinction which we are . . . attempting to draw between medical inspection and treatment. The one runs into the other almost imperceptibly. There are very strong reasons, quite apart

> from the Bill dealing with feeble-minded children, for putting the medical service grant on a better basis. The figures in the accompanying note . . . show . . . that it will be quite possible to include medical inspection in the subject matter of the grants now made in aid of the school medical service at a cost of (say) an additional £34,000 is 1914/15 (PRO ED24/1312, Selby-Bigge to President, 26/5/13: paras 2–3).

The government's decision to introduce a consolidated grant for both medical inspection and treatment represented a major step forward in the development of the school medical service and an important innovation in the history of educational finance. When the government introduced the new grant in August 1913, it said that those authorities which made adequate provision for the conduct of school medical work would receive a grant equal to fifty per cent of the total cost of their recognisable expenditure, and that those authorities which failed to provide an adequate service would have their grants withheld or reduced (PP 1913 Cd. 7041 1, paras 3–4). The principle of relating the size of the government grant to an authority's own expenditure was extended to the rest of public education in 1917, and it continued to play an important part in the financing of public education after the First World War (PP 1917–18 Cd. 8515 xxv: para. 1; 8 & 9 Geo. V Ch. 39, section 44; see also Selby-Bigge 1927: 97–8).

Notes

1 Eichholz represented the Board at a number of international congresses, including an International Congress on the Education of the Deaf in Paris in 1900; an International Congress on the Education of the Feeble-Minded in Augsburg in 1901; an International Congress on the Education of the Blind in Brussels in 1902; the First International Congress on School Hygiene in Nuremberg in 1904; and an International Congress on the Care and Welfare of the Deaf and Dumb in Liège in 1905. His report on the Augsburg conference was published as a Parliamentary Paper: see PP 1902 Cd. 836 xxvii: 595–604.

2 On 16 May 1907 the President of the Board of Education, Reginald McKenna, told Ramsay MacDonald MP, that the Board already employed two 'medical men', and that it was 'mainly on their advice that the Board act in dealing with schools for afflicted children and other matters where technical medical knowledge is especially necessary', but it was clear that this advice did not extend to the organisation of schemes of medical inspection or treatment (Parliamentary Debates, 1907b: col. 1102). I assume that the first of the two medical men was Eichholz, but I have been unable to ascertain the identity of the second.

3 A biography of Newman is long overdue. He began work on an autobiography, but abandoned this in favour of a more wide-ranging historical survey, entitled *The building of a nation's health* (Newman 1939). Newman's diaries and his civil service establishment file are held at the Public Record Office in Kew (PRO MH107/26; MH139/1–6), and other material has been lodged at the Hereford and Worcester Record Office in Hereford (series M4).

4 The Society declined to establish such a section, at least in the short term. However, it did decide to extend membership of the Society to 'Medical Officers appointed by Education Authorities'. The Society's official journal argued that by

taking this step, 'the Society is . . . acting in accordance with the view that it has constantly upheld, namely, that school hygiene is not a distinct speciality, but is an integral part of our system of public health administration' (*Public Health* 1908a).

5 Although this article was unsigned, it is clear from correspondence in the Public Record Office that Mackenzie was the author. See PRO ED50/5, Mackenzie to Newman, 23/12/07. Mackenzie wrote: 'I have just finished a notice of your memorandum for *Nature*. You may think the notice too cold, but it is done out of policy. You will easily see that I have done you justice without gush. I have let the substance speak for itself and quietly backed all your leading positions.'

6 It should be noted that Legge was primarily concerned with the relationship between the medical officer of health (or the school medical officer) and the Director of Education. He was quite happy for the medical officer of health to be appointed school medical officer provided that the medical officer's role was purely consultative. (See PRO ED24/280: Legge to Morant, 14/1/08).

7 It is important to note that these estimates do not take account of those entrants and leavers who were examined after the London County Council had decided to abandon its original plans in the middle of 1909. See Hirst (1981: 293).

8 The Board may also have been concerned that if local education authorities were allowed to establish their own treatment facilities, they would be less likely to hand them over to a unified public health authority in the future. It was also acutely embarrassed by its failure to secure additional government funding for school medical provision before 1912. See Hirst (1989: 324, 336).

9 The estimate of 3520 children receiving treatment is based on the number of children who received treatment for each condition. Some children may have been treated for more than one condition, in which case the actual number of patients would have been less than 3520.

five

The school medical service during the First World War

In the years between 1908 and 1914 George Newman provided a regular account of the progress which the school medical service was making in all parts of England and Wales. By the beginning of 1914, every local education authority had appointed a school medical officer, and in the majority of cases the school medical officer was also the medical officer of health of the local public health district; the vast majority of schoolchildren were being examined at the beginning and end of their school careers, and a growing number were also being examined as 'intermediates'; virtually every local education authority had made some arrangements for medical treatment, and between one-third and one-half of all authorities had established school clinics. In his annual report for 1913, Newman summarised these developments in the following terms:

> As the facts disclosed by medical inspection have become more widely-known and appreciated, Local Education Authorities have come more fully to recognise that expenditure on the discovery of the considerable degree of preventable ill-health which exists is largely wasted unless effectual steps are taken for the prevention and cure of the conditions revealed. An efficient system of medical inspection had already been generally established through England and Wales; consequently the year under review has been mainly a period of development in the work of following-up and treating discovered defects (PP 1914–16 Cd. 7730 xviii: vi).

Newman's confidence in the general health of the school medical service received a further boost from the introduction of government grants for medical treatment in 1912, and for medical treatment and inspection in 1912 and 1913 respectively (PP 1912 Cd. 6138 lxv; PP 1913 Cd. 7041 l). The amount of money expended by local education authorities rose from £107,802 in 1908/9 to £240,179 in 1911/12, and the introduction of the government grants helped to ensure that these increases were maintained. The amount of money spent by local education authorities rose to £285,933 in 1912/13 and £325,735 in 1913/14 (PRO ED24/1312, J.R. Warburton, Expenditure by local education authorities on the school medical service in England and Wales and the amount of grant provided by the Board of Education). In 1914 Newman wrote:

> The stimulus which the school medical service has received from the introduction of an Exchequer grant . . . has been considerable. Local Education Authorities have been . . . encouraged to increase the scope of their medical inspections, to consider improvements in their arrangements for the following-up of defective children, and to inaugurate or extend schemes for the prevention and treatment of defects. . . . The Board hope that the subsidies now offered by the State [will] render possible a well-organised and effective school medical service in the area of every Local Education Authority (PP 1914–16 Cd. 7730 xviii: 15).

The outbreak of war on 1 August 1914 affected these developments in a number of different ways. First, the war clearly imposed a tremendous strain on the ordinary work of the school medical service. The Board of Education and the local education authorities were both under pressure to restrain expenditure, and this meant that a substantial number of planned improvements had either to be either abandoned or postponed. Second, the war also made substantial demands on the personnel of the school medical service, as a growing number of doctors and nurses were recruited to work in military hospitals. However, the war also underlined the importance of school medical work to the country's economic and military future. As Newman again wrote in the preface to his 1913 report:

> Apart from the grave disadvantage that much of the value of the education of children will be lost unless they are physically fit both to profit by the instruction they receive and to perform the individual tasks which await them in the future, it is a matter of grave national concern to secure that physical unfitness and inefficiency in all its forms, due to ill-health or lack of vitality, is reduced to the smallest possible dimensions (PP 1914–16 Cd. 7730 xviii: v).

In addition to assessing the impact of the war on the development and administration of the school medical service, it is also important to try to assess its impact of the war on the health of the school population. In August 1914 many observers, including George Newman, were afraid that the outbreak of war would impose so much hardship on the poorer sections of the population as to pose a major threat to national stability, but by the end of the war he was confident that the average standard of child health had been maintained, or even improved, in the face of war conditions (PRO ED24/1371, Newman to Pease, 4/8/14: para. 1; PP 1917–18 Cd. 8746 xi: 142). The final section of this chapter will examine the extent to which Newman's initial fears and subsequent conclusions were supported by the weight of contemporary evidence (see also Winter 1986; 1988; Waites 1987; Wall 1988).

The impact of war on school medical provision

The outbreak of the First World War, and the subsequent years of conflict, posed two major problems for the day-to-day conduct of school medical work. The war meant that both the Board of Education and the local education authorities were anxious to restrict expenditure to the most essential items, and the needs of the armed forces meant that a significant proportion of school medical staff became directly involved in war work. However, despite these pressures, the Board was determined to ensure that the progress which had been made before 1914 should as far as possible be maintained. In August 1914 the Board informed local authorities that it was of the greatest importance that the work of the school medical service should be maintained throughout England and Wales, and that they should do their utmost to ensure that 'good working arrangements' were made to cover for absent colleagues (PP 1914–16 Cd. 8055 xviii: 2).

The most important weapons in the Board's armoury for dealing with local authorities were the grants for medical inspection and medical treatment which had been introduced in 1912 and 1913. During the early months of the war, the Board endeavoured to ensure that local education authorities continued to satisfy the grant regulations, but it soon became apparent that it would have to interpret the regulations more loosely than it had originally intended. In March 1915 the Board said that it would no longer compel local authorities to inspect all the children in the routine age groups, and that it would continue to pay grants at the same rate as the previous year, provided that the authorities' efforts were 'reasonably satisfactory, regard being had to all the circumstances'. It said that if local authorities were compelled to curtail their activities, they should concentrate on the inspection of 'ailing' children, and the maintenance of existing arrangements for medical treatment (PP 1916 Cd. 8338 viii: 3–4).

We can gain some indication of the impact of these arrangements from Table 5.1, which gives details of the annual expenditure by local education authorities on the school medical service between 1912/13 and 1919/20. The table shows that the total amount of money expended by local authorities increased throughout the war years, although some allowance must be made for inflation in interpreting these figures.[1] The most significant increases in expenditure during the war were on the employment of school nurses, contributions to hospitals and infirmaries and the provision of school clinics. However, there was relatively little change in the amount of money

Table 5.1 Local education authority spending on medical inspection and treatment, 1912/13–1919/20 (£).

	Salaries of medical officers	*Salaries of nurses*	*Travelling expenses of medical officers and nurses*	*Drugs, materials and apparatus*	*Provision of spectacles*	*Contributions to hospitals, infirmaries and nursing associations*	*Provision of clerical assistance, etc.*	*Total*
1912/13	139,774	37,119	15,258	7,378	1,650	23,629	61,185	285,993
1913/14	151,339	43,212	16,779	9,808	2,155	27,459	74,983	325,735
1914/15	180,377	57,856	21,052	14,069	3,681	39,315	95,348	411,428
1915/16	179,579	66,439	17,579	11,440	4,023	43,403	95,407	417,870
1916/17	174,297	71,725	16,620	9,987	4,063	44,843	96,270	417,805
1917/18	181,338	91,163	18,377	14,510	4,826	50,603	111,658	472,475
1918/19	209,250	117,250	21,250	20,750	6,700	58,350	164,050	597,600
1919/20	324,955	172,509	38,294	40,555	11,963	76,861	219,928	885,695

Sources: PP 1920 Cmd. 995 xv: 22; PP 1921 Cmd. 1522 xi: 18.

devoted to the salaries of school medical officers and assistant school medical officers. This figure rose from £151,000 in 1913/14 to £180,000 in 1914/15, but remained virtually unchanged during the remainder of the war.

The Board's willingness to interpret the grant regulations more flexibly was of vital importance, but the greatest problem facing the service was the constantly increasing demand for medical personnel from the armed forces. On 9 March 1915 the Army Council invited the Board of Education to make arrangements with local education authorities to allow school medical officers 'to place their services at the disposal of the Army Council for the duration of the War', and on 29 March the Board issued a Circular (Circular 899) stating that it would not stand in the way of those medical officers who wished to serve in the armed forces, even though this might have an adverse effect on the school medical service in their area (PRO ED50/45, Cubitt to Selby-Bigge; PP 1916 Cd. 8338 viii: 3). In May 1916 the Board issued a second Circular, in which it urged 'all Medical Officers of the school medical service' to offer their services to the military authorities (PP 1916 Cd. 8338 viii: 3–4). In April 1917 the government called up all medical men of military age, and the Board urged all local authorities to secure the services of 'medical substitutes' (i.e. 'women or older men') for the duration of hostilities (PP 1917–18 Cd. 8746 xi: 1–2).

We can gain an impression of the demands which the war placed on the school medical service by examining the statistics of the numbers of school doctors and nurses who served with the armed forces between 1914 and 1918. These statistics are unfortunately incomplete because the Board only began to collect information of this kind after the issue of Circular 899 in March 1915. However, it is clear that the war imposed a substantial burden on the staffing of the school medical service. During the last two years of the war, an average of eighty-three school medical officers, 220 assistant school medical officers, eighty-two specialists and 152 school nurses were engaged in war work (see Table 5.2). During the first three years of the war, Newman reported that local authorities had experienced great difficulty in replacing

Table 5.2 School medical staff absent on military service, 1916–18.

	1 June 1916	*March 1917*	*1917*	*September 1918*
School medical officers	86	85	84	76
Assistant school medical officers	199	231	228	216
Medical officers engaged in school work of a specialist character	53	81	89	104
School nurses	185	163	139	119
Total staff absent on war service	523	560	540	515
Total number of school medical staff[a]	2741	(2741)	2883	3138

[a]The figures showing the total number of school medical staff were based on returns submitted by local authorities. The figure in column 1 is taken from the Chief Medical Officer's annual report for 1915; the figure in column 2 is taken from the annual report for 1916; the figure in column 3 is taken from the annual report for 1917; and the figure in column 4 is taken from the annual report for 1918. The Chief Medical Officer decided not to ask local authorities how many medical staff they normally employed in 1916 and he simply reproduced the 1915 figure in his 1916 annual report. The problems surrounding the collection of these figures were discussed in PRO ED50/34, Lambert to Eaton, 28/3/17, and subsequent correspondence.

The figures themselves include estimates of the total number of medical officers and the total number of nurses. The separate totals are as follows: 1915 and 1916: 1257 medical officers and 1484 school nurses; 1917: 1261 medical officers and 1622 school nurses; 1918: 1373 medical officers and 1765 school nurses.

Sources: PP 1916 Cd. 8338 viii: 2–7; PP 1917–18 Cd. 8746 xi: 1–3; PP 1918 Cd. 9206 ix: 2–4; PP 1919 Cmd. 420 xxi: 1–3.

their medical officers, but by 1918 it was also becoming increasingly difficult to recruit substitute nurses (PP 1916 Cd. 8338 viii: 2; PP 1917–18 Cd. 8746 xi: 1; PP 1918 Cd. 9206 ix: 2; PP 1919 Cmd. 420 xxi: 1).

The absence of a large proportion of the staff of the school medical service forced local authorities to introduce a number of changes to the way in which they made arrangements for school medical work. In Circular 899, the Board advised those local authorities which were unable to maintain their existing level of school medical work to give the highest priority to the inspection of 'ailing' children and the maintenance of their existing facilities for medical treatment. This advice heralded a subtle transformation in the operation of the school medical service during the war years. A substantial number of local education authorities reduced their commitment to routine medical inspection in order to devote more resources to the inspection and treatment of children who were known to be 'ailing'.

The most obvious effect of the war was to initiate a dramatic reduction in the number of children who were subjected to routine medical inspection. In his annual report for 1917, George Newman estimated that approximately 100 local education authorities had abandoned routine medical inspection in favour of the inspection of 'special' children who were already known to be ailing, and a similar number followed the same course of action in 1918 (PP 1918 Cd. 9206 ix: 2; PP 1919 Cmd. 420 xxi: 2). These changes led to a substantial reduction in the number of children who were examined by a doctor between 1914 and 1918. In 1914 approximately 1.4 million children were inspected as either entrants or leavers, and a further 500,000 children were examined as 'specials'. In 1918 only 866,000 children were inspected in the routine age groups (despite the introduction of a third routine age group in April 1915), and the total number of children who were inspected as either routines or specials was just over 1.3 million (see Table 5.3).

In contrast to the impact of the war on medical inspection, the war years also witnessed a substantial increase in the provision of medical treatment. Between 1914 and 1918 a growing number of local authorities employed school nurses, provided school clinics, made contributions to hospitals and provided spectacles (Table 5.4). The number of authorities providing treatment for minor ailments rose from 204 to 260; the number offering dental treatment rose from 130 to 169; and the number offering treatment for defective vision rose from 195 to 242 (Table 5.5). The war years therefore witnessed a significant shift in the distribution of resources within the school medical service. The war forced many local authorities to scale down their plans for routine medical inspection, but they continued to expand the provision of medical treatment to children who were unable to obtain it from other sources.[2]

Table 5.3 Numbers of children medically inspected in England and Wales, 1914–20.[a]

	Routines	*Specials*	*Total*
1914	1,395,133	*c.* 500,000	*c.* 1,900,000
1915	1,448,115	*c.* 500,000	*c.* 1,950,000
1916	–	–	1,446,448
1917	1,007,394	354,669	1,362,063
1918	866,088	451,569	1,317,657
1919	–	–	over 1,800,000
1920	1,819,658	938,016	2,757,674

[a] These figures need to be interpreted with care, since it subsequently emerged that many medical officers failed to distinguish between the number of children inspected and the number of inspections carried out. The figures quoted for 1920 actually refer to the number of inspections. The Board estimated that 325,598 children received both types of examination, so the number of children who were examined was 2,432,076. See PP 1921 Cmd. 1522 xi: 5–6; PRO ED50/72, Marris to Wood, 21/2/22.

Sources: PP 1914–16 Cd. 8055 xviii: 4; PP 1916 Cd. 8338 viii: 5–6; 1917–18 Cd. 8746 xi: 2–3; PP 1918 Cd. 9206 ix: 2; PP 1919 Cmd. 420 xxi: 1–2; PP 1920 Cmd. 995 xv: 2; PP 1921 Cmd. 1522 xi: 5.

Table 5.4 Number of authorities which made arrangements for medical treatment, 1908–20.

	Made some arrangement for medical treatment	*Provided school clinics*	*Contributed to hospitals*	*Made provision for supplying spectacles*
1908	57	7	8	21
1909	88	11	20	37
1910	130	30	34	70
1911	135	56	31	82
1912	167	97	37	101
1913	241	139	53	125
1914	266	179	75	165
1915	279	212	78	210
1916	276	219	87	216
1917	279	231	95	223
1918	287	252	110	235
1919	298	272	127	264
1920	309	288	168	282

Note: The number of Local Education Authorities in each year was as follows: 1908: 328; 1909; 329; 1910; 322; 1911–15: 317; 1916: 319; 1917–19: 318; 1920: 316.

Sources: PP 1910 Cd. 4986 xxiii: 15, 85–102; PP 1910 Cd. 5426 xxiii: 13, 92–122; PP 1911 Cd. 5925 xvii: 15, 126–32, 155–7; PP 1912–13 Cd. 6530 xxi: 6, 118–47; PP 1914 Cd. 7184 xxv: 20, 145–78; PP 1914–16 Cd. 7730 xviii: 3, 104–9, 129–35, 153–6; PP 1914–16 Cd. 8055 xviii: 90–111; PP 1916 Cd. 8338 viii: 1, 60–77; PP 1917–18 Cd. 8746 xi: 52–3; PP 1918 Cd. 9206 ix: 41; PP 1919 Cmd. 420 xxi: 50–1; PP 1920 Cmd. 995 xv: 42; PP 1921 Cmd. 1522 xi: 64.

Table 5.5 Number of authorities providing different kinds of medical treatment, 1908–20.

	Minor ailments	*Dental defects*	*Defective vision*	*Spectacles*	*Enlarged tonsils and adenoids*	*Ringworm (X-ray)*
1908	–	–	–	21	–	–
1909	–	*c.* 10	–	37	–	4
1910	–	16	–	70	–	18
1911	–	29	–	82	–	23
1912	80	61	–	101	–	42
1913	123	88	–	125	–	–
1914	204	130	195	165	83	68
1915	213	147	211	179	93	71
1916	216	146	221	216	102	73
1917	231	151	226	223	110	84
1918	260	169	242	235	129	92
1919	274	203	264	264	151	101
1920	289	235	280	282	198	129

Sources: PP 1910 Cd. 4986 xxiii: 93; PP 1910 Cd. 5426 xxiii: 102, 129–31; PP 1911 Cd. 5925 xvii: 127–8, 179–80; PP 1912–13 Cd. 6530 xxi: 119, 156–7, 122–3; PP 1914 Cd. 7184 xxv: 151, 153, 197; PP 1914–16 Cd. 7730 xviii: 151, 158, 179–83; PP 1914–16 Cd. 8055 xviii: 91; PP 1916 Cd. 8338 viii: 62; PP 1917–18 Cd. 8746 xi: 53; PP 1918 Cd. 9206 ix: 41; PP 1919 Cmd. 420 xxi: 51; PP 1920 Cmd. 995 xv: 42; PP 1921 Cmd. 1522 xi: 65.

War and reconstruction

The development of the school medical service during the First World War testifies to the strength of the foundations which had been laid before 1914, and bears witness to the way in which the war highlighted public health issues.[3] This tendency was also reflected in the development of a series of plans for expanding the scope of school medical provision to cover a wider population. The history of these proposals also illustrates some of the ways in which the outbreak of war highlighted the persistence of interdepartmental rivalries and the power of vested interests. These factors continued to exercise an important influence on the development of social policy after 1918.[4]

One of the most important issues to confront the Board of Education at the outset of the war was the question of school meals. In 1906 Parliament had passed the Education (Provision of Meals) Act, which enabled local education authorities to levy a halfpenny rate to provide free meals to children who were 'unable by reason of lack of food to take full advantage of the education provided them', and by 1913 more than 130 local authorities had decided to put the Act into operation (6 Edw. VII Ch. 57, section 3; PP 1914 Cd. 7184 xxv: 393). However, in August 1914 Parliament passed a further Act, which removed the limit of a halfpenny rate and allowed local authorities to feed children on days when they were not attending school, and this led to a dramatic increase both in the number of authorities providing meals and in the number of children receiving them (4 & 5 Geo. V Ch. 20, sections 1–2; PP 1914–16 Cd. 8055 xviii: 202–4). However, the effect of these changes was short-lived. By the spring of 1915, the majority of local authorities had decided that the number of children in need of meals was much less than the number which they had originally anticipated, and the school meals programme quickly fell back to prewar levels (PP 1916 Cd. 8338 viii: 87). As Table 5.6 shows, the total number of meals provided by local authorities in the last year of the war was less than half the number supplied in 1913/14 (PP 1919 Cmd. 420 xxi: 174–7).

The government's efforts to improve the arrangements for the care and supervision of infants and young children were of much greater significance. During the early years of the twentieth century, Parliament had been happy to leave this issue in the hands of a wide range of voluntary agencies, and it provided very little financial support to these agencies before war broke out. However, in July 1914 the government decided to allow both the Local Government Board and the Board of Education to make grants to different organisations concerned with infant welfare work. The Local Government Board acquired the power to make grants to baby clinics and infant dispensaries, and the Board of Education acquired the power to make grants to schools for mothers (House of Commons Debates 1914: col. 29). At the time, the government hoped that it would be possible for the two departments to cooperate by ensuring that each had a clearly defined set of responsibilities, but the limitations of this view soon became apparent. By 1915, the provision of medical assistance to mothers and young children had become the subject

Table 5.6 Provision of school meals under the Education (Provision of Meals) Acts, 1906 and 1914, in the period 1907/08–1919/20.

	No. of LEAs which fed under the Acts	*Total no. of children fed in the year*	*Total no. of meals supplied in the year*	*Average total cost per meal (d.)*
1907/08	32	–	–	–
1908/09	113	–	14,218,560	1.22
1909/10	126	–	16,102,104	2.00
1910/11	128	–	16,872,997	2.18
1911/12	131	–	16,122,219	2.34
1912/13	137	358,306	19,001,729	2.32
1913/14	98	156,531	14,525,593	2.43
1914/15	134	422,401	29,560,316	2.47
1915/16	116	118,114	9,957,634	4.10
1916/17	94	65,301	5,777,147	5.42
1917/18	88	60,633	6,518,174	5.26
1918/19	86	53,742	5,647,954	5.98
1919/20	117	69,554	6,300,643	7.01

Sources: PP 1917–18 Cd. 8746 xi: 140; PP 1918 Cd. 9206 ix: 128; PP 1919 Cmd. 420 xxi: 175; PP 1920 Cmd. 995 xv: 20; PP 1921 Cmd. 1522 xi: 147.

of heated interdepartmental debate (PP 1914–16 Cd. 7730 xviii: 43; PRO ED24/1363, Memorandum to the Prime Minister – Health work for young children (13/2/17)).

The differences between the two Boards came to a head in July 1915, when the Local Government Board introduced a proposal to extend the Notification of Births Act of 1907 (House of Commons Debates 1915: col. 955). The original Act was a permissive one, which enabled local authorities to compel the father of a new-born child, or some other person in attendance on the mother, to notify the birth to the local medical officer of health (7 Edw. VII Ch. 40). The Local Government Board wished to extend this Act by giving local authorities the power to

> make such arrangements as they think fit, and as may be sanctioned by the Local Government Board, for attending to the health of expectant . . . and nursing mothers, and of children under five years of age who are not being educated in public elementary schools (PP 1914–16 (114) iii, section 2).

The Board of Education objected to the proposal on the grounds that the Local Government Board was seeking to invade its own territory, and when the Notification of Births (Extension) Bill became law, the new powers were only granted to Local Authorities in Scotland and Ireland (5 & 6 Geo. V Ch. 64: sections 2–3).

The disagreements between the Board of Education and the Local Government Board provide a vivid illustration of the way in which interdepartmental rivalries continued to hamper the development of social policy after 1914, and they were highlighted again by the Reports of the Committee on Retrenchment in the Public Expenditure and the Departmental Committee on Prices. In February 1916 the Committee on Retrenchment in the Public Expenditure concluded that the only satisfactory solution to the problem of overlapping would be for 'the control of all institutions . . . providing in any way for the . . . health . . . of mothers or children under school age . . . [to] be handed over . . . entirely to the Local Government Board' (PP 1916 Cd. 8200 xv: para. 52). The Departmental Committee on Prices argued that 'in the present emergency, all Local Authorities (including the London County Council and the Metropolitan Borough Councils) should be urged to start a sufficient number of maternity centres, baby clinics and child nurseries, and should be empowered to provide a certain supply of milk to children under the age of five, and dinner to expectant and nursing mothers' (PP 1916 Cd. 8358 xiv: para. 16).

The Departmental Committee's Report persuaded the Local Government Board to renew its efforts to expand the provision of maternity and child welfare services. In October 1916 the Permanent Secretary of the Local Government Board, Sir Horace Monro, told Selby-Bigge that 'we are desirous of meeting the recommendation of the Food Prices Committee that institutions for infant welfare shall provide milk for infants and dinners for nursing and expectant mothers . . . [and] in order to meet these points, we propose to introduce a [new] Bill conferring on local authorities in England and Wales the same powers as were conferred on local authorities in Scotland and Ireland [in 1915]' (PRO ED24/1363, Monro to Selby-Bigge, 24/10/16). In February 1917 the President of the Board of Education agreed to recognise the Local Government's Board's right to exercise responsibility for the care of mothers and pre-school children, and the President of the Local Government Board offered his support for the Board of Education's campaign to establish public nursery schools (PRO ED24/1363, Fisher to Rhondda, 26/1/17: paras 5–6; 'Health work for young children', 12/2/17: paras 1–2). This agreement paved the way for the introduction of the Maternity and Child Welfare Bill in 1918, and established the general framework for the relationship between the school medical service and the rest of the public health service during the interwar period (PRO ED24/1363, Fisher to Lloyd George, 'Health work for young children', 13/2/17; Local Government Board, 'Maternity and Child Welfare Bill', January 1918).

In addition to these disputes, the Board of Education was also involved in a number of other discussions relating to its own plans for the expansion of school medical work. These discussions revolved around the question of whether local education authorities should be compelled to make arrangements for the medical treatment of elementary schoolchildren, and whether they should have the power to make arrangements for the medical inspection and treatment of secondary schoolchildren. The Board itself was divided on the first issue, and it was only finally persuaded to introduce compulsion as a result of Parliamentary pressure. Its efforts to extend the power to provide medical treatment to secondary schools were much more controversial, and brought the Board into direct confrontation with the British Medical Association.

Shortly after he was appointed to the post of Chief Medical Officer, George Newman suggested that one of the main functions of the Board's Medical Department would be to encourage local authorities to make the greatest possible use of their statutory powers.[5] During the early years of the school medical service, the Board sought to achieve this objective by withholding a proportion of the education grant from those local authorities which failed to make adequate provision for medical inspection, and by introducing special grants for medical inspection and treatment in 1912 and 1913. However, as the war progressed, the Board came under growing pressure to convert the local authorities' power to provide medical treatment into a statutory duty. In 1917 the editor of the *Times Educational Supplement* claimed that 'the attitude of a substantial proportion of the Local Education Authorities towards the school medical service' was 'one of the greatest weaknesses of the position' (*Times Educational Supplement* 1917c), and both the Association of Directors and Secretaries of Education and the National Association of Education Officers said that local authorities should be forced to offer medical treatment to children whose parents were unable to afford it (*Times Educational Supplement* 1917a; 1917b).

Within the Board of Education, the proposal to extend compulsion to medical treatment was the subject of considerable debate. In February 1917 one of the Board's officials suggested that the Board should compel local authorities to provide medical treatment if it felt that their existing arrangements were inadequate, but the Permanent Secretary argued that it would be impossible to lay down 'standards of the amount and kind of medical treatment which it should be the duty of the Authority to provide' (PRO ED24/1369, Pelham to Newman, 28/2/17; Selby-Bigge to Fisher, 6/3/17). The issue of compulsion received relatively direct attention in the debates which accompanied the passage through Parliament of the two Education Bills of 1917 and 1918, but in July 1918 the MP for York, Arnold Rowntree, suggested that the duties which local authorities already possessed with regard to medical inspection should be extended to cover medical treatment (House of Commons Debates 1918: cols 1770–76). Although the President of the Board of Education opposed Rowntree's amendment, he recognised the breadth of support which it commanded, and an appropriate amendment was introduced before the 1918 Education Bill became law (8 & 9 Geo. V, Ch. 39, clause 2 (1) (b)).[6]

Although the proposal to make medical treatment compulsory was undoubtedly important, it attracted far less attention than the Board's own proposal to extend the provision of medical inspection and treatment to secondary schools and continuation classes. After 1908, a number of local education authorities had made some efforts to introduce medical inspection to secondary schools, but they were under no statutory obligation to do so. However, when the government introduced the Education Bill to Parliament in 1917, it included two clauses which greatly extended the range of schools which the school medical service could cover. The first of these clauses, clause 18, said that local authorities should have the duty to make arrangements for medical inspection and the power to make arrangements for medical treatment in secondary schools, continuation schools, Welsh intermediate schools, and any other schools which the local authority provided. The second clause, clause 19, said that local authorities should also have the power 'to make such arrangements as may be appropriate to the industrial and housing conditions of the area . . . for . . . attending to the health, nourishment and physical welfare of children attending nursery schools' (PP 1917–18 (89) i, sections 18–19).

These proposals represented a significant extension of the medical responsibilities of local education authorities, because they extended the scope of the school medical service downwards to include children attending nursery schools and upwards to include children and young persons attending secondary schools and continuation classes, and they attracted enormous opposition from the British Medical Association. In its response to the proposals, the BMA raised three specific objections. First, it said that the proposals would lead to duplication and waste, because the extension of school medical work to nursery schools would lead to conflict with the Local Government Board, and the extension of school medical work to continuation classes would lead to conflict with the national health insurance scheme. Second, it argued that any extension of the medical powers of the local education authorities would jeopardise the government's efforts to create a unified health service under the Ministry of Health. Third, it claimed that the proposals would undermine the interests of the general practitioner, because local authorities would prefer to employ their own medical staffs, and the provision of medical treatment through the school medical service would reduce parents' incentive to consult their own medical practitioner (PRO ED 24/1370, BMA Memorandum, 16/10/17).

The Board discussed these objections with the British Medical Association on 14 December, but its attitude was generally dismissive. It argued that the prospect of duplication could be avoided by careful administration, and that there would still be a need for the kind of legislation proposed in the Bill even if a Ministry of Health was created. The Board also took issue with the suggestion that local authorities would be reluctant to employ private medical practitioners. In a private memorandum, Sir George Newman said that local authorities had always advised parents to consult their own practitioner in the first instance, and that the Board had 'always considered favourably' proposals from local authorities to use private practitioners for the provision of medical treatment (PRO ED 24/1370, [George Newman], Deputation from the BMA). In May 1918 Newman asked W.S. Lambert to draw up a memorandum showing the number of local authorities which relied solely on full-time school medical staff and the number who employed private practitioners. Lambert concluded that forty-seven local authorities relied exclusively on their own staff and that 226 authorities employed private practitioners for the provision of medical treatment (PRO ED24/1370, Newman to Lambert, 13/5/18; Lambert to Newman, 15/5/18: 7).

The Board held a second meeting with the British Medical Association on

30 May 1918. On this occasion the latter appeared to adopt a more conciliatory tone, although it continued to argue that changes were necessary. Its most important recommendation was that a new clause should be inserted into the Bill to limit the extent of the medical service which a local authority could provide (PRO ED24/1370, James Neal to Newman, 29/5/18). In June 1918 the Board agreed to accept an amendment, proposed by Sir William Cheyne, which was designed to prevent local authorities from establishing 'a general domiciliary service of treatment for children and young persons', and to compel them 'to consider how far they can avail themselves of the services of private medical practitioners' in providing whatever treatment they did provide (PP 1918 (57) i, clause 18; House of Commons Debates 1918: col. 1470). The amendment was sharply criticised by a number of MPs, who argued that it was both meaningless and unenforceable, but in spite of this opposition it still became law (House of Commons Debates 1918: cols 1470–74; 8 & 9 Geo. V, Ch. 39, clause 25).

This discussion of the debates surrounding the extension of the school medical service and other services connected with the welfare of children has illustrated some of the problems which confronted social policy makers during the First World War. The war played a vitally important role in highlighting the importance of child welfare and in stimulating proposals for social reconstruction, but it also highlighted the persistence of interdepartmental rivalries and the opposition of vested interests. In the case of the maternity and child welfare service and the extension of school medical services to secondary schools and continuation classes, these obstacles were finally overcome. However, many of the problems which were highlighted by these debates continued to affect the development of the school medical service throughout the interwar period.

War conditions and the health of schoolchildren

The preceding sections have concentrated on the practical development of the school medical service during the First World War and the formulation of plans for the expansion of the service after the war, but one of the main functions of the school medical service was to provide an accurate guide to the health of schoolchildren at any one time. When the war first broke out, the Medical Department expressed considerable concern about the possible effect of war conditions on child health, but it soon concluded that many of its fears were largely unfounded.[7] By the spring of 1915, Newman had become convinced that the war was actually having a much more favourable impact than he had ever anticipated. In his annual report for 1916 he observed:

> The evidence from School Doctors and the Board's Medical Inspectors in all parts of the country is . . . that . . . the children [are] . . . on the whole, better fed and better clothed than at any time since medical

> inspection was introduced . . . there can be no question of the betterment which [has] revealed itself (PP 1917–18 Cd. 8746 xi: 142).

The impact of the First World War on the health of the civilian population has also attracted considerable attention from historians. In 1986 Jay Winter claimed that the war had brought about 'unanticipated gains' in the survival chances of non-combatant men and women, together with the greatest improvements in infant mortality during the first thirty years of the twentieth century (Winter 1986: 107, 117, 142). Winter argued that the main reason for this development was that the war years had witnessed important improvements in civilian living standards. In 1988 he wrote:

> The only conceivable meaning of the concept of *negative* war-related deaths is that the war created conditions which improved the survival chances of men at ages at which they were lucky enough to stay out of the trenches. In the British case, the process which underlay this surprising development was a rise in the standard of living of the working class in general, and in particular, of those strata that had been worst off in the pre-war period (Winter 1988: 14).

Winter's work has been widely cited (see, for example, Drèze and Sen 1989; Wilkinson 1989; Coleman and Salt 1992), but it has not won universal support. Linda Bryder claimed that Winter's arguments were undermined by the fact that tuberculosis mortality rose between 1914 and 1918, and Richard Evans concluded that 'the most that can be said is that standards of living did not deteriorate with anything like the severity they did in Germany' (Bryder 1987; Evans 1991: 347). In addition, a number of writers have questioned the extent to which living standards did improve in the way that Winter described. Winter argued that the most important factors contributing to a rise in living standards were the virtual elimination of prewar patterns of unemployment and underemployment and a significant decline in the birth rate, but these factors may have been offset by increases in the retail price index, food shortages and a deterioration in housing conditions (Winter 1986: 214; Milward 1984: 37; Waites 1987: 139–40, 171–3; Thane 1982: 130–31; Burnett 1983: 271–82; Dewey 1988: 211–12).

Much of the debate between Winter and his critics has focused on the interpretation of different sets of mortality statistics, and relatively little attention has been paid to the school medical records. This is not particularly surprising in view of the doubts which have been expressed over the value of these records and the fact that many local authorities decided to abandon routine medical inspection for the duration of hostilities (Webster 1982: 118–19; 1983b: 79–82). Nevertheless, at least two writers have used the school medical statistics to support the view that domestic living standards improved. In 1987 Bernard Waites drew attention to the remarkable decline in the incidence of malnutrition in Doncaster, which fell from 31 per cent in 1913 to just 5 per cent two years later (Waites 1987: 163). In 1988 Richard Wall showed that there was a steady and continuous decline in the incidence of malnutrition in London, although it was interesting to note that the incidence of 'excellent' nutrition also declined (Wall 1988: 47–50; see also PP 1919 Cmd. 420 xxi: 11–14; 175–6).

The most extensive contemporary survey of children's health and nutrition was conducted by the Board of Education in 1923. In March 1923 the President of the Board of Education, E.F.L. Wood, asked Newman to discover whether unemployment and the rationing of school meals had led to any deterioration in the health of children attending public elementary schools, and the inquiry was subsequently extended to include a consideration of the effects of the First World War. On 15 March Alfred Eichholz asked a total of nineteen school medical officers whether their experience supported the belief that 'the regular wages received during the war resulted in a marked improvement in the physique of schoolchildren', and whether the general health of children was now 'better or worse' than it had been just before the war. In May 1922 Eichholz prepared a summary of the responses for inclusion in Newman's annual report, in which he stated that 'with few exceptions there is a clear statement on the part of School Medical Officers that conditions obtaining during the war resulted in substantial improvement in the physique of the children', but a closer inspection of the original evidence suggests that this conclusion may have been a little too optimistic (PRO ED50/34, [Alfred Eichholz], Annual Report of Chief Medical Officer 1922: Nutritional conditions [15/5/23]; Board of Education 1923: 120–26).

The majority of those who responded to the Board's inquiries agreed that the standard of child health had risen, but their evidence was not always conclusive. The School Medical Officers for Birmingham, Newcastle, Portsmouth and Sheffield all thought that the regular wages received during the war had led to a marked improvement in children's health, and their sentiments were echoed by the Medical Officers for Bradford, Cornwall, Hull, Liverpool, London, St Helens, Shropshire and Swansea.[8] However, several other medical officers thought that conditions had either remained unchanged or deteriorated. The School Medical Officers for Durham, Manchester, Merthyr Tydfil, Rhondda and West Yorkshire said that no clear pattern had emerged, and the Medical Officers for Leeds, Lancashire and North Yorkshire thought that conditions had declined. The School Medical Officer for North Yorkshire said that there had been a definite increase in both slight and grave degrees of malnutrition, and that this had been particularly marked in urban areas (PRO ED50/34, Effect of unemployment and rationing of provision of meals of health of public elementary school children: extracts from replies).

In addition to examining the largely subjective impressions of individual school medical officers, it is also possible to assess the impact of the war by looking at measurements of children's heights. When the school medical service was first created, the majority of local education authorities published statistics showing the average heights of the children who were examined at routine medical inspections, and a number of these authorities continued to publish the statistics during and after the First World War. The study of variations in children's heights has attracted considerable attention from historians and other social scientists in recent years, and many health workers regard these statistics as one of the best available indicators of a population's health and well-being (Fogel 1986; Komlos 1989; Floud *et al.* 1990). In 1991 Phyllis Eveleth and James Tanner wrote:

> A child's growth rate reflects, perhaps better than any other single index, his state of health and nutrition, and often indeed his psychological situation also. Similarly, the average values of children's heights and weights reflect accurately the state of a nation's public health and the average nutritional status of its citizens, when appropriate allowance is made for differences, if any, in genetic potential. This is especially so in developing or disintegrating countries. Thus a well-designed growth study is a powerful tool with which to monitor the health of a population, or to pinpoint sub-groups of a population whose share in economic and social benefits is less than it might be. Indeed as infant mortality rate goes down during a country's development, so the importance of monitoring growth rate increases (Eveleth and Tanner 1991: 1).[9]

The following analysis is based on a study of the average heights of children in twenty-four local authority areas, eighteen of which were situated in England and Wales and six in Scotland. The majority of the English and Welsh areas were situated in the North of England and South Wales, and only five areas were situated in the Midlands, East Anglia or the South of England. Nevertheless, the areas do represent a reasonable cross-section of local authority areas at the time of the First World War. The sample includes a number of large cities, such as Sheffield, Leeds, Bradford and Edinburgh, together with three county areas, and a number of small towns such as Batley, Abertillery and Torquay. It also includes several medium-sized towns, such as Cardiff, Croydon and Nottingham, and the Urban District of Rhondda. Several of the areas included large numbers of coal-miners, while others were heavily involved in the textile trades. The remaining areas included large numbers of agricultural workers, engineering workers, metal workers, dockers and building workers (see Table 5.7).

The main trends in the heights of the children in these areas are shown in Table 5.8. In order to construct this table, the average heights of boys and girls at each age were compared with the distributions of the heights of boys and girls of the same ages in London in 1965, and their heights were then expressed as centiles of the 1965 height distribution[10]. The average value of the heights of all the children was derived from the average value of the heights of the children in each age group. For example, the average height of five-year-old boys in Banffshire in 1914 was 41.99 inches. This figure was less than or equal to the height of 16.24 per cent of the five-year-old boys who were measured in London in 1965, and so the average value of the heights of these children was 16.24. The average values of the heights of seven-year-old and thirteen-year-old boys were 13.17 and 8.54 respectively, and the

Table 5.7 Population size and occupational characteristics in twenty-four areas, 1914–18.

Area	*Admin. unit*	*Population (1911)*	*Principal occupational groups*
England & Wales			
Abertillery	UD	35,415	Coal-mining
Accrington	MB	45,029	Textile manufactures (cotton), general engineering
Batley	MB	36,389	Coal-mining, woollen textiles
Bootle	CB	69,876	Dockwork, construction, general engineering
Bradford	CB	288,458	Woollen and other textiles, construction, commerce
Cambridge	MB	55,812	Professional occupations, domestic service, portering
Cardiff	CB	182,259	Docks, engineering, construction, government and commerce
Carlisle	MB	46,420	Railways, construction, food and drink
Croydon	CB	169,551	Government and commerce, printing, railways
Darwen	MB	40,332	Textile manufactures (cotton), paper manufactures
Leeds	CB	445,550	Coal-mining, textiles, tailoring, engineering, government and commerce
Lincoln	CB	57,285	Construction, food and drink, railways, commerce
Mountain Ash	UD	42,246	Coal-mining
Nottingham	CB	259,904	Coal-mining, textiles, railways, commerce
Rhondda	UD	152,781	Coal-mining
Sheffield	CB	454,632	Coal-mining, iron and steel, metal trades, railways, commerce
Torquay	MB	38,771	Defence, construction, food and drink
Warrington	CB	72,166	General engineering, chemicals, iron and steel
Scotland			
Aberdeen	City	163,891	Merchant shipping, fishing, stone-cutting
Aberdeenshire	County	159,714	Agriculture
Banffshire	County	61,402	Agriculture, fishing
Dumbartonshire	County	139,831	Ship-building, iron manufactures, bleaching and dyeing, food and drink
Edinburgh	City	320,318	Central and local government, railways, iron manufactures, construction, printing
Govan[a]	SB	238,395	Shipping, ship-building, dockwork, iron manufacture

Abbreviations: CB = county borough. MB = municipal borough. UD = urban district. SB = school board.

[a] The School Board of Govan included the whole of the burgh of Govan, together with the burgh of Partick and those parts of the parish of Govan which were included in the City of Glasgow.

Sources: PP 1912–13 Cd. 6258 cxi: Table 8; PP 1913 Cd. 7018 lxxviii: Table 15; PP 1912–13 Cd. 6097, cxix, cxx, vol. I, parts 1–37.

average values of the heights of five-, seven- and thirteen-year-old girls were 18.08, 13.67 and 5.27. The average value of the heights of boys and girls in all three age-groups was therefore (16.24 + 13.17 + 8.54 + 18.08 + 13.67 + 5.27)/6 or 12.50.[11]

The figures in Table 5.8 suggest that the majority of local authority areas did experience increases in the average value of children's heights during the war period. The best evidence comes from those areas which published continuous sets of data throughout the war period. The table shows that the average value of children's heights increased in Dumbartonshire, Edinburgh, Govan, Leeds and Warrington, and declined in Aberdeen (infants and all children), Carlisle, Lincoln and Torquay, but neither the increases nor the decreases were particularly great. The average value of the heights of children in all nine areas was 6.19 in 1914 and 6.11 in 1918.

This impression is reinforced by an examination of the main trends in those areas which only furnished data for individual years either before or after the war period. The average value of children's heights increased in Aberdeenshire (1914–20), Accrington (1914–15), Banffshire (1914–22), Batley (1915–19), Bootle (1915–18), Bradford (1914–18), Cardiff (1914–21), Croydon (1915–18), Mountain Ash (1915–18) and Rhondda (1915–22), and decreased in Abertillery (1915–18), Cambridge (1914–19), Darwen (1914–17), Nottingham (1914–18) and Sheffield (1915–19). However, there is very little evidence that the war made any great difference to the average value of children's heights, and the increases which did occur were much smaller than those which occurred in most parts of Britain between 1918 and 1939 (Harris 1993: 363; 1994: 32–5).

These findings have important implications for our understanding of the impact of the First World War on child health and civilian health generally. Taken together with the results of the Board of Education's own survey in 1923, they suggest that the net impact of the First World War on child health was comparatively small. The majority of areas experienced some improvement, but others experienced little or no change or even a deterioration. The height data do not enable us to reach any firm conclusions about the health of children in different social groups, but there is some evidence of a levelling-up of health standards in certain areas. Nevertheless, so far as the aggregate data are concerned, the overall impression is that the war had relatively little effect on the average standard of child health between 1914 and 1918.[12]

Notes

1 The retail price index almost doubled between 1914 and 1918, but this may not give a true picture of the impact of inflation on the school medical service. Salary payments to school medical officers and assistant school medical officers accounted for between 38 and 46 per cent of local authority expenditure between 1913/14 and 1917/18, but the salaries of public officials failed to rise in line with inflation. See *Public Health* (1919a).

Table 5.8 Heights of schoolchildren in selected local authority areas, 1908–25.

Height in centiles	*1908*	*1909*	*1910*	*1911*	*1912*	*1913*	*1914*	*1915*	*1916*	*1917*	*1918*	*1919*	*1920*	*1921*	*1922*	*1923*	*1924*	*1925*
Aberdeen (infants)	–	–	7.43	11.81	9.32	6.72	12.11	11.12	8.07	8.21	10.67	10.24	11.17	11.62	13.72	14.85	16.06	13.16
Aberdeen (all)	–	–	–	9.30	7.02	6.43	8.92	8.15	6.29	7.37	7.48	7.21	7.79	–	–	–	–	–
Aberdeenshire	–	–	13.19	14.64	13.72	15.23	–	–	–	–	–	–	16.13	16.40	16.09	17.96	17.19	17.49
Abertillery	–	1.54	2.55	2.97	3.51	4.46	4.68	5.02	–	–	4.06	3.41	4.27	–	–	–	–	–
Accrington	6.46	7.37	5.57	5.53	–	5.63	6.70	7.49	–	–	–	–	–	–	–	–	–	–
Banffshire	–	–	–	–	–	13.18	12.50	–	–	–	–	–	–	–	15.72	15.40	16.10	–
Batley	–	2.64	3.37	–	–	3.81	4.32	4.03	–	–	–	6.51	7.10	8.01	7.11	7.60	8.15	7.28
Bootle	2.22	3.90	3.79	–	2.66	4.46	3.13	–	–	–	4.02	5.25	6.74	–	–	–	–	–
Bradford	3.52	3.78	4.16	4.75	4.99	6.55	7.25	–	–	–	8.18	11.07	9.72	–	8.30	9.38	–	11.62
Cambridge	3.58	3.63	4.52	4.47	4.66	5.39	6.91	–	–	–	–	5.82	7.33	7.98	7.42	6.99	11.76	12.86
Cardiff	–	3.58	4.57	4.40	4.41	3.60	3.90	–	–	–	–	–	–	5.35	5.08	–	–	–
Carlisle	–	2.52	2.07	2.24	2.02	3.66	4.27	5.21	4.79	3.08	3.74	4.79	–	–	–	–	–	–
Croydon[a]	7.98	9.74	9.86	–	–	–	–	15.27	16.05	15.62	19.54	16.76	19.64	19.80	20.76	–	–	–
Darwen	–	4.10	4.44	5.06	6.54	6.42	6.09	6.51	6.28	4.92	–	–	–	–	–	–	–	–
Dumbartonshire	–	–	–	–	4.43	4.51	6.20	5.97	5.13	6.55	6.79	6.40	7.56	9.02	10.79	8.17	8.79	11.22
Edinburgh	5.33	4.56	6.04	6.13	6.11	5.85	5.33	5.35	5.07	4.72	6.51	5.75	7.13	8.31	–	9.45	9.62	9.00
Govan	–	2.30	2.92	2.18	1.79	1.97	2.63	2.51	2.73	2.51	2.75	3.29	–	–	–	–	–	–

Leeds	–	2.71	3.39	2.65	2.12	2.53	2.55	3.24	3.41	3.74	3.42	3.41	4.06	4.69	5.25	5.60	6.16	6.99
Lincoln	–	10.03	9.93	10.20	11.06	13.56	13.04	12.27	14.22	11.66	12.14	10.27	–	–	–	–	–	–
Mountain Ash	–	–	4.52	3.25	4.19	4.42	–	4.60	4.11	4.95	4.93	–	–	–	–	–	–	–
Nottingham	–	–	4.68	4.81	4.31	4.87	4.61	–	–	–	3.24	3.93	–	–	–	–	–	–
Rhondda	–	–	–	3.81	2.98	2.97	2.96	2.26	–	–	–	–	–	3.88	3.69	3.89	3.96	4.61
Sheffield	5.49	3.13	3.43	3.35	3.08	4.72	5.72	5.39	–	–	–	3.97	4.68	5.93	–	–	–	–
Torquay	–	–	–	–	–	–	10.12	–	9.72	8.06	8.54	11.37	13.22	13.90	13.65	10.59	–	–
Warrington	–	2.29	2.03	1.98	2.11	2.93	2.69	3.01	2.99	3.81	3.59	2.38	3.06	2.50	2.88	4.08	3.99	6.13

[a] The figures for Croydon between 1915 and 1922 are based on the heights of children attending ten unspecified schools in the borough. The school medical officer failed to record the names of the schools or the numbers of children who were measured in them.

Sources: The original data were derived from the annual reports of the school medical officers for the areas listed in the table. A full list of the school medical reports cited in this study may be found in the Bibliography. Details of the original height statistics have been deposited with the ESRC Data Archive, University of Essex, Wivenhoe Park, Colchester, Essex CO4 3SQ.

2 This may have been less true of the school medical service in Scotland. In 1920 the Scottish Board of Health issued a memorandum stating that 'the war not only stopped further development of the school medical service, but largely suspended the operation of the existing service'. Control of the school medical service in Scotland was transferred from the Scottish Education Department to the Board of Health under the Scottish Board of Health Act of 1919. See *Medical Officer* (1920).

3 This point is developed extensively in Dwork (1987), especially pp. 208–20.

4 There is an enormous literature pertaining to the 'frustration' of social reform in the aftermath of the First World War. For a useful starting point, see Abrams (1963).

5 In his letter to Morant on 6 September 1907, he wrote: 'I want to see the Department not only the best in Europe but in due course I want to see it *leading* all the Education Authorities. Between ourselves, we want to play no LGB games – i.e. half-asleep and following afar off. *If we don't guide and inspire* we may as well go and drown.' See PRO ED24/280, Newman to Morant, 6/9/07.

6 The *Times Educational Supplement* discussed Rowntree's amendment in its leader columns on 11 July 1918. It wrote: 'We are inclined to agree that voluntary effort is the thing that matters, and that the medical service will never be a really national affair unless the local authorities deal with the health of the children as a matter of social rather than of legal duty. . . . [However,] there is a stage in social evolution when men and administrative authorities have to be made to do their duty. . . . Let the Local Authorities know how they actually stand by the imposition of a statutory duty' (*Times Educational Supplement* 1918).

7 On 4 August 1914 Newman wrote: 'It is not possible at this stage of the international crisis to say how soon, or in what degree, it may become necessary for the State to make itself responsible for the feeding of the children. Broadly speaking, the occasion of this necessity is dependent upon three main factors: first, the length of the war and its resulting dislocation of social conditions; second, the economic influences – unemployment and industrial disturbance; and third, the price of food. The three main factors are of course not mutually exclusive or even separable in fact, but I think they are broadly the governing factors affecting the onset of distress. This may come, sooner or later, but in some degree is inevitable.' See PRO ED24/1371, Newman to Pease, 4/8/14: para. 1.

8 The School Medical Officer for Bradford said that 'in Bradford, the impression that the regular wages received during the war resulted in a marked improvement in the physique of the schoolchildren is fairly generally held both by the schoolteachers and the medical profession, official and unofficial. This is also my own impression, although the evidence in my possession does not unreservedly support this view' (PRO ED50/34, Effect of unemployment and rationing . . . extracts from replies, pp. 35–7).

9 For a fuller discussion of the factors influencing children's heights, see Harris (1989: 153–9).

10 For details of the heights of London children in 1965, see Tanner, Whitehouse and Takaishi (1966).

11 The principles which lie behind these calculations are discussed more fully in Harris (1989: 180–82). The computer program which was used to convert the original height data into centiles of the Tanner–Whitehouse distribution was written by Dr Annabel Gregory of Birkbeck College, London.

12 This issue is discussed much more fully in Harris (1993).

six

The school medical service between the wars. I. Finance and administration

The First World War had a rather ambivalent effect on the history of school medical provision. In the short term the war brought major disruption, but in the longer term it highlighted the importance of child life and brought a new sense of urgency to the process of school medical reform. However, even though the school medical service made great progress between 1918 and 1939, its overall record has often been regarded as disappointing. In 1937 the independent research organisation, Political and Economic Planning, concluded that 'the adequacy of the school medical service varies very greatly between the areas of different local education authorities', and that 'economy is undoubtedly hampering the development of a service of which the foundations have been well-laid' (Political and Economic Planning 1937: 123). This was not dissimilar to the conclusion reached by Richard Titmuss in his survey of the history of the school medical service in 1944:

> The school medical service has been said to be static . . . in the sense that its duties had been formulated, although there was naturally a steady growth in the resources devoted to it. On the other hand, the school medical staff had never been evenly distributed throughout the country and the scope of medical treatment differed greatly from area to area (PRO ED138/58, 'Evacuation: the school medical service in wartime and the health of the schoolchild': para. 6).

This chapter examines the development of the school medical service during the interwar period. It is primarily concerned with the finance and administration of school medical work, the organisation of medical inspection, and the provision of medical treatment. The history of the school medical service in this period is closely bound up with debates about the impact of the recession on child health, and this question will be discussed more fully in Chapter 7.

The financing of the school medical service

The financial structure of the local education service in the first part of the twentieth century was determined by the Education Acts of 1902 and 1918. The 1902 Education Act enabled local education authorities to receive a grant from central government based on the average number of children who attended the schools in their area, and this grant was augmented by the introduction of separate grants for medical treatment and medical inspection in 1912 and 1913 (2 Edw. VII Ch. 42, clause 10; PP 1912 Cd. 6138 lxv; PP 1913 Cd. 7041 l). The 1918 Education Act abolished both the attendance grant and the special grants for medical treatment and medical inspection, and replaced them with a 'block grant' covering all aspects of educational spending. The value of the block grant was determined by the authority's rate income, the average number of children in attendance, and expenditure on such items as teachers' salaries, special services and maintenance allowances. The government also introduced a system of 'deficiency grants' to ensure that the total value of the block grant was equal to not less than 50 per cent of the authority's spending (8 & 9 Geo. V Ch. 39, section 44; PP 1950–51 Cmd. 8244 xi: 22–32).[1]

The introduction of the block grant enabled the Board of Education to issue a new set of Special Service Regulations, which explained how local authorities were to be reimbursed for expenditure on medical inspection and treatment, as well as other branches of the special services. Under the new regulations, each local education authority was required to submit a summary of the work it intended to carry out over the next twelve months. This would be used to determine whether the authority intended to comply with the obligations of the Education Act and to assess the value of the grant which it was entitled to receive. The local authorities were required to supply information under a number of headings, including the arrangements for medical inspection, the following-up of cases of defect, the detection and prevention of uncleanliness, and the treatment of minor ailments, eyes, teeth, and enlarged tonsils and adenoids (PP 1920 Cmd. 961 xxxvi: para. 108).

The best guide to the expenditure by local authorities on school medical work is provided by the statistics of net expenditure on special services between 1921 and 1939. The Chief Medical Officer published a complete breakdown of these figures in his annual reports for 1921 and for 1926–38, but the information in the reports for the years 1922–5 was limited to medical inspection and treatment. However, the Board provided information about all items of special service expenditure for this period in the

Memorandum on the Education Estimates for 1926. By piecing together the information in these sources it is possible to build a more complete picture of expenditure on all aspects of the school medical service during the interwar years.

Table 6.1 shows that the interwar period witnessed a significant increase in expenditure on virtually every aspect of school medical provision. The most substantial increases affected medical inspection and treatment and the provision of special schools, but increases were also recorded in expenditure on nursery schools, physical training and school meals. However, the table also reveals a number of interesting variations. Local authority expenditure on medical inspection and treatment fell between 1921/2 and 1924/5 and remained virtually unchanged during the early part of the 1930s. Local authority spending on the provision of school meals reached a peak in 1921/2 and again in 1926/7, but it was generally very low for most of the decade, and only began to rise consistently from 1928/9 onwards.

Historians of social policy have devoted considerable attention to the

Table 6.1 Net expenditure by local education authorities on special services, excluding superannuation payments, 1920/21–1938/39 (£).

	Medical inspection and treatment	*Special schools*	*Physical training*	*Evening play-centres*	*Nursery schools*	*Provision of meals*	*Total*
1920/21	1,330,182	1,253,105	39,872	95,513	11,335	252,891	2,982,898
1921/22	1,362,257	1,393,883	52,717	84,704	13,929	951,482	3,858,972
1922/23	1,193,170	1,293,713	50,665	45,883	12,683	255,850	2,851,964
1923/24	1,182,030	1,257,635	48,827	43,712	11,459	152,429	2,696,092
1924/25	1,253,329	1,293,358	51,369	47,586	12,420	137,589	2,795,651
1925/26	1,380,445	1,353,776	52,152	49,615	13,846	169,358	3,019,192
1926/27	1,450,985	1,387,438	55,338	46,455	12,351	797,969	3,750,536
1927/28	1,558,663	1,448,587	61,283	48,266	13,337	182,673	3,312,809
1928/29	1,643,271	1,494,670	61,702	51,175	16,160	227,107	3,494,085
1929/30	1,751,673	1,574,048	63,992	53,466	21,608	284,461	3,749,248
1930/31	1,882,305	1,637,800	64,294	57,145	37,992	343,259	4,022,795
1931/32	2,004,934	1,719,534	65,259	52,466	52,341	405,571	4,300,105
1932/33	2,007,603	1,860,330	58,773	48,554	58,093	512,580	4,545,933
1933/34	2,019,073	1,890,948	59,386	48,329	61,199	557,316	4,636,251
1934/35	2,089,746	1,995,674	62,150	52,070	63,620	594,162	4,857,062
1935/36	2,188,462	2,110,693	66,649	54,591	74,989	613,425	5,108,809
1936/37	2,312,686	2,191,096	79,752	58,926	83,771	668,156	5,394,387
1937/38	2,446,588	2,289,461	99,277	63,633	104,474	786,857	5,786,290
1938/39	2,605,692	2,380,782	115,818	75,769	124,104	942,803	6,244,968

Note: The figures for 1920/21 and 1925/6–1938/9 are taken from the Chief Medical Officer's annual reports; the figures for 1921/2–1924/5 are taken from the Memorandum on the Board of Education Estimates for 1926. There is a slight discrepancy between the Chief Medical Officer's figures for medical inspection and treatment and the figures given in the Memorandum on the Estimates. According to the Chief Medical Officer, expenditure on medical inspection and treatment in these years was as follows: 1921/2, £1,391,606; 1922/3, £1,223,088; 1923/4, £1,220,268; 1924/5, £1,300,347.

Sources: Board of Education 1922: 22; 1923: 33; 1924: 20; 1925a: 22; 1926: 22; 1927: 170; 1928: 187; 1929: 157; 1930: 138; 1931: 110; 1932: 141; 1933: 165; 1934: 179; 1935: 143; 1936: 146; 1937: 124; 1938: 160; 1940: 68; PP 1926 Cmd. 2688 xxii: para. 27.

reasons behind the 'failure' or 'frustration' of social reform at the end of the First World War. Philip Abrams argued that the government's commitment to social reform was undermined by the weakness of the Ministry of Reconstruction and the ideological limitations of Dr Christopher Addison (Abrams 1963), and Rodney Lowe claimed that the drive towards greater state intervention was eroded by the weakness of new ministries and the government's failure to 'adjust to democracy' (Lowe 1978; 1986). However, other writers have tended to place greater weight on economic factors. Kenneth Morgan argued that the government was committed to social reform and that it only decided to change its policy because 'the cost of social legislation after twelve months of rampant inflation followed by a shattering slump was becoming unacceptable' (Morgan 1979: 97). George Peden concluded that the attack on social expenditure was maintained because the Government wished to return to the gold standard at prewar exchange rates (Peden 1985: 54–5).

The history of school medical provision provides an interesting test of these conflicting interpretations. Although a relatively minor item of government expenditure, it was an important test of the government's commitment to social amelioration.[2] The majority of observers agreed that the war had highlighted the importance of child life and even though the Board expressed reservations about the expansion of school feeding there was widespread support for the extension of school medical services.[3] However, in spite of this, local authority expenditure on medical inspection and treatment fell by approximately 8 per cent between 1921/2 and 1924/5, and expenditure on the special services as a whole fell by nearly 30 per cent over the same period (Table 6.1). The demand for restrictions in school medical expenditure was initiated by the Treasury, but it was subsequently reinforced by the Report of the Geddes Committee on National Expenditure. However, even though the Board of Education identified a number of areas where savings could be made, it was spared the need to impose these restrictions by the actions of the local authorities themselves.

The first attempt to restrict the growth of expenditure on school medical services was made in the second half of 1920. Under the terms of the block grant, local education authorities were entitled to apply for substantive grants to cover a variety of educational services, but they could also apply for a deficiency grant if the total grant was equal to less than half their net expenditure. In August 1920 the Treasury wrote to the Board to complain that local authorities were receiving deficiency grants for services which were not eligible for government support under the normal regulations (PRO ED50/65, extract from Treasury letter dated 19/8/20). In the light of these fears, the Board agreed to scrutinise the authorities' original plans much more carefully, and it instructed local authorities to provide rather more detailed information if they wished to introduce new services in the future (PRO ED50/65, procedural minute M. no. 101).

These changes were designed at least in part to control the growth of school medical expenditure, but they had little immediate impact on the cost of school medical provision. However, in August 1921 the government appointed Sir Eric Geddes to chair a committee of inquiry into the overall level of national expenditure. Although the Committee made little direct reference to the school medical service, it recommended that the total size of the education budget should be reduced from £50.6 million to £34.5 million, a saving of 31.8 per cent. Within this overall figure, it said that expenditure on the special services (including medical inspection and treatment) should be reduced from £3.9 million to £3.0 million, a reduction of 27 per cent (PP 1922 Cmd. 1581 ix: 103–26).[4]

The Board of Education adopted a two-pronged strategy to achieve these reductions in expenditure. In February 1922 (before the Geddes Committee had concluded its deliberations), the Board issued Circular 1192, which reminded local education authorities of their obligations – under the Education (Provision of Meals) Act 1906 and the Local Education Authorities (Medical Treatment) Act 1909 – to recover the cost of school meals and medical treatment from those parents who were able to pay (PRO ED50/104, Draft Circular 1192). On 6 February A.H. Wood sent a further Circular to local education authorities, reinforcing this message:

> It should however be added here that this is a matter to which the Board are now compelled to attach considerable importance, and they will not be able to accept as satisfactory for the purposes of their own administration any arrangements which do not include reasonable schemes for payment by parents who can afford to make them. The Authority's statement should show in each case the date from which these schemes have been in operation (PRO ED50/104, Wood to LEAs, 6/2/22).

The Board decided to remind local authorities of their obligations under these Acts in order to ensure that they recovered as much as possible of the cost of school meals and medical treatment from the parents of those who received them, but it was well aware that such measures were unlikely to lead to any substantial savings in the short term. It recognised that the vast majority of local education authorities were already doing their utmost to recover the cost of school meals, and it was reluctant to impose punitive charges for medical treatment in case parents refused to allow their children to take advantage of it. It therefore instructed local authorities to establish a scale of minimum charges 'in order to get parents used to paying for [the] service without causing any serious injury to it' (PRO ED50/104, Wood to [1] Registry, [2] Mr Moore, 8/8/22).[5]

In view of the practical difficulties raised by the question of charges, it is not surprising that the Board's main line of attack should focus on the question of expenditure itself. In March 1922 A.H. Wood prepared a long memorandum on the financial history of the special services as a whole (with the exception of school meals), and identified a series of savings which could be made in each service. He suggested that expenditure on medical inspection and treatment should be cut by £75,000 and that expenditure on special schools and evening play-centres should be cut by £50,000 and £46,000, respectively. He declined to recommend any reduction in expenditure on physical training, and argued that expenditure on nursery provision was too small for any significant reductions to be achieved (PRO ED50/104, Wood to Newman, 27/3/22).

In the event, the Board was able to avoid imposing any of these cuts on the local authorities, because the authorities themselves were anxious to reduce their own rate-funded expenditure, and as a result expenditure on the services discussed in Wood's memorandum fell by more than £310,000 between 1921/2 and 1922/3 (see Table 6.1). However, Wood's analysis also revealed striking variations in the expenditure which different authorities devoted to different services, and huge disparities in the amount of resources devoted to medical inspection and treatment. He concluded that the Board needed to place the administration of the special services on a more uniform basis, and to establish minimum standards of school medical provision for the country as a whole (PRO ED50/104, Draft Circular on the Special Services of Elementary Education; see esp. para. 3).[6]

The second major period of financial stress occurred at the beginning of the 1930s. During the first half of 1931, the Labour government came under mounting pressure to reduce public expenditure, and in August the Cabinet resigned following a disagreement over unemployment benefit rates (Garside 1990: 58–65). The new National Government launched an immediate campaign to cut public spending by £70 million during the current year (Peden 1985: 92). Over the course of the next two years, expenditure on the special services of education rose by more than £300,000, but the greater part of this increase was taken up by the provision of special schools and free school meals. Expenditure on medical inspection and treatment remained virtually unchanged (see Figure 6.1), and there were reductions in the amounts of money devoted to physical training, evening play-centres and nursery schools.

As was the case during the 1920s, pressure for reductions in school medical expenditure came from a variety of sources. In July 1931 the Committee on National Expenditure (the May Committee) recommended a sharp reduction in educational spending as a whole, and the Treasury called for an immediate reduction of £3.5 million in England and Wales and £0.5 million in Scotland (PP 1930–31 Cmd. 3920 xvi: 191–5; PP 1930–31 Cmd. 3952 xviii: 5). Many of the fears expressed by the May Committee were reiterated by the Committee on Local Expenditure (the Ray Committee) when it reported in December 1932. The Committee highlighted a number of concerns about the administration of the school medical service, and although it made no specific recommendations, it urged the need for a fundamental review of the whole field of special service expenditure (PP 1931–2 Cmd. 4200 xiv: para. 46).

In view of the attention which other writers have devoted to the administration of the school medical service in the interwar period (e.g. Webster 1983b; 1985), it is interesting to examine the criticisms which the Ray Committee put forward. Its most striking observations concerned the persistence of gross disparities in the costs incurred by the school medical service in different areas, despite the comments made by A.H. Wood a decade earlier.

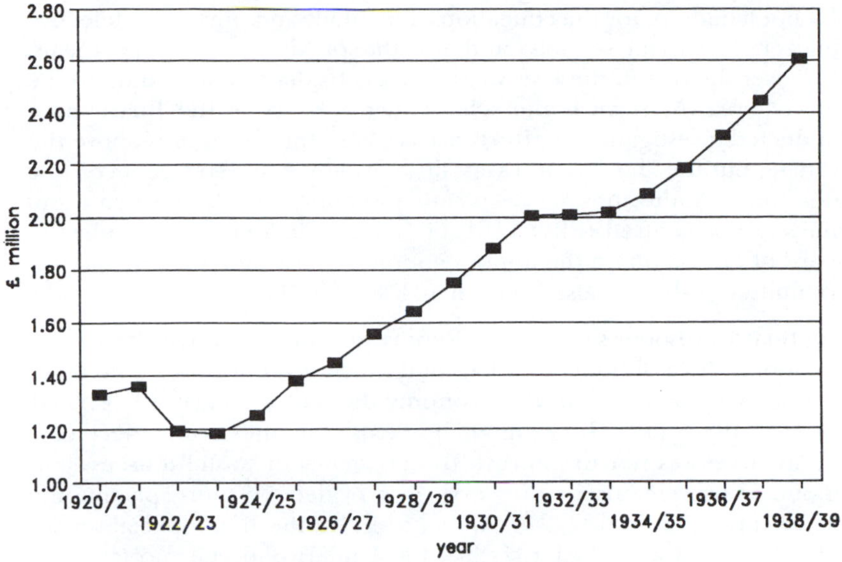

Figure 6.1 Net expenditure by local education authorities on medical inspection and treatment, 1920/21–1938/9.

Source: See Table 6.1.

The Committee argued that these disparities were only partly attributable to differences in provision, and that many of the most striking differences reflected variations in administration and clinical practice. For example, it estimated that in one local education authority area approximately 40 per cent of schoolchildren had their tonsils extracted, whereas the incidence of extraction among schoolchildren in other areas ranged between 2 per cent and 10 per cent (PP 1931–2 Cmd. 4200 xiv: paras 47–51).[7]

Faced with these criticisms, the Board decided to launch an immediate enquiry into the administration of the school medical service in different areas.[8] In all, fourteen areas were selected for investigation, including nine areas which were believed to have above average costs, and five areas with below average costs.[9] However, the Board was able to identify very few instances of 'wasteful expenditure', and its enquiries appear to have had little immediate effect (see PRO ED137/123, 'Staffordshire: investigation of special services expenditure'; PRO ED137/196, 'Darlington: investigation of special services expenditure'; PRO ED137/213, 'Halifax: investigation of special services expenditure'). In March 1934 the Board submitted a report on a somewhat larger number of inquiries to the Treasury. It concluded that:

> The variations in the cost unit of the special services in different areas are due mainly to the wide difference in the amount of provision made by the various Local Education Authorities. Some . . . Authorities make much more complete provision than others for the medical treatment

> of schoolchildren, for the education of mentally and physically defective children in special schools, and for the provision of school meals. Moreover the cost of these services varies considerably according to the type of area. As regards the school medical service the Board have conducted investigations in thirty areas where the cost unit is above the average, but they have found very little evidence of extravagance. The attention of Authorities has been called to minor points in which economies can be secured (PRO T161/664/S/38589, Memorandum by the Board of Education on the minor economies recommended by the Ray Committee: 7–10; see also Welshman 1988: 99–100).

The Board's response to the Ray Report tends to reinforce the view that the economy drive of the early 1930s had much less impact on 'the onward march of social policy' than the economy drive of the early 1920s (Peden 1983: 381; 1985: 110). In general, it seems that the main effect of the economy drive was not to improve the efficiency of wasteful areas, but to postpone improvements in the services provided by more parsimonious areas (see also PRO ED137/249, A. Eichholz, 'Rotherham: special services', 30/10/28: para. 15; PRO ED137/295, J.E. Underwood, 'Glamorgan school medical service', 20/11/29: para. 33). The evidence also suggests that the Board's officials recognised the limitations of the school medical service in these areas and that they felt frustrated by their inability to take firmer action against them. In May 1933 C.W. Woodward wrote to the Local Education Authority in West Hartlepool in the following terms:

> I am directed to state that the Board have had under consideration a report by Dr Robert Weaver, one of their Medical Officers, on his recent visit to the Authority's area, and learn therefrom that within its present restricted scope the work of the school medical service is efficiently conducted.
>
> During the present period of financial stringency, the Board do not propose to suggest any lines of improvement or expansion which would involve an increase in expenditure, but they desire to point out that the existing arrangements for the school medical service do not cover the needs of the area, and that, when conditions improve, it is anticipated that the authority will avail themselves more fully of their powers for safeguarding the health and physical welfare of the children (PRO ED137/279, C.W. Woodward to West Hartlepool LEA, 1/5/33).

The administrative structure of school medical provision

The administrative development of the school medical service after the end of the First World War was shaped by the Education Act of 1918 and the Ministry of Health Act of 1919. The Education Act extended the duty to make arrangements for medical inspection and the power to provide medical treatment to secondary schools, and converted the power to provide medical treatment in elementary schools into a duty. The Ministry of Health Act said that 'all the powers and duties of the Board of Education with regard to the medical inspection and treatment of children and young persons' should be transferred to the Minister of Health, but the latter was given the right to

> make arrangements with the Board of Education respecting the submission and approval of schemes of Local Education Authorities and the payment of grants to Local Education Authorities, so far as such schemes and payment relate to or are in respect of medical inspection and treatment (9 & 10 Geo. V Ch. 5: para. 3 (1) (d)).

This meant that the Board of Education continued to be responsible for the administration of the school medical service after the Ministry of Health was created, and, at the local level, it meant that school medical provision remained in the hands of local education authorities (PP 1919 Cmd. 420 xxi: 36).

Before the Ministry of Health Act was finally passed, the Permanent Secretary of the Board of Education, Sir Lewis Amherst Selby-Bigge, identified three reasons why the Board should retain control of the service it had established. First, Selby-Bigge said that

> if the administration of the powers of the Board of Education relating to medical inspection and treatment [is] transferred bodily to the Ministry of Health, the unity of the school medical service and its coherence with the system of public education . . . will be broken (PRO ED24/958, Selby-Bigge to Fisher, 25/3/19: para. 3).

He pointed out that the school medical service was not only responsible for the administration of medical inspection and treatment, but also for physical training, special schools, nursery schools, school meals and evening play-centres, and he concluded that 'the control of all these activities must remain with the Board of Education' (ibid.: para. 5).

Second, Selby-Bigge argued that Board of Education would be able to exercise greater control over the development of the school medical service because the service would be financed out of the block grant for education as a whole. He claimed that the Board would be able to withhold a proportion of the block grant from those authorities which failed to make adequate arrangements for school medical provision, whereas the Ministry would only be able to withhold grant for the services concerned. He rejected the argument that the school medical service should be transferred from the local education authorities to the local authority public health committees. He said that nothing short of legislation could 'deprive Local Authorities . . . and their Education Committees of the local administration of the school medical service', and he did not believe that such legislation would be forthcoming (PRO ED24/958, 'Sir Philip Magnus' amendment', 17/3/19: para. 5; Selby-Bigge to Fisher, 25/3/19, note).

Selby-Bigge's third argument was that the Board of Education would be in a better position to take account of variations in the circumstances of different local education authorities. He claimed that the Ministry would find it difficult 'to adjust grants to riches and poverty where the expenditure concerned covers only a small field'. By contrast, the Board of Education would be able to take the whole of an education authority's expenditure into account when administering its rate-equalisation formula (PRO ED24/958, Selby-Bigge to Morant, 27/3/19: para. 1).

The Board's determination to retain control of the school medical service represented a major change in the principles on which the service was founded. In 1907 the Board said that it regarded 'the entire subject of school hygiene . . . as an integral factor of the health of the nation' and that its justification 'is not to be measured in terms of money but in the decrease of sickness and incapacity among children and in the ultimate decrease of inefficiency and poverty in after-life arising from physical disabilities' (PP 1910 Cd. 4986 xxiii: 141, 143). However, after 1919 the Board's representatives went to considerable lengths to show that the school medical service was only concerned with the health of the child at school. In 1922 Sir George Newman argued that

> its primary purpose was to fit the children to receive the education provided by the State, and that purpose could only be fulfilled if such medical care was organised as an integral part of the education system of the country, to be undertaken at school age, on school premises, in school hours and with the necessary assistance of school officers, and in association with the school curriculum (Board of Education 1922: 11).

In 1929 Newman wrote:

> It is essential to bear in mind the limitations of the school medical service as well as its opportunities. We must not ask more of it than is reasonable. It is concerned with the physical and mental condition of the child at school. It does not comprise the whole sphere of the health and well-being of the child (Board of Education 1929: 8).

In the memoranda which he prepared for the President of the Board of Education in March 1919, Selby-Bigge said that the school medical service would continue to be regarded as an integral part of the public health service because the overwhelming majority of local education authorities had appointed the local medical officer of health as their school medical officer (PRO ED24/958, Selby-Bigge to Fisher, 25/3/19: para. 3).[10] However, this reassurance failed to satisfy the Society of Medical Officers of Health. In January 1919 the Society's Council complained that the Ministry of Health Bill was unsatisfactory because it failed to bring about the immediate transfer of such 'fundamental matters . . . as the medical inspection and treatment of children and young persons' (*Public Health* 1919b: 51). In December 1922 the editor of *Public Health*, Dr Robert Lyster, said that

> it is not enough to have one officer responsible to two administrative bodies, whether central or local, there must be unity of aim. This can only come by a unification of all the manifold services which centre round the administration of preventive medicine, to which is responsible one local executive agency for carrying out the policy initiated there (*Public Health* 1922: 57–8).

In their history of the school medical service, Samuel and Vera Leff said that the public health and education authorities cooperated closely with each other to ensure that the various branches of the public health service complemented each other efficiently. They claimed that 'the activities of the Board of Education were amalgamated with the maternity and child welfare work of the Ministry of Health' and 'in the localities there was cooperation between the sanitary and education authorities of the area' (Leff and Leff 1959: 63). However, a close inspection of such journals as *Public Health*, the *Medical Officer* and the *British Medical Journal* yields a rather different impression. Contributors to these journals frequently complained that the separation of school medical work from other branches of the public health service was leading to duplication and waste of resources, and that the division between the school medical service and the maternity and child welfare service was leading to the neglect of children between the ages of two and five. These problems were particularly profound in those areas where the school medical officer was not the same as the medical officer of health, but they were not confined to these areas (Wear 1925: 109; *Public Health* 1925).

The biggest difficulties arose as a result of the separation of the school medical service from the maternity and child welfare service. In 1927 Dr Alexander MacGregor told the Annual Meeting of the British Medical Association that

> the remedial and preventive work of the Local Authority and the Education Authority are so closely dovetailed that the multiplication of clinics by the respective authorities . . . is likely to lead to chaos and extravagance. To mention only one point, the provision by both Authorities of dental or ophthalmic or orthopaedic treatment in separate buildings with separate administration is clearly unsound (*British Medical Journal* 1927: 926).

This point was also made by the Medical Officer of Health for Manchester, Dr R. Veitch Clark, who said that he was unable to point to a single area where the school medical service and the maternity and child welfare service had been properly amalgamated. He added:

> An important practical issue arising from the separation of the two services is the waste involved in the establishment of maternity and child welfare centres of whatever type and of school clinics as separate and distinct establishments. This is a condition of affairs existing in many areas. It is not only wasteful of public money, but it involves a duplica-

> tion in one area of the same type of staff for the control and management of such institutions (Clark 1927: 378–9).

The difficulties caused by overlapping and duplication of resources were also reflected in other branches of the public health service. In 1922 Dr J.J. Buchan said that in Bradford

> the Health Authority has considered sanatorium arrangements, hospitals and institutions for pulmonary and surgical tuberculosis, while the Education Authority has considered open-air schools and cripple schools. A residential open-air school is in effect a children's sanatorium, and a residential cripple school is in the largest part a surgical sanatorium. Both Authorities have been considering . . . the same object so far as schoolchildren are concerned and overlapping with each other's work (Buchan 1922: 102).

In 1923 the editor of the *Medical Officer* said that

> the treatment of juvenile tubercle and rickets, of anaemia and of many other diseases associated with debility, clearly should be the result of a single broad-minded action. This is only possible [if there is a] . . . single authority, and [it is] quite impracticable if separate committees are dealing with the same question (*Medical Officer* 1923; see also Clark 1927: 379–80).

Many writers believed that the administrative structure of the school medical service had an adverse effect on the recruitment and career prospects of school medical staff. The interwar years witnessed a substantial increase in the numbers of doctors and nurses employed by the school medical service, but there was widespread concern about their commitment to school medicine, their quality and their general career prospects. In 1920/21 the school medical service employed 316 school medical officers, 720 assistant school medical officers and 967 'additional specialists', together with a total of 2650 nurses. In 1938/9 it employed 1203 assistant school medical officers, 2074 additional specialists, and 6149 school nurses, including orthopaedic nurses and dental attendants. The majority of the doctors who were employed in the school medical service held posts which were directly associated with the public health service, but between 20 and 30 per cent of school medical officers devoted their whole time to school work (Table 6.2).

The employment structure of the school medical service generated two different sets of problems. In the first place, many observers argued that the absence of many senior posts provided little incentive for an ambitious school medical officer to concentrate on school work (*Medical Officer* 1922). In 1927, the School Medical Officer for Swindon, Dunstan Brewer, wrote that

> at present, [the school medical service] . . . is working hard to establish a concrete science of physiological measurement . . . but . . . its ways are hampered [and] its development is halting . . . [because] this, the sum-

Table 6.2 School medical service nursing and medical staff, 1920/21–1938/39.

	SMOs		Assistant SMOs		Additional specialists	School nurses		Total doctors	Total nurses
	Whole-time	*Part-time*	*Whole-time*	*Part-time*		*Whole-time*	*Part-time*		
1920/21	19	297	250	470	967	723	1927	2003	2650
1921/22	17	299	279	418	1069	989	2103	2082	3092
1922/23	18	299	266	417	1162	1052	3083	2162	4135
1923/24	17	300	254	456	1193	1077	3200	2220	4277
1924/25	15	302	237	538	1263	1107	3261	2355	4368
1925/26	317		823		1370	1166	3354	2510	4520
1926/27	13	304	250	656	1456	1209	3570	2679	4779
1927/28	13	304	256	679	1512	1252	3712	2764	4964
1928/29	13	304	254	722	1593	1298	3886	2886	5184
1929/30	13	304	263	739	1677	1365	3907	2996	5272
1930/31	12	305	253	731	1722	1428	4057	3023	5485
1931/32	12	305	265	757	1761	1448	4125	3100	5573
1932/33	11	305	265	760	1773	1435	4195	3114	5630
1933/34	10	306	254	770	1770	1445	4140	3110	5585
1934/35	10	306	256	811	1805	1472	4256	3188	5728
1935/36	10	306	265	831	1814	1527	4117	3226	5644
1936/37	7	309	268	874	1934	1619	4395	3392	6014
1937/38	7	308	264	913	2014	1666	4480	3506	6146
1938/39	6	309	260	943	2074	1715	4434	3592	6149

Notes: The term 'school medical officer' refers to the titular head of the school medical service in each area. In the majority of cases where the school medical officer was employed on a part-time basis, the same officer was also the medical officer of health. The majority of part-time assistant school medical officers also worked in other branches of the public health service, but a significant proportion were in private practice. The majority of part-time school nurses worked in other branches of the public health service or as district nurses. The term 'additional specialists' includes school dentists, ophthalmologists, anaesthetists, radiographers and aural specialists.

Sources: Board of Education 1922: 90; 1923: 145–6; 1924: 159–60; 1925a: 166–7; 1926: 7–8; 1927: 185–6; 1928: 183–4; 1929: 153–4; 1930: 134–5; 1931: 106–7; 1932: 138–9; 1933: 162–3; 1934: 176–7; 1935: 140–1; 1936: 143–4; 1937: 121–2; 1938: 149–50; 1940: 56–7.

> mit of all medicine, is considered the work of a junior, a sideline to be dabbled in by those seeking advancement in their profession, an inferior function to be cast to the novice and to the least experienced (Brewer 1927).

The absence of many senior posts also gave rise to accusations that some local education authorities took advantage of the limited career prospects to employ doctors who could not have hoped to obtain appointments in departments where the school medical service and the public health service were more closely integrated. In 1929 the editor of the *Medical Officer* observed:

> Of the gates to the public health service, the most perilous to enter is the school service of those Authorities in which the Education Department is separated from the general service. Of course, it offers the widest road, and some Education Authorities have staffed their medical departments at less than the recognised scale salaries with practitioners who could not have hoped to obtain public health appointments in fair or open competition (*Medical Officer* 1929b).

Medical inspection between the wars

In recent years, historians have devoted considerable attention to the provision of school medical inspection during the interwar period, and in particular to the question of routine medical inspection. In 1975, the Area Medical Officer for Wakefield, Dr Huw Francis, concluded that

> there are no grounds for believing that the present selective system would not have met the then-perceived medical need, that is, an inspection of all children at school entrance, and of selected children subsequently. There is every reason also to note the subsequent accumulative damaging effect of the routine method on the usefulness and reputation of the school health service (Francis 1975: 189).

These criticisms were echoed by Charles Webster in a paper presented to the Annual Conference of the History of Education Society in 1982. Webster argued that a number of school medical officers had expressed doubts about the validity of routine medical inspection at the outset, and concluded that in practice, 'Newman's system . . . involved so much codification and simplification that it generated accurate data on only the most obvious problems, or on such features as height and weight having little evident usefulness' (Webster 1983b: 79–80).

Before we go on to consider some of the contemporary debates surrounding routine medical inspection, it is important to put the practice of routine medical inspection in the context of the Board of Education's screening procedures as a whole. Table 6.3 shows that approximately one-third of all the children attending public elementary schools were subjected to routine medical examinations in any one year. However, the table also shows that school doctors devoted an increasing proportion of their time to special examinations and to the re-examination of children whom they had already seen. By the end of the 1930s, special examinations and re-examinations accounted for nearly 70 per cent of all the inspections carried out by medical officers in any one year.

During the interwar period, the practice of routine medical inspection was criticised on two main grounds. The first set of critics concentrated on the practice of routine medical inspection itself. They argued that routine medical inspection was an inefficient means of monitoring child health and that the time devoted to routine inspections could be put to better use. The

Table 6.3 Medical inspections carried out by the school medical service, 1921–38.

	No. of areas	*Average attendance*	*Routine inspections*	*Special inspections*	*Reinspections*	*Total inspections*
1921	316	5,205,485	1,886,554	635,022	n/a	n/a
1922	317	5,180,589	1,751,122	635,628	n/a	n/a
1923	317	5,136,032	1,754,919	739,390	1,507,045	4,001,354
1924	317	5,024,544	1,697,561	722,744	1,532,662	3,952,967
1925	317	4,934,197	1,798,397	820,953	1,591,244	4,210,594
1926	317	4,950,343	1,821,577	863,590	1,632,201	4,317,368
1927	317	4,967,394	1,823,775	861,964	1,719,844	4,405,583
1928	317	4,981,101	1,912,747	936,385	1,864,138	4,713,270
1929	317	4,909,404	1,831,637	905,690	1,808,469	4,545,796
1930	317	4,940,381	1,770,779	968,518	1,897,320	4,636,617
1931	317	4,930,076	1,759,186	1,084,467	1,953,708	4,797,361
1932	316	5,005,666	1,845,503	1,192,453	2,015,812	5,053,768
1933	316	5,049,284	1,855,499	1,239,427	1,992,883	5,087,809
1934	316	5,065,963	1,794,963	1,231,663	2,006,936	5,033,562
1935	316	4,907,453	1,729,493	1,257,790	1,998,894	4,986,177
1936	316	4,748,453	1,727,031	1,427,400	2,054,075	5,208,506
1937	315	4,588,298	1,700,078	1,529,136	2,066,082	5,295,296
1938	315	4,526,701	1,677,008	1,563,917	2,182,157	5,423,082

Notes: The phrase 'routine inspection' refers to the number of children who were inspected in the three routine age groups. The phrase 'special inspections' refers to the number of children who were subjected to a special examination after having been selected for such an examination by the medical staff or referred to them by some other agency. The same child might be counted twice if he or she was selected for a special examination in the same year in which he or she was subjected to a routine examination, but no child could receive more than one routine examination or one special examination. The phrase 'reinspections' refers to the number of inspections given to children who had previously received a routine examination or a special examination. See PRO ED50/72, Draft copy of Circular 1321: Revision of statistical tables (1923).

Sources: Board of Education 1922: 89; 1923: 144; 1924: 161; 1925a: 168; 1926: 153; 1927: 159; 1928: 174; 1929: 144; 1930: 126; 1931: 99; 1932: 131; 1933: 155; 1934: 168; 1935: 132; 1936: 141; 1937: 113; 1938: 151; 1940: 59.

second group of critics focused on the statistical results of routine medical inspection. Although the system was designed to provide an accurate snapshot of the general standard of child health, they argued that the results were rendered meaningless by differences of measurement and interpretation.

One of the most prominent critics of routine medical inspection was the School Medical Officer for Manchester, Dr Henry Herd. In 1934, Herd told the North-Western branch of the Society of Medical Officers of Health that the normal system of routine medical inspection provided a 'cross-section picture which we judge by reference to some standard in our own mind . . . of what a child of [a] . . . particular age ought physically to be'. He believed that the practice was flawed because there was no objective standard of normality against which a particular child's health could be judged, and because the length of time between inspections meant that it was impossible to construct a proper system for monitoring child development (Herd 1935a: 125–6).

Herd returned to this subject in a speech to the Royal Sanitary Institute in 1935. On this occasion, he argued that the existing system of routine medical inspection should be replaced and that all children should be weighed and measured at six-monthly intervals. The doctor would then be able to identify those children who were underheight or underweight and subject them to a more detailed examination. He also said that these six-monthly checks should be supplemented by regular nutrition surveys, which would be used to identify children in need of extra food or milk. Although he acknowledged that there were technical difficulties associated with the interpretation of individual heights and weights and with the measurement of 'nutritional status', he believed that the adoption of these two proposals would lead to the discovery of a large number of hitherto undetected medical defects (Herd 1935b: 104–5).[11]

Herd's call for a fundamental reassessment of the role of routine medical inspection was echoed by the School Medical Officer for Birmingham, Dr George Auden, who said that the aims of the school medical service had changed dramatically since 1908, and that the object of the service was no longer 'the discovery and enumeration of defects', but 'the maintenance . . . [and] close supervision of the health and well-being of the whole school population'. He believed that 'in actual experience these routine inspections, other than those of entrants, bring to light an exceedingly small number of defects whose existence is not already known or which could not be discovered at less cost through other means' (Auden 1936). He also thought that the abolition of routine medical inspection would enable school medical officers to devote far more time to the work of 'following-up' defects which had already been discovered. In 1935 he wrote:

> What is wanted is a . . . system of medical inspection which will allow much more time for following-up the children whose parents have sought advice at the clinics and who are reported from various sources to need supervision. . . . [I]f the expenditure on the school medical service is to give a full return, and the full value is to be obtained from the trained experience of the School Medical Officers and School Nurses, then a reconstruction of the whole scheme is of the first importance (Auden 1935; see also Tibbits 1932: 142).

The traditional system of routine medical inspection was also attacked by the Chief School Medical Officer for Hampshire, Dr Leslie Cronk, who argued that 'the present system of inspection . . . results in [the detection of] a number of defects of slight importance . . . and . . . the overlooking of defects . . . of major importance . . . such as . . . nutrition and bodily activity'. He believed that the teacher who observed the children in school every day was in a far better position to assess their health and physical condition than a doctor who examined them every four years. He concluded that the vast majority of the conditions which only came to light at the intermediates' examination could be detected sooner if the teachers made proper use of the attendance register (Cronk 1935: 254; but cf. *Medical Officer* 1935a).

The second major line of criticism concerned the accuracy of the statistics generated by routine medical inspection. This issue had generated considerable controversy before the First World War (e.g. *Medical Officer* 1909) but the Board was confident that the further development of the school medical service would lead to the establishment of more uniform standards. In 1914, the Board's Chief Medical Officer, Sir George Newman, wrote:

> In my earlier reports it has been pointed out that there were various circumstances which rendered it impracticable to furnish anything in the nature of *national* returns or statistics in regard to the physical condition of children attending public elementary schools. We have now, however, the advantage of five years of active development. Medical inspection has become an integral part of the work of every Local Education Authority. Moreover, the work is being carried out on a more or less uniform basis, and thus the results in various areas are, in a broad sense, comparable (PP 1914 Cd. 7184 xxv, para. 28).

One of the earliest indications that this had not been achieved was provided by E.D. Marris of the Board of Education in 1922. Marris was primarily concerned with the way in which local school medical officers compiled their reports and with the use which the Board made of them, but he also made it clear that one of the greatest problems was the absence of any uniform standards of assessment. In order to illustrate this point, he cited a series of returns from ten different authorities which showed wide variations in the estimated incidence of eye and nose and throat defects. He concluded:

> Excluding the absurd Folkestone figure for nose and throat defects, these percentages are fairly evenly spread out between their maximum and minimum, yet in each type of defect the maximum is approximately three times the minimum. The ratio of the incidence of the two types of defect also varies from nearly 2 : 1 to nearly 1 : 2. *Such figures can hardly be summarised without violating a first principle of statistical research, viz. that the average obtained from erratic material is meaningless* (PRO ED50/72, Marris to Wood, 21/2/22: para. 7).[12]

Marris's findings were also discussed by the medical statistician, Dr Major Greenwood, who argued that the cross-sectional variations were only really important if the same observers applied different standards in different years, but even Greenwood agreed that the statistics were too dependent on the individual observer (PRO ED50/72, Greenwood to Newman, 16/3/22: paras 1, 8). The result was that both Greenwood and Marris urged the Board to consider the means by which medical officers could be encouraged to apply more uniform standards (PRO ED50/72, M. Greenwood and E.D. Marris, 'Statistical tables for the use of the school medical service'). However, although the Board agreed to carry out a major review of its statistical tables, it failed to provide any additional guidance on the question of assessment standards (PRO ED50/72, Draft copy of Circular 1321: Revision of statistical tables; see also W.F. Corfield to A.H. Wood, 19/9/23; Tottenham Education Committee, 'Comment upon statistical tables drawn up by the Board of Education').

The problem of varying standards of assessment was also highlighted by the Medical Officer of Health for Stockton-on-Tees, Dr George M'Gonigle, in 1927. M'Gonigle argued that 'the absence of standards has seriously limited the usefulness of the huge mass of clinical data accumulated by the numerous School Medical Officers scattered throughout the country'. In a comparison of the figures recorded in fifteen randomly chosen areas, he found substantial variations in the proportion of all children who required treatment, and in the proportion of children who required either observation or treatment for different conditions (M'Gonigle 1927; M'Gonigle and Kirby 1936: 57–8). In 1939 Cecil Maudslay invited one of the Board's officials to conduct a similar analysis for the country as a whole. The official concluded that 'the above analysis seems merely to confirm, and in some cases to specify, the varying standards adopted by School Medical Officers for different types of defect'. Many of the most striking variations were related to differences in the reported rates of enlarged tonsils and adenoids and visual defects, but there were also substantial differences in the reported rates of bronchitis, anaemia, enlarged cervical glands and other 'deformities' (PRO ED50/196, Anon. (signature illegible) to Maudslay, 3/1/39).

In view of the criticisms voiced by these officers, it is tempting to conclude that the practice of routine medical inspection should have been abandoned long before the outbreak of the Second World War, but the majority of medical officers believed that the basic principle of routine medical inspection was a sound one, even if it was conducted under circumstances which left a lot to be desired.[13] In 1925 the *Medical Officer* wrote that

> routine inspection is often looked upon as monotonous and uninteresting, but only those who are unfitted for the work can so regard it. Laborious it is and sensational it is not – but those who really care for physiological study scarcely expect to achieve anything without labour, and detest the sensational as upsetting and unprofitable (*Medical Officer* 1925).

These comments were echoed by the School Medical Officer for Sheffield, Dr Harold Cohen, in his annual report for 1939:

> In view of the recent discussions of the subject, it is interesting to note that all the Assistant School Medical Officers are in agreement over the value of routine medical inspection. Whilst they appreciate the value of the ancillary examinations, the routine examination remains the basis of the service. . . . In no other way can every child be sure of a complete medical overhaul on the significant occasions in its school career. By this method personal contact is also made with the parents, and in

Sheffield, as detailed elsewhere in the report, the percentage of parents attending these examinations is exceptionally high (*Medical Officer* 1940b).

The development of medical treatment

In focusing attention on the controversies surrounding school medical inspection, it is important to remember that the school medical service was also one of the major sources of medical treatment for schoolchildren in this period, and the interwar years witnessed major changes in the scale of school medical provision and in the range of services provided. By the end of the 1930s, practically every local education authority provided treatment for minor ailments, dental defects and defective vision. The vast majority offered treatment for tonsils and adenoids and more than half provided orthopaedic services and X-ray treatment for ringworm. More than a hundred local authorities provided artificial light treatment for rickets and other 'bony defects'. There were also substantial increases in the number of services provided by individual authorities. By the end of the 1930s, 314 of the 315 authorities provided school clinics, and the average number of clinics in each area had risen to 7.38 (see Tables 6.4–6.5).

Table 6.4 Local education authority provision for medical treatment under the school medical service, 1920–38.

	Minor ailments	*Dental treatment*	*Defective vision*	*Supply of spectacles*	*Adenoids and tonsils*	*Ringworm (X-rays)*	*Orthopaedic treatment*	*Artificial light*
1920	289	235	280	282	198	129	–	–
1921	298	240	290	289	221	141	–	–
1922	303	244	293	294	228	145	–	–
1923	308	250	303	301	234	153	–	–
1924	310	269	309	308	242	161	–	–
1925	311	289	313	310	253	167	85	5
1926	310	294	315	310	258	170	132	18
1927	310	299	315	310	265	171	160	44
1928	311	304	315	310	267	176	183	64
1929	313	307	316	311	271	182	200	78
1930	314	310	316	313	273	188	216	84
1931	313	311	316	313	281	188	222	89
1932	312	312	315	312	281	193	228	93
1933	312	312	315	312	287	196	233	96
1934	312	314	315	313	287	198	238	98
1935	312	314	315	313	287	203	245	105
1936	312	314	315	313	292	204	254	111
1937	311	314	314	312	291	206	262	116
1938	312	314	314	312	292	200	270	118

Sources: PP 1921 Cmd. 1522 ix: 65; Board of Education 1922: 52; 1923: 61; 1924: 32; 1925a: 62; 1926: 38; 1927: 162; 1928: 176; 1929: 146; 1930: 128; 1931: 101; 1932: 133; 1933: 157; 1934: 170; 1935: 134; 1936: 137; 1937: 115; 1938: 157; 1940: 65. The total number of LEAs in each year was as follows: 1920, 316; 1921–31, 317; 1932–36, 316; 1937–38, 315.

Table 6.5 School medical service clinics, 1910–38.

	No. of LEAs with clinics	*No. of clinics*	*Clinics providing for*						
			Minor ailments	*Dental treatment*	*Visual defects*	*Adenoids and tonsils*	*Ringworm (X-rays)*	*Orthopaedic treatment*	*Artificial light*
1910	30	30	21	14	n/a	2	6	–	–
1914	179	350	254	189	n/a	51	38	–	–
1919	272	692	517	437	n/a	76	43	–	–
1920	288	889	679	586	n/a	87	50	–	–
1921	291	976	749	567	n/a	102	51	–	–
1922	297	1029	782	616	n/a	111	49	–	–
1923	304	1076	782	694	n/a	110	48	n/a	–
1924	309	1190	807	822	n/a	93	47	n/a	–
1925	312	1395	891	955	552	82	43	70	3
1926	312	1467	917	998	554	77	47	122	11
1927	312	1520	936	1039	569	80	45	150	26
1928	315	1581	963	1087	593	84	46	191	45
1929	316	1649	1008	1151	606	78	48	228	59
1930	316	1741	1043	1211	633	86	47	257	68
1931	316	1801	1064	1251	644	82	46	271	73
1932	315	1855	1108	1281	660	80	41	282	80
1933	315	1880	1118	1297	673	77	39	287	81
1934	315	1916	1129	1335	670	71	35	300	84
1935	315	2037	1160	1362	694	68	34	324	93
1936	315	2125	1187	1509	718	65	35	335	100
1937	314	2221	1215	1582	737	62	34	358	107
1938	314	2318	1279	1673	774	57	31	382	121

Sources: Board of Education 1926: 53; 1940: 65. The total number of LEAs in each year was as follows: 1910, 322: 1914, 317; 1919, 318; 1920, 316; 1921–31, 317; 1932–6, 316; 1937–8, 315.

The expansion of school medical treatment reflected the increased commitment of local education authorities to the provision of medical services and the development and refinement of new medical techniques. One of the most notable developments in the interwar years was the development of orthopaedic treatment for 'crippled children'. Between 1925 and 1938 the number of authorities providing this form of treatment rose from eighty-five to 270, and the number of clinics offering specialist orthopaedic services rose from seventy to 382. One of the main aims of these services was to enable children who might otherwise have been sent to special schools to remain within the elementary school system. In his annual report for 1930, Newman reported that between 67 and 90 per cent of the 'crippled children' in Leeds, Bath, Staffordshire and Shropshire had been able to return to school or work as a result of orthopaedic treatment provided by the Education Authority. He concluded:

> We have abundant evidence that this result is being achieved by the fact that after treatment and care large numbers of children are rendered capable of attending ordinary schools and of receiving education suitable to their mental capacity. They would otherwise have become and remained physical derelicts (Board of Education 1931: 59).

The interwar years also witnessed a dramatic increase in the use of artificial light for the treatment of rickets, lupus,[14] and various forms of non-pulmonary tuberculosis. In 1928 Newman reported that 'agreement is almost unanimous as to the *tonic* effect of ultra-violet radiation on debilitated children, [as] shown by their improved appetite, activity and nervous stability' (Board of Education 1928: 21). George Auden said that 'a typical result of ultra-violet ray treatment is that poor appetite improves, the tired, languid child becomes bright and active, restless nights give place to sound sleep, and irritability gives place to happiness and content' (ibid.). The School Medical Officer for Tynemouth concluded:

> It is an unquestionable fact that with very few exceptions the patients receiving treatment become more cheerful. The children attend regularly for treatment. In the majority of cases the teachers report their work at school to be more satisfactory and their school attendance improved. Whilst attending the clinic for treatment they are very cheerful – laughing, talking and singing, which at times becomes excessive. Their conduct and general cheerfulness is reminiscent of children one sees in sanatoria, where it is difficult to restrain the excessive energy of the cases which are responding well to treatment (ibid.: 22).

The expansion of medical treatment through the school medical service raised a number of important questions about the relationship between preventive and curative medicine (see Webster 1990: 121–4; PP 1920 Cmd. 693 xvii: para. 6). In 1921 W.J. Howarth told the Society of Medical Officers of Health that

> up to a few years ago there was a clear-cut line of demarcation between [the practitioners of preventive and curative medicine] . . . and we, as Medical Officers of Health, concerned ourselves mainly with work in which the general body of practitioners took only passing interest . . . This detachment and spirit of aloofness ought no longer to exist (Howarth 1921: 39–40).

In 1932 Ralph Crowley told the British Medical Association that

> during the first quarter of the present century we have been passing through the stage of clash between the practitioners of clinical and preventive medicine respectively. The task before us . . . is the welding together of these activities into an organic whole on behalf of the health of the child and its maintenance (Crowley 1932: 576).

However, although many observers recognised the need for a more coordinated approach to the problems of health care, they disagreed over the best means of achieving this. In 1934 Henry Herd told the North-Western branch of the Society of Medical Officers of Health that medical officers of health were already overburdened, and that it was much more likely that both the school medical service and the maternity and child welfare service would soon be placed under separate control (Herd 1935a: 129).

The gap between preventive and curative medicine also had more direct implications for the provision of school medical treatment. Under the terms of the 1918 and 1921 Education Acts, school medical officers were prohibited from offering any form of domiciliary medical treatment, and this imposed severe limitations on the range of services they could provide (8 & 9 Geo. V Ch. 39, clause 25; 11 & 12 Geo. V Ch. 51, clause 80, section 4). In 1921 Howarth said that

> medical treatment of young children remains in a neglected, or at least unsatisfactory position, because the State offers no direct aid, and so long as this deficiency exists the curative efforts of the Local Authority may be likened to trying to fill a bucket with holes in it; it may be filled if there is a large enough inflow, but cessation of this inflow soon empties the bucket (Howarth 1921: 39).

This comment was echoed by Oscar Holden in his address to the Royal Sanitary Institute fourteen years later:

> Any scheme of domiciliary treatment would of necessity entail considerable expense, but it is very probable it would in the outcome prove more economical than the present hit-or-miss methods. Most School Medical Officers could bring forward evidence that children are suffering through the parents' [reluctance], usually on financial grounds . . . to call a doctor. Children in need of regular medical supervision do not obtain it. School clinics do a little, but they are able to meet adequately only a fraction of the need (Holden 1935: 97–8).

Despite the improvements which were made in many aspects of the school medical service, there were substantial deficiencies in the services which it did offer. In 1936 the Chief Medical Officer said that there ought to be one dentist for every 4000 children in rural areas and one dentist for every 5000 children in urban areas, but the ratio of dentists to children in the country as a whole was only 1:7600. As a result, only three-quarters of elementary schoolchildren were examined by a dentist in any one year, and less than two-thirds of the children who were referred for treatment actually received it (Board of Education 1936: 112–18). There were also significant variations in the provision of orthopaedic services. In 1937 Political and Economic Planning reported: 'some areas have no orthopaedic hospital schools, while many have inadequate facilities for remedial exercises. Greater attention should be paid to prevention by such methods as improved seating in schools, improved general school amenities, and physical training' (Political and Economic Planning 1937: 123).

One of the most serious problems facing the school medical service was the 'handicap of locality' (PRO ED136/664, J.A. Glover, 'The school medical service in wartime': 3; PRO ED138/58, 'Evacuation', para. 17). Many local authorities attached considerable importance to the school medical service and allowed their officers to devote both time and resources to it. In 1931 Dr Robert Weaver reported that

> the school medical service of Darlington is an admirable one. In most aspects of municipal life, the town seems to have been progressive, and

in Dr Dawson it has . . . as head of its school medical work [a man] who is full of energy and always on the look-out for ways of improving it' (PRO ED137/196, R. Weaver, 'Darlington: school medical service', 6/11/31, para. 28).

However, the Council's enthusiasm was not shared by all areas. In 1930 Dr John Underwood complained that the Local Education Authority in Warwickshire had failed to implement any of the recommendations which he had made three years previously. He concluded that

> the Authority itself is primarily responsible for this stagnation, but the School Medical Officer . . . is partly to blame [for] . . . his inability or unwillingness to influence a difficult and reactionary Committee (PRO ED137/141, J.E. Underwood, 'Warwickshire: report on special services', 12/3/30, para. 28).

The quality of school medical provision was also influenced by the administrative structures of different local education authorities. It was generally accepted that the school medical service was much better-developed in county boroughs and large urban areas than in county areas, although there were a number of exceptions (see e.g. PRO ED137/119, J.E. Underwood and R. Weaver, 'Salop: Report on Special Services', 21/7/30, para. 29). In February 1932 Dr John Underwood reported that

> at the last inspection of this area [i.e. Blackburn] it was reported that the school medical service was run on comprehensive and progressive lines, but that augmentation was required in the staffs of both nurses and dentists. Since then . . . [i.e. about six years ago], increase in the personnel of both these departments has been made, and . . . all that remains to do, in order to 'complete' the service, is to employ 1.5 additional dentists (PRO ED137/173, J.E. Underwood, 'Blackburn: school medical service', 11/2/32).

However the school medical service in many county areas tended to be much more limited. In 1929 Dr Underwood found that even though the school medical service of Middlesex was well-organised, the number of staff was insufficient, and it was impossible for the existing staff to visit all the schools sufficiently frequently (PRO ED137/87, J.E. Underwood, 'Middlesex: report on special services', 2/3/29, para. 28). In 1931 the Board informed the West Riding Local Education Authority that it 'employ[ed] fewer Medical Officers than the Board would expect to be necessary . . . to cope with the needs of the area', and that 'the lack of a systematic and comprehensive scheme for the treatment of children suffering from crippling defects' had already been brought to the Council's attention (PRO ED137/158, E.R. Turnbull to West Riding Local Education Authority, 13/3/31).

The provision of school medical services was also affected by the system of local government finance and the economic circumstances of poorer areas. As the Geddes Committee pointed out in 1922, the system of percentage

Table 6.6 Local education authorities' expenditure on special services in the Special Areas, 1935–36.

	Average attendance	*Net expenditure on special services*		*Net expenditure on medical inspection and treatment*		*Net expenditure on provision of meals*	
		Total £	*Per head s.d.*	*Total £*	*Per head s.d.*	*Total £*	*Per head s.d.*
County areas							
Breconshire	7,410	5,172	14/0	3,858	10/5	964	2/7
Cumberland	20,422	20,823	20/4	15,879	15/6	2,765	2/8
Durham	112,459	70,541	12/6	22,710	4/0	24,968	4/5
Glamorgan	55,208	41,193	14/11	20,238	7/4	12,105	4/5
Monmouthshire	40,624	31,538	15/6	15,950	7/10	12,502	6/2
Northumberland	42,532	19,607	9/3	11,975	5/8	1,140	0/6
County boroughs							
Gateshead	17,817	11,121	12/6	4,739	5/4	2,097	2/4
Merthyr Tydfil	9,854	8,892	18/0	4,026	8/2	3,703	7/6
Newcastle upon Tyne	37,366	48,724	25/11	14,100	7/7	7,202	3/10
South Shields	17,573	19,349	21/11	4,333	4/11	7,310	8/4
Sunderland	29,573	23,486	15/9	10,556	7/2	4,472	3/0
Tynemouth	9,666	8,853	18/1	2,367	4/11	1,056	2/2
West Hartlepool	10,577	7,118	13/4	2,533	4/10	126	0/3
Boroughs							
Durham	2,382	820	6/11	658	5/6	–	–
Hartlepool	3,143	2,105	13/5	1,585	10/1	134	0/11
Jarrow	5,725	3,150	11/0	1,890	6/6	914	3/2
Pembroke	1,463	1,293	17/8	618	8/5	488	6/8
Port Talbot	6,097	1,606	5/3	1,447	4/9	52	0/2
Wallsend	6,764	3,899	11/6	1,617	4/10	1,763	5/3
Whitehaven	3,811	2,147	11/3	1,301	6/10	289	1/6
Workington	4,407	2,438	11/1	1,588	7/2	753	3/5
Urban districts							
Aberdare	6,789	8,715	25/4	2,646	7/10	2,354	6/11
Abertillery	5,079	8,263	32/7	1,767	6/11	6,278	24/9
Ebbw Vale	4,954	6,712	27/1	1,739	7/0	4,833	19/6
Felling	4,307	2,826	13/1	1,345	6/3	1,350	6/3
Hebburn	4,150	4,228	20/4	2,515	12/1	1,408	6/10
Mountain Ash	6,468	6,983	21/6	3,306	10/3	2,357	7/3
Pontypridd	7,075	7,882	22/2	2,974	8/5	3,399	9/7
Rhondda	22,920	20,693	18/6	7,087	6/4	9,222	8/3
England and Wales							
Counties	1,353,896	1,303,854	13/9	791,265	8/5	126,550	1/4
County Boroughs	1,596,932	1,942,525	23/6	674,134	8/3	319,326	3/11
Boroughs and UDs	611,013	737,416	19/1	394,575	10/2	104,663	2/8
London	444,349	1,228,936	34/10	328,488	14/9	65,681	2/11
Country as a whole	4,006,190	5,212,731	21/10	2,188,462	9/3	616,190	2/7

Source: PRO ED50/181: C.W. Maudslay, 'The need for increased financial assistance to the Special Areas in aid of expenditure on the Special Services', Tables A–C.

grants was designed to encourage local authorities to spend as much as possible on grant-aided services, but this meant that central government was unable to direct resources to areas of greatest need (PP 1922 Cmd. 1581 ix: 105; Crowther 1988: 57–8). In 1927 Dr J.E. Underwood reported that the school medical service in Rhondda was both understaffed and underserviced. It employed only three assistant school medical officers, one dentist, one additional specialist (an ophthalmic surgeon), 4.3 school nurses and two dental attendants, whereas the Board estimated that it required between four and five school medical officers, six dentists, two specialists (an ophthalmic surgeon and an ear, nose and throat specialist), twelve school nurses, 0.5 orthopaedic nurses and six dental attendants. Rhondda provided only one quarter of the number of clinics required for a complete service, and the number of children who received dental treatment was between one-sixth and one-eighth of the number who probably needed it (PRO ED137/296: J.E. Underwood, 'Rhondda: Report on Special Services', 24/3/27).

The financial problems faced by poorer areas were also demonstrated towards the end of the 1930s by a wide-ranging inquiry into the provision of special educational services in the Special Areas. The inquiry showed that areas with very high levels of unemployment tended to spend less on the school medical service than areas with lower levels of unemployment, even though their needs were almost certainly greater. For example, twenty-five out of the twenty-nine local education authorities which contained Special Areas (see Table 6.6) spent below average amounts on school medical provision; sixteen areas had less than the recommended minimum number of school medical officers, and twenty-five areas had less than the recommended minimum numbers of either dentists or nurses. The author concluded:

> In the Special Areas, where the health and nutrition of the children is on the whole below the average of the rest of the country, liberal expenditure on the Special Services is particularly desirable, but speaking generally the expenditure of the Special Areas on these services falls below that of the rest of the country (PRO ED50/181, C.W. Maudslay, 'The need for increased financial assistance to the Special Areas in aid of expenditure on the Special Services', paras 2–7, Tables A–C).

Notes

1 The deficiency grant system was abolished following the publication of the May Report on Public Expenditure in 1931. See PP 1950–51 Cmd. 8244 xi: 29.

2 In 1925 Newman wrote: 'It is interesting to compare the cost of the school medical service in 1923/4 (£1,220,268) with that of the cost of public elementary education as a whole (almost £55,000,000). It will be seen that the school medical service costs about 2.2 per cent of the whole. In other words, out of every £100 spend by Local Education Authorities on elementary education, only £2 4s. goes to the school medical service, not a high premium for health insurance' (Board of Education 1925a: para. 58).

3 In March 1922 George Newman wrote: 'I recognise that the administration of the Provision of Meals Act by Local Education Authorities has been enormously and probably unjustifiably extended until it has become a huge system of relief, having only an indirect relation to education'. He felt that the 'limit' of £300,000 which was placed on local authority spending on school meals was unnecessarily high. See PRO ED50/104, Newman to Wood, 28/3/22: paras 2, 6 and 7.

4 In practice, the Board agreed to limit special service expenditure to £3.4 million, of which £300,000 was earmarked for school meals. See PRO ED50/104, Wood to Newman, 24/3/22.

5 LEAs were advised to invite parents to make an additional contribution to the costs of medical treatment by placing donations in a collecting box (PRO ED50/104, Wood to [1] Registry, [2] Moore, 8/8/22: para. 2 (b)).

6 In his annual report for 1921, the Chief Medical Officer identified the following provisions as 'the essential items of a minimum national standard': the systematic medical and dental inspection of all children at certain ages; facilities for the adequate following up and treatment of the defects found on inspection; and the sanitation of schools, school hygiene and physical training. He also urged the Board to 'review our system of education to make it appropriate and effective from a physical standpoint for all children, whether normal or abnormal'. See Board of Education (1922: 23–4).

7 In 1922, the Board said that 'it is probably correct to say that from five to seven per cent of all schoolchildren in England and Wales suffer from these conditions [i.e. enlarged tonsils and adenoids] in such degree as to call for surgical interference'. See Board of Education (1922: 55).

8 Although the Ray Committee only published its report in December 1932, the Drafting Committee of the Education Sub-Committee discussed its findings with the Board in the third week of August. See PRO ED50/105, C.W. Maudslay to George Newman, 30/8/32: para. 3.

9 The nine high-spending authorities were: Bath, Beckenham, Halifax, Leicester, Manchester, Reigate, Staffordshire, Todmorden and West Sussex. The five low-spending areas were Birmingham, Darlington, Hyde, Shrewsbury and Somerset. The majority of the records pertaining to these enquiries have now been destroyed, and the only surviving records are those for Halifax, Darlington and Staffordshire. For further details, see PRO ED50/105, Expenditure review 1932/33; PRO ED137/123, Staffordshire: investigation of special services expenditure; PRO ED137/196, Darlington: investigation of special services expenditure; PRO ED137/213, Halifax: investigation of special services expenditure.

10 In 1922 there were thirty-seven local authority areas (out of 317) in which the school medical officer was not also the medical officer of health. They included two counties, twenty county boroughs, thirteen boroughs, and two urban districts. The authorities concerned were as follows: Northamptonshire, Carmarthenshire, Birmingham, Blackpool, Bristol, Canterbury, Hastings, Kingston-upon-Hull, Leeds, Leicester, Manchester, Newcastle upon Tyne, Northampton, Portsmouth, Rotherham, Sheffield, Stoke-on-Trent, Sunderland, Walsall, Wolverhampton, Worcester, Newport (Monmouthshire), Barnstaple, Boston, Chipping Wycombe, Dukinfield, Durham (Borough), Hove, Kendal, Kidderminster, Mosley, Newbury, Ossett, Stalybridge, Newport (Isle of Wight), Enfield, and Penge. See PRO ED50/35, Coordination between school medical service and public health staff.

11 In December 1935 the Board issued Circular 1443, which did in fact advise local authorities to conduct these surveys. However, only 50 authorities had succeeded in following the Board's advice by July 1939. See House of Commons Debates 1939a: cols 1141–2.

12 The percentages for the ten areas were as follows:

	Visual defect	*Nose and throat defect*
Walthamstow	5.5	3.3
Acton	2.3	4.5
Newport (Mon)	4.8	2.8
Guildford	5.4	7.0
Surrey	4.6	9.0
Coventry	6.6	5.8
Somerset	7.5	9.0
London	8.6	6.5
Devon	3.0	4.0
Folkestone	7.5	22.1[a]

[a] It subsequently emerged that the 'absurd' figure for Folkestone was a clerical error, and the 'true' figure was 12.1 per cent. See PRO ED50/72, Marris to Wood, 22/3/22: 3.

13 The supporters of routine medical inspection included George Auden's own successor in Birmingham, Dr James Mitchell. See *Medical Officer* (1939b).

14 A form of ulcerous skin disease.

seven

The school medical service between the wars. II. Health and nutrition

During the interwar years the school medical service played a central role in debates about the impact of unemployment on children's health and nutrition. In 1923, the Board's Chief Medical Officer claimed that 'with a few important exceptions, the general view formed by School Medical Officers is that the depression of 1921 and 1922 has not resulted in any substantial depreciation of the physical condition of schoolchildren', and that during 'the last two years of . . . unemployment and financial restriction . . . health conditions have been fairly maintained, and are even now better than before the war' (Board of Education 1923: 123–4). In 1930 he wrote that the combined efforts of the state and voluntary agencies had 'more or less held in check any rapid deterioration in the physique of schoolchildren', and in the country as a whole 'the nutrition of schoolchildren appears to be on the upward grade' (Board of Education 1930: 10). In 1932 he said that 'the depressed state of industry and the need for national economy [do] . . . not appear to have exerted any measurable ill-effect upon the child population' (Board of Education 1932: 107), and in 1933 he concluded that even though there had been a slight increase in the proportion of children who were suffering from malnutrition, 'these slight variations are not of significance . . . they do not, in fact, imply any real increase in malnutrition' (Board of Education 1933: 127).

These claims were greeted with considerable disbelief by many of the Board's opponents, who argued that the real issue was not the failure of unemployment to exercise any significant effect on child health, but the failure of the school medical service to detect such an effect. In 1933 the editor of the *Medical Officer* wrote:

> It is just possible that our children can live on unemployment diet and that our failure to find ill-health . . . is really due to there being no malnutrition to discover. But against this we have such weighty physiological arguments that most of us believe the malnutrition is there and that we are ignorant of the form it takes and so do not detect it (*Medical Officer* 1933b).

In 1936 a deputation from the Standing Joint Committee of Industrial Women's Organisations told the Minister of Health that although

> there had been a definite improvement in the health of the people in recent years, the general health standard was still low in certain sections of the community, and this was due to the fact that, as the result of poverty, these sections were unable to resist disease. The chief poverty factor was defective nutrition (PRO ED50/216, Standing Joint Committee of Industrial Women's Organisations: 1).

In 1937 the National Union of Teachers reported:

> Our knowledge of [the Special Areas] . . . makes us very uneasy about the physical well-being of the children who live in them. It is true that the medical reports on the question of nutrition appear somewhat reassuring, but a close study of them does not leave us with a feeling of confidence, much less complacency. . . . [We] cannot believe that the children . . . [we] teach are adequately fed according to the standards derived from . . . [our] own . . . experience (PRO ED50/175, National Union of Teachers: The Depressed Areas: 4–5).

These debates raise a number of questions about the Board's strategies for measuring and preventing malnutrition, and about the actual impact of unemployment on the health of the child population. In 1979 the historian Jay Winter denied that the depression had any effect on the health of women in childbirth or their infants, and concluded that 'the most important feature of the aggregate data . . . is the persistence of the trend towards better . . . health for the nation as a whole' (Winter 1979: 439–53). However, in 1983 Winter argued that the depression did have a long-term effect on the birth weights of the children and grandchildren of those who were born between 1928 and 1932 (Winter 1983: 254). In 1982 Charles Webster concluded that

> the Depression must be regarded as a significant exacerbating factor, tending to worsen still further prevailing low levels of health, and so contributing towards a crisis of subsistence and health different in kind but similar in gravity to the crises known to students of pre-industrial societies (Webster 1982: 125; see also Webster 1983b; 1985; Mitchell 1985; Whiteside 1987a; 1987b).

This chapter is intended to provide a general account of the role played by the school medical service in measuring the impact of unemployment on child health and protecting children against malnutrition during the inter-war period. The first section examines the arrangements made by the Board of Education for the provision of school meals. The second looks at the development of the 'newer knowledge of nutrition' and its impact on contemporary perceptions of the incidence of poverty and malnutrition. The third section examines the debates which surrounded the construction and interpretation of the Board's 'nutrition statistics' and the history of alternative attempts to measure 'nutrition' by physiological and functional tests. The fourth and final section seeks to shed new light on the relationship between unemployment and child health by examining the available evidence on children's stature.

The provision of school meals

The most important single weapon at the disposal of the school medical service for improving nutrition and combating malnutrition was the provision of school meals. The school meals service was formally established by the Education (Provision of Meals) Act of 1906. The Act allowed local education authorities 'to associate themselves with any committee on which [they] . . . are represented, who will undertake to provide food for [children in attendance at any public elementary school in their area]' and to 'aid that committee by furnishing such land, buildings, furniture and apparatus, and such officers and servants, as may be necessary for the organisation, preparation and service of such meals'. The authorities were not allowed to contribute to the cost of the food itself, and they were expected to recover the costs of the meals from the children's parents. The Act also stated that local authorities could supply free meals to children whose parents were unable to pay for them and who were 'unable by reason of lack of food to take full advantage of the education provided for them', provided that the total amount expended by the authority did not exceed the yield of a halfpenny rate (6 Edw. VII Ch. 57, sections 1–3). In August 1914 the government removed this limitation and allowed the authorities to provide meals on weekends and during school holidays (4 & 5 Geo. V Ch. 20). This Act led to a sharp and immediate increase in the number of children receiving meals, but by the spring of 1915 the extent of school feeding had already reverted to prewar levels (PP 1916 Cd. 8338 viii: 87).

The basic structure of the school meals service, as laid down in the Education Acts of 1906 and 1914, was retained in the Education Act of 1921. Section 82 of this Act gave local education authorities the power to take whatever steps they thought necessary for the provision of school meals to children attending the public elementary schools in their area, both on school days and during weekends and school holidays, provided that they did not incur any costs in respect of the purchase of the food itself. Section 83 gave them the power to charge parents for the food their children received, and to instigate legal proceedings against parents who refused to pay. Section 84 said that if a local education authority believed that any children were unable by reason of lack of food to take full advantage of the education provided for them, and if no other funds were available, then 'it may spend out of the rates such sums as will meet the cost of the provision of such food' (11 & 12 Geo. V Ch. 51, sections 82–4).

We can therefore see that the Acts which governed the provision of school meals contained two distinct elements. They enabled local authorities to provide 'paying' meals to children whose parents were able to pay for them, and free meals to children who were unable by reason of lack of food to benefit from their education and whose parents were unable to pay for them. The Acts placed no limitation on the time at which the meals should be served or the form which they should take. The authorities could provide breakfasts, dinners or teas (or a combination of these), or they could simply provide a bottle of milk. A number of authorities also offered other forms of 'nutritional supplementation' in the form of cod liver oil, dried milk or various proprietary foods (see, for example, Board of Education 1927: 134).

In view of the variety of types of arrangement which local authorities were empowered to make, it is not surprising that it should be difficult to construct a consistent picture of the provisions they made during the interwar period. However, Tables 7.1 and 7.2 enable us to identify some of the main trends.[1] First, it is clear that the period as a whole witnessed a substantial increase in the number of local education authorities which provided school meals, and in the number of children who were fed. Second, the trend in favour of increased school meal provision was much less apparent in the 1920s than it was in the 1930s. Third, the main reason for increases in the consumption of school meals in the first half of the 1920s was an increase in the number of children whose parents paid for the meals they received. Fourth, the number of children receiving free meals declined during the early part of the 1920s and only began to increase consistently from the late-1920s onwards. Finally, the most rapid growth in the field of nutritional supplementation came not from the provision of solid meals, but in the form of milk meals and nutritional supplements (Tables 7.1 and 7.2).

Tables 7.1 and 7.2 also enable us to highlight a number of more specific aspects of the provision of school meals during this period. We have already seen that the total volume of local authority expenditure on school meals rose sharply during the industrial unrest of 1921/2, and this was reflected in the number of meals supplied and the number of children fed. The Board became increasingly concerned about the cost of the school meals service, and on 4 April 1922 the President of the Board of Education announced that the total amount of expenditure on school meals by all local authorities would be restricted to an aggregate figure of £300,000 (House of Commons Debates 1922: col. 1050). This limit was confirmed in Circular 1261, which

Table 7.1 Number of children receiving school meals in England and Wales, 1920/21–1938/39.

	No. of LEAs providing meals	*Children receiving free meals*			*Children paying for meals*	*All children receiving meals*
		Solid meals	*Milk etc.*	*Total*		
1920/21	137	n/a	n/a	n/a	≥18,662[a]	148,082[b]
1921/22	190	n/a	n/a	n/a	≥40,529[a]	592,518[b]
1922/23	156	n/a	n/a	n/a	≥22,040[a]	149,676[b,c]
1923/24	138	n/a	n/a	n/a	≥23,514[a]	103,231[b]
1924/25	132	n/a	n/a	n/a	≥28,040[a]	97,993[b]
1925/26	134	n/a	n/a	n/a	n/a	118,464
1926/27	173	n/a	n/a	n/a	n/a	389,828
1927/28	132	n/a	n/a	82,410	41,267	123,677
1928/29	145	n/a	n/a	132,526	59,952	192,478
1929/30	150	n/a	n/a	150,340	115,053	265,393
1930/31	153	n/a	n/a	185,228	109,893	295,121
1931/32	157	119,617	93,232	206,182	113,533	319,715
1932/33	174	154,383	131,367	268,879	130,498	399,377
1933/34	192	158,543	161,040	298,286	116,500	414,786
1934/35	224	156,448	303,659[e]	401,480	4,901	406,381
1935/36	235[d]	143,179	406,341[e]	479,343	n/a	n/a
1936/37	247[d]	139,662	467,515[e]	535,300	n/a	n/a
1937/38	264[d]	151,538	560,879[e]	614,806	n/a	n/a
1938/39	273[d]	176,767	635,174[e]	687,855	n/a	n/a

[a] The figures for the years 1920/21–1924/25 are based on returns in the Chief Medical Officer's Annual Reports. These returns showed the number of children whose parents contributed all or part of the cost of their meals. The figures for 1920/21 include all areas except Halifax (children whose parents contributed the full cost of their meals) and Rhondda (children whose parents contributed all or part of the cost). The figures for 1921/22 include all areas except the North Riding of Yorkshire and Halifax (full cost) and Oldbury (all or part of the cost). The figures for 1922/23 include all areas except Halifax (all or part of the cost) and London (part of the cost). The figures for 1923/24 include all areas except the East Riding of Yorkshire, Halifax and Oxford (all or part of the cost) and London (part of the cost). The figures for 1924/25 include all areas except the East Riding of Yorkshire (all or part of the cost) and London (part of the cost). The numbers of children whose parents paid all or part of the cost of their meals in these areas in other years were as follows: Halifax: 1920/21 (part of cost): 18; 1921/22 (part of cost): 38; 1924/25 (all or part of cost): nil. Rhondda: 1921/22–1924/25 (all or part of the cost): nil. North Riding: 1920/21: no children fed; 1922/23 (whole cost): 2; 1923/24 and 1924/25: no children fed. Oldbury: 1920/21: no children fed; 1922/23: nil; 1923/24 and 1924/25: no children fed. London: 1920/21: (part of cost): nil; 1921/22: (part of cost): nil. East Riding: 1920/21–1922/23 (all or part of cost): nil. Oxford: 1920/21–1921/22: no children fed; 1922/23 (all or part of cost): nil; 1924/25 (all or part of cost): nil.

[b] These figures should probably be regarded as estimates rather than as exact statements of the number of children who received school meals. The Chief Medical Officer of the Board of Education published detailed breakdowns of the number of children receiving school meals in each area in his reports for 1920–1924; thereafter he only published summary figures for the country as a whole. The returns for 1920/21, 1921/22, 1922/23, 1923/24 and 1924/25 all excluded the East Riding of Yorkshire. The returns for 1921/22 also excluded the returns for the Urban District of Oldbury.

[c] In his Annual Report for 1922, the Chief Medical Officer listed 155 Local Education Authorities who provided meals for 149,586 children.

[d] Free meals only.

[e] Milk meals only.

Sources: Number of Local Education Authorities providing meals (1920/21–1934/35): Board of Education 1935: 147; Number of Local Education Authorities providing free meals (1935/36–1938/39): Board of Education 1938: 159; 1940: 67; Number of children receiving meals for payment (1920/21–1924/25): PP 1921 Cmd. 1522 xi: 218–23; Board of Education 1922: 104–08; 1923: 159–63; 1924: 173–6; 1925a; 180–3; Number of children receiving free and paying meals (1920/21–1934/35): Board of Education 1935: 147; Number of children receiving free meals (1935/36–1938/39): Board of Education 1938: 159; 1940: 67.

Table 7.2 Number of school meals provided in England and Wales, 1920/21–1938/39.

	Total number of free meals in PESS			*Total number of free and paying meals in PESS*		
	Solid	*Milk etc.*	*Total*	*Solid*	*Milk etc.*	*Total*
1920/21	n/a	n/a	8,579,490	8,406,951	3,460,983	11,867,934
1921/22	n/a	n/a	n/a	54,125,778	6,550,239	60,676,017
1922/23	n/a	n/a	n/a	13,731,984	3,429,706	17,161,690
1923/24	n/a	n/a	n/a	8,085,049	2,890,171	10,975,220
1924/25	n/a	n/a	n/a	6,644,976	3,560,814	10,205,790
1925/26	n/a	n/a	9,666,286	8,621,058	4,555,325	13,176,383
1926/27	n/a	n/a	n/a	64,913,651	5,131,847	70,045,498
1927/28	9,253,860	2,087,860	11,341,720	10,071,894	5,803,446	15,875,340
1928/29	11,267,927	3,765,625	15,033,552	12,092,855	8,038,180	20,131,035
1929/30	14,148,354	9,394,173	23,542,527	15,055,776	17,681,261	32,737,037
1930/31	15,189,493	12,394,905	27,584,398	16,327,120	23,986,831	40,313,951
1931/32	18,311,975	17,179,022	35,490,997	19,618,608	28,239,607	47,858,215
1932/33	25,194,461	23,585,637	48,780,098	26,471,620	35,833,021	62,304,641
1933/34	25,818,569	30,385,544	56,204,113	27,256,743	41,586,538	68,843,281
1934/35	25,492,938	42,183,271[a]	67,676,209	25,939,470	42,183,271	68,122,741
1935/36	22,959,362	63,710,297[a]	86,669,659	23,480,027	63,710,297	87,190,324
1936/37	21,709,627	78,299,008[a]	100,008,635	n/a	n/a	n/a
1937/38	22,690,807	97,667,750[a]	120,358,557	n/a	n/a	n/a
1938/39	26,819,108	114,961,182[a]	141,780,290	n/a	n/a	n/a

[a] Milk meals only.

Sources: Number of free meals: PP 1922 Cmd. 1718 vii: 14; PP 1927 Cmd. 2866 viii: 114; PRO ED138/56, Annual Report of the Chief Medical Officer of the Board of Education for 1939: 27; Number of free and paying meals: Board of Education 1922: 95–103; 1923: 152–8; 1924: 166–72; 1925a: 174–9; 1926: 118; 1927: 135; 1928: 100; 1929: 72; 1930: 112; 1931: 113; 1932: 144; 1933: 168; 1934: 182; 1935: 146; 1936: 149.

was issued to local authorities on 17 May (PRO ED24/1372, Memorandum by M. Branch relating to the limitation of expenditure on which the Provision of Meals grant will be payable in respect of the year 1922/23). The Board also advised local authorities to make every effort to cooperate with Poor Law authorities and to recover the cost of school meals from Boards of Guardians when they fed children whose parents were being relieved by them (Board of Education 1922: 41; 1923: 118).

The Board's desire to limit costs continued to play a major part in the development of school meals policy throughout the 1920s, even though the expenditure limit was abandoned in February 1924 (House of Commons Debates 1924: cols. 1009–10). In January 1924 the President of the Board of Education instructed his officials 'to consider whether the removal of the purely financial restriction might not be accompanied by some tightening up of our administration', and the Permanent Secretary suggested that this might be achieved by 'insisting upon close coordination between the school medical service . . . and the provision of school meals' (PRO ED50/77, Selby-Bigge to Attwood and Newman, 28/1/24). This advice was received enthusiastically by the Board's Chief Medical Officer, and in July 1925 the Board advised local education authorities that 'provision must be made for associating the school medical service with the planning and administration of [provision of meals] arrangements' (PRO ED50/77, Newman to Selby-Bigge, 29/1/24: para. 5; Board of Education 1925a: para. 23 [iv]). However, even though the Board continued to insist on the merits of medical selection, there was still a good deal of variation in the policies pursued by individual local education authorities (Board of Education 1928: 102–3). In 1944 E.D. Marris recalled:

> Between 1920 and 1930 the Board had assumed that the children might be selected for free meals either because of poverty or because of malnutrition. The matter was left very much to Authorities and the position was rather obscure. The Board's Legal Adviser had indicated . . . that if [an] . . . Authority passed the necessary resolution under Section 84 of the [1921 Education] Act . . . it became a matter for the . . . Authority what charge, if any, should be made to the parents of . . . children who received meals at school (PRO ED138/60, E.D. Marris, 'War history of school meals and milk', para. 50).

The question of medical selection returned to the fore at the beginning of the 1930s. In July 1931 the May Committee called for cuts in public expenditure, and the Board of Education '[was] subsequently compelled to insist that a child could not receive a meal at less than the cost of food unless he were both "necessitous" and "undernourished"' (ibid.). This policy was bitterly condemned by Eleanor Rathbone M.P., and in 1934 the Medical Officer of Health for Smethwick, Dr Hugh Paul, claimed that as a result of the Board's regulations children were required to undergo a period of 'trial starvation' in order to qualify for free meals (House of Commons Debates 1934: cols 1055–62; Leff and Leff 1959: 84). In September 1934 the Board advised local authorities to offer school meals to any child who showed signs of 'sub-normal nutrition', and in 1935 it urged them to carry out periodical nutrition surveys 'at which all children not receiving meals would be passed under review' (PRO ED50/81, Circular 1437, para. 3; PRO ED138/59, Circular 1443: para. 7). This had the somewhat paradoxical effect of ensuring that the overall level of school feeding continued to rise, even though economic conditions were beginning to improve.

In addition to the provision of both solid and milk meals under sections 82–4 of the Education Act, local education authorities were also able to supply milk to schoolchildren under a number of different schemes associated with the National Milk Publicity Council. Under the terms of the original milk-in-schools scheme, launched in 1923, the Council agreed to supply bottles containing one-third of a pint of milk to children whose parents were prepared to pay 1d. per bottle. During the remaining part of the 1920s, a series of reports appeared, extolling the nutritional properties of milk and its beneficial impact on children's growth, and by the early 1930s the scheme had been adopted by 150 local authorities, so that milk was being supplied to about 800,000 elementary schoolchildren (Board of Education 1923: 118–19; 1924: 118–20; 1928: 104–5; 1929: 71–2; 1930: 114–16; 1931: 46–7; 1932: 109–10; 1934: 27–8).

The campaign to increase the consumption of milk in schools received a further boost from the launch of the Milk Marketing Board's milk-in-schools scheme on 1 October 1934. The government agreed to make a grant of £500,000 to enable the Marketing Board to supply milk to schools at reduced rates, and parents were able to obtain milk for their children for $^1/_2$d. per bottle instead of 1d. per bottle. The introduction of the scheme led to a dramatic increase in the number of children who received milk under the Education Acts and under the milk-in-schools scheme. By the end of the 1930s, 635,000 children were receiving free milk under the Education Acts, and 2.7 million children were receiving milk, either free or for payment, under the milk marketing scheme (see Table 7.3).

The provision of school meals and the development of the milk-in-schools scheme represented a major extension of public welfare provision, but it is important to recognise the limitations of this record as well as its strengths. Even though there was a considerable increase in the total number of children who received school meals, the majority of the 'meals' provided in the second half of the 1930s were milk meals and supplements, and the number of children who received solid meals rarely exceeded 2–3 per cent of the school population (Hurt 1985: 191–7; Webster 1983: 77–8). The number of children who were reported as being malnourished often bore little relationship to the number being fed. In 1938 the Parliamentary Secretary of the Board of Education reported that even though 12.5 per cent of the children in Brentford and Chiswick showed signs of slightly sub-normal

Table 7.3 Provision of milk under the milk-in-schools scheme, 1935–39.

<table>
<tr><th colspan="3">Percentage of departments providing milk</th><th colspan="4">Percentage of children receiving milk</th></tr>
<tr><th></th><th>Under scheme</th><th>Outside scheme</th><th colspan="2">Under scheme</th><th colspan="2">Outside scheme</th></tr>
<tr><th></th><th></th><th></th><th>For payment</th><th>Free</th><th>For payment</th><th>Free</th></tr>
<tr><td>31/3/35</td><td>78.7</td><td>8.6</td><td colspan="2">48.7</td><td colspan="2">3.0</td></tr>
<tr><td>1/10/35</td><td>79.9</td><td>7.1</td><td colspan="2">44.9</td><td colspan="2">2.4</td></tr>
<tr><td>31/3/36</td><td>81.7</td><td>8.5</td><td colspan="2">45.8</td><td colspan="2">3.3</td></tr>
<tr><td>1/10/36</td><td>82.4</td><td>7.3</td><td>6.3</td><td>39.3</td><td>0.3</td><td>2.2</td></tr>
<tr><td>31/3/37</td><td>83.3</td><td>8.5</td><td colspan="2">49.0</td><td colspan="2">3.5</td></tr>
<tr><td>1/10/37</td><td>83.3</td><td>7.3</td><td>7.1</td><td>42.1</td><td>0.3</td><td>2.2</td></tr>
<tr><td>31/3/38</td><td>85.2</td><td>8.2</td><td colspan="2">53.0</td><td colspan="2">3.2</td></tr>
<tr><td>1/10/38</td><td>86.1</td><td>6.9</td><td>9.0</td><td>44.8</td><td>0.4</td><td>1.9</td></tr>
<tr><td>31/3/39</td><td>86.9</td><td>n/a</td><td colspan="2">55.6</td><td colspan="2">n/a</td></tr>
</table>

Sources: Board of Education 1936: 33; 1937: 32–3; 1938: 27; 1940: 23–4; PP 1938–9 Cmd. 6013 x: 45; PRO ED138/56, Annual Report of the Chief Medical Officer of the Board of Education 1939: 29.

or bad nutrition, only 3.6 per cent were being fed, but in the neighbouring borough of Ealing, 2.5 per cent of the children showed signs of slightly sub-normal or bad nutrition, and 11.8 per cent were fed (House of Commons Debates 1938: cols 1542–4). The defects of the school meals service were particularly apparent in the depressed areas of Durham and Northumberland and South Wales (PRO ED50/181, C.W. Maudslay, 'The need for increased financial assistance to the Special Areas': para. 8). In 1936 the Ministry of Health and the Board of Education conducted a joint investigation into the provision of school meals in South Wales and Monmouthshire, and found that between 25 and 44 per cent of the children whose nutrition was found to be slightly sub-normal or bad were not receiving any form of nutritional support (PRO MH55/629, J. Pearse, T. Wade, T. Evans and J. Underwood, 'Inquiry into present conditions as regards the effects of continued unemployment on health in certain areas of South Wales and Monmouth', pp. 17–31; see also Welshman 1988: 166–7).

The problem of insufficient quantity was compounded by the fact that many local education authorities fed their children in dirty and overcrowded premises, and provided meals which contained very little nutritional value. In 1935 Dr Muriel Bywaters visited two school feeding centres in Radcliffe, and found that

> the accommodation was poor, the premises were dark, over-crowded and badly-ventilated, and there was barely sufficient seating accommodation and of course no training of any kind (PRO ED137/73, M. Bywaters, 'Radcliffe: report on special services', 15/4/35: paras 12, 17; see also PRO ED50/214, Extracts from reports: 2).

Dr Bywaters also found that many of the meals provided by Local Education Authorities contained little or no nutritional value. The menu offered by one Local Education Authority consisted of little more than 'stew, soup or potato pie, followed by milk pudding', whilst another Local Authority attempted to safeguard the nutrition of its children with 'a thin soup containing potatoes, onions, a little barley, an infinitesimal portion of meat . . . and a piece of bread' (PRO ED50/214, Extracts from reports). In 1938 the Board appointed an 'Inspector of Provision of Meals Arrangements', but her appointment had little immediate effect. In her first annual report, in 1939, she concluded:

> The methods by which Authorities organise this service frequently leave much to be desired. . . . In the 54 areas visited . . . about five per cent of the arrangements are really good. Of the remainder approximately 20 per cent are entirely unsatisfactory while most of those which fall between these extremes . . . cannot be looked upon as up to any reasonable standard (PRO ED138/60, E.D. Marris, 'War history of school meals and milk': para. 6).

The newer knowledge of nutrition

During the second half of the 1930s the Board of Education came under growing pressure from critics who argued that it had failed to take sufficient account of new developments in nutritional science (M'Gonigle and Kirby 1936; Orr 1936; 1937). By the early years of the twentieth century, it was well known that most foods contained a combination of fats, carbohydrates, proteins and lipids, but it was becoming increasingly apparent that many foods also contained a number of 'accessory food factors', or vitamins, which were equally necessary for the maintenance of health (Mayhew 1988: 445). The emergence of the 'newer knowledge of nutrition' forced many investigators to recognise that a large proportion of the working-class population was living in poverty and that the number of people who were living on inadequate diets was much higher than they had previously believed (Macnicol 1980: 46–7). In 1935 F.C. Kelly observed:

> Different lines of study began to converge showing that individuals and communities, while not exhibiting signs of obvious disease, are functioning at levels far below those normally attainable under optimal conditions of feeding, and that the effective activities of a race may be seriously limited by the prevalence of a great deal of veiled undernutrition (Kelly 1935: 65–6).

The first clear evidence for the existence of vitamins was provided by N. Lunin in Basle in 1881. Lunin discovered that when mice were fed with an artificial mixture containing all the fats, proteins and carbohydrates which were normally found in milk, they failed to survive. This led him to conclude that 'a food such as milk must therefore contain besides these principal ingredients small quantities of unknown substances essential to life' (Medical Research Council 1932: 11–12). By 1915, scientists had succeeded in identifying two such substances, called 'fat-soluble A' and 'fat-soluble B', together with a third 'anti-scorbutic' vitamin, which became known as vitamin C. During the 1920s and 1930s 'fat-soluble A' was broken down into vitamins A and D and the multiple nature of the vitamin B complex was also apprehended (McCollum and Simmonds 1929; Medical Research Council 1932). In 1940 R.H.A. Plimmer observed:

> The medical profession was at first rather sceptical as to the part played by vitamins in maintaining the resistance of the body to disease. Now the tendency is to welcome synthetic vitamins as the latest things in drugs and to prescribe them in the pure state. Such a procedure should, however, be for emergency use only. The right way to take our daily dose of vitamins is not in tablet form but as they occur in a properly-balanced diet providing minerals, protein and other essentials in the form of fruits and vegetables, wholemeal flour, nuts and legumes, and in milk, butter, cheese, eggs, liver and fish (Plimmer 1940: 194).

In addition to their research into vitamins, interwar nutritionists also investigated the nutritive properties of milk. Between 1922 and 1926 H.C. Corry Mann conducted a famous investigation into the effects of different dietary supplements on the growth rates of 220 boys attending the Dr Barnardo's home in Woodford, and in 1926 and 1927 John Boyd Orr conducted a similar enquiry into the growth of over 1000 children in Scotland. Both sets of investigations showed (or appeared to show) that milk was an important factor in the promotion of growth, but the investigators were unable to agree on the reasons for this. Corry Mann believed that milk promoted faster growth because it contained fat-soluble vitamins, but Boyd Orr and Mabel Clark attributed its growth-promoting properties to the influence of calcium (Mann 1926: 55–6; Orr 1928: 202–3).[2] In 1930 they investigated the diets of 607 families in Scotland, and concluded that 24.5 per cent of the families consumed less than the recommended minimum intake of calcium for adults, and that more than 75 per cent of the families in Dundee consumed less than the amount needed to ensure optimum growth in children (Orr and Clark 1930: 598).

The 'newer knowledge of nutrition' had important implications for the study of poverty in interwar Britain. Between 1923 and 1932 poverty surveys were carried out in nine separate areas, including Bolton, Northampton, Reading, Stanley, Warrington, London, Merseyside, Southampton and Sheffield (Bowley and Hogg 1925; Smith 1930–35; Jones 1934; Ford 1934; Owen 1933). The investigators compared the income of each family with a 'poverty line' based on the cost of a list of essential items, and concluded that between 10 and 21 per cent of the working-class population in different parts of Britain was living in poverty (Ford 1934: 121; George 1937: 74–6; Stevenson 1984: 134). However, in 1937 the statistician R.F. George recalculated their results in the light of recent advances in nutrition. He concluded:

> The outstanding feature is that in every case the total minimum cost of the items considered on the revised basis is greatly in excess of the estimates hitherto accepted. For the married couple, the new standard is above those of the previous surveys by amounts varying from about one shilling to three shillings weekly; for the married couple with a child of school age, the excess varies from 3/3 to 5/8; and for the family of a man and wife with one child of, and one child below, school age, the revised estimate exceeds former standards by amounts varying from 6/2 to 7/6 weekly. The excess of the revised standard increases with the number of children. This is almost entirely due to the present conception of minimum food requirements. Even for the married couple, the revised minimum cost of food is greater than the cost hitherto generally accepted, and this tendency becomes strongly pronounced as children come into the family. . . .
>
> The result of these calculations is that the minimum needs standards should be significantly higher than those hitherto accepted, with the

result that the extent of absolute poverty has been under-estimated (George 1937: 91–2).

These conclusions were reinforced by a series of dietary surveys which were carried out during the second half of the 1930s. The first and arguably the most important was carried out by the Rowett Research Institute in 1935. The researchers divided the population into six different income groups, and concluded that the majority of the population consumed a diet which was insufficient for the maintenance of 'maximum health' (Orr 1937: 41–2; see also Lloyd 1936; Orr 1936). In 1937 W. Crawford and H. Broadley compared the dietary standards used in this survey with those employed by the British Medical Association and the Technical Committee of the League of Nations (Table 7.4). They concluded that at least 8 million people were unable to afford the minimum diet, and that between 12 and 22 million people consumed an inadequate diet because they spent their money unwisely (Crawford and Broadley 1938: 148–61).

These conclusions were also reinforced by evidence derived from local studies. In 1936–7 C.F. Brockington examined the diets of two different groups of children in West Sussex. He found that 62.7 per cent of the children consumed a diet which fell 'below sufficiency' in terms of total food, and that more than half consumed a diet which fell below sufficiency in terms of first-class protein (Brockington 1938a; 1938b; 1939: 307–10). In 1938 the School Medical Officer for Ipswich, Dr A.M.N. Pringle, carried out a special survey for the local branch of the Committee Against Malnutrition. He found that the diets of virtually all the families in the survey were deficient in milk, butter, cheese, fruit and green vegetables, and that the amount of protein was deficient in both quantity and quality (*Medical Officer* 1938).

Table 7.4 Estimated numbers of individuals consuming inadequate quantities of the various nutritive constituents of foodstuffs (millions).

	Compared with BMA diet	*Compared with Stiebeling (Food, health and income) minima*	*Compared with League of Nations stands*
Calories	15	16	18
Proteins	18	10	20
Calcium	25	31	35
Phosphorus	20	25	37
Iron	33	19	34
Vitamin A	37	–	44
Vitamin B_1	24	–	38
Vitamin C	21	27	33

Source: Crawford and Broadley (1938: 158); see also Stiebeling (1933); Orr (1936: 32–3; 1937: 38–9).

Further evidence of nutritional deficiency was provided by surveys in Edinburgh and the West Riding of Yorkshire. In 1939 Dr T.N.V. Potts conducted an analysis of the diets of 205 families in the West Riding of Yorkshire. All the diets contained enough calories, but the diet of the working-class population was deficient in proteins and protective foods, and the extent of the deficiency was directly related to the size of the family (*Medical Officer* 1940a). In 1941 the Children's Nutrition Council examined the diets of over 100 families in Edinburgh: only 10 per cent of the families had enough money to purchase an adequate diet, and out of 53 families who kept adequate records, only one had a diet 'of more than seventy per cent adequacy'. Seventy per cent of the people in these families were children under the age of eighteen (*Public Health* 1941a).

During the 1920s and 1930s it was often assumed that problems of ill health and malnutrition were essentially urban phenomena, but this was not necessarily the case (see Burnett 1983: 306). In 1936 W.B. Stott investigated the family budgets of 204 families in the Urban Districts of Cuckfield and Burgess Hill, and the Rural District of Cuckfield. He found that 34.4 per cent of the children whose parents spent less than 7s. per head on food per week showed signs of sub-normal nutrition, and that 91 per cent of the children whose parents spent more than 7s. per head showed signs of nutrition which was 'good', 'very good' or 'excellent'. However Stott's report also highlighted one of the major difficulties facing health workers in the interwar period. As E.H. Wilkins pointed out, the fact that sixty per cent of the children whose parents spent less than 3s. per head a week on food failed to show signs of sub-normal nutrition merely underlined the fact that the medical profession had still not devised an adequate method of measuring 'nutritional status' (East Sussex Education Committee 1937: 22–6; Stott 1937; Wilkins 1937).

The measurement of children's 'nutrition'

The absence of any agreed system for defining, measuring or classifying nutrition was one of the greatest difficulties facing the school medical service in the interwar years. Between 1934 and 1941 more than half a dozen surveys were carried out in different parts of Britain which suggested that more than half the British population was failing to obtain an adequate diet, and that the overwhelming majority of the child population experienced a period of deprivation during their growing years. However even though many school medical officers recognised that large numbers of children were inadequately fed, they found it difficult to prove that this was having an adverse effect on their health and condition. In 1933 the editor of *Medical Officer* observed:

> We must find out the clinical signs of malnutrition, for these we do not know. We know that at the present time a very large proportion of the

population is imperfectly fed, but we cannot find the signs of it. We have districts where the amount spent on food is inadequate to cover the necessities, and we report the observed nutrition of the children . . . as 90 to 95 per cent good. We know that this is false, and those who quote these results as proof that all is going well . . . know that it is false also (*Medical Officer* 1933a; see also *Medical Officer* 1929a; 1932; 1934; 1935b; 1936a; 1936b).

In the Circular which it issued to local education authorities on 23 January 1908, the Board of Education instructed school medical officers to classify the nutrition of children as good, normal, below normal or bad (PP 1910 Cd. 4986 xxiii: 152). However, the Board failed to offer any clear guidance as to how children should be placed into the different categories, and many medical officers used an entirely different classification system. In the winter of 1934–5, Dr R.H. Simpson investigated the arrangements made by medical officers in eleven separate local authority areas, and found that different officers used different classification systems and attached different meanings to the same terms. The School Medical Officers for Smethwick and Blackburn classified the nutrition of children as 'good', 'fairly good' and 'bad', but the School Medical Officer for Smethwick thought that 'fairly good' meant 'normal', whereas the School Medical Officer for Blackburn thought that 'fairly good' meant 'sub-normal'. The School Medical Officer for Plymouth distinguished between malnutrition requiring observation and malnutrition requiring treatment, while the School Medical Officer for Ebbw Vale managed to use no formal classification system at all (PRO ED50/51, Dr Simpson's enquiry).

The second problem with the nutrition returns concerned the relationship between the way in which school medical officers classified nutrition at the time of their inspections, and the way in which they reported the results of those inspections in their annual reports. We have already seen that medical officers used a variety of systems to classify nutrition, but they were then required to translate the results of this analysis into two separate lists of children suffering from malnutrition requiring observation and children suffering from malnutrition requiring treatment. It might be argued that the differences between the various classification systems would be unimportant if all the figures were converted into a common form, but the result was that the published figures often bore little relationship to the original estimates. In 1935 Dr J.R. Marrack wrote:

> The children are classified . . . by the inspecting Medical Officers in four categories: 'good', 'normal', 'sub-normal' and 'bad'. The 'sub-normal' and 'bad' children are later reclassified by some obscure and variable process, and a fraction of these . . . appear in the reports under the headings 'malnutrition requiring treatment' and 'malnutrition requiring observation'. In London, for example, 4.7 per cent of the children fall in categories 'sub-normal' and 'bad': only 0.6 per cent are reported under the heading 'malnutrition requiring treatment' and 0.35 per cent

> are reported under the heading 'malnutrition requiring observation'. It is these edited figures . . . that Sir George Newman . . . quotes with the respect due to the first-hand results of careful observation (Marrack 1935: 14; see also Board of Education 1934: 17–19).

The third problem with the nutrition returns was that the standards used by different medical officers were subject to a wide range of variation, so that even when medical officers used the same system of classification, it was still impossible to compare their results. In 1933 Dr J.C. Spence wrote:

> There are at present no definite standards or formulae by . . . which the physique and state of nutrition can be estimated with mathematical accuracy. An expression of poor physique must therefore be regarded as an opinion, the validity of which will vary with the experience of the observer and the methods which he [*sic*] uses (City and County of Newcastle upon Tyne 1934: 16).

This opinion was echoed by the Medical Officer of Health and School Medical Officer for Cumberland, Dr Kenneth Fraser, in his annual report for 1934. He wrote that

> as a consequence of economic distress, and unemployment, and so on, there can be no doubt that large numbers of the children in this area . . . are badly fed . . . [but] only a proportion of these children could possibly be classified as malnourished. . . . The weak point in the argument . . . is that there is no known standard in the matter, and that there is no satisfactory way of assessing nutrition or malnutrition (Cumberland Education Committee 1935; qu. Harris 1937: 225).

Faced with these criticisms, the Board decided to adopt a new system for classifying children's nutrition at the end of 1934. It issued new guidelines for assessing nutrition and abandoned the somewhat invidious distinction between 'malnutrition requiring observation' and 'malnutrition requiring treatment'. The original four-point scale was replaced by a new scale in which nutrition was assessed as 'excellent', 'normal', 'slightly sub-normal' or 'bad'. The new Chief Medical Officer, Sir Arthur MacNalty, summarised the various issues which needed to be taken into account in the following terms:

> The main issue is to estimate the general well-being of the child. Such general assessment cannot as a rule be based upon any single criterion, such as any ratio of age, sex, height and weight, but should also have regard to other data derived from clinical observation: for example, the general appearance, facies, carriage, posture, the condition of the mucous membranes, the tone and functioning of the muscular system, the amount of subcutaneous fat. An alert, cheerful child, with bright eyes and a good colour, may usually be accepted as well-nourished without demur. On the other hand, a child who appears dull, listless and tired, who has a muddy complexion or stands slackly, is at once under sus-

> picion and should be further examined. Too much reliance on a single sign may lead to error. Carious teeth and other local defects should not in themselves be regarded as evidence of faulty nutrition. It is the general impression which decides the issue (Board of Education 1935: 27).

In his annual report for 1934, MacNalty argued that these changes would 'secure a more precise, uniform and comparable classification than those used by many Authorities in recent years', but the new system failed to meet the need for uniform standards (Board of Education 1935: 26). In 1937 R. Huws Jones of the University of Liverpool told the Royal Statistical Society that 'the distribution of nutrition in a given population and the number and identity of the boys assessed sub-normal are largely dependent on the particular doctor who makes the assessments', and this meant that 'the method of assessing nutrition at present followed by School Medical Officers, on the direction of the Board of Education, is unreliable' (Jones 1938: 33). In 1940 the Board's Senior Medical Inspector, Dr J.A. Glover, examined the returns submitted by a large number of medical officers over the previous five years and discovered that a large proportion 'differ entirely from expectation or probability'. He concluded:

> The [present] writer has tried to defend the method of clinical assessment on many occasions, and the obvious conclusion of this examination is painful to him, but it cannot be denied that a very large proportion of the returns are so unreliable as to be valueless for any purpose. 'A gem cannot be polished without friction, nor a method perfected without adversity.' Clinical assessment, however . . . has so many intrinsic flaws that with the friction of common use it flies to pieces (PRO ED50/204, J.A. Glover, 'A critical examination of the nutrition returns over a period of five years', p. 23).

In view of the obvious problems associated with clinical assessment, it is interesting to consider some of the alternative methods which were tried by school medical officers and other researchers during the interwar period (see also PRO ED50/201, 'The improvement of nutrition': 13–18). Some of the most important attempts focused on the use of anthropometric measurement and 'nutrition quotients'. In 1933 Dr J.C. Spence compared the heights and weights of 125 well-to-do children in Newcastle upon Tyne with those of 124 children 'from the poor districts of the city'. He found that 12.9 per cent of the well-to-do children fell below the 'normal zone' for weight and 4.8 per cent fell below the 'normal zone' for height, but the equivalent figures for the poor children were 55.2 per cent and 47.0 per cent, respectively (City and County of Newcastle upon Tyne 1934: 15–17; see also Miller 1938). Dr Victor Freeman calculated the weight–height ratios of 914 children in Heston and Isleworth and compared them with a set of United States standards. He found that 46.7 per cent of the children whose weight–height ratio was more than 10 per cent below the US standards showed signs of physical defect, as did 42.3 per cent of the children whose weight–height ratio was within ±5 per cent of the standard. However, the proportion of physical defects among children whose weight–height ratio was more than 10 per cent above the standard was 26.1 per cent (Freeman 1934).

These results suggested that weight–height ratios and similar statistics could be used to identify sub-groups of the population more likely to show signs of physical defect, but it was more difficult to show how they could be used to identify individual children who were actually malnourished. In 1935 R.H. Jones examined twenty-five separate 'nutritional indexes' in order to see which gave the best results in comparison with the clinical judgements of an experienced medical observer. The most 'successful' index was the Tuxford index, which was the only index to take account of differences in children's ages and to provide separate figures for each sex.[3] However, even this index picked out some children whom the doctors regarded as well nourished and rejected others whom they regarded as malnourished. The basic problem was that the Tuxford index could only be tested by comparing it with a method which was itself open to question. In 1937 Dr A. Bradford Hill told the Royal Statistical Society:

> Our index may be a very good one. We have no way of knowing for we have no true discrimination of satisfactory nutrition and malnutrition against which to check it. That seems to me to be a logical difficulty from which there is at present no means of escape (Jones 1938: 32–5; see also PRO ED50/51, Dr Simpson's Report, p. 10; Frazer 1938: 21–7; Dublin and Gebhart 1924: 3–23).

The second major attempt to devise an alternative system of measuring nutrition was concerned with the use of various types of 'functional test'. In 1846 Dr John Hutchinson claimed that it was possible to test an individual's 'vital capacity' by measuring 'the greatest voluntary expiration, following the deepest inspiration' of air into the lungs (Hutchinson 1846: 143). Hutchinson's method was tested by Lucy Cripps, Major Greenwood and Ethel Newbold and by Alfred Mumford and Matthew Young in 1922 and 1923 respectively, but both sets of researchers concluded that the results were far too variable to serve any practical purpose. (Cripps *et al.* 1923: 326–36; Mumford and Young 1923: 133). However, in 1917 Group Captain Martin Flack developed a modified form of Hutchinson's test for use with aircraft pilots, and in 1925 J.G. Woolham and J.V. Simpson adapted Flack's test for use with schoolboys (Flack 1920: 98–9). Both Woolham and Simpson found that the tests could be used to compare the fitness levels of different groups of children, but they were less useful in individual cases (Manchester Education Committee 1926: 64–71; Torquay Education Committee 1926: 54–8). In 1926 Simpson concluded:

> The Flack-Woolham tests are very important as an aid to the assessment of physical fitness: marked physical weakness is easily shown by comparison of the rowing boys with those at the open-air school, but the diffi-

culty is to find a limiting range. Woolham suggests 0.4 to 0.5 as probably correct, but products under 0.4 may be due either to 'flabbiness' or loss of tone, or to actual disease – because . . . many boys [who] were below 0.4 [at the start of the enquiry] . . . easily came over the figure [after training] (Dunlop 1926: 54–8; see also Magee *et al.* 1935: 719–23; Dreyer 1920).[4]

Many researchers tried to measure the physical fitness of children by subjecting them to various kinds of strength, coordination and endurance test. The most common tests were the dynamometer test, which measured the strength of the arm, back, lumbar and thigh muscles; Romberg's test, which measured children's ability to stand still with their eyes closed; and the hanging-bar test, which measured their ability to remain suspended from a horizontal bar without their feet touching the ground. In 1934 Dr Marcus Milligan used the dynamometer and hanging-bar tests to compare the fitness levels of the children of employed and unemployed parents, and found that the 'employed' children achieved better results than the 'unemployed' children, but the results were subject to such a wide range of variation that it was impossible to use them for diagnostic purposes (Glossop Education Committee 1935: 19–23; see also Manchester Education Committee 1936: 66–7; Milk Nutrition Committee 1939: 27). This conclusion was echoed by Dr C.A. Paulusz in Warrington in 1935. Paulusz compared the results obtained from a battery of physical tests with the results of his own observation and a haemoglobin test, and concluded that 'the only test of value, apart from one's own clinical observation, of all those experimented with, appears to be the haemoglobin test, by means of which any deficiency of the haemoglobin of a child's blood can be detected' (Warrington Education Committee 1936: 64–5).

The problems associated with the use of nutrition quotients and with tests of physical and vital capacity led an increasing number of researchers to investigate the use of tests for specific dietary deficiencies. In 1936 Leslie Harris described tests for the detection of deficiency in vitamin A (the photometer or dark adaptation test), vitamin B_1 (a urinary excretion test), vitamin C (a urinary excretion test or Göthlin's capillary resistance test), and vitamin D (the blood phosphatase test) (Harris 1936). However, many of these tests were open to the objection that they were difficult to perform and that the results were subject to a wide range of possible interpretations. One of the most widely discussed tests was the photometer or dark adaptation test, but although the test appeared to work quite well in individual surveys, there were problems when it was applied on a more routine basis (Maitra and Harris 1937: 1012–14). In 1937 two American researchers concluded that children who took the test on more than one occasion tended to improve their scores by practice, and that 'more data concerning the quantitative relationships between Vitamin A nutrition and dark adaptation tests are needed' (*Public Health* 1937; *Lancet* 1937; Jones 1938: 36).

In addition to these tests for vitamin deficiencies, there were also a number of tests for various forms of mineral deficiency (Harris 1936: 968). The most widely used test was the haemoglobin test for iron deficiency. J.C. Spence used this test to compare the nutrition of well-to-do and poor children in Newcastle in 1933, and C.A. Paulusz used it to compare the nutritional status of children examined at routine medical inspections with those who had been specially selected for supplementary feeding (City and County of Newcastle upon Tyne 1934: 10–11; Warrington Education Committee 1935: 64–5). However, although the amount of haemoglobin varied according to the socio-economic and nutritional status of the different groups, it was difficult to know how to interpret the results or how to apply them to individual children. In 1935 H.E. Magee told the Royal Society of Medicine that 'it would . . . be unwise in the present state of knowledge to regard anaemia in children as nutritional in origin without dietary evidence pointing in the same direction' (Magee *et al.* 1935: 718). This conclusion was echoed by John Boyd Orr in 1937:

> Records of the incidence of nutritional anaemia would give a good indication of the adequacy of the diet. Unfortunately the incidence of anaemias and the extent to which they are due to causes other than diet cannot be stated with any degree of confidence (Orr 1937: 48).

Unemployment and stature in interwar Britain

In his celebrated study of *Poverty and population*, Richard Titmuss drew his readers' attention to the fact that Britain possessed no reliable statistics of the general state of health of those who lived among the people whose deaths were recorded in the annual mortality statistics. He pointed out that the school medical service had been designed to provide such information in the form of the nutrition statistics collected at routine medical examinations, but the absence of any uniform standards meant that 'no reliance can be placed on either the local, regional or national figures' (Titmuss 1938: 101; see also ibid.: 309). However, some school medical officers did reproduce information about the average heights and weights of the children in their areas. This information can be used to shed new light on the health and nutrition of the school population during the interwar period.

The basic principles which lie behind this analysis were discussed in Chapter 5. Although some interwar researchers expressed doubts about the value of anthropometric data, it is now recognised that the average height of a population provides an accurate guide to its health and well-being, and changes in the average height of a population over time can be used to measure changes in its standard of living (Board of Education 1924: 137–8; Eveleth and Tanner 1991: 1). The present writer has been able to identify forty-five local education authorities whose medical officers published height and weight statistics during the interwar period, and in eleven of these areas it has been possible to combine these data with local unemployment statistics. These data have been used to generate new findings about the relationship between unemployment and child health between 1923 and 1938.

The names of the eleven local authorities, and details of their occupational and demographic characteristics, are given in Table 7.5. Three areas – Cambridge, Croydon and Reading – were situated in the prosperous south-eastern quarter of England, and benefited from the growth of new industries during the interwar period. Croydon was an important engineering centre, and Cambridge continued to be dominated by the University. The largest employer in Reading was the Huntley and Palmer biscuit factory, but there was also a considerable amount of employment in general engineering, motor and aircraft manufacture. Reading was one of the five towns studied by Bowley and Hogg (1925). They found that the percentage of the population which was living below the poverty line declined from 29 per cent in 1912 to 11.9 per cent in 1924 (Fogarty 1945: 8, 395–6; Bowley and Hogg 1925: 125).

Four of the sample areas were situated in the West Riding of Yorkshire. Leeds and Huddersfield both enjoyed periods of growing prosperity during the interwar years. Leeds witnessed a substantial increase in the number of people employed in tailoring and administration, and this helped to compensate for declines in the engineering and boot and shoe trades.[5] Huddersfield was also able to avoid the worst effects of the recession because of its varied industrial base. By contrast, both Bradford and Wakefield were less favourably placed. In Bradford 43 per cent of all insured workers were employed in the woollen industry or in textile finishing, and the rate of unemployment fluctuated around the national average. The worst-affected area was Wakefield, which was heavily dependent on coal-mining and engineering. In 1932 25.7 per cent of the insured workers in Wakefield were registered as unemployed (Fogarty 1945: 32, 243–8; Meadowcroft 1980: 430–31).

Blackburn and Warrington provide examples of two contrasting areas in the North-West of England. Blackburn was heavily dependent on the cotton textile industry, and the decline of this industry after the end of the First World War produced very high levels of unemployment among both male and female workers. Between 1929 and 1936 the average rate of unemployment in Blackburn was almost twice the national average, and in 1935 and 1936 the unemployment rate was higher than that of the Scottish Special Area. Warrington also suffered from high levels of unemployment, but it was not affected to anything like the same extent as Blackburn. The main industry in the area was wire-making, but there was also a substantial amount of employment in other branches of the iron and steel industry, in leather and clothing manufacture, brewing, saw-milling, paper-making and printing (Fogarty 1945: 218–19, 226–7; see also Bowley and Hogg 1925: 83–108).

The final two areas are Glasgow and Rhondda. Both of these areas suffered very high levels of unemployment during the interwar period. The majority

Table 7.5 Population size and occupational characteristics of eleven areas, 1918–39.

Area	*Admin. unit*	*Population (1931)*	*Principal occupational groups*
Blackburn	CB	122,697	Metalwork, textiles, wood and furniture, construction, transport and communication, commerce, finance and insurance, personal services
Bradford	CB	298,041	Agriculture, metalwork, textiles, electrical trades, woodwork, construction, painting and decorating, transport and communication, commerce, finance and insurance
Cambridge	MB	66,789	Metalwork, construction, transport and communication, commerce, finance and insurance, professional occupations, personal services, clerical occupations
Croydon	CB	233,032	Metalwork, electrical trades, tailoring and dress-making, woodwork, printing and photography, painting and decorating, transport and communication, commerce, finance and insurance, professional occupations, personal services
Glasgow	City	1,088,461	Commercial occupations, metalwork, transport and communication, personal service, clerical work, other and undefined (mainly unskilled)
Huddersfield	CB	113,475	Metalwork, textiles, woodwork, construction, transport and communication, commerce, finance and insurance, professional occupations, personal service, clerical occupations
Leeds	CB	482,809	Coal-mining, metalwork, textiles, tailoring, construction, painting and decorating, transport and communication, commerce, finance and insurance, professional occupations, personal services, clerical occupations
Reading	CB	97,149	Agriculture, metalwork, textile goods and articles of dress, food manufacture, wood and furniture, construction, transport and communication, commerce, finance and industry, personal services, clerical occupations, warehousing
Rhondda	UD	141,346	Coal-mining, metalwork, construction, transport and communication, commerce, finance and insurance, personal services, clerical occupations
Wakefield	CB	59,222	Mining and quarrying, metalwork, textiles, transport and communication, commerce, finance and insurance, personal services, clerical occupations
Warrington	CB	79,317	Metalwork, textiles, construction, transport and communication, commerce, finance and insurance, clerical occupations

Abbreviations: CB = country borough. MB = municipal borough. UD = urban district.

Sources: HMSO (1932: 41, 47; 1934).

of Glasgow's workers were employed in ship-building, marine engineering and heavy engineering, and all three industries suffered considerable damage following the collapse of the ship-building industry after the end of the First World War. In December 1932 the total number of registered unemployed workers reached 130,000, and Allen Hutt estimated that approximately half the city's population was dependent on some form of public relief. The situation was at least as bad in the mining district of Rhondda in South Wales. In 1936, when the Pilgrim Trust visited the area, 44.5 per cent of insured male workers were unemployed, and 63 per cent of these had been out of work for more than one year (Gibb 1983: 148; Hutt 1933: 97–8; Pilgrim Trust 1938: 15).

In order to examine the relationship between changes in unemployment and changes in height in these areas, it was necessary to obtain more detailed information about changes in local unemployment rates for the whole period. The Ministry of Labour published a monthly digest of local unemployment statistics between 1927 and 1939, but there are no comparable figures for the years before 1927. However, the Public Record Office holds copies of the original unemployment registers which contain details of the number of insured workers who registered at the employment exchanges, and these figures have been used to generate new estimates of the incidence of unemployment in each area from 1923 onwards.[6] The figures are not

Table 7.6 Effect of changes in the average annual rate of unemployment on changes in the average value of children's heights in three groups of areas, 1925–38.

		Constant	ΔU_{-1}	R^2	*d**	*Sig. F*
Group A	1925–38	1.32	−1.07	0.04	3.46	0.51
Group B	1925–38	0.93	−0.58	0.31	2.25	0.04
Group C	1925–38	0.79	−0.46	0.33	2.35	0.03
		Constant	ΔU_{-2}	R^2	*d**	*Sig. F*
Group A	1926–38	1.26	−0.86	0.04	3.46	0.53
Group B	1926–38	0.85	−0.45	0.22	1.53	0.11
Group C	1926–38	0.91	−0.41	0.26	2.75	0.07

Group A: Cambridge, Croydon, Reading. Group B: Bradford, Huddersfield, Leeds, Warrington. Group C: Blackburn, Glasgow, Rhondda, Wakefield.

Method: OLS.

Sources: The original unemployment statistics were derived from the following records: PRO LAB85/19–22; 41–44; 117–21; 161–4; 187–90. Height statistics were derived from the Annual Reports of the School Medical Officers for the areas listed in the text. A full list of the school medical reports cited in this study may be found in the Bibliography. Details of the original height statistics have been deposited with the ESRC Data Archive, University of Essex, Wivenhoe Park, Colchester, Essex CO4 3SQ. The statistics used in the preparation of this table can also be found in Harris (1989: 218–48, 275–81).

Table 7.7 Effect of changes in the average annual rate of unemployment on changes in the average value of children's heights in individual areas, 1927–37.

		Constant	ΔU_{-1}	R^2	*d**	*Sig. F*
Blackburn	1928–37	1.18	−0.32	0.28	1.66	0.02
Bradford	1927–37	0.74	−1.45	0.70	0.75	0.00
Cambridge	1926–37	1.64	−4.54	0.40	0.77	0.03
Croydon	1930–37	0.74	−0.14	0.00	3.46	0.92
Glasgow	1926–37	0.71	−0.05	0.01	1.59	0.72
Huddersfield	1926–37	1.00	−1.28	0.72	1.45	0.00
Leeds	1926–37	0.78	−0.55	0.57	2.04	0.00
Reading	1926–37	1.08	0.41	0.02	2.79	0.67
Rhondda	1926–37	0.77	−0.17	0.26	1.85	0.09
Wakefield	1931–37	0.64	−0.31	0.55	2.15	0.06
Warrington	1926–37	1.34	−0.07	0.01	1.54	0.80
		Constant	ΔU_{-2}	R^2	*d**	*Sig. F*
Blackburn	1928–37	1.11	−0.06	0.01	1.20	0.78
Bradford	1927–37	0.77	−0.98	0.29	0.59	0.09
Cambridge	1927–37	1.66	−5.09	0.50	0.90	0.02
Croydon	1930–37	0.81	−0.84	0.07	3.59	0.54
Glasgow	1927–37	0.72	−0.11	0.06	1.44	0.47
Huddersfield	1927–37	1.10	−1.35	0.75	2.25	0.00
Leeds	1927–37	0.80	−0.61	0.64	2.36	0.00
Reading	1927–37	1.12	0.47	0.03	2.72	0.64
Rhondda	1927–37	0.80	−0.12	0.11	1.60	0.33
Wakefield	1931–37	0.86	−0.47	0.92	1.72	0.00
Warrington	1927–37	1.32	−0.47	0.35	1.77	0.05

Method: OLS.

Sources: See Table 7.6

directly comparable with the official unemployment returns because the number of unemployed workers has been divided by the local population, and not by the number of insured workers, and the analysis has been based on the returns for adult male unemployment, because the incidence of female *employment* varied so widely between different areas.[7]

The analysis itself was carried out in two stages. In the first stage, the eleven areas were divided into three groups, based on the level of unemployment in each group during the interwar period. Group A included the three south-eastern towns of Cambridge, Croydon and Reading; group B included Bradford, Huddersfield, Leeds and Warrington; and group C included the 'high-unemployment' areas of Blackburn, Glasgow, Rhondda and Wakefield. The object of the analysis was to use least-squares regression equations to estimate the effect of a change in the average annual rate of unemployment in each group of areas on changes in the average height of the children in those areas. In Table 7.6, ΔU is the change in the adult male unemployment rate between one year and the next, and ΔH is the change in the average value of children's heights between one year and the next. The average value of children's heights was measured in centiles of the Tanner–Whitehouse distribution, and the equations were estimated with lags of one and two years.[8]

The results of this analysis suggest that there was little relationship between changes in unemployment and changes in average height in areas of low unemployment, but there was a somewhat closer relationship in areas of moderate and high unemployment. These results are not particularly surprising because we would not expect changes in the average rate of unemployment to have an effect on the *average* value of children's heights in areas where levels of unemployment rates were generally low. However, although changes in the average rate of unemployment were related to changes in the average value of children's heights in the group B and group C areas, the size of the relationship was not very great. This suggests that unemployment was only one of the factors which led to changes in child health in the course of this period.

In addition to examining the relationship between changes in unemployment and changes in average height in groups of areas, we can also examine the relationship between the two variables in individual areas. In this case, the equations have again been estimated with one- and two-year lags, but the data have been 'smoothed' with a three-year moving average. The results tend to reinforce the conclusions derived from the previous analysis. Changes in the average value of children's heights were related to changes in the annual rate of adult male unemployment in a number of different areas, but the strength of this relationship varied from area to area. The two variables were quite closely related in Bradford, Huddersfield, Wakefield and Leeds, but they were much less closely related in Blackburn, Glasgow and Rhondda (Table 7.7).

These findings have important implications for our understanding of the social consequences of unemployment in interwar Britain. In the first place, they suggest that changes in the average rate of unemployment did have an effect on the average value of children's heights, even though the strength of this relationship varied from area to area. The contrast between those areas where the two variables were closely related and those where they were less closely related demonstrates the importance of the local context within which unemployment occurred (see, for example, Nicholas 1986; Harris 1990). Secondly, we need to know much more about the relationship between unemployment benefits and local wage rates, and about differences in the welfare provisions made by different local authorities and voluntary agencies. Historians have devoted considerable attention to the national unemployment insurance scheme, but there were also substantial variations in the benefits provided by different local authorities and local charities (Harris 1989: 274). Finally, we also need to place the history of interwar unemployment in its wider social context. Many of the areas which experienced the highest levels of unemployment were also characterised by low wage rates, poor housing and high rates of disease, and it is much more difficult to identify the social consequences of unemployment in these areas than in areas where the standard of living of the employed population was relatively high (Harris 1988: 177; see also McKibbin 1990: 253–8).

Notes

1 For details of local education authority expenditure on the school meals service, see Table 6.1.
2 For a more critical assessment of the research into the growth-promoting qualities of milk, see Petty 1987a; 1987b.
3 The formula for boys was

$$\frac{weight\ (grams)}{height\ (centimetres)} \times \frac{381 - age\ (months)}{54}$$

and that for girls

$$\frac{weight\ (grams)}{height\ (centimetres)} \times \frac{354 - age\ (months)}{48}$$

See Jones (1938: 17); Liverpool Education Committee (1938: 20–21); Tuxford (1917: 66).
4 Simpson used Flack's tests (or the 'Flack–Woolham tests') to measure the physical fitness of four groups of boys. Group 1 consisted of boys who rowed frequently over a three-month period, group 2 consisted of boys who rowed less frequently, and group 3 included boys who were unfit for rowing. The boys in group 4 were definitely unfit, and were attending an open-air school for delicate children. He found that the rowers achieved higher scores at the end of the period than they had done at the beginning, and that there was a significant difference between the results obtained in groups 1–3 and the results obtained in group 4 (Torquay Education Committee 1926: 54–8).
5 It should also be noted that Leeds was characterised by a notoriously high incidence of slum housing. In 1934 a government survey revealed that nearly 23 per cent of the population was living in slum accommodation. See Bowley (1945: 218–19).
6 The registers were originally filed in the EDS2 and EDS10 series, and subsequently reclassified in the LAB85 series. For a full account of the procedures which were used to convert the raw data into unemployment 'percentages', see Harris (1989: 264–7).
7 For example, in 1931 the proportion of women over the age of fourteen who were described as 'occupied' in Blackburn (62.2 per cent) was nearly six times as great as the proportion of women who were described as occupied in Rhondda (11.4 per cent). See HMSO (1934).
8 Note that the division of the eleven areas into three groups differs slightly from that employed in Harris (1988). I have also taken advantage of the opportunity to correct one or two minor errors in the transcription of the original data.

eight

The school medical service during the Second World War

In December 1940, in the introduction to his unpublished report on the health of the schoolchild in 1939, Sir Arthur MacNalty reviewed the impact of the Second World War on the operation of the school medical service in the following terms:

> Since the advent of War the school medical service has undergone much dislocation and has been subjected to severe strain. It has been a kinetic and not a static service. Successive waves of evacuation have broken [over?] it. There have also been the ebb-tides of trickle evacuation from country districts back to London and the big towns, with the consequent need for new improvisation to meet the needs of emergency; the dislocation of work already planned to meet conditions which were constantly changing; the bombing of schools; their closure or requisition for war needs; the depletion of medical, nursing and teaching personnel; and countless other difficulties, which it would take volumes to enumerate (PRO ED138/56, The health of the schoolchild 1939: 1).

This chapter seeks to delineate the impact of the Second World War on the development of the school medical service on a somewhat smaller canvas than MacNalty considered necessary. It also seeks to build on the unpublished accounts of E.D. Marris and Sophia Weitzman, as well as the more recent accounts provided by Michael Davies, Peter Gosden, and John Welshman (PRO ED138/3, Brief history of education: Vol. 1: Special Studies; ED138/60, Nutrition of the schoolchild; Gosden 1976: 163–209; Welshman 1988: 312–65). The chapter itself is divided into five main sections. The first considers the impact of evacuation, and the second focuses on the more general history of school medical provision in wartime. The third and fourth sections concentrate on the history of the school meals service and the problems of postwar reconstruction, respectively. The final section examines the overall impact of the Second World War on the health of the school population in terms of nutrition, morbidity and mortality.

The impact of evacuation

The evacuation of thousands of British schoolchildren (and others) between 1939 and 1945 provides one of the clearest indications of the way in which the conduct of war was transformed during the first half of the twentieth century (Crosby 1986: 12–27). As Sir Arthur MacNalty pointed out in his annual report for 1938, it had traditionally been assumed that the safest location for a civilian population in time of war was a fortified town. However, the introduction of bombing raids towards the end of the First World War revolutionised military thinking, and demonstrated the need to transport vulnerable sections of the population to less densely populated areas (Board of Education 1940: 6–7). In May 1938 the government appointed the Anderson Committee to consider 'various aspects of the problem of transferring persons from areas which are likely to be exposed to continuous air attack' and to establish the general principles on which detailed plans for evacuation should be based. The Committee recommended that 'plans should be prepared . . . for the transfer of children of school age . . . from vulnerable areas to places of greater safety' and that 'the scheme relating to schoolchildren [should have] first claim on transport and reception facilities' (PP 1937–8 Cmd. 5837 x, para. 91).

Following the publication of the Anderson Report, the Ministry of Health drew up plans for dividing the whole of England and Wales into three different types of area. There were to be eighty-one *evacuation areas*, which were areas containing large centres of population from which children were to be evacuated, and 1100 *reception areas*, which were chiefly rural areas to which children would be sent; the remaining areas, which would neither send children out nor receive them, were designated *neutral areas* (*Times* 1939; Glover 1940: 400). The government made strenuous efforts to provide 'billets' for those children who were evacuated, but although these efforts were largely successful, they had to overcome considerable resistance. In one of the first contemporary studies of the evacuation, Margaret Cole reported:

> From the day on which the evacuation was completed the complaints began to arise. Most of these, naturally, came from the hosts. . . . The character of the complaints was fairly uniform over all areas. Apart from cases of obvious mistakes . . . the hosts complained that their guests were verminous, bed-wetters, liars, petty thieves without respect for property, of unclean habits, ill-equipped, rude and quarrelsome; conversely, that

> they were stuck-up, would give no assistance in the home, and were too expensive to keep. As time went on it was added that the care of them was very exhausting and that their parents were a nuisance (Cole 1940: 72).

Richard Titmuss identified three 'big waves' of evacuation, each smaller than the last and connected 'by a slender diminishing trickle' (Titmuss 1950: 355). The first wave took place during the first few weeks of the war and involved the movement of approximately 1.45 million people, including 830,000 unaccompanied children.[1] The second wave began during the second half of 1940, and involved approximately 1.3 million people, of whom approximately half a million were unaccompanied children. The third and smallest wave was sparked off by the threat of rocket attacks in the summer of 1944, and involved approximately 1 million people, of whom just over 300,000 were unaccompanied children (Titmuss 1950: 255; see also Table 8.1).

The movement of so many children around Britain would have imposed a considerable burden on the administration of the school medical service, regardless of the additional dislocations which were caused by the war itself. When the government drew up its evacuation plans, it assumed that school medical officers would be able to examine children as part of the normal operation of the school medical service, but it failed to anticipate the extent to which medical officers would be diverted to civil defence duties, or the problems which were likely to emerge if the evacuation took place at the end of the school holidays. The second omission was particularly important, because when the order to commence evacuation was finally given, the children had been out of school for up to five weeks, and this may well have contributed to the problems which were subsequently encountered by medical officers in the reception areas (PRO ED136/664, J.A. Glover, 'The school medical service in wartime', p. 6; PRO ED138/56, Health of the schoolchild 1939: 34; PRO ED50/207, Interview Memorandum, 24/11/39, para. 2).

The second major difficulty concerned the administration of the school medical service in the reception areas themselves. In the notes which he prepared on the history of evacuation, Titmuss identified three factors which were a source of particular distress. First, the majority of the children were evacuated to lightly populated areas which tended to have comparatively underdeveloped school medical services. Second, the host families were less inclined to put themselves out to obtain medical services for other people's children than they were for their own. Third, the medical staff who moved from the evacuation areas to the reception areas were accustomed to work in urban districts, and had little experience of the particular difficulties associated with work in rural areas (PRO ED138/58, Evacuation, para. 17).

The third set of difficulties involved the evacuation areas themselves. In many of these areas, the operation of the school medical service was effectively suspended, because school medical staff were diverted to civil defence work or to other areas, and because the schools themselves were closed.

Table 8.1 Government evacuation scheme: total number billeted in all areas.

	Unaccompanied children	*Mothers and children*	*Teachers and helpers*	*Other adults*[a]	*All classes*
England and Wales					
Sep 1939	765,000	426,500	89,000	18,000	1,298,500
Jan 1940	420,000	56,000	43,400	3,380	522,780
Aug 1940	421,000	57,000	27,000	14,000	519,000
Feb 1941	480,500	571,000	25,000	262,200[b]	1,338,700
Sep 1941	435,700	450,000	21,000	157,000	1,063,700
Mar 1942	332,000	279,000	18,000	109,000	738,000
Sep 1942	236,000	196,000	13,000	85,000	530,000
Mar 1943	181,000	148,000	9,000	68,000	406,000
Sep 1943	137,000	124,000	6,400	55,000	322,400
Mar 1944	124,000	132,000	5,400	58,000	319,400
Sep 1944	284,000	601,000	6,800	121,000	1,012,800
Mar 1945	132,000	243,000	4,000	59,000	438,000
Sep 1945	13,250	–	–	–	13,250
Scotland					
Sep 1939	62,000	99,000	13,000	1,000	175,000
Jan 1940	37,600	8,900	3,100	200	49,800
Aug 1940	17,900	7,400	1,600	100	27,000
Feb 1941	11,800	15,700	1,000	1,500	30,000[c]
Sep 1941	25,600	85,000	1,300	29,700	141,600[d]
Mar 1942	18,400	47,400	1,400	13,400	80,600[d]
Jun 1942	13,600	31,500	1,200	8,200	54,500[d]
Dec 1942	9,500	23,000	1,000	6,500	40,000[d]
Jun 1943	7,800	18,800	900	5,500	33,000[d]
Dec 1943	6,000	15,700	700	7,600	30,000[e]
Jun 1944	5,100	15,900	400	6,000	27,400[f]
Apr 1945	1,700	11,200	100	3,200	16,200[g]
Oct 1945	150	3,550	–	1,800	55,000[h]

[a] Includes homeless persons, expectant mothers, children in nurseries, camps and hostels, invalids, old people, the crippled, the blind, civil defence personnel, emergency medical service staff and war workers up to April 1942. The last three groups are excluded thereafter.
[b] Mainly homeless people; including 66,200 such people billeted in evacuation areas.
[c] Includes 11,700 evacuees from English areas billeted in Scotland.
[d] Includes an unknown number of evacuees from English areas billeted in Scotland.
[e] Includes 4300 evacuees from English areas billeted in Scotland.
[f] Includes 5100 evacuees from English areas billeted in Scotland.
[g] Includes 10,600 evacuees from English areas billeted in Scotland.
[h] Includes 850 evacuees from English areas billeted in Scotland.

Source: Titmuss (1950: 562).

However, it is important to remember that more than half the school-age children in these areas remained at home, and many of those who joined the evacuation scheme 'trickled back' within weeks of their departure (PRO ED138/56, Health of the schoolchild 1939: 40).[2] As a result of these difficulties, a large number of children received very little supervision from the school medical service during the first months of the war. In November 1939 the President of the Board of Education, Kenneth Lindsay, told the House of Commons that:

> In neutral areas, where the schools are opening, the school medical service is operating. As I have said before, it is not so easy where there is only a skeleton service – as in the evacuation areas – but they are trying to keep the children clean, and . . . the service is being extended day by day. Some authorities have displayed great resource. Others have been so handicapped by the demands of civil defence, the commandeering of clinics and cleansing stations, and in other ways, that they have neglected this aspect of the problem (House of Commons Debates 1939b: cols 896–7).

Many of the problems faced by the school medical service in the first months of the war reflect the fact that relatively little attention had been given to the maintenance of school medical services before war broke out. It was generally assumed that the outbreak of war would be followed by a large-scale bombing campaign, and the government's main priority was to ensure the safe transfer of as many children as possible from the target areas (PRO ED138/56, Health of the schoolchild 1939: 33). However, once it became apparent that this had not taken place, the Board began to turn its attention to the longer-term problem of how the school medical service was expected to function under war conditions. On 14 December the Board advised local authorities that 'the school health services, which have been built up with so much labour during the last thirty years, and which form so valuable a part of the education system of this country, must not be allowed to lapse because of the stress of the war' (PRO ED138/59, Circular 1490: para. 17). In order to ensure that an adequate standard of provision was maintained, the Board advised all local authorities to allow school medical staff who had been diverted to civil defence duties to resume their original work. Local authorities in evacuation areas were advised to reopen their school clinics, and authorities in reception areas were reminded that evacuated children were entitled to the same standard of medical care as the children who normally resided there (ibid.: paras 2–4, 8).

The Board also issued a questionnaire which invited local authorities to indicate the extent to which they had been able to restore the school medical service to its prewar level (Table 8.2). The responses to this questionnaire were surprisingly encouraging, and in February 1940 one of the Board's officials concluded that 'the position is better than might have been anticipated, and . . . the dislocation of the health services due to the war and the evacuation scheme has in most cases been satisfactorily remedied' (PRO ED50/207, Summary of replies to Circular 1490: para. 2). The same official also observed that

> the difficulties of staffing and premises are less than might have been anticipated; that some provision is as a rule being made for the inspec-

> tion and treatment of children who are not yet attending school; that the routine medical inspection of children attending school is in most cases being conducted normally; that the evacuated children are in nearly all the reception areas participating fully in the local health service; and that the provision of free meals and milk is functioning normally in the great majority of cases (ibid.: para. 7).

However, although these results were undoubtedly reassuring, some difficulties remained. First, it was clear that many of the reception areas possessed insufficient staff to cater fully for the needs of both local and evacuated children; and although the majority of the evacuation areas had made some arrangements for the inspection and treatment of children who were not yet attending school, 'it is not always stated whether an attempt will be made to deal with all such children within the period . . . contemplated by . . . the Circular' (ibid.: paras 3, 5). It is also important to realise that the summary statistics excluded the Education Authority of the London County Council, where the difficulties caused by evacuation were particularly severe.[3] In 1940 Joan Simeon Clarke reported:

> There are long waiting lists for the reduced numbers of nutrition sessions now being held, and for the two remaining aural (nose and throat) centres [*sic*]. Children often have to travel farther than before the War for dental treatment, and children with corrective dental appliances have been unable to have these adjusted at the appropriate intervals. The school medical inspections will not be able to function normally until the children are finally settled in schools in which they will remain. . . . [Although] medical inspections have been held . . . it will be long before the resultant confusion and the uncoordinated advice given . . . at these . . . inspections can be straightened out (Clarke 1940: 207–8; see also Titmuss 1950: 145).

Historians of wartime evacuation have devoted considerable attention to the question of personal uncleanliness (Titmuss 1950: 125–36; Macnicol 1986: 16–18; Welshman 1988: 312–65). In May 1939 the Board warned local authorities to make special efforts for the detection and prevention of contagious diseases, and drew particular attention to the threat posed by scabies, impetigo, ringworm and pediculosis (Board of Education 1939: para. 14). However, in spite of these warnings, the Board failed to anticipate the degree of uncleanliness which would be reported by medical officers in the reception areas. The School Medical Officer for Shrewsbury reported that 31 per cent of the children evacuated to his area had unclean heads, and the School Medical Officer for West Suffolk reported an incidence of 32.49 per cent (PRO ED138/56, Health of the Schoolchild 1939: 35). The School Medical Officer for East Suffolk, where 23 per cent of the evacuees were found to be 'verminous', reported that 'some of the heads were in a terrible condition, and an experienced School Nurse told me that she had never seen such heads in this area since 1920' (Women's Group on Public Welfare 1943: 66).

Table 8.2 The restoration of school medical services in wartime.

Evacuation areas (51 replies from 61 areas)[a]	*Satisfactory*	*Fairly satisfactory*	*Not satisfactory*	*Not applicable as no information given*
Reply to 'staff' question	31	17	3	–
Reply to 'premises' question	40	6	4	1
Reply to question about children not at school	34	11	5	1
Reply to 'RMI' question	24	11	15	1
Reply to continuance of arrangements for free meals and/or milk	41	5	5	–
Reply to milk-in-schools scheme	26	15	9	1
Neutral areas (83 replies from 86 areas)				
Reply to 'staff' question	63	19	1	–
Reply to 'premises' question	71	10	1	1
Reply to question about children not at school	44	5	2	32
Reply to 'RMI' question	75	2	4	2
Reply to continuance of arrangements for free meals and/or milk	74	6	–	3
Reply to milk-in-schools scheme	74	5	–	4
Reception areas (135 replies from 168 areas)[b]				
Reply to 'staff' question	73	55	6	1
Reply to 'premises' question	127	7	–	1
Reply to question about children not at school	23	5	2	105
Reply to 'RMI' question	115	9	9	2
Provision for evacuated children	120	5	1	9
Reply to continuance of arrangements for free meals and/or milk	119	8	2	6
Reply to milk-in-schools scheme	99	31	2	3

[a] In some cases only part of the area was 'zoned' as an evacuation area.

[b] In many county areas part of the area was also 'zoned' as neutral, and in some cases a small part of the area was 'zoned' as an evacuation area.

The 'replies' in this table refer to the following questions (the number allocated to each question in the Board's original questionnaire is given in square brackets). [1] To what extent is the normal medical, dental and nursing staff of the Authority available? [4] To what extent is the operation of the school health services restricted by the use of school clinics or other essential premises for civil defence or other purposes connected with war? [5] What arrangements have been made for the operation of the school health services in the case of children who are not attending school? [6] In the case of children who are attending school, is the routine medical inspection of the prescribed age-groups being carried out? [7] In reception areas, are the services provided for the evacuated children of the same standard and scope as those provided for local children? [8] Is the Authority's provision of free meals and milk for necessitous undernourished local children functioning normally? [9] Is the milk-in-schools scheme functioning normally for the local children who are attending school?

Sources: PRO ED138/59, Circular 1490, Appendix; PRO ED50/207, The school health services in wartime: summary of replies to Circular 1490.

These findings suggested that the incidence of pediculosis was much higher than had been suggested by the Board's prewar medical inspection statistics, and they threatened to undermine the credibility of its screening procedures (Women's Group on Public Welfare 1943: 66–8; Titmuss 1950: 129–31). The Board responded by claiming that the figures were exaggerated because the children had been away from school for a significant period and that many of the evacuees were drawn from homes in which the problem of uncleanliness was particularly severe (PRO ED138/56, The health of the schoolchild 1939: 35). However it was difficult to reconcile this explanation with Professor Kenneth Mellanby's claim that 16.1 per cent of the boys and 35.3 per cent of the girls who were admitted to hospitals in Sheffield were infested with lice or nits (PRO ED50/196, K. Mellanby, 'Suggestions for an investigation on the prevalence of lousiness in Britain', 4/12/39). In February 1940 the Board invited Mellanby to conduct a much larger enquiry into the incidence of pediculosis in seven large cities, five county boroughs, two municipal boroughs, and six rural areas. He concluded that there was 'a very high degree of infestation . . . in the industrial cities', and that the incidence of louse infestation in these areas was substantially higher than the figures reported in the Reports of the local school medical medical officers (PRO ED50/196, Board of Education Circular 1544: 1–2; Mellanby 1941; 1943).[4]

In addition to the problem of pediculosis, school medical officers were also required to devote attention to the problems of ringworm and scabies. The incidence of scabies had been increasing in many areas before the war, but it rose substantially between 1939 and 1942. There was also a sharp increase in the incidence of ringworm, although this was more apparent in some areas than in others (Ministry of Education 1947a: 37–40).[5] The reason for these increases is not entirely clear, but it seems likely that the population movements associated with evacuation played a significant role. In one case, a group of children contracted scabies after being evacuated to a seaside town and placed in billets which had previously been occupied by holidaymakers. The householders had not had sufficient time to change the bedclothes, and this 'interesting example . . . of "reverse lend-lease"' led to a marked increase in the incidence of the disease when the children returned to their home districts (PRO ED58/138, Evacuation: para. 12).

Although historians have drawn considerable attention to the impact of evacuation on contagious diseases, they have devoted less attention to its impact on the incidence of infectious diseases. Before the war broke out, many observers predicted that the introduction of evacuation would lead to increased rates of infection among both the host and evacuee populations. the *Medical Officer* argued that there was 'a definite danger of serious disturbance of the epidemiological balance of the districts into which . . . [the] town-dwellers are introduced', and the Medical Officer of Health for Lambeth predicted an increase in diarrhoea and enteric disorders among the evacuees (*Medical Officer* 1939a; Thompson 1939; Forrest 1939; see also *Lancet* 1939). However, these fears proved to be largely though not entirely unfounded. In 1941 Percy Stocks concluded that the notification rates for diphtheria and scarlet fever had declined in evacuation areas and remained roughly unchanged for evacuated children in reception areas. Nevertheless, there was a significant though short-lived increase in the notification rates for both diseases among children who were normally resident in the reception areas (Stocks 1941; 1942; see also Glover 1940).

The introduction of evacuation also had important implications for the development of child guidance services. When the government drew up its evacuation plans, it made arrangements for the provision of a small number of hostels for 'difficult' or 'maladjusted' children who could not be placed with host families. However, it soon became apparent that the number of children who required such places – for whatever reason – was much greater than had originally been supposed, and this led to a substantial increase in the number of hostels provided (Welshman 1988: 360–61).[5] The demand for hostel places helped to focus attention on the more general question of child guidance. The number of local authorities providing child guidance clinics rose from twenty-two in 1939 to sixty-two in 1942 and to seventy-nine in 1945. In 1946 sixty-six local authorities provided their own clinics, and forty-nine authorities used clinics provided by voluntary bodies and other local education authorities (Ministry of Education 1947a: 66; Ministry of Education 1958: 146).[6]

School medical provision in wartime

The problems associated with evacuation dominated the attention of the school medical service during the first months of the war, but the main challenge was posed not by evacuation, but by the more general demands of the war itself. As the war progressed, the Board of Education was able to maintain and even increase the amount of money devoted to the special services, but it experienced rather more problems in maintaining both the number and the quality of school medical staff. As a result of these difficulties, the Board was forced to accept a number of modifications in school medical practice.

The best guide to expenditure on the school medical service is provided by the Memoranda on the Education Estimates which were published by the Board (and subsequently the Ministry) of Education between 1939 and 1946, but the figures are not entirely comparable with those produced elsewhere in this book for earlier years. In the first place, the estimates relate to calendar years rather than financial years; secondly, the figures for some years are limited to expenditure on special services as a whole; and thirdly, the basis of calculation changed towards the end of the war as a result of the changes introduced under the 1944 Education Act. Nevertheless, the figures show that there was a small but significant increase in the expenditure on medical inspection and treatment and on the provision of special schools, and a much larger increase in expenditure on the provision of school milk and meals. Expenditure on the provision of medical inspection and treatment in both elementary and secondary schools increased by 47 per cent (in money terms) between 1942 and 1945, and expenditure on the special services as a whole increased by 140 per cent between 1939 and 1944 (Table 8.3).[7]

It is also difficult to produce reliable estimates of the number of people employed by the school medical service during the war. In 1938 the school medical service employed the equivalent of 728 full-time school medical officers, and by the end of 1940 this figure had increased to 750, but these figures do not represent any real increase in efficiency. The Board itself admitted that a large proportion of school medical officers and assistant school medical officers now devoted a greater part of their time to other services; that a substantial number of officers had remained in evacuation areas even though the majority of their children had been evacuated; and that the number of officers in the reception areas was too low to cater for local needs (PRO ED138/56, Memorandum by the Board of Education on the school health services: para. 13). As the war progressed, moreover, the

Table 8.3 Local education authorities' expenditure on special services, 1939–45 (£ thousands).

	Medical inspection and treatment	*Special schools*	*Physical training*	*Evening play-centres*	*Nursery schools*	*Provision of milk and meals*	*Total*
Expenditure on the special services of elementary education[a]							
1939	n/a	n/a	n/a	n/a	n/a	n/a	5,790
1940	n/a	n/a	n/a	n/a	n/a	n/a	5,822
1941	n/a	n/a	n/a	n/a	n/a	n/a	6,709
1942[b]	n/a	n/a	n/a	n/a	n/a	n/a	8,993
1943[c]	n/a	n/a	n/a	n/a	n/a	n/a	10,650
1944[c]	n/a	n/a	n/a	n/a	n/a	n/a	13,900
Expenditure on selected educational services[d]							
1942[e]	2,898	1,854	n/a	n/a	n/a	3,716	n/a
1943[f]	3,033	2,011	n/a	n/a	n/a	6,161	n/a
1944[f]	3,338	2,124	n/a	n/a	n/a	9,178	n/a
1945[g]	4,250	2,250	n/a	n/a	n/a	11,620	n/a

[a] Pre-1944 basis.
[b] Provisional figure derived from 1944 estimates.
[c] Estimate derived from 1944 estimates.
[d] Figures based on the revised classification of schools under the Education Act 1944.
[e] Provisional figure derived from 1945 estimates.
[f] Provisional figure derived from 1946 estimates.
[g] Estimate (including supplementary estimates) derived from 1946 estimates.

Sources: PP 1941–2 Cmd. 6343 vii: 6; PP 1942–3 Cmd. 6429 ix: 6; PP 1943–4 Cmd. 6508 vii: 6; PP 1944–5 Cmd. 6581 ix: 6; PP 1945–6 Cmd. 6629 xx: 6.

number of school medical staff showed a definite decline. Between 1940 and 1945 an increasing number of medical personnel were called up for military service, and the total number of officers employed by the school medical service fell accordingly (see Table 8.4).[8]

During the period between 1939 and 1945, the Board issued a series of memoranda setting out procedures for releasing school medical officers for the armed forces and the measures which should be taken to compensate for this. During the early stages of the war, both doctors and dentists were included in the list of reserved occupations whose members were excused from compulsory military service, but the government was obliged to remove these exemptions in May 1940 (Supplement to the *British Medical Journal* 1940a; 1940b). In March 1941 the government invited all local authorities to consider the release of medical staff 'in the light of the circumstances of [their] . . . area[s]', and in April 1942 it announced that 'public health services, including school medical services, are to release further doctors . . . for the services' (Supplement to the *British Medical Journal* 1941; 1942). One of the main problems was the impossibility of ensuring that equal numbers of medical officers were recruited from different areas. Some local education authorities lost half or even two-thirds of their medical personnel,

Table 8.4 Medical and nursing staff in schools, 1938–45.

	1938	*1944*	*1945*[a]
Whole-time SMOs	6	6	4
Part-time SMOs	309	298	143
Total SMOs	315	304	147
Whole-time ASMOs	260	192	179
Part-time ASMOs	943	769	818
Total ASMOs	1203	961	997
Total school nurses	3313	3112	3024
Whole-time equivalent school nurses	2195.3	1916.0	1822.2
Total district nurses	2118	1871	2113
Whole-time equivalent district nurses	n/a	350.0	307.0
Total nursing attendants	n/a	148	145
Whole-time equivalent nursing attendants	n/a	127.5	127.7
Whole-time dental officers	425	325	317
Part-time dental officers	584	495	408
Total dental officers	1009	820	725
Toatal dental attendants	563	681	659
Whole-time equivalent dental attendants	512.5	615.3	595.4

[a]Under the Education Act 1944, the Part III local education authorities were abolished, thus reducing the number of senior school medical officers from 315 to 147.

Source: Ministry of Education (1947a: 140–41).

while other areas, whose medical officers were above military age, were largely unscathed (Ministry of Education 1947a: 33–45).

The growing demand for medical personnel forced the Board of Education to issue a series of guidelines governing the conduct of school medical services in wartime. In August 1940 the Board issued Circular 1523, which urged local authorities to make every effort to maintain a complete school medical service, and advised adjacent authorities to pool their staffs if there were any shortages. If this proved impossible, the Board said that all children should be inspected as soon as possible after they first entered school, and that school medical officers should carry out 'rapid surveys' of selected children at least once a term (PRO ED138/56, Circular 1523, para. 4). In July 1941 the Board advised local education authorities to consider 'whether the surveys . . . now conducted by Medical Officers might not be undertaken by School Nurses . . . and whether less highly-trained staff might not be more widely employed . . . in connection with surveys for the detection of lice' (PRO ED138/56, Circular 1559, para. 3). In August 1942 it said that 'School Medical Officers should examine all the children on or as soon as possible after their admission to school' and 'in the last year of school life'. In order to facilitate the retention of these examinations, it recommended that 'the inspection of the intermediate age group should be discontinued' (Board of Education 1942, para. 2).

We can gain some insight into the impact of these changes on the work of the school medical service from Table 8.5, which shows the number of children who were inspected or treated by the school medical service between 1938 and 1945. The table suggests that despite the advice contained in these Circulars, a large number of local education authorities continued to inspect children in all three age groups throughout the war, although there was a decline in the numbers inspected between 1942 and 1945.[9] The majority of local education authorities also succeeded in maintaining provision for the treatment of minor ailments, although there was a decline in the number of children receiving treatment for visual and dental defects, and for defects of the nose and throat. On the other hand, the war years witnessed an increase in the provision of child guidance clinics and – more surprisingly – in the development of speech therapy (PRO ED138/58, Evacuation: para. 21).

The maintenance of an adequate school dental service was a source of particular difficulty throughout the war years. One of the main problems was that the average age of school dentists was comparatively low, and this meant that a high proportion of dental officers were recruited by the armed forces (Ministry of Education 1947a: 45). The Board tried to rectify this situation by urging local authorities to make greater use of private practitioners and to impose stricter guidelines on the provision of services. In August 1940 the Board advised local authorities that conservative dentistry should be limited to 'the children of parents who have already shown their appreciation of conservative treatment', and that 'the treatment of children whose parents have failed to take advantage of past opportunities should . . . be limited to

Table 8.5 Children inspected and treated in public elementary schools in England and Wales, 1938–45 (thousands).[a]

	1938	*1939*	*1940*	*1941*	*1942*	*1943*	*1944*	*1945*
Medical inspection and treatment								
Children inspected in routine medical inspections[b]	1677	1294	1595	1599	1619	1335	1297	1322
Special inspections and reinspections[c]	3746	3050	2922	2835	3046	2868	2725	2268
Defects treated or under treatment								
Minor ailments	1121	987	968	1189	1238	1304	1269	1124
Defective vision or squint	285	241	238	241	248	248	242	233
Defects of nose or throat	142	105	75	72	90	97	89	86
Dental inspection and treatment								
Children inspected[b]	3531	3040	3224	3195	3324	3220	3177	2751
Children found to require treatment	2498	2123	2251	2256	2131	1966	1862	1615
Children treated	1635	1431	1431	1420	1414	1310	1239	1093

[a] Including all maintained and assisted schools from 1/4/45.
[b] No child is included more than once in the figures for any one year.
[c] The same child may be included more than once in any one year.

Source: Central Statistical Office (1948: Table 95).

extractions' (PRO ED138/56, Circular 1523: paras 6–9). It also recommended that treatment sessions should be extended from two-and-a-half to three hours, and that sessions should be held on Saturday mornings as well as during school holidays (ibid.: paras 5–6). However, in spite of these measures, the service continued to struggle. The number of children inspected, which had been inadequate before the war, fell by 22.1 per cent between 1938 and 1945, and the number of children treated fell by 33.1 per cent (Table 8.5; see also PP 1943–4 Cmd. 6565 iii, paras 43–7).

The provision of school meals and milk

In 1950 Richard Titmuss argued that the Second World War witnessed a fundamental change in attitudes to social policy. The evacuation of mothers and children, the retreat from Dunkirk, and the shared horrors of the Blitz reinforced 'the war-warmed impulse of people for a more generous society' and moved forward the goals of welfare provision (Titmuss 1950: 507–8). However, other historians have claimed that Titmuss exaggerated the war's impact and misrepresented the nature of the changes which occurred. In

1986 John Macnicol concluded that the initial wave of evacuation only served to reinforce traditional social attitudes and that 'the ideological consensus of wartime, so stressed by Titmuss and some historians, was something of a myth' (Macnicol 1986: 27–8).

The history of the school meals service provides an interesting focus for these debates. Titmuss almost certainly exaggerated the role played by humanitarian 'generosity' in the development of the service, but we should not ignore the significance of the changes which took place (see also Burnett 1994: 55). During the early stages of the war, the government's main concern was to ensure that there was an adequate supply of 'paying' meals to evacuated children in reception areas, but it subsequently decided to make the provision of both free and paying meals to all children an essential part of its military strategy (Board of Education 1939: para. 17; PRO ED138/59, Circular 1520: para. 1).[10] This consideration was reinforced by the need to supply school meals to children whose mothers were employed in war-related industries (PRO ED138/59, Circular 1567: para. 1). The cumulative impact of these developments represented a major change in the state's attitude to school feeding. As the editor of *Public Health* observed in November 1941:

> The new 'push' for school feeding, recently announced by the President of the Board of Education and, in an expanded statement, by the Minister of Food, is really a national effort to overcome the deficit of the coupon. It can only be a partial measure because there are other members of the community . . . who [also] have special needs. . . . [However,] the statement shows the determination of the Government to ensure an approved meal for the schoolchildren . . . and neither in the Lords nor the Commons was a word said about the delegation of parental responsibility (*Public Health* 1941b).[11]

The statistical history of the provision of school meals in wartime is summarised in Tables 8.6 and 8.7.[12] The tables show that we can divide the wartime history of the school meals service into four main periods. During the first nine months of the war, relatively little attention was devoted to school meals, and the number of elementary schoolchildren receiving meals actually declined. There was a slow increase in the number of meals provided between July 1940 and October 1941, but the vast majority of children continued to take dinners elsewhere. The first major expansion in the coverage of the school meals service occurred between October 1941 and May 1943, and this culminated in the provision of school meals to more than 20 per cent of elementary schoolchildren and more than 47 per cent of secondary schoolchildren by the Spring of 1943. The school meals service continued to expand after this period, and by the end of the War more than one-third of elementary schoolchildren and approximately half of all secondary schoolchildren were receiving school dinners (Tables 8.6 and 8.7).[13]

When the government drew up its initial plans for the maintenance of the school meals scheme, it concentrated its attention on the provision of meals to evacuees. It said that local authorities in reception areas should consider

Table 8.6 Numbers of children receiving school meals in England and Wales and Scotland, 1939–45.

	England and Wales				*Scotland*	
	Number of dinners[a]		*% of numbers present receiving dinners*		*Number of children receiving meals*[b]	
	Primary	*Secondary*	*Primary*	*Secondary*	*Number*	*% of school population*
1938/39	150,000	n/a	4.4	n/a	90,900[c]	n/a
1939/40	n/a	n/a	n/a	n/a	85,625[d]	n/a
1940/41	n/a	n/a	n/a	n/a	104,185[e]	n/a
Jun 1940	n/a	n/a	2.7	n/a	n/a	n/a
Jul 1940	130,000	n/a	3.5	n/a	n/a	n/a
Feb 1941	179,000	100,000	4.3	n/a	n/a	n/a
May 1941	n/a	n/a	5.1	n/a	n/a	n/a
Oct 1941	289,000	128,000[f]	6.9	n/a	n/a	n/a
Dec 1941	377,000	n/a	8.9	n/a	50,000	n/a
Feb 1942	447,000	160,000	11.5	37.2	82,850	11.1
May 1942	n/a	n/a	12.8	n/a	84,940	n/a
Oct 1942	660,000	183,000	16.3	45.0	106,930	n/a
Feb 1943[g]	809,000	217,000	20.7	47.0	144,510	19.3
May 1943	n/a	n/a	22.4	n/a	n/a	n/a
Oct 1943	1,077,000	230,000	26.5	53.4	159,420	n/a
Feb 1944[h]	1,202,000	265,000	30.1	53.8	191,480	25.5
Jun 1944	1,258,000	n/a	30.7	n/a	n/a	n/a
Oct 1944	1,245,000	250,000	31.2	56.0	n/a	n/a
Feb 1945[i]	1,329,000	291,000	33.8	55.6	201,490	26.7
Jun 1945[j]	1,186,000	498,000	34.4	46.3	n/a	n/a
Oct 1945[k]	1,209,000	616,000	35.9	49.4	n/a	n/a

[a] Excluding dinners served to boarders.
[b] The term 'meal' includes dinners, lunches and soup meals. The figures for 1938/39, 1939/40 and 1940/41 refer to the numbers of children who received meals regularly during the years ending 31/7/39, 31/7/40 and 31/7/41, and are not directly comparable with the figures for the remaining years, which refer to the number of children fed on a particular day.
[c] 51,000 children paid for the meals and 39,900 children received free meals.
[d] 40,310 children received 'solid' meals and 45,315 children received 'light' meals.
[e] 47,270 children received 'solid' meals and 56,915 children received 'light' meals.
[f] In February 1942 one of the Board's officials estimated that the number of secondary schoolchildren receiving school dinners in October 1941 was 145,000 (PRO ED136/662, S. Goodfellow to D. Serpell, 27/2/42).
[g] The total number of dinners supplied in England and Wales also included 22,000 dinners in junior technical schools.
[h] The total number of dinners supplied in England and Wales also included 28,000 dinners in junior technical schools.
[i] The total number of dinners supplied in England and Wales also included 30,000 dinners in junior technical schools.
[j] The total number of dinners supplied in England and Wales also included 10,000 dinners in junior technical schools and 6,000 dinners in nursery schools.
[k] The total number of dinners supplied in England and Wales also included 8,000 dinners in junior technical schools and 7,000 dinners in nursery schools.

Sources: PRO ED136/662, Miscellaneous papers showing numbers of breakfasts, dinners and teas, and bottles of milk, consumed in public elementary schools in England and Wales between December 1941 and February 1945; PRO ED138/59, J.E. Brown, 23/3/48; Central Statistical Office (1948: Table 94); Clark (1948: 21, 25); PP 1940–1 Cmd. 6317 iv: 18; PP 1941–2 Cmd. 6370 iv: 12–13; PP 1942–3 Cmd. 6452 iv: 9–10; PP 1943–4 Cmd. 6540 iii: 8–9; PP 1945–6 Cmd. 6667 xi: 8–9.

Table 8.7 Numbers of children receiving milk at school in England and Wales and Scotland, 1939–45.

	England and Wales				*Scotland*	
	Number of children receiving milk[a]		*% of numbers present receiving milk*		*Number of children receiving milk*	
	Primary	*Secondary*	*Primary*	*Secondary*	*Number*	*% of school population*
1938/39	2,500,000	n/a	55.0	n/a	n/a	n/a
Mar 1939	n/a	n/a	n/a	n/a	362,000	46.9
Oct 1939	2,748,000	n/a	55.6	n/a	n/a	n/a
Jan 1940	n/a	n/a	n/a	n/a	186,000	n/a
Jul 1940	2,100,000	n/a	n/a	n/a	n/a	n/a
Oct 1940	2,022,000	n/a	50.1	n/a	361,000	n/a
Feb 1941	2,239,000	240,000	n/a	n/a	n/a	n/a
Apr 1941	n/a	n/a	n/a	n/a	415,000	56.1
Oct 1941	2,994,000	217,000[b]	n/a	n/a	458,000	61.0
Feb 1942	3,115,000	271,000	79.8	61.0	n/a	66.6
Oct 1942	3,089,000	245,000	76.5	59.3	510,000	67.4
Feb 1943	3,086,000	285,000	78.9	59.8	506,000	67.4
Oct 1943	3,100,000	262,000	76.4	59.9	513,500	67.6
Feb 1944	3,122,000	306,000	78.3	60.2	520,000	68.8
Oct 1944	3,036,000	264,000	76.0	58.4	n/a	n/a
Feb 1945	2,955,000	310,000	75.1	57.5	501,000	66.1
Jun 1945	2,566,000	615,000[c]	74.5	56.6	n/a	n/a
Oct 1945	2,591,000	724,000[c]	77.0	57.4	n/a	n/a

[a] Including milk supplied to boarders.
[b] In February 1942 one of the Board's officials estimated that the number of secondary schoolchildren receiving milk in October 1941 was 261,000. See PRO ED136/662, Goodfellow to Serpell, 27/2/42.
[c] The increase in the figures for secondary schools from June 1945 onwards is accounted for mainly by the reclassification of schools as secondary under the Education Act 1944.

Sources: PRO ED138/59, J.E. Brown, 23/3/48; Central Statistical Office (1948: Table 94); PP 1940–1 Cmd. 6317 iv: 18; PP 1941–2 Cmd. 6370 iv: 12–13; PP 1942–3 Cmd. 6452 iv: 9–10; PP 1943–4 Cmd. 6540 iii: 8–9; PP 1945–6 Cmd. 6667 xi: 8–9.

the provision of 'paying' meals because this would relieve local householders of some of their domestic responsibilities, but denied that there would be any need to expand the provision of free meals because the host families received a billeting allowance of between 8s. 6d. and 10s. 6d. per week to provide full board and lodging (Board of Education 1939: para. 17). The Board repeated this advice in Circulars 1475 and 1484, which were issued on 31 August and 21 November, respectively (PRO ED138/59, Circulars 1475, 1484). On 14 December the Board reminded all local authorities of the need to carry out regular nutrition surveys, and urged local authorities in evacuation areas to make every effort to maintain their school meals service, despite the problems caused by school closure (PRO ED138/59, Circular 1490: paras 6, 9–12).

The first major step towards the development of an expanded school meals service came with the publication of Circular 1520 in July 1940. The Board acknowledged that 'the provision, which was insufficient before the war, is now even less adequate', and urged all local authorities 'to survey the position in their areas and to consider as a matter of urgency what increase of provision is required' (PRO ED138/59, Circular 1520, para. 2). It also announced that local authorities which provided school meals would receive a minimum grant of 50 per cent, and that the grants paid to authorities which currently received grants in excess of 30 per cent would be increased by a further 20 per cent (ibid., para. 14). In December the Board announced an important symbolic change in the arrangements for the provision of free meals to necessitous children. It abolished the traditional distinction between feeding centres and school canteens, and declared that 'in future all these types of provision will be known officially as school canteens' (PRO ED138/59, Administrative Memorandum no. 267).[14]

The Board announced a further change in the administration of the school meals scheme in October 1941. It said that the rate of grant in respect of expenditure on the provision of school meals would be increased by a further 10 per cent (up to a maximum of 95 per cent), and that the minimum grant would be increased to 70 per cent. It also introduced a number of new measures which were designed to increase the nutritional value of school meals and to enable school canteens to take advantage of the services provided by the Ministry of Food's cooking depots (see Hammond 1956: 421–3). In an ironic echo of the language used by its critics in the 1930s, it abandoned its earlier policy of insisting on proof of both necessitousness and malnutrition as criteria for the provision of free meals. It stated that 'since the aim of these proposals is to maintain a high standard of nutrition and to prevent malnutrition, rather than to remedy it after symptoms have appeared, Authorities may in future base their provision of free milk and free or part-payment meals solely on evidence of financial need' (PRO ED138/59, Circular 1567: paras 1, 2, 9).[15]

The final phase in the development of the school meals service was initiated by the publication of Circular 1629 in May 1943. The Board declared that ' it will not be possible to hold that schoolchildren have been made as secure as . . . possible . . . against nutritional dangers . . . until the majority of them are able to have a hot mid-day meal at school', and that 'the Government's objective will not be reached until school meals are available for . . . 75 per cent of the children' (PRO ED138/59, Circular 1629: paras 1–2). In order to achieve this target, the government announced a series of measures which were designed to ensure the fullest possible cooperation between local education authorities and the Ministry of Works in the construction and equipment of school canteens (ibid.: paras 3–10). It also recognised that the continued expansion of the school meals service was closely related to the value of the meals provided. It therefore reminded authorities of the need to maintain food quality and expressed the hope 'that the provision of dinners which . . . are seriously unsatisfactory may soon be looked upon as a thing of the past' (ibid.: para. 11).

In addition to an expansion in the provision of school meals, the war also witnessed a parallel growth in the provision of school milk. This service had grown rapidly during the second half of the 1930s as a result of the milk-in-schools scheme, but its growth was halted by the outbreak of war. The immediate cause of this cessation of growth was the dislocation resulting from evacuation, but it soon became apparent that many dairy producers were reluctant to supply milk at reduced prices when they could sell it more freely on the open market. In February 1941 the President of the Board of Education, Herwald Ramsbotham, persuaded the Treasury to increase the price paid to the producers, and the number of children taking milk rose rapidly. By the end of 1941, more than 75 per cent of children were taking milk at school, and this figure was maintained throughout the remainder of the war (Table 8.7; Gosden 1976: 201–4).

One of the most important issues facing the school meals service was the question of food quality. During the early stages of the war, the Board's main concern had been to ensure that school meals were 'off the ration', and it had therefore acquiesced in the introduction of food allowances which meant that the nutritional value of school meals fell below prewar levels (PRO ED136/662, E.D. Marris, 'Lord Woolton's letter to Ernest Brown', 5/4/42: para. 6). However, it soon became apparent that such a situation was incompatible with a policy of increasing school meals provision. Following the publication of Circular 1567 in October 1941, the Board urged 'that as a general rule school dinners should be planned to provide per child energy value amounting to 1000 calories, first class protein amounting to 20 to 25 grams and fat in all forms amounting to 30 grams'. In order to achieve these targets, the allowances of meat and sugar were doubled, the allowance of jam was almost doubled, and a special allowance of cooking milk was introduced (PRO ED138/60, Marris, 'War history of school meals and milk': paras 39–51). School canteens were also given special assistance to obtain cocoa powder, starch food powders, rice, suet, pulses and oatmeal, together with dried fruits, processed eggs and certain canned foods (Gosden 1976: 196–9).[16]

War and reconstruction

Towards the end of 1940, the Principal Assistant Secretary of the Board of Education's Teacher Training Branch, S.H. Wood, wrote to a number of his colleagues to suggest 'that some of the Board's officials should be authorised to make a cooperative and continuing study of the educational problems which may arise when the war is over' (PRO ED136/212, S.H. Wood, 'Educational reconstruction', n.d.). Wood's proposal was taken up by the Permanent Secretary, Maurice Holmes, and the first meeting of the Board's 'Office Committee' took place on 9 November (PRO ED136/212, M. Holmes, 'Post-war educational reconstruction', 5/11/40). On 17 January 1941 the Board's Deputy Secretary, R.S. Wood, summarised the progress which the Committee had made over the previous two months:

> While policy will have to command the support of the main elements in all parties, it is clear that the War is moving us in the direction of Labour's ideas and ideals, and the planning for a new 'national order' will be more towards the left than may generally be imagined now. . . . In these circumstances, it is clear that it will be fatal for officials to formulate their ideas in any spirit of timidity: we must 'dare boldly' in a fair cause. . . . Planning on bold and generous lines is what is looked for, and it may well be necessary to free our minds from conceptions that from long familiarity seem almost sacred and immutable: in short, to think in new terms for new times (PRO ED136/212, R.S. Wood, 'Policy and planning for postwar reconstruction', 17/1/41: para. 3).

Although many of the most heated debates concentrated inevitably on the broad principles of educational reform, the Board was also anxious to consider the impact of war and educational reconstruction on the school medical service, and this sense was reflected within the Medical Department itself. In May 1941 J.E. Underwood wrote to the new Chief Medical Officer, Sir Wilson Jameson, to suggest the appointment of a small informal committee of school medical officers 'to consult with the Medical Branch of the Board on medical problems connected with Special Services (school medical service, special schools, provision of meals etc.)'. He suggested that such a committee could play an invaluable role in advising the Board on the day-to-day administration of the school medical service in wartime, and on its reconstruction after the war was over. He concluded:

> It is no exaggeration to say that in some areas the school medical service is in the melting pot. After the war it will have to be reconstructed, though not necessarily on the same plan as it was founded. For example, it may be desirable to revise the system of routine medical inspection; to extend the scope of treatment, particularly specialist treatment; to extend the school medical service to children under five. All this will have to be carefully considered and a policy formulated which can be applied as soon as the period of reconstruction begins. . . . We want help and advice immediately on the organisation of special services in wartime and on the policy of reconstruction after it. We shall want it in the future when the medical services of the country generally may undergo profound reorganisation (PRO ED50/192, Underwood to Chief Medical Officer, 1/5/41).

The Board's initial proposals for the reform of the school medical service were drafted by the Principal Assistant Secretary of the Medical Branch, N.D.

Bosworth-Smith, at the beginning of 1941, and a final draft was agreed by the Office Committee towards the middle of May (PRO ED50/192, 'The health and physical well-being of the schoolchild').[17] Although the war created the circumstances in which they were prepared, the proposals reflected many of the debates which had taken place within and around the school medical service over the previous thirty years. In the first place, the Board proposed that the provision of medical inspection was 'more or less adequately covered', and that the main question was whether it would be desirable to modify the ages at which routine medical inspections took place in the light of changes which were being proposed elsewhere in the education system.[18] The Board also raised the question of 'whether more of the routine supervision of children might not be left to school nurses, the medical staff being used among other things for more detailed forms of inspection than can be practised under present arrangements' (PRO ED50/192, 'The health and physical well-being of the schoolchild': para. 67).

The Board's other suggestions concerned the future provision of medical treatment and the care and supervision of children between the ages of two and five. The Board said that although provision for medical treatment was made by all local education authorities, the standard of provision was far from even and there were 'wide disparities' in the scope of the services which different authorities offered. In order to rectify these difficulties, it proposed that the duty to provide medical treatment should be extended to cover both elementary and secondary education, and that the scope of the services provided by local authorities should be more clearly defined (ibid.: para. 68). The Board also argued that one of the main problems faced by the school medical service during the interwar years was the absence of a complete medical service for children between the ages of two and five years. It therefore proposed that the responsibilities of the maternity and child welfare service should be limited to children under the age of two, and that the Board of Education should assume responsibility for the medical care of all children from the age of two onwards (ibid.: para. 69).

These proposals were circulated confidentially to a number of interested parties, including the members of the Board's Consultative Committee, in the summer of 1941.[19] The majority of the Board's respondents welcomed the proposals, but there were some disagreements. The Workers' Educational Association (WEA) thought that there should be a minimum of five medical inspections, and both the WEA and the Association of Municipal Corporations expressed concern about the suggestion that more of the 'routine' work of the school medical service might be discharged by school nurses (PRO ED136/218, Green Book Discussions: WEA: 6; ED136/243, Green Book Discussions: Association of Municipal Corporations: para. 16). The most controversial proposal concerned the suggestion that local education authorities should assume complete responsibility for the medical care and supervision of two- to five-year-olds. This proposal was strongly supported by the main educational organisations and vigorously opposed by the Society of Medical Officers of Health (PRO ED136/218, Green Book Discussions: Association of Directors and Secretaries: 6; ED136/243, Association of Education Committees). The Society argued that 'the reasons given in support of the suggestion . . . were unsound' and that it would reinforce the separation of the school medical service from the rest of the public health service (PRO ED136/243, Green Book Discussions: Society of Medical Officers of Health: 1).[20]

The disputes over the division of responsibility for the care of pre-school children played a central role in discussions about the way in which the Board expected local education authorities to discharge their responsibility to secure the provision of medical treatment. When the Board drew up its proposals, it suggested that the duties of local education authorities should be extended to include the treatment of both elementary and secondary schoolchildren and that the scope of medical treatment should be more precisely defined, but it made no attempt to link these proposals to the broader question of a national health service (see Webster 1988: 24–34). In October 1942 Bosworth-Smith complained that 'the Green Book had been written long before any announcement of the Minister of Health's hospital policy and could not therefore take [it] into account' (PRO ED136/243, Green Book Discussions: Society of Medical Officers of Health: 2). Nevertheless, the absence of any reference to health service reform was a major weakness in the Board's proposals, because there was a clear risk of overlap between an expanded school medical service and a comprehensive national health service for the population as a whole (ibid.: 1).

These issues were discussed by the Board and the Ministry of Health in February 1943. The Board agreed that local education authorities would continue to make arrangements for the medical inspection of both elementary and secondary schoolchildren, and that they would also make arrangements for medical treatment. However the Board also agreed that local authorities should make the maximum possible use of existing facilities and that their direct responsibility for the provision of medical services would be transferred to the National Health Service at a later date (PRO ED136/378, Bosworth-Smith, 'Notes on conclusions reached at a discussion . . . between officers of the Board and the Ministry of Health', 17/2/43; Bosworth-Smith to Dawes, 17/2/43). These conclusions were restated in the White Paper on Educational Reconstruction and the White Paper on the National Health Service. The White Paper on Educational Reconstruction stated that:

> The setting up of a comprehensive National Health Service will eventually ensure that all forms of treatment which schoolchildren require will be available for them through that service. When this stage is reached it will no longer be necessary for Local Education Authorities to provide treatment and their functions will be confined to providing medical inspection and seeing that the children and parents are properly advised and encouraged to seek . . . any treatment the children may need (PP 1942–3 Cmd. 6458 xi: para. 94).[21]

The Board's decision to separate the medical inspection of schoolchildren from medical treatment provoked a number of criticisms. The MP for Islington North, Dr Haden Guest, complained that

> the great picture of an extended and improved educational system . . . is an inspiring one, but its physical basis must be a well-nourished, well-cared for and well-developed body, and on that side of education the school medical service of inspection and . . . treatment is an essential part of the machinery of education under the control of the education authority (Guest 1943).

The editor of the *Medical Officer* claimed that 'the separation of examination and diagnosis from the dispensing of treatment would largely destroy medical interest and enterprise, and greatly limit the benefit . . . which the two services, combined under the same personnel, would effect' (*Medical Officer* 1943). However, the proposal also won the support of many individual school medical officers. The Deputy County Medical Officer for Devonshire, Dr F.J.G. Lishman, said that the separation of inspection and treatment was a small price to pay for the establishment of an integrated national health service, and that it would

> open the door to the development of an entirely new type of school medical service . . . in which the medical personnel would become real specialists, not only in their own eyes, but also in those of the medical and teaching professions as a whole (Lishman 1944: 35).

In addition to these issues, which concerned the overall framework of school medical provision, the Board also held discussions on the future staffing of the school medical service and the organisation and development of routine medical inspection. During the war, a number of observers suggested that the time had come to expand the employment of specialist paediatricians within the school medical service. Dr F. Hall argued that 'child welfare centres and school clinics are staffed, or should be staffed, by expert paediatricians assisted by highly-qualified trained nurses' (Hall 1941: 38) and Dr J.L. Newman claimed that 'the Diploma in Public Health is almost entirely useless as a qualification for [school medical] work, and could with advantage be replaced by a Diploma of Child Health, provided this was not made a requirement for entry' (Newman 1944: 141). The Chief Medical Officer of the Board of Education, Sir Wilson Jameson, said that he was 'in favour of the employment of young paediatricians for routine medical examinations' and that there had been 'a change of heart among paediatricians and that they were anxious to become guardians of children's health rather than doctors of sick children' (PRO ED50/192, Consultative Committee of School Medical Officers [second meeting], 25/2/42). In 1944 the Board's Senior Medical Officer, J.E. Underwood, said that 'paediatricians were obviously becoming interested in children's health as well as their diseases [and] the problem was how best to use paediatricians in school and child welfare work' (PRO ED50/192, Consultative Committee of School Medical Officers [fourth meeting], 19/1/43).

The Board also held a number of discussions with school medical officers and other groups concerning the future of routine medical inspection. This question had been brought to a head not only by the suggestion in the Green Book, but also by the need to make more efficient use of medical staff time during the war. In 1942 the Chief Medical Officer said that he did not believe that the routine medical examination 'was very valuable from a strictly medical point of view', and that 'the actual inspection could be done almost as well by a nurse' (PRO ED50/192, Consultative Committee of School Medical Officers [second meeting], 25/2/42). However, this view was not shared by the majority of practising school medical officers. The School Medical Officer for Portsmouth, Ernest Roberts, said that even though there may be changes in the frequency and scope of routine medical inspection, 'the school medical service has done pioneer work in establishing the importance of a procedure which will certainly become an essential feature of the future State medical service' (PRO ED50/213, T.E. Roberts, 'The future of the school medical service': 4). The Assistant School Medical Officer for Birmingham, Dr Edgar Wilkins, said that:

> The school medical service is unique in periodically examining *all* children, and in this it is a model in preventive medicine. But only when ideals of human health and physique are inculcated in our medical schools and the possibilities of health teaching more fully explored and applied, will the periodic medical examination attain anything like its full potential of social usefulness (Wilkins 1943).[22]

The impact of the war on child health

One of the clearest indications of the way in which the war focused attention on the importance of public and child health was the large number of investigations undertaken by the Ministry of Health and the Board of Education, in conjunction with other government departments, to monitor the health of the population. Towards the end of 1940, the Ministry of Food and the Ministry of Health initiated a regular programme of food monitoring to investigate changes in family diets (Bransby 1946a). In 1942 the Ministry of Health began to carry out systematic surveys of the nutritional status of different sections of the population, and in 1943 the Medical Research Council initiated the first national haemoglobin survey (Committee on Haemoglobin Surveys 1945). In addition to these investigations, the Board of Education conducted systematic surveys of changes in children's heights and weights, and a large number of separate inquiries were undertaken into the effects of different forms of nutritional supplementation (Bransby 1944; 1946b; Magee 1944; 1946; 1947; Marrack 1947; Medical Research Council 1947: 96–130).

In view of the interest which has been shown in the demographic impact of the First World War, it is interesting to compare the different ways in which the two wars may have affected health status. Both wars witnessed sharp reductions in the level of unemployment, a decline in the birth rate, and increases in average earnings, although the beneficial effects of these changes may have been at least partially offset by increased working hours, food restrictions, poor housing, and price increases (Milward 1984; Winter 1986). However, the Second World War was also characterised by a much more concerted attempt to use the power of the state to compensate for these disadvantages by the introduction of such measures as food rationing, school meals and the distribution of priority foods (Magee 1947).

Some of the most comprehensive attempts to assess the impact of the war on children were made by E.R. Bransby in his studies of changes in the average height of schoolchildren in different parts of England, Scotland and Wales between 1936 and 1944 (Bransby 1944; 1946b; Ministry of Education 1947a: 20–22). Bransby found that the growth rates of the majority of schoolchildren were well maintained or even improved during the first three to four years of the war. A number of areas experienced a deterioration in average height between 1939 and 1942, but these declines were usually but not invariably made up in 1943 (Bransby 1944: 212–13). There was no consistent pattern of change between 1943 and 1944–5, but the majority of areas reported increases in average height over the war as a whole. When Bransby compared the average heights and weights of boys and girls in twenty-one areas with the corresponding figures for the period 1936–8, he found that seventeen areas reported increases in the average height of boys and fourteen areas reported increases in the average height of girls. Only one area reported a decline in boys' heights and two areas reported declines in girls' heights; the remaining areas saw no change (Table 8.8).[23]

It is interesting to compare these results with those obtained from an analysis of changes in the average height of children in ten of the areas which have been discussed elsewhere in this study. The list includes seven areas which were also examined by Bransby (Croydon, Glasgow, Huddersfield, Leeds, Sheffield, Wakefield and Warrington), together with Cambridge,

Table 8.8 Comparison of 1944 and prewar height data, showing the number of areas where 1944 data were better than, worse than or the same as prewar.

	Better	*Worse*	*Same*
Height: boys	17	1	3
Height: girls	14	2	4
Weight: boys	19	2	–
Weight: girls	20	1	–

Sources: Bransby (1946b: 59); Ministry of Education (1947a: 21).

Dumbartonshire and Rhondda. In view of the extent to which the two data sets overlap, it is not surprising that there should be a strong similarity between the results, but the new data do enable us to construct a somewhat clearer picture of the pattern of change from one year to the next. Overall, seven areas showed clear evidence of improvement, two areas (Cambridge and Rhondda) showed evidence of deterioration followed by improvement, and one area (Warrington) saw a net decline in average height between 1939 and 1944 (Table 8.9).[24]

In addition to examining changes in the average height of children, we can also examine data on nutritional status. We have already seen that the Board's 'nutrition statistics' came under increasing attack during the 1930s, and by the end of the 1930s even the Board's own officials had been forced to concede that fundamental changes were necessary (PRO ED50/204, J.A. Glover, 'Notes on a paper on physical indices and clinical assessment of the

Table 8.9 Changes in the average heights of boys and girls at different ages, 1939–45.

	Sex	*Age group*	*Height in inches*						
			1939	*1940*	*1941*	*1942*	*1943*	*1944*	*1945*
Cambridge	Male	Entrants	43.19	42.85	43.11	43.10	43.26	43.23	43.27
		Intermediates	50.04	49.57	49.85	49.78	49.77	50.02	50.08
		Leavers	56.99	57.09	57.44	57.25	57.94	57.79	57.61
	Female	Entrants	43.10	43.03	42.69	42.75	42.63	42.69	43.26
		Intermediates	49.55	49.34	49.58	49.54	50.71	50.09	49.80
		Leavers	57.97	58.10	58.17	58.18	57.89	58.23	58.20
Croydon	Male	Entrants	41.80	n/a	n/a	n/a	43.20	n/a	43.30
		Intermediates	49.00	n/a	n/a	n/a	51.10	n/a	51.30
		Leavers	58.40	n/a	n/a	n/a	58.00	n/a	58.00
	Female	Entrants	41.20	n/a	n/a	n/a	42.90	n/a	43.30
		Intermediates	50.90	n/a	n/a	n/a	49.40	n/a	50.70
		Leavers	58.80	n/a	n/a	n/a	58.90	n/a	59.00
Dumbartonshire	Male	Entrants	42.43	42.18	42.71	42.71	42.67	42.63	42.66
		Intermediates	49.64	n/a	49.87	48.63	49.91	49.80	49.81
		Leavers[a]	59.44	59.51	59.02	58.87	58.87	57.99	58.82
	Female	Entrants	42.13	42.68	42.03	42.32	42.40	42.19	42.39
		Intermediates	49.34	49.61	49.61	48.33	49.42	49.23	49.38
		Leavers[a]	60.48	59.68	59.50	59.25	59.20	59.61	59.61
Glasgow	Male	Entrants	41.70	n/a	42.16	41.99	41.91	41.82	41.95
		Intermediates	50.20	n/a	50.59	50.88	50.69	50.71	50.93
		Leavers	57.60	n/a	58.33	58.35	58.39	58.54	58.62
	Female	Entrants	41.50	n/a	41.84	41.62	41.49	41.45	41.62
		Intermediates	49.80	n/a	50.66	50.46	50.33	50.26	50.48
		Leavers	58.50	n/a	58.90	58.89	59.17	59.10	59.30
Huddersfield	Male	Entrants	43.00	43.45	43.42	43.38	43.54	44.11	44.00
		Intermediates	49.17	49.26	49.14	49.37	49.65	50.72	50.00
		Leavers	56.52	56.24	56.52	56.79	56.03	57.00	57.91

Table 8.9 Continued

	Sex	*Age group*	*Height in inches*						
			1939	*1940*	*1941*	*1942*	*1943*	*1944*	*1945*
	Female	Entrants	42.43	42.66	42.16	42.53	41.34	42.00	41.97
		Intermediates	48.86	49.10	48.96	48.76	48.62	49.59	49.21
		Leavers	57.29	57.22	57.01	57.72	57.95	56.52	57.50
Leeds	Male	Entrants	42.10	42.60	42.40	42.30	42.20	42.30	42.30
		Intermediates	48.60	48.90	48.80	48.60	48.60	48.60	49.50
		Leavers	55.60	56.10	56.00	55.90	56.00	56.00	56.20
	Female	Entrants	41.60	42.00	42.10	42.00	41.60	41.90	42.20
		Intermediates	48.20	48.60	48.40	48.60	48.30	48.20	48.60
		Leavers	56.50	56.90	56.70	56.30	56.70	56.50	56.50
Rhondda	Male	Entrants[b]	40.96	40.93	39.97	40.64	40.66	41.36	41.10
		Intermediates	48.34	48.02	48.62	47.66	47.07	48.68	49.12
		Leavers	55.99	56.16	56.00	58.20	56.06	55.92	55.91
	Female	Entrants[b]	40.53	38.69	40.45	40.11	40.25	41.01	40.50
		Intermediates	47.88	48.34	48.39	48.82	48.38	47.58	48.59
		Leavers	56.31	56.81	56.31	55.94	56.22	56.77	56.42
Sheffield	Male	Entrants	42.56	42.68	42.87	42.53	43.14	42.76	42.93
		Intermediates	49.29	49.41	49.45	n/a	n/a	n/a	n/a
		Leavers[c]	57.80	58.19	58.54	58.27	59.02	58.85	59.10
	Female	Entrants	42.20	42.44	42.60	42.25	42.86	42.46	42.64
		Intermediates	49.17	49.17	49.13	n/a	n/a	n/a	n/a
		Leavers[c]	58.74	59.33	59.76	59.26	59.96	59.90	60.02
Wakefield	Male	Entrants	41.25	41.75	41.50	41.50	41.25	41.50	41.50
		Intermediates	48.75	49.00	48.50	48.75	48.50	48.75	n/a
		Leavers	54.00	54.50	54.75	54.25	54.75	54.50	54.75
	Female	Entrants	40.75	41.00	41.25	41.50	41.25	41.25	41.75
		Intermediates	48.50	48.50	48.75	49.00	48.75	49.00	n/a
		Leavers	54.50	54.75	54.50	54.75	54.75	54.75	55.00
Warrington	Male	Entrants	41.40	41.20	41.30	40.50	41.20	41.20	n/a
		Intermediates	48.60	48.50	50.20	49.00	48.50	48.60	n/a
		Leavers	55.50	55.30	56.20	55.90	55.80	56.20	n/a
	Female	Entrants	41.20	41.10	41.10	41.60	40.90	41.10	n/a
		Intermediates	48.50	48.30	48.30	48.20	48.10	48.34	n/a
		Leavers	56.50	56.20	56.30	55.50	56.60	56.60	n/a

[a] The apparent decline in the heights of school-leavers in Dumbartonshire is probably attributable to a change in the age at which the children were measured.
[b] The figures for 'entrants' in Rhondda are based on the average heights of children aged between four and six.
[c] The figures for school-leavers in Sheffield are based on the heights of children aged thirteen to fourteen. The number of children measured in this age group in 1939 was comparatively small.

Sources: The original data were derived from the Annual Reports of the School Medical Officers for the areas listed in the table. A full list of the school medical reports cited in this study may be found in the Bibliography. Details of the original height statistics have been deposited with the ESRC Data Archive, University of Essex, Wivenhoe Park, Colchester, Essex CO4 3SQ.

nutrition of schoolchildren', p. 9; 'A critical examination of the nutrition returns over a period of five years', p. 23). The Board responded to these criticisms by advising school medical officers to pay particular attention to evidence of nutritional defect, and this meant that the 'standards' adopted by many school medical officers may have become more rigorous as the war progressed (Ministry of Education 1947a: 16). In view of this, it is interesting to note that in the country as a whole, school medical officers' subjective assessments of children's nutritional status showed an increase in the number of children with 'excellent' or 'normal' nutrition, and a decline in the number of children whose nutrition was described as 'slightly sub-normal' or 'bad' (Table 8.10).

Further evidence of changes in child health during the war can be gleaned from the statistics of morbidity and mortality. The evidence here is slightly more mixed, although child mortality rates as a whole (0–14 years) fell by 4.88 per cent between 1939 and 1945 (see Table 8.12). Table 8.11 shows the main changes in disease notification rates for the principal epidemic diseases of childhood. The reported incidence of diphtheria fell by more than 60 per cent as a result of a highly successful immunisation campaign, but there was little change in the figures for whooping cough and measles, and only a small decline in the incidence of scarlet fever (Ministry of Education 1947a: 59–61).[25] The war witnessed a substantial decline in the number of deaths attributed to diphtheria, and a somewhat smaller decline in the number of deaths attributed to bronchitis, pneumonia and heart disease. The number of deaths attributed to violence increased, while other death rates remained relatively unchanged (Table 8.12).

Table 8.10 Summary of the assessment of nutrition of elementary schoolchildren (aged between five and fourteen) seen in routine medical inspection in England and Wales, 1939–45.

	Number examined	*Assessments (%)*			
		A (excellent)	*B (normal)*	*C (slightly sub-normal)*	*D (bad)*
1939[a]	1,098,367	14.7	73.8	11.0	0.5
1940	1,591,824	15.6	73.0	10.8	0.4
1941	1,584,979	14.8	74.2	10.6	0.4
1942	1,599,339	14.6	74.7	10.3	0.3
1943	1,288,910	15.3	74.3	10.1	0.3
1944	1,272,562	15.9	74.4	9.4	0.3
1945	1,268,951	16.3	74.5	8.9	0.3

[a] First two terms only.

Source: Ministry of Education (1947a: 16).

Table 8.11 Notifications in England and Wales, including those of non-civilians and from port health districts 1939–45.

	1939	*1940*	*1941*	*1942*	*1943*	*1944*[a]	*1944*[b]	*1945*
Diphtheria	47,343	46,281	50,797	41,404	34,662	29,949	23,199	18,596
Measles	n/a	409,251	409,715	286,341	376,104	159,041	158,479	446,796
Scarlet fever	78,101	65,302	59,433	85,084	116,034	94,859	92,671	73,687
Whooping cough	n/a	53,607	173,330	66,016	96,136	94,217	94,044	62,691

[a] Uncorrected figures.
[b] Revised figures taking account of changes in diagnosis.

Sources: Ministry of Health (1946: 18–19); General Register Office (1947: 286).

Table 8.12 Child mortality rates, 1939–45 (per million).

	1939	*1940*	*1941*	*1942*	*1943*	*1944*	*1945*
Children up to four years							
Appendicitis	44	46	41	34	31	39	34
Bronchitis and pneumonia	2,539	3,704	3,732	2,570	2,950	2,478	2,478
Congenital causes	6,307	3,343	3,201	3,354	3,151	3,257	3,122
Diarrhoea[a]	1,016	1,003	1,050	1,194	1,204	1,227	1,206
Diphtheria	292	338	416	255	183	117	81
Heart disease	15	15	15	14	11	12	9
Measles	88	252	334	136	225	73	202
Tuberculosis (all forms)	427	473	639	485	479	420	419
Violence	592	992	1,070	741	669	810	695
Other causes	2,337	5,451	5,934	5,214	5,138	4,844	4,031
Total	13,658	15,618	16,432	13,997	14,041	13,276	12,276
Children aged five to fourteen							
Appendicitis	53	59	52	53	45	54	47
Bronchitis and pneumonia	80	101	95	73	74	64	55
Congenital causes	17	31	31	31	30	34	35
Diarrhoea[a]	12	0	0	0	0	0	0
Diphtheria	201	229	212	160	108	79	59
Heart disease	76	67	60	51	55	57	48
Measles	9	17	25	11	15	4	12
Tuberculosis (all forms)	151	161	200	164	156	151	159
Violence	217	524	580	334	322	412	323
Other causes	432	480	448	386	411	358	310
Total	1,248	1,669	1,703	1,263	1,215	1,214	1,049

[a] This category was redefined as 'diarrhoea under 2' in 1940.

Sources: General Register Office 1944a: 1, 162; 1944b: 1, 170; 1945: 1, 170; 1946: 1, 170; 1947: 1, 174; 1948: 1, 174; 1949: 1, 174.

In addition to these general health indicators, it is also interesting to examine the impact of the Second World War on two other aspects of child health, namely the mental health of schoolchildren and the condition of their teeth. There is little direct evidence on the subject of children's mental health during the war, but a number of investigations were carried out towards the end of 1940 to discover the effects of aerial bombardment in London.[26] In general, these investigations suggested that children were standing up remarkably well to the mental strain of bombing, but some observers felt that the lack of sleep was exacting a physical toll. The following report was fairly typical:

> I find that the children are standing up to the air-raids even better than their parents. The important thing is the attitude of the mother. If she is not nervous the children are not; if she is nervous then the children are frightened. More intelligent parents stay in their own homes or sleep in the Anderson shelters and make their children very comfortable. Most of these children sleep through the night and know very little of the raids. They regard sleeping in the Anderson shelter or new sleeping arrangements at home as a special treat. Many of the children, however, look tired although neither they nor their parents complain of their tiredness (PRO ED50/206, Children's reactions to the war/nervous strain in childhood).

One of the more remarkable consequences of the war was its effect on the condition of children's teeth. In 1948 May and Helen Mellanby reported that there had been a sharp decline in the incidence of dental caries among five-year-old children in London between 1929 and 1943, and between 1943 and 1947. They were unable to say how much of this decline was directly attributable to the war, but their figures for 1929 were very similar to those discovered by J.D. King in south-east London ten years later (Marrack 1947: 234; Mellanby and Mellanby 1948). Further evidence that the decline in dental caries was war-related was provided by the School Medical Officers of Glasgow, Cambridge and West Bromwich. The percentage of five-year-old children whose mouths were free from dental caries increased from 18 per cent to 48 per cent in Glasgow, and from 32.3 per cent to 53.6 per cent in West Bromwich, between 1938 and 1944 (*Medical Officer* 1945a: 3; 1945b). In Cambridge, the Principal Dental Officer reported that the percentage of carious deciduous teeth declined from 21.5 per cent in 1938 to 14.3 per cent in 1942 and 11.0 per cent in 1945 (Ministry of Education 1947a: 49; Weaver 1950: 231).[27]

Notes

1 The Board of Education calculated that the precise number of schoolchildren who were evacuated in England and Wales was 734,883, excluding those who made their own arrangements independently of the official scheme. See PRO ED138/56, Health of the schoolchild 1939: 34.

2 The Board estimated that 316,441 evacuees (43.06 per cent of the total) had left the reception areas by the end of 1939 (PRO ED138/56, Health of the schoolchild 1939: 40; see also Padley 1940: 46–7).
3 The official explained that 'a separate note on the position in London has already been sent to the President' (PRO ED50/207, Summary of replies to Circular 1490: para. 3).
4 For example, the number of cases in Stoke-on-Trent increased from 115 in 1944 to 400 in 1945 (Ministry of Education 1947a: 39).
5 The Board's own investigations suggested that many of the hostels were used initially as 'dumping-grounds' for children whom no one else would take. See Gosden (1976: 176, footnote 57).
6 The earlier history of child guidance is discussed in Thom (1992); Hendrick (1994: 149–76).
7 C.H. Feinstein's estimates suggest that prices in the economy as a whole rose by 40.7 per cent between 1939 and 1944, and by 14.2 per cent between 1942 and 1945. The price of goods and services purchased by public authorities rose by 44.5 per cent during the first period and by 16.4 per cent during the second period (Feinstein 1972: Table 61).
8 According to Samuel and Vera Leff, 'from 1938 to 1945, the number of whole-time school medical officers had been reduced by more than fifty per cent (part-time by about 20 per cent), and whole-time dental officers by 25 per cent (part-time by 30 per cent). The number of whole-time school nurses fell by 12 per cent' (Leff and Leff 1959: 95–6; Hendrick 1994: 194). However the authors failed to reveal the original source of these calculations. The figures presented in Table 8.4 suggest that the number of whole-time school medical officers (including assistant school medical officers) fell by 31.2 per cent, and that the number of part-time officers fell by 23.2 per cent. The number of *senior* school medical officers fell by 53.33 per cent, but this was caused by the reducation in the number of local education authorities under the 1944 Education Act (PP 1942–3 Cmd. 6458 xi: paras 111–18; 7 & 8 Geo. VI Ch. 31: section 6).
9 The total number of children seen at routine medical examinations fell by 17.5 per cent between 1942 and 1943. If all local education authorities had abandoned the intermediate examination, the number would have fallen by approximately 33 per cent (see Table 8.5).
10 In July 1940 the Board argued that 'the maintenance of the nutrition of schoolchildren is at all times a matter of vital national importance, but in time of war it is specially important to safeguard the health of the rising generation by ensuring that they receive adequate quantities of nutritive food' (PRO ED138/59, Circular 1520: para. 1). The statement reflected Lord Woolton's observation that food was 'one of the munitions of war' (quoted in Gosden 1976: 196).
11 *Public Health* returned to this subject in August 1942. It wrote: 'To those familiar with the history of the school medical service the interesting thing is the absence of public cant on the ground of usurpation of parents' rights or anything of that kind, even when the service extends far into the nutritional field' (*Public Health* 1942).
12 For an account of the development of the school meals service in Scotland, see Watt (1948).
13 Table 8.6 gives details of the numbers of children receiving school dinners at various times between 1939 and 1945. The Board of Education also collected information about the number of children receiving breakfasts and teas in public elementary schools in England and Wales. The relevant details are as follows: Dec. 1941: breakfasts, 2443; dinners, 376,501; teas, 1759; Oct. 1942: breakfasts, 2829; dinners, 660,372; teas, 7043; Feb. 1943: breakfasts, 3083; dinners, 809,219; teas,

10,349; May 1943: breakfasts, 4033; dinners, 912,079; teas, 12,234; Oct. 1943: breakfasts, 4342; dinners: 1,076,651; teas, 14,292; Feb. 1944: breakfasts, 4721; dinners, 1,202,117; teas, 15,493; Jun. 1944: breakfasts, 4236; dinners, 1,257,566; teas, 15,016; Oct. 1944: breakfasts, 3810; dinners, 1,245,201; teas, 11,296; Feb. 1945: breakfasts, 3459; dinners, 1,329,437; teas, 13,227 (PRO ED136/662, Miscellaneous papers showing numbers of breakfasts, dinners and teas, and bottles of milk, consumed in public elementary schools in England and Wales between December 1941 and February 1945).

14 During the interwar years, free meals had been supplied in feeding centres, and 'paying' meals had been supplied in school canteens. See Clark (1948: 19).

15 This comment recalls the observation, attributed to Dr Hugh Paul, the Medical Officer of Health for Smethwick, that the Board's policy on medical selection required children to undergo a 'period of trial starvation' before they qualified for supplementary feeding (Leff and Leff 1959: 84). The British Medical Association had also argued that 'to wait for clinical evidence [of incipient malnutrition] was bad preventive practice' (*British Medical Journal* 1935).

16 The target of 1000 calories was based on the assumption that the average elementary schoolchild required a daily calorie intake of 2500 calories, and that two-fifths of this could reasonably be supplied by the midday meal (PRO ED136/662, J.A. Glover, 'The school medical service in wartime': 16). Some observers believed that the target of 1000 calories was unnecessarily high, and it is likely that many local education authorities experienced difficulties in meeting it. See Marrack (1946: 179); Stewart (1948: 86); Hurt (1985: 201).

17 This document formed Chapter 6 of the Board's 'Green Book'. See PRO ED136/214, Board of Education, *Education after the War*: paras 66–80.

18 Bosworth-Smith was referring to the proposal that all children should move from elementary (or primary) schools to secondary schools at the age of eleven, and that the school leaving age should be raised to fifteen.

19 The Board attracted considerable criticism for its refusal to make the proposals available publicly. See Gosden (1976: 265–7).

20 The proposal also brought the Board into conflict with the Ministry of Health, and it was agreed to retain the existing division of responsibility. The Board retained responsibility for the medical supervision of all children who were attending recognised places of instruction, and the Ministry retained responsibility in all other cases. See PRO ED136/377, Allocation or reallocation of functions between government departments, 23/4/43: 4–5; ED136/378, Notes for discussion with the Ministry of Health on postwar nursery policy, 9/2/43).

21 The White Paper on the National Health Service stated that 'the Education Authorities will retain as part of their educational machinery the functions of inspection of children in the school group (the supervision, in fact, of the state of health in which the child attends school and of the effect of school life and activities on the child's health) together with the important function of using the influence of the school and the teacher and the whole school relationship with child and parent to encourage the recourse of the child to all desirable medical treatment. But, as from the time when the new health service is able to take over its comprehensive care of health, the child will look for its treatment to the organisation which that service provides – and the Education Authority, as such, will give up responsibility for medical treatment' (PP 1943–4 Cmd. 6502 viii: 39).

22 In 1944 the Board circulated a number of organisations, including the Society of Medical Officers of Health, the Medical Officers of Schools Association (an organisation of medical officers in private schools) and the British Paediatric Association for their views on the retention and development of routine medical inspection. The Society of Medical Officers of Health said that all children should

be examined at six-monthly intervals between the ages of two and seven, and that older children should be examined at the ages of seven, ten and thirteen. In the longer term, it argued that all children should be examined once a year between the ages of seven and eleven, and once every two years between eleven and fifteen. See PRO ED50/213, Society of Medical Officers of Health, 'School medical inspection'.

23 Bransby collected data on the following areas: Barrow, Birkenhead, Bromley, Chadderton, Crewe, Croydon, Ebbw Vale, Gillingham, Glasgow, Halifax, Huddersfield, Ilford, Jarrow, Leeds, Leyton, Newport, Sheffield, Southampton, Wakefield, Warrington and Wrexham. These areas contained a total elementary school population of approximately 395,000, of whom 160,000 attended schools in Glasgow (Bransby 1946b: 59; Ministry of Education 1947a: 21).

24 The Medical Officer of Health for Warrington was one of very few medical officers to express a very clear view that the overall impact of the war had been negative. In his annual report for 1945 he stated that: 'The shortage of fats, sugars and variety in the diet, combined with the irksome difficulties of getting even basic necessities, and the after-effects of war strain and prolonged war effort, have all combined to bring about a condition of physical and nervous "tiredness" which increases the liability to sub-acute conditions such as nervous complaints, catarrhs, muscular lack of tone etc., of which there is plenty of evidence' (qu. in *Medical Officer* 1946).

25 Measles and whooping cough only became notifiable in November 1939. The fluctuations which occurred during the war reflect the normal periodicity of these diseases. See Ministry of Education (1947a: 61).

26 One might examine childhood suicide rates, but the numbers involved were far too small to reveal any definite trend. The numbers of children aged five to fourteen who committed suicide between 1939 and 1945 were as follows: 1939, three; 1940, five; 1941, four; 1942, seven; 1943, four; 1944, four; 1945, seven. See General Register Office 1944a: Table 24; 1944b: Table 24; 1945: Table 24; 1946: Table 24; 1947: Table 24; 1948: Table 24; 1949: Table 24.

27 Although most observers agreed that the condition of children's teeth had improved during the war, there was less agreement about the reasons for this. Some observers stressed the importance of a general improvement in diet (and in particular the increased consumption of liquid milk), while others cited the effects of a reduction in sugar consumption. The debate is summarised in Weaver (1950).

nine

The school health service, 1945–74

The Second World War represented a major watershed in the history of school medical provision. During the war, the movement for social reconstruction produced a fundamental reform of the public education system and the development of wide-ranging plans for the creation of a comprehensive national health service. The war also highlighted many of the inadequacies of the existing school medical service. It revived a long-standing debate about the value of routine medical inspection and generated fresh doubts about the accuracy of school medical statistics. It also demonstrated the inadequacy of the treatment services which were provided by a large number of local authorities, and created a new determination to 'universalise the best'. These developments provided the basis for a wide-ranging debate about the future of the school medical service and the development of child health services as a whole.

The transformation of the school medical service continued after 1945. The school medical service was renamed the school health service, and many of its specialist services were transferred to the new National Health Service. The establishment of the National Health Service conferred new rights to medical care on the whole population, and this enabled a much larger proportion of the school population to be treated by a general practitioner. The postwar period also witnessed a dramatic improvement in the overall standard of child health, and this led to a renewed debate about the need for routine medical inspection. There was a sharp reduction in the proportion of children who required treatment for physical defects, and this enabled school medical officers to devote an increasing amount of time to the development of 'psychological' services such as child guidance and speech therapy.

The structure of the school health service

The basic framework for the development of the school health service after 1945 was determined by the Education Act of 1944 (7 & 8 Geo. VI Ch. 31). Section 1 of the new Act abolished the Board of Education and transferred its powers to the Ministry of Education. Section 6 created a unified system of local administration for both primary and secondary schools by abolishing the so-called part III authorities which had previously been responsible for public elementary schools. Section 7 established a progressive system of public education which enabled all children to pass from primary schools to some form of secondary school at the age of eleven. Section 48 (1) imposed a duty on every local education authority 'to provide for the medical inspection . . . of pupils in attendance at any school or county college [i.e. college of further education] maintained by them', and gave them the power 'to provide for [the] . . . inspection of senior pupils in attendance at any other educational establishment maintained by them'. Section 48 (3) gave local authorities the duty 'to make . . . arrangements for securing the provision of free medical treatment' for pupils at both primary and secondary schools and at county colleges, and the power to make similar provision for senior pupils attending other maintained establishments.

Although the Act failed to specify the precise form which these arrangements might take, the government expected local education authorities to make full use of existing health services, and to transfer their own treatment services to the new national health service when it was eventually created. The White Paper on Educational Reconstruction stated that

> the setting up of a comprehensive National Health Service will eventually ensure that all forms of treatment which schoolchildren require will be available for them through that service. When this stage is reached it will no longer be necessary for Local Education Authorities to provide treatment, and their functions will be confined to providing medical inspection and seeing that the children and parents are properly advised and encouraged to seek through the new channels any treatment the child may need (PP 1942–3 Cmd. 6458 xi: para. 94).

The White Paper on the National Health Service said that

> the conception underlying both the [Education] Bill and the present paper is that the Education Authorities will retain as part of their educational machinery . . . the supervision . . . of the state of health in which the child attends school and . . . the effects of school life and activities on child's health, together with the important function of using the influence of the school . . . to encourage the recourse of the

> child to all desirable medical treatment. But as from the time when the new National Health Service is able to take over its comprehensive care of health, the child will look for its treatment to the organisation which that service provides – and the Education Authority, as such, will give up responsibility for medical treatment (PP 1943–4 Cmd. 6502 viii: 39).

The officials who drew up the initial plans for health and educational reform hoped that the Education Act and the new National Health Service might come into being together, but this expectation was frustrated by the long delays involved in the establishment of the National Health Service (Webster 1988: 44). These delays forced the Ministry of Education to issue a Circular to local authorities setting out the steps which they should take to comply with their obligations under Section 48 of the 1944 Education Act. The Ministry advised the authorities to 'concentrate on improving and perfecting their existing schemes by providing that all the normal facilities of the school medical service shall be readily available for all pupils who need them, at no cost to the parent' (PRO ED50/287, Circular 29: para. 2). It also encouraged them to make their own arrangements with local hospitals to extend the range of services which they currently provided (ibid.: para. 5). This led to a series of complicated negotiations with local hospitals to determine the level of fees to be charged for hospital services (PRO ED50/287, Bosworth-Smith to Cleary, 27/2/45; Ministry of Education 1949: 49–51).

The most controversial negotiations during the passage of the National Health Service Bill concerned the future of the school dental service. During the Second World War, the Interdepartmental Committee on Dentistry had called on the government to establish a comprehensive dental service as part of its plans for the creation of the National Health Service, but it recognised that such a service could not be established overnight, and it recommended that priority should be given to the needs of expectant and nursing mothers, schoolchildren and adolescents (PP 1943–4 Cmd. 6565 iii: paras 82–90). The Ministry of Education seized on this recommendation to argue that local education authorities should retain responsibility for the provision of dental inspection and treatment after the National Health Service had been created (PRO ED50/351, Maud to Douglas, 19/7/46). The Ministry of Health rejected this argument on the grounds that it would undermine the long-term goal of establishing a comprehensive dental service for the population as a whole, but it accepted that local authorities would need to continue to provide dental treatment for schoolchildren for the foreseeable future (ibid., Douglas to Maud, 27/9/46; 17/10/46).

The Ministry issued a further set of guidelines following the establishment of the National Health Service in 1948. It said that local education authorities should retain responsibility for medical inspection and for the treatment of minor ailments such as ringworm, scabies, impetigo, various forms of ear and eye defect, and minor injuries (Ministry of Education 1948b: paras

3, 12). They also retained responsibility for child guidance and speech therapy, both of which were regarded as primarily educational services to be conducted in close association with the school authorities (ibid.: paras 18–21). The most significant changes concerned the provision of specialist services, such as orthopaedic treatment and artificial light treatment, which were transferred to the regional hospital boards of the National Health Service (ibid.: paras 4–6). However, although local education authorities surrendered responsibility for most of these services, they continued to provide ophthalmic services, and they retained control of the school dental service (ibid.: paras 8, 14). They also retained the power to provide 'any specialist service for schoolchildren which it appears to them desirable to provide notwithstanding the facilities otherwise available' (ibid.: para. 7).

When the new proposals for the National Health Service were first mooted, many school medical officers expressed concern that the removal of medical treatment would make the profession of school medicine even less attractive than it already seemed (e.g. Jolly 1943). However, as the shape of the new service became clearer, the general mood became significantly more optimistic (see also Lishman 1944). In 1946 the School Health Service Group of the Society of Medical Officers of Health expressed the view that the new school health service would provide a valuable 'integrating factor . . . preventing over-insistence on the remedying of some defect or another without reference to the whole interests of the child' (*Public Health* 1946: 104). In 1948 the Group's President, G.H. Hogben, predicted that the advent of the new service would offer fresh opportunities for the practice of preventive medicine. He concluded:

> With the time and the opportunity for research authorised in Section 47 [of the School Health Service Regulations], and with the promised improvement in financial recompense of Medical Officers in local government, the school health service should become attractive equally to those who wish to practise preventive medicine as distinct from curative medicine (Hogben 1949: 83–4).[1]

Finance and personnel

During the Second World War, the government introduced a number of emergency measures to safeguard educational provision. The grant for elementary education in each area was fixed at the same percentage as the grant for 1937/8, and special grants were introduced for particular services, such as air-raid precautions, emergency teacher training and school meals and milk. Following the introduction of the 1944 Education Act, the government introduced an interim grant formula to tide the authorities over until a final settlement of the financial relationship between central and local government could be reached. As part of this formula, local authorities received a uniform grant for the provision of both primary and secondary education, together with a number of special grants for school meals and milk and the removal of air-raid precautions and defence works. A figure of approximately £2 million was set aside for poorer areas and areas with sparse populations (PP 1950–51 Cmd. 8244 xi: 30–31).

The long-term arrangements for financing public education were resolved during the second half of 1947, and took effect in April 1948. The 'main grant' included a capitation grant, based on the number of children in average attendance, and a percentage grant, based on the net recognisable expenditure of the authority, with a reduction based on the rateable value of the properties in each area. This grant was intended to cover the majority of local authority services, including the school health service and the provision of special schools. The 'main grant' was supplemented by a series of special grants for the provision of school meals and milk, teacher training, and removal of air-raid shelters and wartime defence works (Ministry of Education 1947b; 1948a). In 1958 Parliament agreed to abolish the 'main grant', and the majority of education services were financed out of the general grant provided by the Ministry of Housing and Local Government (PP 1959–60 Cmnd. 1088 xii: 8–9, 97–101). The Ministry of Education (and later the Department of Education and Science) continued to make separate provision for the school meals and milk service until 1967 (PP 1966–7 Cmnd. 3226 xxvii: 50; Department of Education and Science 1966c, para. 6).

The history of local education authority spending on the school health service is summarised in Table 9.1, which also includes details of expenditure on special schools and school meals, together with information about local authority spending as a whole. The table shows that local authority spending on the school health service rose sharply in the immediate aftermath of the war, before falling back at the end of the 1940s. Expenditure rose steadily during the 1950s and 1960s, and increased at a somewhat faster rate during the late 1960s and early 1970s. However, expenditure on the school health service rose less rapidly than expenditure on the education service as a whole. During the period between 1945/6 and 1973/4, local authority spending on the school health service rose by 178 per cent in real terms, while expenditure on special schools and the provision of school meals rose by 1071 per cent and 347 per cent, respectively. The ratio of school health service expenditure to total expenditure declined from 3.1 per cent to 1.6 per cent over the same period.[2]

In view of the debates surrounding the cost of health services since 1945, it is interesting to compare expenditure on the school health service with expenditure on the National Health Service as a whole. In his study of *The politics of the National Health Service*, Rudolf Klein suggested that the National Health Service faced an almost impossible battle to control health service costs because of the development of new techniques, the constant desire for better health, and the accelerating increase in the number of elderly people (Klein 1989: 33–40, 67–73; see also Ham 1992: 38–44). However, even

Table 9.1 Current expenditure (excluding loan charges) by local education authorities on selected services, at constant (1949/50) prices, 1945/6–1973/4 (£ thousands).

	School health service	*Special schools*	*Provision of meals*	*Total expenditure by LEAs*	*Total expenditure by government and LEAs*
1945/46	5,173	2,047	13,218	166,325	n/a
1946/47	7,308	2,347	16,047	188,250	n/a
1947/48	8,828	2,340	18,392	198,161	n/a
1948/49	6,757	2,636	20,603	212,145	n/a
1949/50	5,552	3,163	22,610	224,790	n/a
1950/51	5,674	3,552	20,706	227,421	n/a
1951/52	5,747	4,144	21,015	249,274	n/a
1952/53	5,834	4,490	30,147	259,879	274,871
1953/54	6,082	4,688	27,559	263,566	276,830
1954/55	6,345	5,125	29,342	283,755	294,982
1955/56	6,806	5,319	31,757	296,270	307,353
1956/57	7,110	5,879	33,193	325,866	337,363
1957/58	7,188	6,331	30,006	344,176	356,427
1958/59	7,351	6,556	30,282	356,760	369,409
1959/60	7,956	7,081	31,183	385,357	398,770
1960/61	8,254	7,551	31,917	406,773	420,950
1961/62	8,593	7,982	34,085	435,238	450,044
1962/63	8,985	8,725	35,387	475,408	495,794
1963/64	9,396	9,370	35,205	505,444	527,821
1964/65	9,541	9,392	38,943	527,684	552,237
1965/66	10,095	10,331	42,058	587,181	605,876
1966/67	10,335	10,888	44,953	617,838	637,182
1967/68	10,808	11,781	50,371	664,767	685,099
1968/69	11,448	12,535	43,518	681,282	703,065
1969/70	11,776	13,609	44,244	711,595	732,719
1970/71	12,626	14,937	44,418	746,643	767,955
1971/72	13,093	19,909	42,972	796,823	818,545
1972/73	13,983	22,370	48,086	854,585	876,866
1973/74	14,378	23,961	59,077	889,571	912,401

Notes: Details of current expenditure were obtained from the *Annual Abstract of Statistics 1938–48*, the annual reports of the Ministry of Education and the annual volumes of *Statistics of Education* published from 1960 onwards. These figures were deflated by a price index for the economy as a whole obtained from Feinstein (1972) and Central Statistical Office (1975).

Sources: Central Statistical Office 1949: Table 90; PP 1947–8 Cmd. 7426 xi: Table 87; PP 1948–9 Cmd. 7724 xiv: Table 84; PP 1950 Cmd. 7957 ix: Table 89; PP 1950–1 Cmd. 8244 xi: Table 93; PP 1951–2 Cmd. 8554 x: Table 98; PP 1952–3 Cmd. 8835 ix: Table 96; Ministry of Education 1963a: Tables 57, 60; Department of Education and Science 1969a: Tables 2, 6; Department of Education and Science 1976: Tables 3, 5; Feinstein 1972: Table 61 (column 7); Central Statistical Office 1975a: Table 17 (price index for GDP at factor cost).

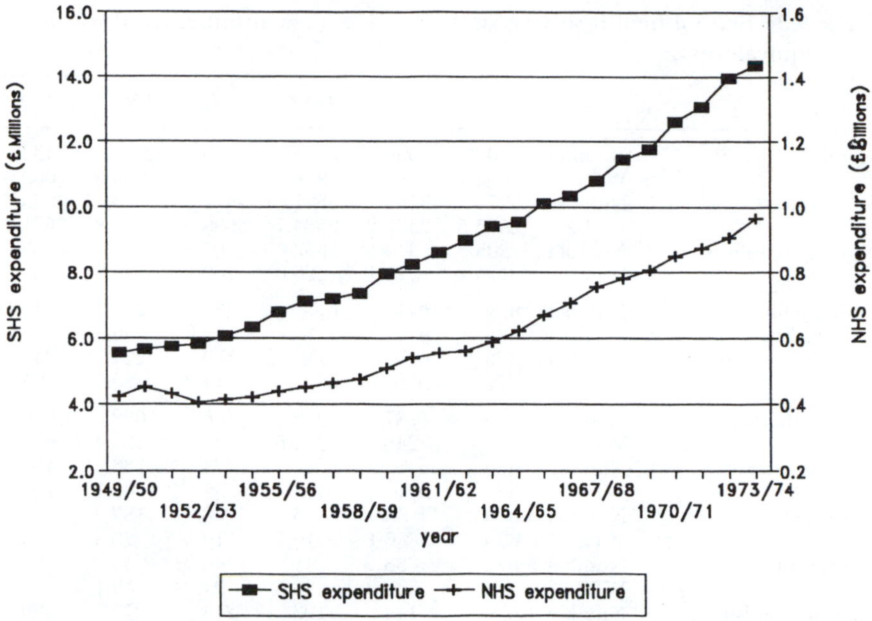

Figure 9.1 Current expenditure on the National Health Service and school health service, 1949/50–1973/74 (at 1949/50 prices).

Sources: School health service expenditure: see Table 9.1. National Health Service expenditure: Adapted from PP 1979–80 Cmnd. 7615 lvi: Table E6. For details of the price index used to deflate both sets of figures, see Table 9.1.

though the school health service accounted for a declining proportion of the education budget, the figures depicted in Figure 9.1 suggest that school health service expenditure grew more rapidly than expenditure on the National Health Service as a whole between 1949/50 and 1973/4. The real cost of the school health service increased by 43.30 per cent between 1949/50 and 1959/60, by 48.01 per cent between 1959/60 and 1969/70, and by 22.10 per cent between 1969/70 and 1973/4. The equivalent figures for the National Health Service were 25.17 per cent, 58.56 per cent and 21.75 per cent, respectively.

In addition to examining the finances of the school health service, we can examine the growth of school medical provision by looking at changes in staffing levels. Table 9.2 shows that there was a substantial increase in both the number and range of staff employed in school medical work. The number of school medical officers, expressed as whole-time equivalents, increased from 832.1 in 1947 to 1062.9 in 1972, and the number of school nurses (including district and orthopaedic nurses) increased from 2505.5 to 3371.3. However, the most remarkable increases came in the range of specialist services provided by the school health service. The number of speech therapists rose from 246.4 in 1952 to 616.5 in 1972, and the number of psychiatrists and educational psychologists rose from 151.9 to 800.7.

Table 9.2 School health service staff, 1947–72 (raw numbers and whole-time equivalents).

		1947	*1952*	*1957*	*1962*	*1967*	*1972*
Medical officers	Number	1608	2098	2341	2509	2914	3433
	WTE	832.1	898.1	978.4	971.7	930.6	1062.9
School nurses	Number	5273	5700	6641	7471	8823	9986
	WTE	2505.5	2528.2	2584.7	2683.6	2888.8	3371.3
Nursing assistants	Number	205	343	362	507	569	736
	WTE	175.1	229.1	226.0	260.1	285.2	365.7
Ophthalmic specialists	Number	n/a	n/a	n/a	232	265	342
	WTE	n/a	n/a	n/a	47.8	56.3	67.7
Other specialists	Number	n/a	n/a	n/a	169	224	245
	WTE	n/a	n/a	n/a	14.2	20.7	25.0
Speech therapists	Number	n/a	287	379	486	652	926
	WTE	n/a	246.4	334.6	392.3	434.4	616.5
Audiometricians	Number	n/a	n/a	n/a	73	133	193
	WTE	n/a	n/a	n/a	52.8	82.1	122.7
Chiropodists	Number	n/a	38	45	108	187	245
	WTE	n/a	6.1	10.7	19.3	23.6	35.0
Orthoptists	Number	n/a	33	41	40	54	64
	WTE	n/a	22.0	23.6	21.0	19.1	27.0
Physiotherapists	Number	n/a	144	193	214	273	420
	WTE	n/a	93.3	134.1	134.2	161.6	236.9
Others (excluding clerical staff)[a]	Number	n/a	59	136	57	223	264
	WTE	n/a	48.0	94.5	38.1	132.7	197.5
Psychiatrists	Number	n/a	148	195	260	318	404
	WTE	n/a	53.6	65.6	95.0	129.7	162.3
Educational psychologists	Number	n/a	164	209	290	446	694
	WTE	n/a	131.3	163.3	226.7	375.6	638.4
Psychiatric social workers	Number	n/a	125	151	192	256	
	WTE	n/a	107.9	124.3	144.6	185.8	
							518
							438.0
Social workers	Number	n/a	n/a	n/a	n/a	194	
	WTE	n/a	n/a	n/a	n/a	127.3	
Others (excluding clerical staff)[b]	Number	n/a	207	145	289	329	1392
	WTE	n/a	160.5	104.0	177.5	250.0	957.5
Dental officers	Number	1063	1117	1534	1775	1821	1967
	WTE	921.2	849.8	1014.5	1165.0	1272.2	1449.9
Dental attendants	Number	1011	1045	1284	1563	1801	2299
	WTE	939.2	926.9	1105.3	1316.0	1555.0	1742.0
Dental auxiliaries	Number	–	–	–	42	162	233
	WTE	–	–	–	41.0	140.9	188.5
Dental health education personnel	Number	n/a	n/a	n/a	n/a	25	31
	WTE	n/a	n/a	n/a	n/a	11.2	15.6
Others (including clerical staff)	Number	n/a	n/a	n/a	33	143	154
	WTE	n/a	n/a	n/a	23.4	106.9	119.7

[a] Includes remedial gymnasts.

[b] Includes paediatricians, psychotherapists, play therapists and remedial teachers. The figure for 1952 also includes clerical staff.

Sources: Ministry of Education (1949: 139–40; 1954: 130–2; 1958: 199–201); Department of Education and Science (1964: 129, 145; 1969b: 115–6, 125; 1974a: 54–6, 64).

There was also a substantial increase in the number of school dentists, the number of dental officers rising from 921.2 in 1947 to 1449.9 25 years later.

However, although these statistics represent a significant increase over interwar levels, it is important to remember that the school population was also increasing, and changes in the number of school medical staff look rather less impressive when compared with the number of children they

Table 9.3 School health service staff per 10,000 pupils attending maintained schools in England and Wales, 1946–73 (whole-time equivalents).

	Number of pupils	*Number (WTE)*			*Number per 10,000 pupils*		
		Medical officers	*School nurses*	*Dental officers*	*Medical officers*	*School nurses*	*Dental officers*
1946	6,103,302	708.1	2,417.6	752.8	1.16	3.96	1.23
1947	6,126,136	832.1	2,505.5	921.2	1.36	4.09	1.50
1948	6,377,458	831.7	2,579.0	880.0	1.30	4.04	1.38
1949	6,474,678	861.0	2,516.0	732.0	1.33	3.89	1.13
1950	6,523,085	907.1	2,473.8	717.2	1.39	3.79	1.10
1951	6,561,573	893.8	2,522.5	712.8	1.36	3.84	1.09
1952	6,740,094	898.1	2,528.2	849.8	1.33	3.75	1.26
1953	6,898,614	898.6	2,559.7	945.0	1.30	3.71	1.37
1954	7,012,061	932.4	2,568.5	978.9	1.33	3.66	1.40
1955	7,098,064	945.9	2,556.1	1,007.9	1.33	3.60	1.42
1956	7,179,212	971.3	2,573.2	1,023.8	1.35	3.58	1.43
1957	7,213,632	978.4	2,584.7	1,014.5	1.36	3.58	1.41
1958	7,178,353	940.6	2,602.5	1,032.0	1.31	3.63	1.44
1959	7,168,537	948.0	2,670.2	1,015.8	1.32	3.72	1.42
1960	7,144,479	958.8	2,640.7	1,030.1	1.34	3.70	1.44
1961	7,131,982	953.9	2,664.0	1,069.3	1.34	3.74	1.50
1962	7,095,367	971.7	2,683.6	1,165.0	1.37	3.78	1.64
1963	7,017,945	977.9	2,628.0	1,214.9	1.39	3.74	1.73
1964	7,084,253	983.0	2,689.3	1,243.3	1.39	3.80	1.76
1965	7,122,255	1,036.9	2,856.9	1,264.1	1.46	4.01	1.77
1966	7,199,307	949.0	2,929.0	n/a	1.32	4.07	n/a
1967	7,342,336	930.6	2,888.8	1,272.2	1.27	3.93	1.73
1968	7,555,944	1,035.0	3,020.0	n/a	1.37	4.00	n/a
1969	7,751,465	980.9	3,334.6	1,325.8	1.27	4.30	1.71
1970	7,959,529	1,057.7	3,312.9	1,357.2	1.33	4.16	1.71
1971	8,165,472	1,078.4	3,643.7	1,421.3	1.32	4.46	1.74
1972	8,364,346	1,062.9	3,371.3	1,449.9	1.27	4.03	1.73
1973	8,511,519	1,140.1	3,460.0	1,593.2	1.34	4.07	1.87

Sources: Numbers of pupils in maintained schools (Simon 1991: 576); SHS staff: Ministry of Education 1949: 139–40; 1952a: 81; 1952b: 126–8; 1954: 130–2; 1956b: 166–8; 1958: 199–201; 1960: 205–7; 1962c: 225–7; Department of Education and Science 1964: 129, 145; 1966d: 118–20, 138; 1969b: 115–6, 125; 1972c: 104–6, 115; 1973: Table 33; 1974a: 54–6, 64; Henderson 1975: 49–50, 56.

were expected to serve. During the period between 1947 and 1973, the number of children attending maintained schools in England and Wales increased by 39 per cent, while the numbers of school medical officers and school nurses increased by 37 per cent and 38.1 per cent, respectively (Simon 1991: 576). Over the period as a whole, the ratio of school doctors and school nurses to pupils remained virtually unchanged, while the ratio of school dentists increased only fractionally from one dentist for every 6650 children in 1947 to one dentist for every 5344 children 26 years later (Table 9.3).[3]

One of the main aims behind the establishment of both the school health service and the National Health Service had been to secure a more even distribution of medical staff throughout Britain (Klein 1989: 147–52; Ham 1992: 190–98). However, in spite of this, staffing levels continued to vary widely. In January 1966 the number of medical officers per 10,000 pupils ranged from 1.26 in the Eastern region and North Midlands to 1.64 in Wales, and nearly thirty areas (out of a total of 162) reported doctor–pupil ratios of more than 2:10,000 or less than 1:10,000.[4] The most striking variations were observed in the school dental service. The number of dental officers varied from 1.09 dentists per 10,000 pupils in the North Midlands to 2.11 in Greater London and 2.39 in the South-West of England. The number of

Table 9.4 Number of medical officers, school nurses and dental officers (full-time equivalents) on the staff of local education authorities in England and Wales, per 10,000 children, January 1966.

	Medical officers	*School nurses*	*Dental officers*
Northern	1.27	4.49	2.11
Yorkshire (East and West Ridings)	1.46	4.88	1.72
North-Western	1.43	4.86	1.67
North Midland	1.26	3.38	1.09
Midland	1.31	4.35	1.61
Eastern	1.26	3.39	1.78
South-Eastern	1.50	3.41	2.16
Southern	1.27	4.03	2.00
South-Western	1.44	4.09	2.39
Greater London	1.71	5.19	2.11
England	1.41	4.34	1.86
Wales	1.64	3.67	1.68
England and Wales	1.43	4.30	1.85

Note: This table is based on the summary table on p. 124 of *Health of the schoolchild* 1964–5, but the figures have been recalculated using the individual returns for each area. Information about the numbers of children in each area is given in Appendix I of the same report. The composition of each region is described in Department of Education and Science (1967: 7–8, para. 34).

Source: Department of Education and Science (1966d: 121–4).

school nurses per 10,000 pupils ranged from 3.38 in the North Midlands and 3.39 in the Eastern region to 4.88 in Yorkshire and 5.19 in Greater London (Table 9.4).

Medical inspection and treatment

Despite the changes introduced by the National Health Service, the core of the school health service remained its ability to carry out medical inspections, detect the signs and symptoms of disease, and secure the provision of effective medical treatment. Nevertheless, the performance of all these tasks underwent significant changes after 1945. The Ministry of Education relaxed the regulations surrounding routine medical inspection in 1953 and 1959, and this led to a substantial reduction in the number of children who were routinely examined. The establishment of the National Health Service meant that many of the specialist services which had previously been provided by the school medical service were transferred to the regional hospital boards, and the expansion of the general practitioner service enabled a much higher proportion of schoolchildren to obtain treatment from their own doctor.[5] The development of the school health service was also affected by the general improvement in child health and the growing emphasis on 'emotional' and 'psychological' disorders (Hendrick 1994: 211–88). There was a sharp reduction in the number of children receiving treatment for physical 'defects', and a corresponding increase in the number of children receiving speech therapy or child guidance.

The regulations governing the conduct of routine medical inspection were established by the Handicapped Pupils and School Health Service Regulations of 1945 (Ministry of Education 1945b). Paragraph 49 of the new regulations stated that all children should be examined as soon as possible after their admission to a maintained primary school, during the last year of their attendance at such a school, and during the last year of their attendance at a maintained secondary school. However, during the 1950s the Ministry of Education modified these regulations in two important ways. In 1953 it stated that 'there may be fewer than three general inspections for any pupil who attends schools maintained by the Authority for less than the period of his compulsory school age, or, if the Minister approves, for all pupils' (Ministry of Education 1953: para. 10). In 1959 it decided to abandon its insistence on routine medical inspection altogether, and urged local authorities to consider alternative ways of carrying out more selective schemes (Ministry of Education 1959a). On 24 March 1959 the Ministry advised local authorities that:

> Where it is possible . . . for the school doctor to visit schools regularly . . . it may be found preferable for him to see on each occasion such children as are brought to his attention by parents, teachers or the school nurse, instead of seeing all the children of a particular age group

> at infrequent intervals. The Minister hopes that this practice will continue to be developed, as being likely to increase the efficiency of the preventive work of the school health service (Ministry of Education 1959b: para. 8).

One of the most influential critics of routine medical inspection was Allan Withnell, a lecturer in social medicine at Sheffield University. Withnell argued that the general improvement in the standard of child health had led to a radical change in the overall pattern of children's diseases. There had been a marked reduction in the incidence of physical defects, which were detected largely by signs, and an apparent increase in the incidence of emotional and psychological disorders, which were detected by symptoms. However, even though the character of the defects discovered by school medical officers had changed, there had been little change in the arrangements for detecting them. Withnell concluded that the 'changing pattern . . . [of] disease in child[hood] has . . . an important bearing on the screening procedures required to detect these conditions' (Withnell 1957: 28–32; see also Ministry of Education 1958: 75).[6]

In addition to highlighting the changing pattern of childhood disease, Withnell also argued that many of the screening procedures which were used in the course of routine medical inspections had been superseded by the growth of new specialist services, such as dentistry, audiometry and chiropody. In the winter of 1956–7 he conducted his own investigation into the use of audiometers to test children's hearing. He found that the audiometer was much more effective than any of the techniques which the school medical officer could use during a routine examination, and concluded that there was no need for the medical officer to test children's hearing if they had previously been tested with an audiometer (Withnell 1957: 32–3; 1958: 5–6).

Withnell's arguments received powerful support from the Principal Medical Officer of the Ministry of Education, Dr Peter Henderson. Henderson pointed out that routine medical inspection was only one of the ways in which school medical officers became aware of children's 'defects', and that approximately one-third of all the defects discovered by school medical officers were encountered at special examinations which had nothing to do with the routine examination.[7] He also argued that the effectiveness of routine medical inspection was often undermined by the failure to maintain proper records. One school medical officer, who had examined the records of 400 children who left school between 1952 and 1955–6, found that in 236 cases there was no record of the entrant's examination and in 116 cases no record of the leaver's examination. On another occasion, a different school medical officer, who had been asked to examine twenty school-leavers, was given twenty blank cards because none of the children's earlier records could be found (Henderson 1957: 43–7).

Henderson also questioned the statistical value of the results generated by routine medical inspection, because the returns for neighbouring areas showed wide variations. In 1955, the average proportion of children who were found to require treatment for defective vision at periodic medical inspections in England and Wales was 51.4 per thousand, but the returns for two neighbouring areas were 20 per thousand and 85 per thousand respectively. The average proportion of children requiring treatment for defective heart conditions was 2.3 per thousand, but the returns for two groups of adjacent areas ranged from 0.5 to 13 per thousand, in the first instance, and from 0 to 8 per thousand in the second. The average proportion of children suffering from serious lung defects was 6 per thousand, but the returns for neighbouring areas ranged from 4 to 31 per thousand, and from 2 to 26 per thousand (Henderson 1957: 43–7).[8]

In view of these arguments, it is not surprising that a substantial number of local education authorities took advantage of the new regulations to abandon the traditional system of routine medical inspection. Between 1953 and 1967 two local authorities abandoned the routine examination of school entrants; seventy-one authorities abandoned the routine examination of intermediates; and twenty-two authorities abandoned the routine examination of school-leavers (Department of Education and Science 1972c: 9; Lunn 1967: 303–5). The number of children who received a routine examination fell from 2.15 million in 1956 to 1.54 million seventeen years later. However, the postwar years also witnessed an even more substantial decline in the number of special examinations and reexaminations. During the second half of the 1940s, school medical officers conducted nearly 1.2 million special inspections and 1.5 million reinspections each year. By 1970, the number of special inspections had fallen to 478,000, and the number of reinspections to 1.2 million (Table 9.5).

In addition to changes in the system of medical inspection, the postwar period witnessed a number of changes in the provision of medical treatment. These changes were associated with a number of factors, including the establishment of the National Health Service, the increased availability of general practitioners, and the general improvement in child health. The number of children who received treatment for some conditions was also affected by changes in medical practice.[9] As a result of these changes, there was a substantial decline in the number of children who received treatment for physical defects. The period also witnessed a number of important developments in the provision of effective forms of vaccination against tuberculosis and poliomyelitis. The administration of these vaccines represented an important addition to the work of the school health service from the mid-1950s onwards.

Table 9.6 contains a summary of the number of children who received treatment for various conditions as a result of the school health service. The most notable change concerns the sharp decline in the number of children who received treatment for physical defects. During the period between 1947 and 1973, the number of children receiving treatment for skin diseases fell by 120,000, the number receiving treatment for various forms of eye disease (excluding errors of refraction and squint) fell by nearly 50,000, and the

Table 9.5 Medical inspections by local education authorities, 1946–73.

	Routine inspections	*Special inspections*	*Reinspections*	*Special inspections and reinspections*	*Total inspections*
1946	1,633,560	n/a	n/a	2,647,132	4,280,692
1947	1,652,357	1,169,264	1,481,947	2,651,211	4,303,568
1948	1,798,802	n/a	n/a	2,882,680	4,681,482
1949	1,834,742	1,174,921	1,512,807	2,882,680	4,522,482
1950	1,866,958	n/a	n/a	2,582,183	4,449,141
1951	1,879,376	1,146,970	1,384,284	2,531,254	4,410,630
1952	1,978,303	1,125,246	1,366,007	2,491,253	4,469,556
1953	2,057,965	1,107,027	1,281,873	2,388,900	4,446,865
1954	2,127,374	1,084,528	1,269,628	2,354,156	4,481,530
1955	2,119,454	1,036,560	1,178,629	2,215,189	4,334,643
1956	2,148,765	978,641	1,151,613	2,130,254	4,279,019
1957	2,106,157	924,387	1,109,160	2,033,547	4,139,704
1958	2,078,803	809,226	1,043,559	1,852,785	3,931,588
1959	2,138,616	703,948	1,041,375	1,745,323	3,883,939
1960	2,112,353	701,759	1,060,046	1,761,805	3,874,158
1961	2,056,221	723,589	936,523	1,660,112	3,716,333
1962	2,110,143	673,411	947,672	1,621,083	3,731,226
1963	2,010,215	665,614	925,314	1,590,928	3,601,143
1964	1,972,071	n/a	n/a	1,538,383	3,510,454
1965	1,886,524	601,183	876,985	1,478,168	3,364,692
1966	1,892,000	n/a	n/a	1,393,000	3,285,000
1967	1,870,126	n/a	n/a	1,364,193	3,234,319
1968	1,803,000	n/a	n/a	1,291,000	3,094,000
1969	1,796,511	n/a	n/a	1,215,003	3,011,514
1970	1,786,329	477,809	701,506	1,179,315	2,965,644
1971	1,746,000	n/a	n/a	1,245,000	2,991,000
1972	1,631,496	n/a	n/a	1,176,648	2,808,144
1973	1,536,911	n/a	n/a	1,143,475	2,680,386

Sources: Ministry of Education 1949: 141; 1952a: 82; 1952b: 129; 1954: 133; 1956b: 171; 1958: 204; 1960: 210; 1962c: 230; Department of Education and Science 1964: 132; 1966d: 125; 1969b: 117; 1972b: 107; 1973: Table 32; 1974a: 57; Henderson 1975: 51.

number receiving treatment for conditions of the ear, nose and throat (including the operative treatment of tonsils and adenoids) fell by nearly 80,000. The number of children receiving treatment for orthopaedic and postural defects fell by more than 60,000 between 1950 and 1973. At the same time, there was also a substantial increase in the numbers of children receiving treatment in the form of child guidance and speech therapy. The number of children who were known to have received treatment at child guidance clinics rose by nearly 65,000, while the number receiving treatment for speech defects increased by 93,000.

One of the most important functions of the school health service during the 1950s and 1960s was its involvement in the public health campaigns against tuberculosis and poliomyelitis. Local education authorities played an

Table 9.6 The provision of medical treatment through the school health service, 1947–73.

	Skin diseases	*Miscellaneous minor ailments and injuries*[a]	*Eye diseases (excl. squint)*	*Defective vision and squint*	*Ear, nose or throat defects*	*Orthopaedic or postural defects*	*Child guidance*	*Speech therapy*
1947	271,686	773,060	74,795	322,263	178,678	n/a	16,000	16,000
1948	266,611	885,930	105,380	363,483	245,061	n/a	18,000	18,000
1949	227,736	844,821	104,077	367,201	204,600	n/a	21,149	25,098
1950	211,006	987,978	86,756	369,862	198,642	141,000	22,379	24,340
1951	208,721	938,628	91,741	398,879	217,924	140,000	25,123	28,132
1952	217,414	870,358	92,975	423,344	214,640	136,000	26,859	33,874
1953	216,897	819,808	91,482	441,409	211,125	130,000	28,458	39,532
1954	215,664	788,608	84,132	456,190	204,278	137,000	29,889	44,840
1955	212,318	721,492	74,267	477,960	177,870	126,000	30,994	47,794
1956	188,415	798,879	64,643	491,455	172,722	119,000	31,067	45,824
1957	173,824	857,321[b]	64,603	494,936	145,551	121,000	32,010	49,817
1958	177,523	1,036,051[b]	56,314	496,379	164,206	128,000	34,594	51,949
1959	165,251	1,046,426[b]	53,449	515,211	149,901	129,000	36,281	56,291
1960	168,697	1,072,871[b]	54,132	505,445	148,928	121,000	39,519	57,536
1961	170,394	1,203,741[b]	48,306	490,452	133,780	119,000	46,350	58,640
1962	161,734	1,074,394[b]	47,313	518,008	125,561	109,000	44,248	62,217
1963	156,532	960,020[b]	47,570	526,429	127,909	105,000	49,133	61,297
1964	157,728	905,532[b]	45,278	532,697	127,545	105,000	46,303	58,087
1965	158,713	893,667[b]	51,432	502,023	124,957	94,000	54,418	61,755
1966	n/a	n/a	n/a	n/a	117,000	89,000	57,000	65,000
1967	178,094	341,918[c]	35,678	450,940	117,000	85,000	61,532	67,894
1968	n/a	n/a	n/a	n/a	110,000	79,000	64,000	81,000
1969	180,181	319,741[c]	29,602	404,305	104,000	79,000	65,654	82,307
1970	164,833	292,505[c]	25,810	409,053	102,000	71,000	69,321	88,164
1971	n/a	n/a	n/a	n/a	99,000	70,000	69,256	94,445
1972	156,193	296,924[c]	28,130	380,232	95,000	69,000	74,696	103,909
1973	150,735	294,241[c]	25,699	362,889	90,000	79,000	79,265	109,628

[a] The Chief Medical Officer used the term 'minor ailments' to describe a number of different categories of defect during the period under review. In 1946/47 and 1948/49 he used term to describe skin diseases, eye diseases (excluding errors of refraction and squint), ear defects and miscellaneous injuries. In his reports for 1950/51–1954/55 he used the term to describe skin diseases, eye diseases and miscellaneous injuries only. Between 1956/57 and 1964/65 the figure for miscellaneous injuries included children who received convalescent treatment (presumably for tuberculosis) and the number of children who were given the BCG vaccine. From 1966/68 onwards, the term 'minor ailments' was reserved for children receiving treatment for minor injuries. In this table, the column headed 'miscellaneous minor ailments and injuries' refers to the number of children receiving treatment for miscellaneous conditions (including convalescent treatment) between 1946/47 and 1964/65, and to the number of children receiving treatment for minor ailments and convalescent treatment between 1966/68 and 1973, except where otherwise stated.
[b] Includes children receiving convalescent treatment and the BCG vaccine.
[c] Includes children receiving convalescent treatment.

Sources: Orthopaedic and postural defects (1950–73): Central Statistical Office 1955: Table 103; 1965: Table 97; 1975: Table 104; Ear, nose and throat defects (1966–73): Central Statistical Office 1975b: Table 104; Child guidance and speech therapy: 1947–48: Central Statistical Office 1955: Table 103; 1966, 1968: Central Statistical Office 1975b: Table 104; All other treatment statistics: Ministry of Education 1949: 144–5; 1952a: 85–6; 1952b: 133–5; 1954: 138–9; 1956b: 175–7; 1958: 209–11; 1960: 215–7; 1962c: 236–7; Department of Education and Science 1964: 137–40; 1966d: 131–2; 1969b: 119–20; 1972b: 109–10; 1974a: 58–9; Henderson 1975: 51–2.

important part in the development of mass radiography (for the detection of pulmonary tuberculosis) during the 1940s, and in the early 1950s they also took part in tests using tuberculin jelly. However, it was not until the mid-1950s that local authorities began to make extensive use of the Bacille Calmette–Guérin (BCG) vaccine on a routine basis (Ministry of Education 1952a: 72–4; 1952b: 79–80; 1956b: 78–80; 1958: 161). During the early years of the scheme, vaccination was limited to children between the ages of thirteen and fourteen, but in 1959 the Ministry of Health extended the provision to children who were approaching the age of thirteen and to children aged fourteen and over, and in 1961 it gave local authorities permission to vaccinate all children over the age of ten (Ministry of Education 1960: 144–5; 1962c: 190). By the early 1960s, every local education authority had made some provision for the vaccination of schoolchildren, and more than 400,000 children were vaccinated by school medical officers each year (Department of Education and Science 1964: 36; 1966d: 45–6).

The school health service also played an active role in the campaign against poliomyelitis. Polio vaccine first became available in January 1956, and in February 1956 the Ministry of Health drew up plans to inoculate between 250,000 and 500,000 children between the ages of two and nine (Ministry of Education 1956b: 83). In September 1957 the Ministry extended provision to all children under the age of fifteen, and the Chief Medical Officer warned local authorities to expect their medical officers to 'be busily engaged on this work during the early part of 1958' (Ministry of Education 1958: 163–4). In 1961 the Minister of Health announced that an oral vaccine had been developed by Dr Albert Sabin in the United States, and this led to a sharp increase in the supply of polio vaccine to pre-school children (Ministry of Education 1962c 195; Department of Education and Science 1964: 37–8). There was also a corresponding decline in the number of children requiring vaccination after entering school, but the Chief Medical Officer continued to emphasise the need for vigilance. In his report for 1969–70 he concluded:

> Children on entry to school should have a course of three doses of oral vaccine at specified intervals if unvaccinated or not fully vaccinated; a further booster dose should be given to those children who have not been fully immunised in infancy. It is probable that most areas of England and Wales have a level of vaccination which is high enough, if maintained, to prevent a major outbreak, but there may still be pockets of unprotected individuals among whom infection would spread. The Netherlands has recently experienced just such an incident in a village where the number of objectors to vaccination was high. Neither the community nor parents can afford to neglect vaccination (Department of Education and Science 1972b: 89).

The school dental service

During the early years of the Second World War the condition of the dental profession attracted considerable attention. During the 1930s, the average age of the profession had been gradually increasing, and the supply of new recruits dwindled still further after 1939 (PP 1943–4 Cmd. 6565 iii: para. 33). The seriousness of this condition was underlined by the fact that 98 per cent of children leaving public elementary schools showed signs of past or present dental caries, and 86 per cent of female recruits and 90 per cent of male recruits required dental treatment when they joined the Army (PRO MH77/124, Report of a Committee on Postwar Dentistry: para. 3; PP 1943–4 Cmd. 6565 iii: Appendix B). In April 1943 the government appointed an Interdepartmental Committee (the Teviot Committee) to consider 'the progressive stages by which . . . provision for an adequate and satisfactory dental service should be made available for the population' (PP 1943–4 Cmd. 6565 iii: para. 1). The Committee recommended that 'a comprehensive dental service should be initiated as an integral part of the National Health Service at its inception', but it recognised that it would take some time before a comprehensive dental service could be achieved (ibid.: paras 72–80; recommendation no. 1). It therefore suggested that special attention should be paid to the needs of three 'priority classes' – nursing and expectant mothers, children and adolescents (ibid.: para. 83). It welcomed the fact that local education authorities were obliged to provide medical inspection and treatment (including dental inspection and treatment) under Section 48 (3) of the 1944 Education Act, and concluded that 'we regard a big expansion of the dental service available to schoolchildren as one of the essential foundations of a comprehensive service' (ibid.: para. 85).

The status of the school dental service became the focus of further discussion following the introduction of the National Health Service Bill in 1946. Section 40 of the National Health Service Bill required the new executive councils to make arrangements with local dental practitioners regarding the supply of dental services in their area, but these arrangements were much more limited than the arrangements for the National Health Service as a whole (PP 1945–6 (94) iii, section 40). The Ministry of Education was afraid that some local education authorities might take advantage of this clause to abandon their own dental treatment schemes even though the Bill failed to establish a comprehensive dental service in their area, and it urged the Ministry of Health to make it clear 'that section 40 does not affect . . . [the] powers [of local education authorities] under Section 48 (3) of the Education Act' (PRO ED50/351, Maud to Douglas, 19/7/46). The Ministry of Health rejected this proposal on the grounds that it would undermine the agreement between the two departments that all treatment functions would eventually be transferred to the National Health Service (PP 1943–4 Cmd. 6502 viii: 39; PRO ED50/351, Douglas to Maud, 17/10/46). However, it recognised that 'the stage at which a sufficient general dental service is likely to be available . . . seems pretty remote' and it said that local education authorities would continue to provide dental treatment for a considerable time to come (PRO ED5O/351, Douglas to Maud, 27/9/46; 17/10/46).[10]

Although the establishment of the National Health Service had little immediate effect on the administrative position of the school dental service, it had an important effect on the provision of child dental services as a whole. During the early years of the National Health Service, it is likely that the majority of schoolchildren continued to receive dental treatment from the school dentists, but as the general dental service expanded, a growing number of children became registered with ordinary dental practitioners. It is difficult to obtain reliable statistics on this point, but it has been estimated that by the mid-1960s National Health Service dentists provided approximately 4.5 million courses of treatment to children between the ages of five and fifteen, and carried out more than 6 million individual fillings (Department of Education and Science 1966d: 99).[11] The establishment of the National Health Service also had a dramatic effect in the short term on Local Authority staffing levels. The introduction of new salary scales for NHS dentists meant that large numbers of school dentists left the school dental service in order to obtain better remuneration elsewhere (Ministry of Education 1952a: 46). As a result, the number of school dentists, expressed in terms of whole-time equivalents, fell from 921 at the end of 1947 to 880 at the end of 1948 and to 732 at the end of 1949 (ibid.). The school dental service still employed the equivalent of less than 1000 full-time dentists at the end of 1954, and the ratio of dentists to pupils did not regain its former level until the early 1960s (see Table 9.3).

The problems faced by local education authorities in recruiting dental officers were discussed in two official reports in 1955 and 1956. The McNair Committee on Recruitment to the Dental Profession pointed out that the difficulties faced by the school dental service needed to be placed within the context of dental recruitment as a whole, and called for the number of places for students in dental schools to be increased from 650 to 1000 (PP 1955–6 Cmd. 9861 xiv: para. 126).[12] The Guillebaud Committee on the Cost of the National Health Service argued that in the short term some attempt should be made to ensure that there was a degree of parity between the remuneration available to local authority dentists and dentists working in the National Health Service. It concluded:

> One lesson to be learnt from these last seven years is that if the Local Authority services and the general dental service are to be developed in step, then it is essential that the relationship between the two types of remuneration should be kept in balance (PP 1955–6 Cmd. 9663 xx: para. 538).

In addition to the problem of poor (or relatively poor) remuneration, the development of the school dental service was also hampered by the poor status enjoyed by school dental officers within the school health service. During the second half of the 1950s, a number of school dentists argued that the school dental service should become entirely independent of the school health service, while others said that the Principal School Dental Officer should at least enjoy a substantial degree of autonomy in dental matters (Ministry of Education 1960: 34). The Ministries of Health and Education discussed the issue with representatives of the various Local Education Authority Associations, the British Dental Association, and a number of individual school medical officers and school dental officers, and in 1962 they issued a joint Circular setting out some of the ways in which local authorities could make employment in the school dental service a more attractive proposition (Ministry of Education 1962c: 186). In addition to recommending the appointment of more 'chairside assistants', they advocated the creation of a larger number of senior dental posts. They argued that the creation of such posts would not only lead to increased efficiency, but would also enhance the career prospects of individual officers (Ministry of Education 1962b).

The most important changes in the development of the school dental service followed the publication of a scathing report by the House of Commons Select Committee on the Estimates in December 1962 (PP 1962–3 (40) v). The Committee pointed out that there was a marked lack of uniformity in the local administration of the school dental service, and urged local authorities to do more to recruit and retain dental staff (ibid., paras 53, 57–8). It also drew attention to the fact that, while the 'productivity' of dentists in the National Health Service appeared to be increasing, the productivity of school dentists was declining (ibid., paras 61–6). It criticised the Ministry of Education for its failure to take effective measures to improve the service, and for its reluctance to urge local authorities to take full advantage of the National Health Service (ibid., paras 72, 77). In its conclusions, it said that 'the responsible Departments [i.e. the Ministry of Education and the Scottish Home and Health Department] should bring to the notice of all Local Authorities the desirability of entrusting the local responsibility for the school dental service to their Health Committees or to Joint Committees including members of their Health Committees', and that 'the responsibilities for the school dental service . . . [which are currently] exercised . . . by the Minister of Education should be assumed by the Minister of Health (ibid., paras 103 (12), 103 (17)). It also urged

> the responsible departments . . . [to] take a close interest in the progress of all schemes involving cooperation between local education authorities and executive councils, and . . . [to] communicate the details of any which prove to be successful to all local education authorities, so that they may be put into operation in other areas (ibid.: para. 103 (19)).

In its response to the Committee's report, the government declined to transfer responsibility for the school dental service from the Ministry of Education to the Ministry of Health, but it accepted many of the Committee's other recommendations. The Chief Dental Officer of the Ministry of Health was given the additional title (and duties) of Chief Dental Officer of the Ministry of Education, and the dental staffs of the two departments were merged to form the Joint Dental Staff (Department of Education and Science 1966b: Appendix 1, para. 1). The two Ministries sought to improve the efficiency of the school dental service by instituting a programme of annual inspections, and by revising the form on which local authorities submitted their statistical returns (ibid.: paras 3–4, 6). They also advised local authorities to improve the degree of coordination between the school dental service and the maternity and child welfare dental service, and between each of these services and the National Health Service (ibid.: para. 5). They attached particular importance to the question of dental personnel. They advised local authorities to continue their efforts to recruit additional dentists by offering better promotion prospects and higher rates of pay, and they tried to improve the efficiency of school dentists by providing postgraduate and refresher courses, and by encouraging them to take up sessional appointments in the dental departments of local hospitals (ibid.: Appendix 2, paras 3–4).

In addition to these developments, the 1960s witnessed the appointment of the first dental auxiliaries. The school medical service began to employ dental attendants (or chairside assistants) in 1908 but the Dentists Act of 1921 prevented any person other than a registered dentist from providing dental treatment (PP 1910 Cd. 4986 xxiii: 100–1; 11 & 12 Geo. V Ch. 21, section 1 (1)). During the Second World War the armed forces had employed a small number of dental hygienists, and in 1946 the Teviot Committee recommended that 'a general scheme for the training of dental hygienists should be initiated forthwith' (PP 1945–6 Cmd. 6727 xi: paras 169, 190). However, it was not until 1956 that Parliament passed legislation which permitted the General Dental Council to establish a category of ancillary dental workers 'to undertake dental work . . . amounting to the practice of dentistry under the . . . [1921] Dentists' Act' (4 & 5 Eliz. II Ch. 29, section 18). The first 'ancillary dental workers', or dental auxiliaries, were appointed in 1962, and by the end of 1973 they represented the equivalent of 197.9 full-time workers (Henderson 1975: 62). In 1969 the Chief Medical Officer observed that 'these girls are providing a useful addition to the service and . . . in many areas where there is an insufficient number of dental officers the additional assistance has been invaluable' (Department of Education and Science 1969b: 38). In 1972, 'these girls' were directly responsible for the treatment of 81,000 pupils, and for the provision of 282,000 individual fillings (Department of Education and Science 1974a: 52).

The postwar period also witnessed two important developments in the kinds of treatment provided by the school dental service. The most obvious development concerned the relationship between fillings and extractions. During the Second World War, the Board of Education had advised school dentists to limit conservative dentistry to 'the children of parents who have already shown their appreciation of conservative treatment' (PRO ED138/56, Circular 1523: para. 9), and the Ministry of Education continued to advise local authorities to exercise 'caution' in the filling of temporary teeth after 1945 (Ministry of Education 1949: 65). However, as the number of school dentists began to increase, the Ministry began to take a more optimistic view of the possibilities of conservative treatment. The number of fillings began to rise rapidly after 1951, and the number of fillings exceeded the number of extractions for the first time in 1957 (Ministry of Education 1958: 212).[13] In 1973, during the last full year of the 'independent' school health service, school dentists carried out 2.3 million permanent fillings and 1.1 million temporary fillings. By contrast, the total number of extractions of both permanent and temporary teeth was less than 1.2 million (Henderson 1975: 58).[14]

The second major development was the gradual expansion of orthodontic treatment. Many local education authorities began to provide orthodontic services at the end of the Second World War, with the general approval of the Chief Medical Officer (Ministry of Education 1949: 66).[15] However, in 1948 he warned local authorities 'to exercise discretion . . . in making . . . [this service] available to the public' (ibid), and in 1950 he said that in view of 'the present . . . shortage of dental officers . . . the need for strictly limiting the amount of orthodontic work . . . should . . . be evident to all concerned' (Ministry of Education 1952a: 49). In 1955 the Ministry adopted a more relaxed attitude and expressed the hope that local education authorities would expand their services 'as quickly as other considerations permit', but it also said that orthodontic work should not be undertaken at the expense of ordinary treatment, and advised local authorities to notify the regional hospital board if they required assistance. It is difficult to obtain comprehensive statistics, but the available evidence suggests that the number of children who received orthodontic treatment through the school dental service increased only slowly from this point onwards. In 1956 school dentists fitted 30,101 removable appliances and 3,424 fixed appliances. The equivalent figures for 1973 were 42,684 and 2,773, respectively (Ministry of Education 1958: 64; Henderson 1975: 58).

School milk and meals

In addition to the changes made to the school health service, the 1944 Education Act also had a major impact on the provision of school milk and meals. Section 49 of the Act stated that 'regulations made by the Minister shall impose upon Local Education Authorities the duty of providing milk, meals and other refreshment for pupils in attendance at schools and county colleges maintained by them' (7 & 8 Geo. VI Ch. 31, section 49). In 1945, the Provision of Milk and Meals Regulations stated that the arrangements for the provision of these services would be known collectively as the school meals service (Ministry of Education 1945a: para. 2). Under the terms of the Regulations, each local education authority was expected to appoint an organiser of school meals with suitable qualifications in dietetics and cookery and experience of planning, preparing and serving meals on a large scale (ibid.: para. 13). The meals themselves were expected to be 'adequate in quantity and quality so as to be suitable as the main meal of the day', and local authorities were instructed to keep suitable records of the ingredients used (ibid.: para. 8).

The cost of providing school dinners was divided between the government and local authorities, on the one hand, and the children's parents, on the other. The government continued to pay the full cost of capital expenditure and between 70 and 95 per cent of the local authorities' current expenditure until the introduction of the unit grant system in 1947. Under this system, the Ministry agreed to reimburse local authorities for the whole of their 'reasonable expenditure', provided that this figure had been agreed in advance on the basis of estimates prepared by the authorities (PP 1950–51 Cmd. 8244 xi: 30–31).[16] Local authorities were also expected to recover part of the cost of the school meals service by charging the children's parents an amount not exceeding the cost of the food provided (Ministry of Education 1945a: para. 10). The government was forced to abandon plans for the introduction of a universal free meals service, but local authorities were given the power to provide free or subsidised meals to those children whose parents were unable to pay (Ministry of Education 1945a: para. 10; PP 1947–8 Cmd. 7426 xi: 57).

The development of the school meals service after 1945 continued to be dominated by financial considerations. The government imposed restrictions on capital expenditure in 1948 and these remained in force for much of the 1950s, but in spite of this there was still a substantial reduction in the number of schools which lacked canteen facilities.[17] The government sought to control the level of current expenditure by raising meal prices, and tried to protect the poorest parents by raising the income scales which were used to calculate fee remissions. Between 1945 and 1963, local authorities were allowed to set their own income scales, but these were replaced by national scales in May 1963 (PP 1963–4 Cmnd. 2316 xi: 33; PP 1964–5 Cmnd. 2612 xiii: 52).[18]

The impact of these changes on the development of the school meals service can be seen from Table 9.7. The table shows that in spite of the restrictions which were imposed at different times on both capital and current expenditure, the total number of pupils receiving school dinners continued to rise. Over the whole period from 1946 to 1973, the number of children receiving school dinners increased from 2.3 million to 5.8 million, and the proportion of children taking school dinners increased from 47 per cent to 70.1 per cent. However, the table also shows that there was a disproportionate increase in the number of children receiving free meals from 1955 onwards. The number of children rose particularly sharply in 1968, when the government automatically provided free meals to all children with three or more siblings under the age of nineteen (PP 1968–9 Cmnd. 3950 xxviii: 52; Department of Education and Science 1968a, para. 2). Over the period as a whole, however, the proportion of children receiving free meals increased from 3.7 per cent in 1958 to 9.6 per cent 15 years later.

The postwar years were also marked by a series of negotiations with teaching organisations over the role played by teachers in the supervision of school meals, and by the continuation of efforts to improve the quality and variety of the meals provided. The Provision of Milk and Meals Regulations granted local education authorities the power to 'require teachers of any

Table 9.7 The provision of school meals in England and Wales, 1946–74.

	Day pupils present (thousands)	*Day pupils taking dinners (thousands)*			*Day pupils taking dinners as percentage of those present*		
		Free	*On payment*	*Total*	*Free*	*On payment*	*Total*
1946	4788	n/a	n/a	2252	n/a	n/a	47.0
1947	4994	n/a	n/a	2536	n/a	n/a	50.8
1948	5213	n/a	n/a	2743	n/a	n/a	52.6
1949	5354	n/a	n/a	2851	n/a	n/a	53.2
1950	5445	n/a	n/a	2745	n/a	n/a	50.4
1951	5630	n/a	n/a	2824	n/a	n/a	50.2
1952	5838	n/a	n/a	3009	n/a	n/a	51.5
1953	6025	n/a	n/a	2734	n/a	n/a	45.4
1954	6188	n/a	n/a	2850	n/a	n/a	46.1
1955	6246	226	2792	3018	3.6	44.7	48.3
1956	6386	n/a	n/a	3059	n/a	n/a	47.9
1957	6205	n/a	n/a	2847	n/a	n/a	45.9
1958	6471	239	2854	3093	3.7	44.1	47.8
1959	6507	254	2978	3232	3.9	45.8	49.7
1960	6499	247	2978	3408	3.8	48.6	52.4
1961	6584	238	3161	3560	3.6	50.4	54.1
1962	6510	261	3322	3652	4.0	52.1	56.1
1963	6506	289	3391	3849	4.4	54.7	59.2
1964	6577	281	3808	4089	4.3	57.9	62.2
1965	6672	308	4053	4361	4.6	60.7	65.4
1966	6810	330	4325	4655	4.8	63.5	68.4
1967	6974	404	4442	4847	5.8	63.7	69.5
1968	7160	841	4179	5020	11.7	58.4	70.1
1969	7378	594	4575	5169	8.1	62.0	70.1
1970	7587	635	4521	5148	8.4	59.6	67.9
1971	7788	805	3853	4658[a]	10.3	49.5	59.8
1972	7929	851	4229	5080[b]	10.7	53.3	64.0
1973	8198	795	4621	5416	9.7	56.4	66.1
1974	8240	750	5023	5773	9.1	61.0	70.1

[a]According to the Annual Abstract of Statistics for 1975, the total number of children receiving meals in England and Wales was 4,659,000 (Central Statistical Office 1975b: Table 105).

[b]According to the Annual Abstract of Statistics for 1975, the total number of children receiving meals in England and Wales was 5,076,000 (Central Statistical Office 1975b: Table 105).

Sources: 1946–57: Central Statistical Office (1956: Table 101); 1955: Number of pupils receiving dinners free and on payment: Ministry of Education (1956a: 2; 1958: Table 102); 1958–9; Number of pupils present: Central Statistical Office (1960: Table 102); Number of pupils receiving dinners free and on payment: Ministry of Education (1960: 219; 1960–70); Number of pupils present: Central Statistical Office (1971: Table 104); Number of pupils receiving dinners free and on payment: PP 1961–2 Cmnd. 1737 xiii: 27–8; PP 1962–3 Cmnd. 1990 xi: 27; PP 1963–4 Cmnd. 2316 xi: 33; PP 1964–5 Cmnd. 2612 xiii: 52; PP 1966–7 Cmnd. 2938 xxvii: 47; PP 1966–7 Cmnd. 3226 xxvii: 50; PP 1967–8 Cmnd. 3564 xix: 49; PP 1968–9 Cmnd. 3950 xxviii: 52; Department of Education and Science (1970: 47; 1971: 21); 1971–4: Number of pupils present in England and Wales: Central Statistical Office (1975b: Table 105); Number of pupils present in Wales: Welsh Office (1976: Table 8.01); Number of pupils receiving dinners free and on payment in England: Department of Education and Science (1974b: 7; 1975: 7); Number of pupils receiving dinners free and on payment in Wales: Welsh Office (1976: Table 8.01).

school to supervise pupils partaking of dinners upon days on which the school is open for instruction', but both the government and the teachers were concerned by the size of the burden teachers faced (Ministry of Education 1945a: para. 14). In April 1946 the Ministry advised local authorities to appoint supervisory assistants to assist teachers with midday supervision (PP 1947–8 Cmd. 7426 xi: 57), and in 1959 it advised them to review their arrangements for the appointment of these assistants and provide additional clerical support (PP 1959–60 Cmnd. 1088 xii: 29). In 1963 it said that although local education authorities were entitled to assume some 'voluntary assistance', teachers should not be subjected to any 'unreasonable burdens' (Ministry of Education 1963b: para. 3). In 1967 the National Union of Teachers withdrew its support for the school meals service in eighteen local authority areas, and the government agreed to establish a Joint Working Party to consider the question further. The Working Party recommended that local authorities should no longer be able to require teachers to supervise school meals, and this recommendation was accepted by the Department of Education and Science in August 1968 (PP 1967–8 Cmnd. 3564 xix: 50; Department of Education and Science 1968b: para. 2).

The Ministry of Education and the Department of Education and Science also played a leading role in the development of efforts to improve the quality and variety of children's diets. In 1941 the Board of Education established formal standards for the nutritional content of school dinners, and these standards were retained after 1945 (Ministry of Education 1949: 19–20; 1952a: 12–13; 1955). In 1962 the Ministry of Education introduced a number of changes in the regulations governing the supply of heavy equipment in small kitchens and the calculation of grants for school premises (Ministry of Education 1962a), and in 1965 the Department of Education and Science established a Departmental Working Party on the nutritional standard of the school dinner (Department of Education and Science 1965). The Working Party recommended that the number of meat dinners should be reduced from four to three, and that the amount of meat served at each meal should be increased. It also recommended increases in the supply of fish, eggs, cheese, fresh and dried fruit, and vegetable fats (Department of Education and Science 1966a, paras 6–7). In 1967 the Department asked all local education authorities to supply details of the menus used over a four-week period in order to monitor the implementation of the Working Party's recommendations (PP 1967–8 Cmnd. 3564 xix: 49). The recommendations themselves were restated, with some modifications, by the Working Party on the Nutritional Aspects of School Meals in 1975 (Department of Education and Science 1975b).

The development of the milk-in-schools scheme followed a slightly different path to that taken by school dinners. In 1945 the government decided to transfer the cost of the school milk service to the Ministry of Food, and it only reverted back to the Ministry of Education in 1954. The Ministry invited local education authorities to issue tenders for the supply of school milk from April 1955 onwards, but their efforts to comply with this request met with concerted opposition from the milk producers (Gosden 1983: 124). By the end of May it was estimated that approximately 73 per cent of counties and 78 per cent of county boroughs were still paying the maximum retail price, and more than eighty local education authorities were still paying the maximum price at the end of the year (PP 1955–6 Cmd. 9785 xiv: 42). However, by the end of the 1950s, virtually every local education authority had secured some form of agreement, and the average size of the discounts obtained by local education authorities ranged between 5.8 per cent in county areas and 7.5 per cent in county boroughs (PP 1960–61 Cmnd. 1439 xiii: 36).

The postwar period also witnessed a number of important changes in the scope and coverage of the school milk scheme. The Provision of Milk and Meals Regulations 1945 required every local education authority to ensure the provision of enough milk to enable every pupil to obtain a minimum of one-third of a pint of liquid milk each day (Ministry of Education 1945a: para. 7). Local authorities were also expected to charge half a penny for each third of a pint consumed, provided that the children's parents were able to pay, but this provision was abandoned following the introduction of family allowances in July 1946 (Ministry of Education 1946). The government continued to supply free milk to all children attending maintained primary and secondary schools until 1968, when the service was withdrawn from secondary schools and from senior pupils in all-age schools (PP 1968–

Table 9.8 The provision of school milk in England and Wales, 1946–74.

	Day pupils and boarders (thousands)	*Number taking milk (thousands)*	*Percentage taking milk*		*Day pupils and boarders (thousands)*	*Number taking milk (thousands)*	*Percentage taking milk*
1946	4798	4438	92.5	1961	7204	5927	82.3
1947	5006	4395	87.8	1962	7131	5867	82.3
1948	5225	4614	88.3	1963	7118	5855	82.3
1949	5369	4666	86.9	1964	7180	5904	82.2
1950	5456	4638	85.0	1965	7250	5868	80.9
1951	5652	4748	84.0	1966	7383	5912	80.1
1952	5865	4938	84.2	1967	7536	5969	79.2
1953	6052	5126	84.7	1968	4575[a]	4182	91.4
1954	6163	5208	84.5	1969	4666[a]	4265	91.4
1955	6354	5379	84.7	1970	4806[a]	4383	91.2
1956	6989	5843	83.6	1971	2075[b]	1962	94.6
1957	6724	5607	38.4	1972	2095[b]	1985	94.7
1958	7093	5954	83.9	1973	2075[b]	1966	94.7
1959	7132	5969	83.7	1974	2084[b]	1976	94.8
1960	7117	5832	81.9				

[a] The provision of free school milk was withdrawn for secondary school pupils and for senior pupils attending maintained all-age schools in September 1968.
[b] The provision of free school milk for primary schoolchildren over the age of eight was withdrawn in September 1971.

Sources: Central Statistical Office (1956: Table 101; 1958: Table 102; 1960: Table 102; 1971: Table 104; 1975: Table 105).

9 Cmnd. 3950 xxviii: 53), and in 1971 the incoming Conservative government introduced further restrictions on the supply of free milk to children over the age of eight (Department of Education and Science 1972a: 10–11). These changes led to a reduction in the number of children who received milk at school from 7.5 million in 1967 to 2.1 million seven years later (Table 9.8).

The health of the schoolchild, 1945–74

It is generally acknowledged that there was a substantial improvement in the average standard of child health between 1945 and 1974, and this improvement was reflected in the debates over routine medical inspection and in the declining numbers of children who came forward for medical treatment. The general improvement in child health was also reflected in the decline of infant and child mortality, and in the statistics of children's heights and 'general condition'. The postwar years witnessed the virtual elimination of many of the extreme forms of physical disability which had disfigured the lives of earlier generations, and a substantial reduction in the recorded incidence of the most common infectious diseases (Court and Alberman 1988; McPherson and Coleman 1988; Coleman and Salt 1992: 238–304).

A full explanation of these developments lies beyond the scope of this study, but a number of factors spring immediately to mind. The period between 1945 and 1974 witnessed a substantial improvement in real wage rates, and an even more substantial increase in the family wage as a result of the increase in female labour-force participation rates (Price and Bain 1988: 179–84). These developments were reinforced by changes in the occupational structure of the labour force, which saw an increasing proportion of workers enter more highly-paid occupations, and by the maintenance for much of the period of full, or nearly full, employment (ibid.: 174; Routh 1980: 5–9). The postwar period also witnessed the development and consolidation of the welfare state, which provided the whole population with access to an increased range of welfare services, the expansion of local authority housing, and the creation of the National Health Service (Lowe 1993, *passim*). The number of doctors per head of population increased by 31.5 per cent between 1951 and 1978, and the development of new vaccines, such as the BCG and Salk vaccines, provided increased protection against some of the most common childhood diseases (McPherson and Coleman 1988: 452; Jones 1994: 125).

The impact of these developments on the health of the child population can be demonstrated in a number of ways. During the 1930s and early 1940s, the Board of Education had become increasingly aware of the futility of its efforts to measure children's 'nutrition', and in 1947 the Ministry of Education decided to abandon the term altogether in favour of the equally vague, but less 'scientific', 'general condition' (Ministry of Education 1949:

12). The years between 1950 and 1955 witnessed a steady increase in the number of children whose condition was described as 'fair' or 'good', and a decline in the number whose condition was described as 'poor' (Table 9.9). In 1956 the Ministry decided to classify all children as either 'satisfactory' or 'unsatisfactory', and between 1956 and 1965 the proportion of children whose condition was described as 'unsatisfactory' declined from 2.47 per cent to 0.36 per cent.

The general improvement in the standard of child health can also be demonstrated by looking at children's heights and, to a lesser extent, at the ages at which girls began to menstruate (Eveleth and Tanner 1991). The average height of five-year-old boys in London increased by 0.35 inches between 1949 and 1966, and the average height of five-year-old girls increased by 0.28 inches (Cameron 1979: 514). The average height of five-year-old boys in Sheffield increased by 0.41 inches between 1945 and 1968, and that of five-year-old girls increased by 0.45 inches (Sheffield Education Committee 1946: 12; 1969: 50). The average age at which London girls began to menstruate declined by 2 months between 1954 and 1959, but there does not appear to have been any further decline after that date (Tanner 1962: 152–

Table 9.9 Classification of the general condition of pupils undergoing routine medical inspections, 1950–65.

	Number	*Condition (number)*			*Condition (%)*		
		Good	*Fair*	*Poor*	*Good*	*Fair*	*Poor*
1950	1,866,958	728,501	1,072,163	66,293	39.02	57.43	3.55
1951	1,879,376	766,957	1,057,098	55,318	40.81	56.25	2.94
1952	1,978,303	867,449	1,081,471	50,562	43.85	54.67	2.56
1953	2,057,965	920,898	1,090,708	46,573	44.75	53.00	2.26
1954	2,127,374	1,019,470	1,068,843	40,061	47.92	50.24	1.88
1955	2,119,454	1,078,580	1,008,707	31,042	50.89	47.59	1.46

	Number	*Satisfactory*	*Unsatisfactory*	*Satisfactory*	*Unsatisfactory*
1956	2,148,765	2,095,657	53,018	97.53	2.47
1957	2,106,157	2,069,827	36,330	98.28	1.72
1958	2,078,803	2,047,440	32,363	98.49	1.56
1959	2,138,616	2,114,290	24,326	98.86	1.14
1960	2,112,353	2,094,356	17,997	99.15	0.85
1961	2,056,221	2,042,223	13,998	99.32	0.68
1962	2,110,143	2,097,127	13,016	99.38	0.62
1963	2,010,215	1,999,340	10,875	99.46	0.54
1964	2,012,528	2,003,576	8,952	99.56	0.44
1965	1,954,036[a]	1,946,925[a]	7,111	99.64	0.36

[a] These figures include 40,457 pupils who were found not to warrant a medical examination.

Sources: Ministry of Education (1952b: 130; 1954: 134; 1956b: 172; 1958: 205; 1960: 211; 1962c: 231); Department of Education and Science (1964: 133; 1966d: 126).

5; 1973). However, there is some evidence that age at menarche may have continued to decline in other parts of the country after the 1950s (Danker-Hopfe 1986: 100–03).

These improvements were also reflected in changes in infant and child mortality rates and in disease notification rates. Between 1945 and 1974, the mortality rate among children aged up to four declined from 12.28 deaths per thousand to 3.45, and the mortality rate among children aged between five and fourteen fell from 1.05 to 0.29 (General Register Office 1947: Tables 1, 19; Office of Population Censuses and Surveys 1977: Tables 1, 10). These trends reflected the impact of improved resistance to disease as well as that of reduced exposure. Between 1945 and 1975, the recorded incidence of the principal infectious diseases of childhood was dramatically reduced. The figures for scarlet fever and whooping cough fell by 86 per cent and 89 per cent, respectively, and diphtheria and polio were virtually eliminated. The recorded incidence of measles fell by 65 per cent over the same period (for sources see Table 9.10).

These statistics represent a formidable achievement, although it is debatable how far the school health service itself was directly responsible for it. However, while it would be wrong to ignore the overall improvement in health standards, it would be equally unwise to overlook some of the deficiencies which remained. The most obvious blemishes concerned the persistence of health inequalities. It is now well known that children from more affluent backgrounds are taller and freer from disease than children from less affluent backgrounds, and children from different ethnic backgrounds tend to suffer disproportionate amounts of social and economic disadvan-

Table 9.10 Disease notification rates per thousand population, 1945–75.

	1945	*1950*	*1955*	*1960*	*1965*	*1970*	*1975*
0–4-year-olds							
Scarlet fever	5.28	5.65	2.90	2.67	1.90	0.95	0.74
Diptheria	1.05	0.07	0.01	0.00	0.00	0.00	0.00
Whooping cough	13.25	27.20	14.07	8.91	1.99	2.30	1.63
Measles	74.60	55.79	106.06	23.56	71.64	44.61	19.81
Poliomyelitis	0.07	0.72	0.53	0.04	0.00	0.00	0.00
5–14-year-olds							
Scarlet fever	8.32	6.79	3.21	3.11	2.60	1.11	0.77
Diphtheria	1.67	0.07	0.01	0.00	0.00	0.00	0.00
Whooping cough	6.29	9.11	4.68	3.64	0.65	0.93	0.37
Measles	34.99	26.11	50.01	10.69	29.56	16.37	10.22
Poliomyelitis	0.05	0.45	0.40	0.02	0.00	0.00	0.00

Sources: General Register Office (1947: Tables 1, 28A; 1952: Tables 1, 32; 1956: Tables 1, 32; 1962: Tables 1, 30; 1967: Tables 1, 30); Office of Population Censuses and Surveys (1972: Tables 1, 30; 1976: Table 3; 1978: Table 1).

tage (Coleman and Salt 1992: 305–64; Jones 1994: 172–92). The persistence of these patterns was discussed by a number of occasions by the Chief Medical Officer (Ministry of Education 1949: 15–17; 1952a: 9; 1954: 11; 1956b: 23; 1958: 71–4; 1962c: 10–12). In his report for 1961, he revealed that children in the poorer districts of Liverpool and Sheffield were between 0.6 and 2.6 inches shorter than children in more affluent districts (Ministry of Education 1962c: 11). In 1981 the Department of Health and Social Security showed that there was still a substantial 'social gradient in height' among pre-school children in the mid-1970s (Department of Health and Social Security 1981: 75–81, 95–7).

The second disquieting feature of the school medical returns was the fact that even though the average standard of child health appeared to be improving, the number of conditions which were noted by school medical officers as requiring either observation or treatment at routine medical inspection actually increased (Table 9.11). The reasons for this increase can probably be found in the increased sensitivity of school medical officers to different types of disease, but the statistics themselves are no less disturbing. They suggest that even in 1970, 15 per cent of the children who were examined at routine medical inspections suffered from some form of visual defect, and at least 5 per cent of children suffered from defects of the ears, nose or throat. These figures show that even though the days of the independent school health service may have been numbered, the need for some form of regular medical supervision of child health was undiminished (see also PP 1976–7 Cmnd. 6684 xi: 39–54).

Table 9.11 Percentage of children seen at routine medical inspection who were found to be suffering from defects requiring either observation or treatment, 1947–70.

	1947	*1952*	*1957*	*1962*	*1967*	*1970*
Skin	1.48	1.85	2.46	3.01	3.57	3.66
Eyes	9.77	10.89	13.48	15.08	15.41	15.08
Ears	0.97	2.37	2.80	3.67	5.07	5.86
Nose or throat	10.95	10.22	6.92	6.49	6.46	5.38
Speech	0.60	0.99	1.24	1.56	1.89	2.23
Lymphatic glands	–	2.77	1.94	1.79	1.49	1.37
Heart and circulation	–	1.57	1.27	1.37	1.48	1.47
Lungs	–	2.84	2.49	2.27	2.45	2.46
Developmental	–	1.24	1.66	2.07	2.60	2.82
Orthopaedic	–	7.77	7.79	6.98	6.01	5.55
Nervous	–	0.70	0.77	0.89	1.08	1.26
Psychological	–	1.42	2.00	2.97	4.11	4.72
Abdomen	–	–	0.34	0.59	0.78	0.86
Other	–	3.60	2.34	2.11	2.64	2.91

Sources: Ministry of Education (1949: 143; 1956b: 174; 1958: 207–8); Department of Education and Science (1966d: 128–9; 1969b: 118; 1972b: 108).

Notes

1 Section 47 gave local education authorities the power 'to afford facilities in educational establishments . . . for the conduct of research in matters relating to the school health service', and the duty to afford such facilities if requested to do so by the Minister. The Chief Medical Officer summarised the research carried out by school medical officers in his biennial reports. See Ministry of Education (1948a, section 47).

2 These figures compare current expenditure on the school health service with current expenditure on education as a whole. The figures do not include capital expenditure, and loan charges have also been excluded.

3 It is worth recalling that in 1936 the Chief Medical Officer of the Board of Education estimated that there should be one dentist for every 4000 children in rural areas and one dentist for every 5000 children in urban areas. In 1956 the Chief Medical Officer said that in view of the increasing variety of work undertaken by the school dental service, 'a ratio of at least one [full-time] dentist to 3000 children would be required' (Board of Education 1936: 112–18; Ministry of Education 1956b: 57).

4 The authorities concerned (with the number of medical officers per 10,000 pupils in parentheses) were as follows. 'High-staffing' areas: Barking (4.79); Kingston upon Thames (3.96); Blackpool (3.83); Isles of Scilly (3.72); West Hartlepool (2.43); Stoke-on-Trent (2.31); Swansea (2.30); Bury (2.28); Bexley (2.25); Montgomeryshire (2.24); Monmouthshire (2.13); Inner London Education Authority (2.10); Rochdale (2.04); Merioneth (2.01); Chester (2.01). 'Low-staffing' areas: Norwich (0.98); Suffolk West (0.98); Hounslow (0.97); Suffolk East (0.97); Wallasey (0.92); Luton (0.90); Oxfordshire (0.86); Grimsby (0.84); Rutland (0.84); Darlington (0.83); Middlesborough (0.78); Redbridge (0.78); Tynemouth (0.60); Harrow (0.55). See Department of Education and Science (1966d: 121–4).

5 The number of registered medical practitioners increased from 7.5 doctors per 10,000 population in 1951 to 10.8 in 1968 and 11.7 in 1978 (McPherson and Coleman 1988: 452). The proportion of patients living in 'underdoctored' areas (i.e. areas where patient lists were exceptionally large) fell from 51.5 per cent to 18.6 per cent between 1952 and 1958 (Klein 1989: 53).

6 In order to demonstrate the way in which the pattern of children's diseases had changed, Withnell compared the incidence of a number of defects in Leith in 1906 with the incidence of the same defects in Manchester in 1955. In 1906, 13.6 per cent of Leith children had rickets, 7.6 per cent had curvature of the spine, 44.8 per cent had eye disease or refractive error, and 52.9 per cent had affections of the nose or throat. The numbers of children suffering from these conditions in Manchester in 1955 were 0 per cent, 0.6 per cent, 18.2 per cent and 17.6 per cent, respectively. See British Medical Journal (1907b); Withnell (1957: 30).

7 In 1957 school medical officers discovered 1,003,587 defects requiring observation or treatment at routine inspections and 573,431 defects at special inspections. These figures do not include 247,900 children who were found to be suffering from infestation by nits or lice during examinations by school nurses (Ministry of Education 1958: 207–8, 213).

8 It would be wrong to conclude that these variations, which echoed the results of similar surveys before the Second World War, were peculiar to the school health service. In 1958 a study by twelve general practitioners showed that 'the degree of accuracy at the first consultation ranged from 25.6 per cent to 72.4 per cent, the average being 55.5 per cent'. The authors concluded that 'we must, it seems,

examine the diagnostic habits of doctors with great care, and bear these wide differences in mind when we interpret any figures collected from general practice'. See Ministry of Education (1958: 28).

9 After 1945, the Chief Medical Officer continued to devote considerable attention to the number of children who received tonsillectomies. In 1958 he wrote: 'The number of school leavers who had tonsillectomy was below the national average in Lancashire, St Helens and Salford and slightly above in Leicester. The experience of these four areas supports the opinion that a periodic review of all children [a]waiting tonsillectomy would considerably reduce the number of operations' (Ministry of Education 1958: 100).

10 The Education (Miscellaneous Provisions) Act, 1953, required every local education authority 'to make . . . arrangements for securing that there are available for pupils for whom . . . education is provided by them comprehensive facilities for free dental treatment either . . . by the Authority . . . or . . . under arrangements made by a Regional Hospital Board or the Board of Governors of a Teaching Hospital within the meaning of the National Health Service Act 1946' (1 & 2 Eliz. II Ch. 33, section 4).

11 In the same year (1965), school dentists provided 1.3 million courses of treatment and carried out 2.6 million fillings (Department of Education and Science 1966d: 139–40).

12 In fact, as the Guillebaud Committee had pointed out nine months earlier, the number of students who took places in dental schools reached a peak of 654 in 1947 and fell to 478 seven years later (PP 1955–6 Cmd. 9663 xx: para. 528).

13 The number of individual teeth filled first exceeded the number of extractions in 1959 (Ministry of Education 1960: 218).

14 In 1946 school dentists performed 1,124,000 fillings and 1,976,000 extractions (Ministry of Education 1949: 146).

15 He commented that 'the immediate benefits of this treatment are twofold. In the first place, the value to a girl or boy of being freed of a disfiguring dental irregularity is very considerable. . . . Secondly, the high regard which patients and parents and the public generally have for this work reflects credit on the school dental service as a whole, and encourages a better acceptance of the more ordinary kinds of dental attention' (Ministry of Education 1949: 66).

16 In December 1966 the Department of Education and Science announced that expenditure on the provision of school milk and meals would no longer qualify for 100 per cent grant, and that support for these services would henceforth be provided by the rate support grant. The new system came into effect on 1 April 1967. See Department of Education and Science (1966c: para. 6).

17 The number of schools or departments which remained unserved by a canteen fell from 2622 in October 1948 to 539 ten years later. See PP 1948–9 Cmd. 7724 xiv: 73; PP 1958–9 Cmnd. 777 xi: 34.

18 The price of school meals was increased on eight occasions between 1945 and 1974, as follows: January 1950, 6d. (from 5d.); April 1951, 7d.; March 1953, 9d.; September 1956, 10d.; April 1957, 1s.; April 1968, 1s. 6d.; April 1970, 1s. 9d.; April 1971, 2s. 5d. A further planned increase (to 2s. 10d.) was abandoned in April 1973 as part of the government's counter-inflationary strategy. See PP 1950–1 Cmd. 8244 xi: 68; PP 1951–2 Cmd. 8554 x: 43; PP 1953–4 Cmd. 9155 xi: 18; PP 1956–7 Cmd. 223 x: 22; PP 1957–8 Cmd. 454 x: 24; PP 1968–9 Cmd. 3950 xxviii: 52; Department of Education and Science (1971: 21; 1972d: 10; 1974b: 6).

ten

The school health service and the reorganisation of the National Health Service

This book has sought to provide a general overview of the development of school medical provision in England and Wales from the 1870s onwards. During the last thirty years of the nineteenth century, the concept of medical provision in schools was largely confined to the medical inspection of school buildings and the prevention of the spread of infectious diseases. Towards the end of the nineteenth century, medical officers of health became increasingly concerned with the health of the individual child, and this concern culminated in the establishment of the school medical service in 1907. Over the course of the next 67 years, the government's central education departments worked with local education authorities to provide a wide range of medical services. The school medical service was renamed the school health service in 1945, but by the end of this period it employed the equivalent of more than a thousand full-time medical officers, 1500 dental officers and three thousand school nurses, together with a large number of additional specialists and other workers. It was responsible for the conduct of nearly 2.7 million separate medical examinations, and it provided a range of medical treatment services from minor ailments and injuries to child guidance and speech therapy (Henderson 1975: 49–63).

The history of school medical provision from 1907 onwards was marked by a number of impressive achievements. When the school medical service was first established, it represented the first concerted attempt to furnish national statistics about the state of child health, and even though these statistics have often been criticised, they made a very important contribution to the development of health policy.[1] Both the school medical service and the school health service made a vital contribution to the improvement of child health by alerting parents to the presence of disease and encouraging them to obtain medical treatment, and for much of this period they were one of the major sources of medical treatment for the school-age population. The school health service was directly involved in the mass immunisation programmes of the 1950s and 1960s, and it played a leading role in the development of health education. It also played an important part in the identification of children with special needs.

However, despite the importance of these achievements, many health workers continued to regard the school health service as a 'Cinderella' service which was isolated from the rest of the National Health Service and offered few opportunities for stimulating work or personal advancement (*Public Health* 1971: 95). The most important problem was the isolation of the service from the rest of the National Health Service. In 1972 the editor of *Public Health* wrote that

> the school health service has certainly suffered from its separation from pre-school child health work, in that too often by the time the child came under its care opportunities had been missed and substantial damage . . . might have been done. It has also been hampered by difficulties in liaison with the clinical agencies (*Public Health* 1972: 105).

Many observers believed that the school health service was a 'dead-end' job which offered little hope of personal advancement beyond the administrative sphere. In 1977 Dr C. Simpson Smith recalled:

> The historical background of the service with its slavish adherence to routine medical inspection . . . poor recruitment, lack of adequate in-service training and general lack of insight into the purpose of the service all helped to create a bad image. Many former Medical Officers of Health regarded the clinical posts as either stepping stones for senior administrative appointments or the purview of male doctors with no ambition or for 'pin-money' girls (Smith 1977: 306).

The reputation of the school health service was also hampered by its continued association with the question of routine medical inspection. By the end of the 1960s the majority of local education authorities had replaced at least one of the standard 'routine' examinations with a selective examination of those children who were recommended to them, but in spite of this, more than 1.5 million children were still receiving a routine examination at the beginning of the 1970s (Henderson 1975: 51). Even though many doctors had previously defended the institution of routine medical inspection, the majority now accepted the view that it had outlived its usefulness (see e.g. Lunn 1973; Francis 1973; 1975: 181–90). In 1976 Dr Hugh Jolly, a consultant paediatrician, observed:

> For the doctor, faced with a queue of children outside the door, it becomes a weary soul-destroying chore with minimal chances of uncovering any serious medical problem. Such problems should have been detected by properly conducted medical examinations in baby clinics provided for the pre-school child and run by the family doctor or the infant health doctor employed by the Area Health Authority (Jolly 1976).

Many observers hoped that the problems faced by the school health service would be resolved by the passage of the National Health Service Reorganisation Act of 1973. This Act abolished the tripartite division between hospital services, general practitioner services and local authority services which had been introduced in the 1946 Act, and replaced it with a cumbersome and ultimately unsuccessful network of Regional Health Authorities, Area Health Authorities and District Management Teams (Klein 1989: 90–9; Ham 1992: 26–7). The Government took advantage of the opportunity provided by reorganisation to transfer the school health service from the local education authorities to the new area health authorities, and it repeated its earlier advice to local authorities to abandon the general provision of routine medical inspection in favour of a more selective system (1973 Ch. 32: section 5; Department of Health and Social Security 1974: para. 15; 1976: para. 9.10).[2] The majority of school medical officers welcomed the new arrangements on the grounds that they would lead to the creation of a more unified system of child health surveillance (see, for example, Francis 1973). However, even though the Act represented a major step forward on the road to unification, it failed to achieve all the goals that its supporters anticipated. As a result, many observers continued to call for changes in the organisation of child health services and for the introduction of new methods of medical screening. (PP 1976–7 Cmnd. 6684 xi; Fitzherbert 1982; Jepson 1982; Latham 1982; Whitmore and Bax 1982; Newby and Nicholl 1985; Peckham, Stark and Moynihan 1985; Harrison and Gretton 1986; National Children's Bureau 1987; British Paediatric Association 1987; 1993).

The origins of reorganisation

The history of National Health Service reorganisation has been told on a number of occasions, but its impact on the school health service has received relatively little attention (Levitt 1976; Brown 1979; Klein 1989; Ham 1992). However it would be wrong to view the transfer of the school health service to the National Health Service as a simple by-product of National Health Service reorganisation (Gosden 1983: 131). The decision to initiate this change was directly related to the promise made by the Board of Education in 1907, when it said that the school medical service should rest 'upon a broad basis of public health' and that 'in all steps taken the progressive unification of the medical services and the needs and circumstances of each community must continually be borne in mine' (PP 1910 Cd. 4986 xxiii: 142–3, 150). At the same time, it also reflected the conclusions of a series of reports from the early-1960s onwards, in which the disadvantages of a divided administration and the need for greater coordination received considerable emphasis (PP 1962–3 (40) v; Ministry of Health 1967; Department of Education and Science 1968c; 1972c).

One of the earliest and most critical reports on the development of the school health service after 1945 was the report produced by the Select Committee on the Estimates in 1962. The Committee identified a large number of defects in the administration and performance of the school dental service, including its failure to inspect more than 60 per cent of the school population, the absence of any proper system of financial management, the variety of local administrative arrangements, the poor status and recruitment of school dental staff, and the failure to make sufficient use of the National Health Service (PP 1962–3 (40) v: paras 50–76). Even though the Committee recognised that many of these problems were beyond the immediate control of the school health service, it was extremely critical of both the leadership and the administration provided by the Ministry of Education. It had no hesitation in recommending 'that the responsibilities for the school dental service . . . at present exercised on behalf of the Minister of Health by the Minister of Education should be assumed by the Minister of Health' (ibid.: paras. 77–83).

The administration of the school health service was also discussed by the Sheldon Committee in 1967. This Committee was primarily concerned with the administration of health services for children under the age of five, but it found that it was impossible to consider these issues without considering their impact on the child health services as a whole. It thought that the separation of the school health service from the child health service was particularly harmful in the case of children between the ages of two and five, and that unification of the two services would provide a more efficient service for the child, save administrative time, prevent duplication, and simplify the links with general practice and hospital paediatrics. It concluded that 'we can see nothing but benefit to be obtained from unification of the clinical work of the two services' and that 'there would seem to be much to be said in favour of a unified service . . . for the whole of childhood from birth to school leaving age' (Ministry of Health 1967: paras 36, 140).

The future of the school health service was also discussed by the Summerfield Committee in its report on *Psychologists in Education Services.* The Committee recognised that the Education Authorities were not the only bodies with an interest in child guidance, but insisted that 'it would be inappropriate for other departments of Local Authorities to appoint psychologists for work with children' (Department of Education and Science 1968c: para. 3.1). However, although the Committee was anxious to ensure that child guidance work remained within the educational sphere, it also called for a number of important changes in the way in which these services were organised. In particular, it said that 'continuing efforts should be made to develop collaboration with hospital psychiatric services', and that 'the organisation of psychological work within the field of education on a much larger scale than at present would be conducive to a high standard of service, to efficiency, and to economy of man-power' (ibid.: paras 6.37, 6.72–6.75).[3]

The Department of Education and Science also played an important part in the inquiry into the growth and development of speech therapy services. These services had developed rapidly after the Second World War, and by 1971 the total number of practising speech therapists in England and Wales had risen to 1,097. The majority of these practitioners were employed by local education authorities, but a substantial number worked in hospitals or in private practice (Department of Education and Science 1972c: para. 5.05).[4] The enquiry concluded that the division between local authority speech therapists and hospital speech therapists had hampered the development of the service and created a damaging degree of professional isolation (ibid.: paras 4.27–4.32). Although the majority of speech therapists were employed by local education authorities, the Committee believed that speech therapy was an essentially medical activity (ibid.: para. 8.18). It therefore concluded that local authority speech therapy services should be taken out of the hands of local education authorities and placed under the unified control of the local health authority (ibid.: paras 8.09–23).

Although there was strong support within the Ministry of Health for the incorporation of the school health service within the National Health Service, there was no reference to the school health service in Kenneth Robinson's Green Paper on the reorganisation of the National Health Service in 1968, and this led to speculation that the government might be preparing to abandon the school health service altogether (Ministry of Health 1968a: 113; 1968b; Department of Health and Social Security 1970a: 102; Smith 1977: 305). However, when the government issued its second Green Paper, in February 1970, it stated unequivocally that 'the main services making up the school health service will be brought within the integrated National Health Service' (Department of Health and Social Security 1970b: para. 32). The Labour party lost office at the 1970 General Election, and in March 1971 the five major local education authority associations persuaded the incoming Conservative government to refer the whole issue to the Working Party on Collaboration between the National Health Service and Local Government (Times 1971a; 1971b; Department of Health and Social Security 1973a: 121).[5] However, despite the continued opposition of the Secretary of the Association of Education Committees, Sir William Alexander, the Committee concluded that 'it would [not] be desirable for the furtherance of the health of children . . . [for] responsibility for the health of children receiving ordinary education . . . [to] be divided between two Authorities' (Department of Health and Social Security 1973a: para. 6.15; see also 1973b: 10, 16–22.).

The government signalled its decision to accept the recommendations of the Working Party to the House of Commons on 13 July 1972. The Secretary of State for Health, Sir Keith Joseph, said that he welcomed the proposed transfer of the health inspection and treatment functions of local education authorities and that this would facilitate the future development of health services for children, and the Secretary of State for Education, Margaret Thatcher, said that she was confident that local education authorities would continue to play a major part in the planning of child health services (House of Commons Debates 1972: written answers, cols 400–1; 445–6). Sir Keith also announced that he intended to set up a much more wide-ranging inquiry into the organisation of child health services generally (House of Commons Debates 1972: written answers, col. 446; PP 1976–7 Cmnd. 6684 xi). The government included a proposal to transfer control of the school health service to the National Health Service in the White Papers on the Reorganisation of the National Health Service which it published in August 1972, and a similar proposal was included in the National Health Service Reorganisation Bill at the end of the year (PP 1971–2 Cmnd. 5055 xvi: para. 20; PP 1971–2 Cmnd. 5057 xvi: para. 5; PP 1972–3 (79) iv: section 3). The National Health Service Reorganisation Act was passed on 5 July 1973.[6]

The impact of reorganisation

The government set out its immediate plans for the development of the school health service in the Department of Health and Social Security's Circular on the Operation and Development of Services (Circular HRC[74]5) in January 1974. It stated that the main aim of the reorganised National Health Service in the field of child health was to establish a comprehensive range of integrated health services for children. The government charged the area health authorities with the duty of coordinating the child health service (for pre-school children), the school health service and the hospital and specialist services, and ensuring that all these services were fully maintained (Department of Education and Science 1974c; Department of Health and Social Security 1974: paras 1–2). The Joint Working Party on Collaboration had recommended that area health authorities should work with local education authorities to promote the interests of the children through the establishment of Joint Consultative Committees, and this recommendation was included in the National Health Service Reorganisation Act (Department of Health and Social Security 1973a: paras 6.24–6.35; 1973 Ch. 32: section 10). The Circular instructed area health authorities to keep in close touch with local education authorities through these committees 'as well as by the officers concerned working and planning together' (Department of Health and Social Security 1974: para. 2).

The Circular also described the staffing arrangements for the new authorities. The three senior officers were the Area Medical Officer, the Area Dental Officer and the Area Nursing Officer, each of whom had their own separate staffs. The staff of the Area Medical Officer included the Specialist in Community Medicine (Child Health) who assumed responsibility for the day-to-day administration of the child health service. The posts of Area Medical Officer, Area Dental Officer and Area Nursing Officer were replicated at the level of each District by the District Community Physician, the District Dental Officer and the District Nursing Officer (Department of Health and Social Security 1974: paras 46–53). When the government introduced the National Health Service Reorganisation Act, it said that the Secretary of State for Health should have the power to transfer the employment contracts of all staff who had previously been employed by the local health authority or the local education authority to the appropriate area health authority (1973 Ch. 32: section 18). The area health authorities took over these responsibilities on 1 April 1974, and those officers who had failed to obtain an administrative post were employed as clinical medical officers, clinical dental officers and clinical nurses (Department of Health and Social Security 1974: paras 28, 54).

The DHSS Circular also provided a detailed account of the range of services which area health authorities would be expected to provide. It said that 'everything possible should be done to maintain the high standards already achieved in school health services and to continue their development (Department of Health and Social Security 1974: para. 12). It advised Area Health Authorities to continue to make arrangements for the medical examination of all pupils at or around the start of their primary school careers, and to carry out more selective examinations at older ages (ibid.: para. 15). It said that area health authorities would continue to make arrangements for the provision of school clinics, although it recognised that 'the pattern of provision may need to be revised in consultation with local education authorities and . . . general practitioners' (ibid.: para. 17). It reminded the authorities of their obligation to make arrangements for the supply, repair and replacement of optical appliances, and it said that they would also be responsible for the provision and repair of various types of hearing aid (ibid.: paras 22–3).

The second major factor to influence the development of the school health service was the Report of the Committee on Child Health Services (the Court Committee) in 1976. This Committee was appointed in 1973 by Sir Keith Joseph to review the existing child health services and issue proposals for their integration. Its primary recommendation was that 'the organisational structure of the child health service should be changed to provide an integrated two-tier system based on comprehensive primary care firmly linked with supporting consultant and hospital care' (PP 1976–7 Cmnd. 6684 xi: 1, 368). It said that the provision of primary care should be firmly based in general practice, and that all health services for children should be provided by a new type of general practitioner, the general practitioner paediatrician, working closely with a child health visitor (PP 1976–7 Cmnd. 6684 xi: 105–8, 368). It also advocated the creation of a new type of consultant community paediatrician, who would be the specialist counterpart of the general practitioner paediatrician, with special skills in developmental, social and educational paediatrics (PP 1976–7 Cmnd. 6684 xi: 110–1, 369).

The Court Committee also made a number of more specific recommendations regarding the future of the school health service. It argued that the arrangements for the health surveillance of schoolchildren should be planned as a continuation of the arrangements for pre-school children, and that all children should receive a thorough and detailed medical examination on entering school. It recognised that the provision of this examination would require a large input of medical time, and it therefore recommended that the routine examinations of older children should be discontinued. It said that every child should have an annual interview with the school nurse, and an interview with the school doctor at the age of thirteen. It recommended that every school should have its own school doctor, drawn from the list of local general practitioner paediatricians, and a specially-trained school nurse, working under the supervision of the child health visitor. There should be a minimum of one medical session per fortnight in each primary school and two sessions a week in each secondary school (PP 1976–7 Cmnd. 6684 xi: 106–7, 147–52, 374–5).

The Court Committee's proposals received a predictably fierce response. There was very widespread support for the general aims of the report, but equally widespread opposition to the means of achieving them. The British Medical Association was strongly opposed to the creation of a separate class of general practitioner paediatricians, because it thought that this would lead to the fragmentation of general practice (*British Medical Journal* 1977b). The Society of Medical Officers of Health (which was now known as the Society of Community Medicine) argued that there was a fundamental difference between the preventive outlook of the community physician and the curative outlook of the general practitioner, and that the implementation of the proposals would lead to the elimination of the clinical medical officer (*Public Health* 1977; see also *British Medical Journal* 1977a; Horner 1977). The Education Authorities thought that the proposals were impractical and that they focused too heavily on the doctors' interests at the expense of the educationists' (Johnson 1977: 248). The Inner London Education Authority thought that the concept of preventive medicine would be damaged, and that the inevitable delay between the appearance of the proposals and their implementation would produce a dangerous hiatus in the development of school medical provision (*Education* 1977).

The government's response to the Court Committee reflected the force of the opposition the Report had provoked.[7] It accepted 'the central recommendation of the . . . Committee . . . that the various health services for children should be welded together into an integrated child health service' but it rejected the proposal to create a new class of child health specialists in the form of general practitioner paediatricians, child health visitors, consultant community physicians and child health nurses. The Secretary of State for Health and Social Services, David Ennals, said that he understood the fear 'that the creation of these special groups would integrate the services for children at too high a price in disintegrating the mainstream of our services', but he was prepared to allow individual health authorities to carry out local experiments if the practitioners concerned were happy to do so. The Government's other recommendations were very limited. It said that the existing specialist paediatric services should be extended into the community, that the number of health visitors should be increased, and that all general practitioners should be trained in paediatric care. It also invited Professor Jerry Morris to chair a working group on improvements in the quality of child health provision (Department of Health and Social Security 1978a: Appendix A; 1978b: 77; House of Commons Debates 1978: written answers, cols 824–5).

The administrative structure of the school health service was also affected by the government's decision to reorganise the National Health Service for a second time in 1982. Under the new arrangements, the regional health authorities were retained, but the area health authorities and the district management teams were replaced by a new administrative unit called the district health authority. The new structure was designed to simplify the decision-making process and to reduce the amount of money devoted to administration, but it also meant that one of the key principles of the earlier reform – the coterminosity of the area health authorities and the local authorities – had been abandoned. The responsibility for the school health service was transferred from the area health authorities to the district health authorities, but these often bore little relationship to the existing local government boundaries. This inevitably gave rise to fears that one of the results of the 1982 reorganisation would be to sunder the lines of communication between the health authorities and the education authorities (*Education* 1980; Jepson 1982; Harrison and Gretton 1986: 25–7; Klein 1989: 133–40; Ham 1992: 27–30).

The school health service after reorganisation

The transfer of the school health service to the National Health Service in 1974 led to a significant reduction in the amount of publicly-available information about the extent of school medical provision. The government abandoned the publication of the biennial reports on the health of the schoolchild which had previously been published by the Department of Education and Science, and it only included the briefest of reports in the Annual Reports of the Chief Medical Officer of the Department of Health and Social Security. The supply of statistical information about the development of school health services also declined. The Department of Health and Social Security (and subsequently the Department of Health) provided information about the number of staff employed by the school health service, and the number of medical examinations, in England, and the Welsh Office recorded the number of children who received a dental examination in Wales. Neither Department published information about the health of the children examined at medical inspections, although details of children's heights and weights were available for Scotland (Central Statistical Office 1990: 35).

In view of the paucity of the available information, it is not surprisingly difficult to build up a complete picture of changes in the provision of school health services since 1974. These difficulties are compounded, in the case of school health service staff, by changes in the job descriptions of different workers. However the overall evidence suggests that the amount of staff time devoted to the school health service was reasonably well-maintained between 1974 and 1986, and the number of medical officers, expressed in terms of whole-time equivalents, actually increased (Table 10.1). There was a substantial decline in the number of children who received a routine medical examination and in the number of children who were examined for signs of infestation. The number of children who were found to be suffering from infestation declined from 172,000 in 1976 to 91,000 in 1987/8 (Table 10.2).

We can gain a deeper insight into the changing nature of school health service provision from the work of Sue Lucas and Anthony Harrison and John Gretton. In 1980 Lucas compared the take-up of school medical services in 1977 with the results of a previous survey in 1964. She found that the proportion of children whose parents said that they had seen a school doctor during the year had not changed significantly since the earlier survey, and even though fewer than half the parents had attended the examination with their children, the overwhelming majority (93 per cent) continued to believe

Table 10.1 School health service staff in England 1974–1986 (whole-time equivalents, in thousands).

	Medical officers	*Senior nursing officers and nursing officers*	*Health visitors*	*Other registered nurses*	*Enrolled nurses*[a]	*Other nursing staff*[a]	*Total*
1974	791	n/a	1993[b]	1837	172	231	5024[b]
1975	868	n/a	1050	1850	205	181	4154
1976	923	103	968	1896	228	219	4337
1977	923	101	876	1968	262	188	4318
1978	938	98	866	2036	234	167	4339
1979	929	112	898	2110	245	204	4498
1980	943	34[c]	71	2190	225	170	3633
1981	964	27[c]	127	2404	205	228	3955
1982	949	27[c]	150	2434	225	272	4057
1983	959	20[c]	157	2445	218	233	4032
1984	917	35[c]	148	2443	219	251	4013
1985	944	38[c]	137	2493	189	248	4050
1986	905	33[c]	77	2482	182	215	3894

[a] Includes special school staff.
[b] Includes duplication.
[c] Senior nurses.

Sources: Department of Health and Social Security (1978c: Table 6.3; 1982: Table 6.3; 1985: Table 6.3); Department of Health (1988: Table 6.3).

Table 10.2 Numbers of pupils examined at routine medical examinations and other examinations in England, 1974–1987/8 (thousands).

	Pupils inspected at routine medical inspection	*Pupils seen by nurses*	*Pupils referred by nurses for medical examination*	*Pupils examined for infestation*	*Pupils suffering from infestation*
1974	1391	n/a	n/a	n/a	n/a
1975	1399	n/a	n/a	n/a	n/a
1976	1405	n/a	n/a	12,392	172
1977	1319	n/a	n/a	n/a	n/a
1978	1247	n/a	n/a	13,905	138
1979	1169	4027	n/a	14,500	161
1980	1125	4533	n/a	14,573	180
1981	1077	4579	n/a	14,223	189
1982	1010	4621	257	12,795	170
1983	962	4492	236	11,682	173
1984	917	4450	251	9,402	132
1985	868	4510	251	7,288	106
1986	847	4426	259	6,090	95
1987/8	783	4079	233	4,536	91

Sources: Department of Health and Social Security (1978c: Table 6.3; 1982: Table 6.4); Central Statistical Office (1988: Table 7.21); Department of Health (1990: Table 6.3).

that school medicals were a good idea (Lucas 1980: 216). Harrison and Gretton conducted a much more extensive study of the school health services provided by more than 120 health authorities throughout the United Kingdom. They found that 95 authorities (out of 128 who replied to the question) conducted routine examinations of school entrants, and 20 authorities conducted routine examinations of children aged between seven and thirteen, but the majority now relied on selective examinations for the majority of the children in their care. They also found that there had been a substantial increase in the proportion of children who received a dental examination, and that about one quarter of the authorities in their survey claimed that school health services had improved between 1981 and 1986 (Harrison and Gretton 1986: 27–31).[8]

When the government originally suggested that the school health service should be transferred to the National Health Service, the five main local education authority organisations predicted that 'the school health service effectively could cease to exist . . . unless a way . . . [is] found to coordinate the role of the health and education services', and the Secretary of the Association of Education Committees, Sir William Alexander, claimed that the National Health Service was under such strong pressure to provide curative services 'that the school health service, which is essentially preventive, may not get the attention it needs' (*Times* 1971a; 1971b; Ingram 1972).

The statistics reported in the previous two paragraphs suggest that these fears may have been exaggerated, but many of the advantages which were expected to flow from reorganisation failed to materialise. The main reason for transferring the school health service to the National Health Service was the hope that this would pave the way for a more integrated child health service, but this goal was only partially achieved, and there was considerable evidence that the ties between the school health service and the education service may have been weakened.

The most immediate aim of reorganisation, with regard to the school health service, was to abolish the distinction between the local authority service for pre-school children and the school health service. In 1986, Harrison and Gretton found that 115 of the 127 authorities which responded to their enquiries said that they had introduced a joint school and child health service, and although one or two of these authorities admitted that this had not quite happened on the ground, only eight authorities reported that the two services were run entirely separately (Harrison and Gretton 1986: 27). However, although there was now a good deal of cooperation between the pre-school and school health services, there was still a considerable gulf between the pre-school and school health services and the hospital and general practitioner services. In 1988 Aidan Macfarlane and Ross Mitchell observed:

> Reviews of the ways in which health care was delivered to children were undertaken in the late 1960s: the findings for Scotland were published in the Brotherston Report (1973) and for England and Wales in the Court Report (1976). Both reports criticised the separation between primary health care, hospital services and services in the community . . . and recommended that children's services should be more clearly identified by integrating the general practitioner, hospital and community components into a single child health service. . . . However, despite much discussion and expressions of intent, the recommendations of these reports have not been implemented. . . . General practitioners provide the bulk of treatment and some of the preventive care . . . doctors in the community child health clinics and school clinics . . . are responsible for much of the preventive care and school health work; and consultants in hospitals and clinics undertake the more specialised forms of care . . . including the management of complex forms of health relating to education (Macfarlane and Mitchell 1988: 159).

One of the most important examples of 'non-integration' concerned the failure to establish proper channels of communication between the school health service and the other child health services. When the Court Committee published its Report, it attempted to bridge the gap between the school health service and the general practitioner service by creating a new class of 'general practitioner paediatricians', but this proposal was firmly rejected by the British Medical Association and the Community Medical

Officers (PP 1976–7 Cmnd. 6684: 368; *British Medical Journal* 1977a; 1977b; *Public Health* 1977). However there was still considerable evidence that the gap between the different types of health service was one of the major deficiencies of school health service provision. In 1977 C. Simpson Smith commented that 'there is still a great need to improve communications between the different workers for children, and the medical profession still has much to do in this direction' (Smith 1977: 310). In 1980 Sue Lucas reported that even though

> similar proportions of children had seen a school doctor in 1977 as in 1964 . . . communication between the school doctor and the general practitioner did not appear to have improved. Parents attended less than half the school medicals and were less likely than in 1964 to discuss with their general practitioner a problem about which the school doctor had offered them advice (Lucas 1980: 209).

In addition to the problem of poor communication between different sections of the health service, the school health service was also criticised for breaking its lines of communication with the education service. When the National Health Service was first reorganised, local education authorities had derived some reassurance from the fact that the new area health authorities were coterminous with their own boundaries, and they expressed considerable disquiet when this safeguard was removed in 1982 (*Education* 1980; Jepson 1982). In the same year as the new structure came into operation, Katrin Fitzherbert found that many teachers were strikingly ill-informed about the work of the school health service and did not even realise that there was such a person as a named school doctor attached to their school (Fitzherbert 1982: 102). In 1986 Harrison and Gretton examined the degree of communication between the school health service and the head teachers. They found that the majority of health authorities supplied some information to the head teacher, but this ranged widely in quality and scope. Twenty-nine health authorities, out of a total of 133, provided no information at all, and 48 authorities only transmitted information about children with special needs (Harrison and Gretton 1986: 31).

The future of the school health service

The years since 1974 have seen a large number of important changes in both the health and education services. The Government introduced further modifications to the administrative structure of the National Health Service in 1984 (the establishment of district general manager posts) and 1986 (the reform of family practitioner services), and in 1989 in published a White Paper on *Working for Patients* (National Children's Bureau 1987: 45–6; PP 1988–9 Cm. 555 xlvi). This in turn formed the basis of the National Health Service and Community Care Act of 1990, which established the internal market in health care (Ham 1992: 53–5; see also 1990 Ch. 19). The last fifteen years have also seen major changes in education policy. The Education Act of 1981 made area health authorities (and subsequently district health authorities) directly responsible for the ascertainment of children with special needs, and the 1988 Education Act gave individual schools more control over their own affairs (1981 Ch. 60: section 10; 1988 Ch. 40: sections 33–51). The Children Act of 1989 strengthened the ties between the school health service and the social services by giving school nurses and community paediatricians a leading role in child protection work (1989 Ch. 41; see also Department of Health 1991: paras 3.1–3.5; 1992a: 4–5).

These changes have had an important effect on the development of health service provision in schools. The changes within the National Health Service have seen an increased emphasis on the role of preventive medicine (PP 1990–1 Cm. 1523 lii), and the 1981 Education Act strengthened the opportunities for collaboration between the health authorities and the education authorities. The Children Act offered new opportunities for collaboration between the health and social services. However many other developments have pointed in the opposite direction. The changes which have been made to the administrative structure of the National Health Service have increased the scope for local variation at the expense of national coordination, and the creation of the internal market has led to difficulties in areas where the hospital and community services are provided by separate trusts (British Paediatric Association 1993: 8). The introduction of local management of schools and the creation of grant-maintained schools have exacerbated fears that the contribution of the school health service may be increasingly devalued (ibid.: 10).

The pace of change in both the health and education services has ensured that the school health service has continued to be the subject of debate, but the future of the service remains uncertain. There is now far greater coordination between the school health service and the health service for preschool children, and there is closer cooperation between the community health services and the general practitioners, but the links between the school health service and the local education authorities have been weakened, and there is still a significant gap between the community health services and the hospital and consultant services (Macfarlane and Mitchell 1988: 196; British Paediatric Association 1993: 8). In 1989 the Secretary of State for Health, Kenneth Clarke, told the President of the British Paediatric Association that

> I appreciate the reasons for the BPA's concern that implementation of the White Paper [on *Working for Patients*] should not impede progress towards the integration of comprehensive hospital and community services for children. I am aware that successive expert studies . . . have described the need for integration and I have no doubt that this is necessary for the effective delivery of services (British Paediatric Association 1991: 2; see also Department of Health 1992b: 139).

However, while there is clearly very widespread support for the principle of integration, the goal of achieving this remains some way off.

Notes

1 It is important to remember that even during the 1930s, when the Board of Education's nutrition statistics were much-criticised and eventually discredited, they were still capable of providing as much ammunition for the Government's opponents as they were for its supporters. See e.g. House of Commons Debates 1936: cols 1229–1351; Hannington 1937: 43–55.

2 The obligation placed on the Secretary of State for Health and Social Security to provide for medical and dental examination and treatment of pupils attending local authority schools was reaffirmed in Section 5 of the National Health Service Act 1977. See 1977 Ch. 49: section 5.

3 The distinctive nature of the child guidance service was reflected in the arrangements which were made for the continuation of the service after 1974. See Department of Education and Science 1974d.

4 In 1971 there were 1097 practising speech therapists in England and Wales, of whom 850 were employed in public practice. 532 worked in the school health service, 192 in hospitals, 12 were joint appointments, and 32 worked in schools and clinics run by independent bodies. The equivalent figures for Scotland were: LEAs: 94; hospitals: 33; joint appointments: 10; independent bodies: 4; private practice: 45. See Department of Education and Science 1972c: para. 5.05.

5 The organisation concerned were the County Councils Association, the Association of Education Committees, the Association of Municipal Corporations, the Welsh Joint Education Committee, and the Inner London Education Authority. See *Times* 1971a; 1971b.

6 By a curious coincidence, the National Health Service Reorganisation Act entered the Statute Book exactly 25 years to the day after the original NHS Act was put into operation.

7 The Government's initial response to the Court report was spelt out by the Minister of State, Lord Wells-Pestell, during the House of Lords debate on child health services on 16 February 1977. See House of Lords Debates (1977: cols 1605–53).

8 The Court Committee reported that only 56 per cent of children between the ages of 5 and 16 had been examined by a school dentist in 1974. By contrast, Harrison and Gretton found that three quarters of children received a dental examination a decade later. See PP 1976–7 Cmnd. 6684 xi: 206–7; Harrison and Gretton 1986: 30.

Bibliography

Acts of Parliament

38 & 39 Vict. Ch. 55, An Act for consolidating and amending the Acts relating to public health in England.

56 & 57 Vict. Ch. 42, An Act to make better provision for the elementary education of blind and deaf children in England and Wales.

2 Edw. VII Ch. 42, An Act to make further provision with respect to education in England and Wales.

6 Edw. VII Ch. 57, An Act to make provision for meals for children attending public elementary schools in England and Wales.

7 Edw. VII Ch. 40, An Act to provide for the early notification of births.

7 Edw. VII Ch. 43, An Act to make provision for the better administration by the central and local authorities in England and Wales of the enactments relating to education.

8 Edw. VII Ch. 63, An Act to amend the laws relating to education in Scotland, and for other purposes connected therewith.

9 Edw. VII Ch. 13, An Act to provide for the recovery by Local Education Authorities of costs for medical treatment of children attending public elementary schools in England and Wales.

3–4 Geo. V Ch. 12, An Act to enable the provision of medical treatment for children attending schools in Scotland.

4 & 5 Geo. V Ch. 20, An Act to amend the Education (Provision of Meals) Act, 1906.

5 & 6 Geo. V Ch. 64, An Act to extend the Notification of Births Act, 1907, to areas in which it has not been adopted, and to make further provision in connection therewith for the care of mothers and young children.

8 & 9 Geo. V Ch. 39, An Act to make further provision with respect to education in England and Wales and for purposes connected therewith.

9 & 10 Geo. V Ch. 5, An Act to establish a Ministry of Health to exercise in England and Wales powers with respect to health and local government, and confer upon the Chief Secretary certain powers with respect to health in Ireland, and for purposes connected therewith.

11 & 12 Geo. V Ch. 21, An Act to amend the Dentists Act 1878 and the provisions of the Medical Act 1886 amending that Act.

11 & 12 Geo. V Ch. 51, An Act to consolidate the enactments relating to education and certain enactments relating to the employment of children and young persons.

7 & 8 Geo. VI Ch. 31, An Act to reform the law relating to education in England and Wales.

1 & 2 Eliz. II Ch. 33, An Act to amend the law relating to education in England and Wales, and to make further provision with respect to the duties of Education Authorities in Scotland as to dental treatment.

4 & 5 Eliz. II Ch. 29, An Act to amend the law relating to dentists.

1973 Ch. 32, An Act to make further provision with respect to the national health service in England and Wales and amendments of the enactments relating to the national health service in Scotland; and for purposes connected with those matters.

1977 Ch. 49, An Act to consolidate certain provisions relating to the health service for England and Wales, and to repeal certain enactments relating to the health service which have ceased to have any effect.

1981 Ch. 60, An Act to make provision with respect to children with special educational needs.

1988 Ch. 40, An Act to amend the law relating to education.

1989 Ch. 41, An Act to reform the law relating to children; to provide for local authority services for children in need and others; to amend the law with respect to children's homes, community homes, voluntary homes and voluntary organisations; to make provision with respect to fostering, child-minding and day-care for young children and adoption; and for connected purposes.

1990 Ch. 19, An Act to make further provision about health authorities and other bodies constituted in accordance with the National Health Service Act 1977; to provide for the establishment of National Health Service trusts; to make further provision about the financing of the practices of medical practitioners . . . and for connected purposes.

Parliamentary Papers

PP 1871 C. 252 lv, 303, *Minute of the Right Honourable the Lords of the Committee of the Privy Council on Education establishing a new Code of Regulations.*

PP 1878–9 C. 2287 lvii, 95, Education Department, *New Code of Regulations . . . by the Right Honourable the Lords of the Committee of the Privy Council.*

PP 1882 C. 3152 l, 511, *Minute of 6 March 1882, establishing a new Code of Regulations, by the Right Honourable the Lords of the Committee of the Privy Council.*

PP 1884 (293) lxi, 259, *Elementary schools: Dr Crichton-Browne's Report.*

PP 1898 C. 8746 xxvi, 1, *Departmental Committee on Defective and Epileptic Children.*

PP 1900 Cd. 323 xv, 1, *Sixty-second Annual Report of the Registrar-General for England and Wales, for 1899.*

PP 1901 Cd. 513 lv, 743, Board of Education, *Code of regulations for day schools and schedules and appendices.*

PP 1902 Cd. 836 xxvii, 1, *Education in Germany.*

PP 1903 Cd. 1507 xxx, 1, Royal Commission on Physical Training (Scotland), *Report and Appendix.*

PP 1903 Cd. 1508 xxx, 123, Royal Commission on Physical Training (Scotland), *Evidence and Index.*

PP 1904 Cd. 2032 xix, 411, *Report of the Interdepartmental Committee on the Model Course of Physical Exercises.*

PP 1904 Cd. 2175 xxxii, 1, Interdepartmental Committee on Physical Deterioration, *Report and Appendix.*

PP 1904 Cd. 2210 xxxii, 145, Interdepartmental Committee on Physical Deterioration, *List of witnesses and Evidence.*

PP 1904 Cd. 2186 xxxii, 655, Interdepartmental Committee on Physical Deterioration, *Appendices and Index.*

PP 1905 Cd. 2618 xviii, 1, *Supplement to the sixty-fifth Annual Report of the Registrar-General of Births, Marriages and Deaths in England and Wales 1891–1900, Part I.*

PP 1906 (143) ii, 199, *A Bill to provide secular education, periodical medical examination and food for children attending state-supported schools.*

PP 1906 (160) i, 895, *A Bill to make further provision with respect to education in England and Wales.*

PP 1906 (317) i, 925, *A Bill to make further provision with respect to education in England and Wales, as amended in Committee.*

PP 1906 (327) i, 949, *A Bill to make further provision with respect to education in England and Wales, as amended in Committee and on Report.*

PP 1906 Cd. 2779 xlvii, 1, Interdepartmental Committee on Medical Inspection and Feeding of Children Attending Public Elementary Schools, *Report and Appendices.*

PP 1906 Cd. 2784 xlvii, 157, Interdepartmental Committee on Medical Inspection and Feeding of Children attending Public Elementary Schools, *List of witnesses, Evidence, Appendices and Index.*

PP 1907 (22) i, 793, *A Bill to make provision for vacation schools, and for the medical inspection and treatment of schoolchildren.*

PP 1907 (83) i, 801, *A Bill to make provision for the better administration by the central and local authorities in England and Wales of the enactments relating to education.*

PP 1907 (288) vi, *Report from Standing Committee B on the Education (Administrative Provisions) Bill with the Proceedings of the Committee.*

PP 1908 (112) ii, *A Bill to regulate the conditions on which public money may be applied in aid of elementary education in England and Wales, and for other purposes incidental thereto.*

PP 1908 Cd. 4158 lxxxii, 303, *Code of Regulations for Public Elementary Schools in England (excluding Wales and Monmouth) with Schedules.*

PP 1909 (143) iii, 513, *A Bill to provide for the recovery by Local Education Authorities of costs for medical treatment of children attending public elementary schools in England and Wales.*

PP 1910 Cd. 4986 xxiii, 1, *Annual Report of the Chief Medical Officer of the Board of Education for 1908.*

PP 1910 Cd. 5426 xxiii, 175, *Annual Report of the Chief Medical Officer of the Board of Education for 1909.*

PP 1911 Cd. 5925 xvii, 449, *Annual Report of the Chief Medical Officer of the Board of Education for 1910.*

PP 1912 Cd. 6138 lxv, 519, Board of Education, *Regulations under which grants in respect of medical treatment and care of children attending public elementary schools and certain special schools in England and Wales will be made by the Board of Education during the year ending March 31, 1913.*

PP 1912–13 (213) iii, 993, *A Bill to make further and better provision with respect to feeble-minded and other mentally-defective persons.*

PP 1912–13 Cd. 6258 cxi, 1, *Census of England and Wales 1911. Vol I: Administrative areas.*
PP 1912–13 Cd. 6097, cxix, cxx, *Census of Scotland, 1911.*
PP 1912–13 Cd. 6530 xxi, 439, *Annual Report of the Chief Medical Officer of the Board of Education for 1911.*
PP 1913 (60) ii, 461. *A Bill to amend the law relating to the education of defective and epileptic children in England and Wales.*
PP 1913 Cd. 6986 xxii, 507, *The 78th Report of the Commissioners of National Education in Ireland (school year 1911/12).*
PP 1913 Cd. 7041l, 79, Board of Education, *Regulations under which grants in respect of the medical inspection and medical treatment of children attending public elementary schools and the medical treatment and care of children attending certain special schools in England and Wales will be made by the Board of Education during the year ending March 31, 1914.*
PP 1913 Cd. 7018 lxxviii, 1, *Census of England and Wales 1911. Vol. X: Occupations and industries.*
PP 1914 Cd. 7184 xxv, 401, *Annual Report of the Chief Medical Officer of the Board of Education for 1912.*
PP 1914 Cd. 7484 lxv, 121, *Minute of the Board of Education dated 24 June 1914, modifying the Regulations for Public Elementary Schools 1912 in England and Wales, as already modified by the Minute dated 4 July 1913.*
PP 1914–16 (114) iii, 245, *A Bill to extend the Notification of Births Act, 1907, to areas in which it has not been adopted and to make further provision in connection therewith for the care of mothers and young children.*
PP 1914–16 Cd. 7730 xviii, 277, *Annual Report of the Chief Medical Officer to the Board of Education for 1913.*
PP 1914–16 Cd. 8055 xviii, 665, *Annual Report of the Chief Medical Officer of the Board of Education for 1914.*
PP 1916 Cd. 8200 xv, 181, *Final Report of the Committee on Retrenchment in the Public Expenditure.*
PP 1916 Cd. 8338 viii, 149, *Annual Report of the Chief Medical Officer of the Board of Education for 1915.*
PP 1916 Cd. 8358 xiv, 731, *Departmental Committee on Prices . . . Interim Report on meat, milk and bacon.*
PP 1917–18 (89) i, 337, *A Bill to make further provision with respect to education in England and Wales and for purposes connected therewith.*
PP 1917–18 Cd. 8515 xxv, 85, Board of Education, *Regulations under which supplementary grant will be paid to Local Education Authorities for elementary education, if provision is made by Parliament for the purpose.*
PP 1917–18 Cd. 8746 xi, 89, *Annual Report of the Chief Medical Officer of the Board of Education for 1916.*
PP 1918 (57) i, 231, *A Bill (as amended in Committee) to make further provision with respect to education in England and Wales and for purposes connected therewith.*
PP 1918 Cd. 9206 ix, 99, *Annual Report of the Chief Medical Officer of the Board of Education for 1917.*
PP 1919 Cmd. 420, xxi, 149, *Annual Report of the Chief Medical Officer of the Board of Education for 1918.*
PP 1920 Cmd. 995 xv, 149, *Annual Report of the Chief Medical Officer of the Board of Education for 1919.*
PP 1920 Cmd. 693 xvii, 1001, Consultative Committee on Medical and Allied Services, *Interim Report on the future provision of medical and allied services.*
PP 1920 Cmd. 961 xxxvi, 145, Board of Education, *Consolidated Regulations relating to*

the Special Services of Elementary Education (other than nursery schools) for promoting the healthy physical and mental development of children.

PP 1921 Cmd. 1522 xi, 109, *Annual Report of the Chief Medical Officer of the Board of Education for 1920.*

PP 1922 Cmd. 1581 ix, 1, *First Interim Report of the Committee on National Expenditure.*

PP 1922 Cmd. 1718 vii, 413, *Report of the Board of Education for the year 1920/21.*

PP 1926 Cmd. 2688 xxiii, 463, Board of Education, *Memorandum on the Board of Education Estimates 1926.*

PP 1927 Cmd. 2866 viii, 653, *Report of the Board of Education for the year 1925/26.*

PP 1930–31 Cmd. 3920 xvi, 1, *Report of the Committee on National Expenditure.*

PP 1930–31 Cmd. 3952 xviii, 371, *Memorandum on the measures proposed by H.M. Government to secure reductions in national expenditure.*

PP 1931–2 Cmd. 4200 xiv, 1, *Report of the Committee on Local Expenditure (England and Wales).*

PP 1937–8 Cmd. 5837 x, 607, *Report of Committee on Evacuation.*

PP 1938–9 Cmd. 6013 x, 661, *Education in 1938, being the Report of the Board of Education and the Statistics of Public Education for England and Wales.*

PP 1940–1 Cmd. 6317 iv, 223, *Summary Report of the Department of Education for Scotland in the years 1939 and 1940.*

PP 1941–2 Cmd. 6343 vii, 65, Board of Education, *Memorandum on the Board of Education Estimates 1942.*

PP 1941–2 Cmd. 6370 iv, 201, *Summary Report of the Department of Education for Scotland for the year 1941.*

PP 1942–3 Cmd. 6452 iv, 281, *Summary Report of the Department of Education for Scotland for the year 1942.*

PP 1942–3 Cmd. 6429 ix, 39, Board of Education, *Memorandum on the Board of Education Estimates 1943.*

PP 1942–3 Cmd. 6458 xi, 21, Board of Education, *Educational reconstruction.*

PP 1943–4 Cmd. 6502 viii, 315, Ministry of Health and Department of Health for Scotland, *A National Health Service.*

PP 1943–4 Cmd. 6508 vii, 47, Board of Education, *Memorandum on the Board of Education Estimates 1944.*

PP 1943–4 Cmd. 6540 iii, 195, *Summary Report of the Department of Education for Scotland for the year 1943.*

PP 1943–4 Cmd. 6565 iii, 169, Ministry of Health and Department of Health for Scotland, *Interim Report of the Interdepartmental Committee on Dentistry.*

PP 1944–5 Cmd. 6581 ix, 63, Ministry of Education, *Memorandum on the Ministry of Education Estimates 1945.*

PP 1945–6 (94) iii, 67, *A Bill to provide for the establishment of a comprehensive health service for England and Wales, and for purposes connected therewith.*

PP 1945–6 Cmd. 6667 xi, 399, *Summary Report of the Department of Education for Scotland for the year 1944.*

PP 1945–6 Cmd. 6727 xi, 169, Ministry of Health and Department of Health for Scotland, *Final Report of the Interdepartmental Committee on Dentistry.*

PP 1945–6 Cmd. 6629 xx, 167, Ministry of Education, *Memorandum on the Ministry of Education Estimates 1946.*

PP 1947–8 Cmd. 7426 xi, 515, *Education in 1947, being the Report of the Ministry of Education and the Statistics of Public Education in England and Wales.*

PP 1948–9 Cmd. 7724 xiv, 345, *Education in 1948, being the Report of the Ministry of Education and the Statistics of Public Education in England and Wales.*

PP 1950 Cmd. 7957 ix, l, *Education in 1949, being the Report of the Ministry of Education and the Statistics of Public Education for England and Wales.*

PP 1950–51 Cmd. 8244 xi, 261, *Education 1900–50. The Report of the Ministry of Education and the Statistics of Public Education for England and Wales for the year 1950.*
PP 1951–2 Cmd. 8554 x, 247, *Education in 1951, being the Report of the Ministry of Education and the Statistics of Public Education for England and Wales.*
PP 1952–3 Cmd. 8835 ix, 379, *Education in 1952, being the Report of the Ministry of Education and the Statistics of Public Education for England and Wales.*
PP 1953–4 Cmd. 9155 xi, 561, *Education in 1953, being the Report of the Ministry of Education and the Statistics of Public Education for England and Wales.*
PP 1955–6 Cmd. 9663 xx, 833, *Report of the Committee of Enquiry into the Cost of the National Health Service* (Guillebaud Report).
PP 1955–6 Cmd. 9785 xiv, 609, *Education in 1955, being the Report of the Ministry of Education and the Statistics of Public Education in England and Wales.*
PP 1955–6 Cmd. 9861 xiv, 207, *Report of the Interdepartmental Committee on Recruitment to the Dental Profession* (McNair Report).
PP 1956–7 Cmnd. 223 x, 921, *Education in 1956, being the Report of the Ministry of Education and the Statistics of Public Education for England and Wales.*
PP 1957–8 Cmnd. 454 x, 537, *Education in 1957, being the Report of the Ministry of Education and the Statistics of Public Education for England and Wales.*
PP 1958–9 Cmnd. 777 xi, 269, *Education in 1958, being the Report of the Ministry of Education and the Statistics of Public Education in England and Wales.*
PP 1959–60 Cmnd. 1088 xii, 637, *Education in 1959, being the Report of the Ministry of Education and the Statistics of Public Education in England and Wales.*
PP 1960–61 Cmnd. 1439 xiii, 549, *Education in 1960, being the Report of the Ministry of Education and the Statistics of Public Education in England and Wales.*
PP 1961–2 Cmnd. 1737 xiii, 61, *Education in 1961, being the Report of the Ministry of Education for England and Wales.*
PP 1962–3 (40) v, 27, *First Report from the Estimates Committee, together with part of the minutes of the evidence taken before sub-committee C appointed by the Estimates Committee in session 1961–2, and appendices.*
PP 1962–3 Cmnd. 1990 xi, 503, *Education in 1962, being the Report of the Ministry of Education for England and Wales.*
PP 1963–4 Cmnd. 2316 xi, 183, *Education in 1963, being the Report of the Ministry of Education for England and Wales.*
PP 1964–5 Cmnd. 2612 xiii, 287, *Education in 1964, being the Report of the Department of Education and Science.*
PP 1966–7 Cmnd. 2938 xxvii, 1, *Education in 1965, being a Report of the Department of Education and Science.*
PP 1966–7 Cmnd. 3226 xxvii, 153, *Education in 1966, being a Report of the Department of Education and Science.*
PP 1967–8 Cmnd. 3564 xix, 393, *Education in 1967, being a Report of the Department of Education and Science.*
PP 1968–9 Cmnd. 3950 xxviii, 871, *Education in 1968, being a Report of the Department of Education and Science.*
PP 1971–2 Cmnd. 5055 xvi, 197, *National Health Service reorganisation: England.*
PP 1971–2 Cmnd. 5057 xvi, 269, *National Health Service reorganisation: Wales.*
PP 1972–3 (79) iv, *A Bill . . . to make further provision with respect to the National Health Service in England and Wales and amendments to the enactments relating to the National Health Service in Scotland, and for purposes connected with these matters.*
PP 1976–7 Cmnd. 6684 xi, 457, *Fit for the future: Report of the Committee on Child Health Services* (Court Committee).
PP 1979–80 Cmnd. 7615 lvi, *Report of the Royal Commission on the National Health Service.*
PP 1988–9 Cm. 555 xlvi, *Working for Patients.*

PP 1990–1 Cm. 1523 lii, *The health of the nation: a consultative document for England.*

Parliamentary Debates

Parliamentary Debates (1903), *Parliamentary Debates*, 4th series, vol. 124.
Parliamentary Debates (1905), *Parliamentary Debates*, 4th series, vol. 149.
Parliamentary Debates (1906a), *Parliamentary Debates*, 4th series, vol. 150.
Parliamentary Debates (1906b), *Parliamentary Debates*, 4th series, vol. 158.
Parliamentary Debates (1906c), *Parliamentary Debates*, 4th series, vol. 160.
Parliamentary Debates (1906d), *Parliamentary Debates*, 4th series, vol. 162.
Parliamentary Debates (1906e), *Parliamentary Debates*, 4th series, vol. 165.
Parliamentary Debates (1906f), *Parliamentary Debates*, 4th series, vol. 167.
Parliamentary Debates (1907a), *Parliamentary Debates*, 4th series, vol. 169.
Parliamentary Debates (1907b), *Parliamentary Debates*, 4th series, vol. 174.
Parliamentary Debates (1907c), *Parliamentary Debates*, 4th series, vol. 180.
Parliamentary Debates (1907d), *Parliamentary Debates*, 4th series, vol. 181.
Parliamentary Debates (1907e), *Parliamentary Debates*, 4th series, vol. 182.
Parliamentary Debates (1907f), *Parliamentary Debates*, 4th series, vol. 184.
House of Commons Debates (1909a), *House of Commons Debates*, 5th series, vol. 1.
House of Commons Debates (1909b), *House of Commons Debates*, 5th series, vol. 16.
House of Commons Debates (1913a), *House of Commons Debates*, 5th series, vol. 46.
House of Commons Debates (1913b), *House of Commons Debates*, 5th series, vol. 55.
House of Commons Debates (1914), *House of Commons Debates*, 5th series, vol. 65.
House of Commons Debates (1915), *House of Commons Debates*, 5th series, vol. 72.
House of Commons Debates (1918), *House of Commons Debates*, 5th series, vol. 107.
House of Commons Debates (1922), *House of Commons Debates*, 5th series, vol. 152.
House of Commons Debates (1924), *House of Commons Debates*, 5th series, vol. 169.
House of Commons Debates (1934), *House of Commons Debates*, 5th series, vol. 292.
House of Commons Debates (1936), *House of Commons Debates*, 5th series, vol. 314.
House of Commons Debates (1938), *House of Commons Debates*, 5th series, vol. 337.
House of Commons Debates (1939a), *House of Commons Debates*, 5th series, vol. 349.
House of Commons Debates (1939b), *House of Commons Debates*, 5th series, vol. 353.
House of Commons Debates (1972), *House of Commons Debates*, 5th series, vol. 840.
House of Commons Debates (1978), *House of Commons Debates*, 5th series, vol. 942.
House of Lords Debates (1909), *House of Lords Debates*, 5th series, vol. 2.
House of Lords Debates (1977), *House of Lords Debates*, 5th series, vol. 379.

Public Records Office sources

PRO ED24/279, National League for Physical Education and Improvement.
PRO ED24/280, Formation of Medical Department.
PRO ED24/282, British Medical Association.
PRO ED24/590, Anson papers.
PRO ED24/958, Board of Education on Ministry of Health Bill, 1919.
PRO ED24/1312, Grants for medical inspection and treatment.
PRO ED24/1363, Responsibility for the care of the preschool child.
PRO ED24/1369, Ministry of Reconstruction on treatment.
PRO ED24/1370, Medical aspects of the 1917 Education Bill.
PRO ED24/1371, Meals (school feeding arrangements in August 1914).

PRO ED24/1372, Meals during strikes (1921–6).
PRO ED50/1, Duties of Medical Officers of Health.
PRO ED50/3, British Medical Association on medical inspection.
PRO ED50/5, Circular 576.
PRO ED50/6, Circular 582.
PRO ED50/7, Circular 596.
PRO ED50/34, Correspondence with school medical officers on contents of Chief Medical Officer's annual reports.
PRO ED50/35, Coordination of public health and school medical services.
PRO ED50/45, General.
PRO ED50/51, Nutrition enquiries.
PRO ED50/65, Expenditure cuts (1920–21).
PRO ED50/72, School medical service statistics (1923).
PRO ED50/77, Meals (1921–33).
PRO ED50/81, Milk Act 1934.
PRO ED50/104, Rationing of special services (1922/23).
PRO ED50/105, Expenditure review (1932/33).
PRO ED50/175, Depressed areas (1931–45).
PRO ED50/181, Financial assistance to Special Areas for provision of special services.
PRO ED50/192, School medical officers' ideas re reconstruction of school medical service post-World War 2.
PRO ED50/196, Heights and weights etc.
PRO ED50/201, Conduct of special services.
PRO ED50/204, Nutrition: improvement and assessment.
PRO ED50/206, Clinics in reception areas (1939–45).
PRO ED50/207, The school medical service in wartime (1939–40).
PRO ED50/213, Proposals for improvement of school medical service.
PRO ED50/214, Nutrition.
PRO ED50/216, Malnutrition: representations by Children's Minimum Council.
PRO ED50/287, Circular 29 (1945–6).
PRO ED50/351, Special services. M. Files. Dental treatment (1946–7).
PRO ED125/8, Precedent files – implementation of Administrative Provisions Act.
PRO ED136/212, Education after the war. Green Book drafting papers. Preliminary papers.
PRO ED136/214, Board of Education, *Education after the War* (Green Book).
PRO ED136/218, Green Book. Summaries of discussions.
PRO ED136/243, Green Book. Minutes of discussion with various associations.
PRO ED136/377, Education Bill: Miscellaneous correspondence.
PRO ED136/378, Preparation of the Education Bill, 1944. Volume 1. Secretary's papers 1942–3.
PRO ED136/662, Provision of school meals and milk in wartime.
PRO ED136/664, School health services in wartime.
PRO ED137/73, Radcliffe Borough Council Local Education Authority: School health service 1935–45.
PRO ED137/87, Middlesex County Council: School health service 1929–52.
PRO ED137/119, Shropshire County Council LEA: School health service 1930–53.
PRO ED137/123, Staffordshire County Council: School health service 1932–52.
PRO ED137/141: Warwickshire County Council LEA: School health service 1930–52.
PRO ED137/158, Yorkshire West Riding County Council LEA: School health service 1930–52.
PRO ED137/173, Blackburn County Borough Council LEA: School health service 1932–52.

PRO ED137/196, Darlington County Borough Council: School health service 1931–52.
PRO ED137/213, Halifax County Borough Council: School health service 1932–52.
PRO ED137/279: West Hartlepool County Borough Council LEA: School health service 1933–52.
PRO ED137/296: Rhondda Urban District Council LEA: School health service 1927–49.
PRO ED138/3, Brief history of education. Vol. 2. Special services.
PRO ED138/56, Medical etc. Annual reports.
PRO ED138/58, Medical etc. Evacuation etc.
PRO ED138/59, Nutrition of the schoolchild 1907–45. School milk and meals. Miscellaneous notes. Circulars and administrative memoranda.
PRO ED138/60, Nutrition of the schoolchild. War history of school milk and meals. Mr Davidson's file containing draft by Mr E.D. Marris – Board of Education.
PRO LAB85/19–22, 41–4, 117–21, 161–4, 187–90, Employment Department Statistics.
PRO MH55/629, Inquiry into conditions affecting health through unemployment in South Wales and Monmouthshire.
PRO MH77/124, National health services. Dental services policy (1943–6).
PRO MH107/26, Sir George Newman.
PRO MH139/1–6, Diaries of Sir George Newman, 1907–46.
PRO PC 8/584, Physical Deterioration Committee (Chancery Lane).
PRO T/161/664/S/38589, Education. Restrictions on capital expenditure and memorandum on Ray Committee recommendations.

Other references

A School Medical Officer (1922), 'School medical service and the Ministry of Health', *Public Health*, 35, 99–101.
Abrams, P. (1963), 'The failure of social reform', *Past and Present*, 24, 43–64.
Allan, F.J. (1915), 'The public health service as a career', *Medical Officer*, 14, 99.
Amery, L.S. (1900), *The Times History of the War in South Africa 1899–1900*, vol. 1, London: Sampson Low, Marston and Co. Ltd.
Annual reports of the School Medical Officer for Aberdeen.
Annual reports of the School Medical Officer for Aberdeenshire.
Annual reports of the School Medical Officer for Abertillery.
Annual report. of the School Medical Officer for Accrington.
Annual reports of the School Medical Officer for Banffshire.
Annual reports of the School Medical Officer for Batley.
Annual reports of the School Medical Officer for Blackburn.
Annual reports of the School Medical Officer for Bradford.
Annual reports of the School Medical Officer for Cambridge.
Annual reports of the School Medical Officer for Cardiff.
Annual reports of the School Medical Officer for Croydon.
Annual reports of the School Medical Officer for Darwen.
Annual reports of the School Medical Officer for Dumbartonshire.
Annual reports of the School Medical Officer for Edinburgh.
Annual reports of the School Medical Officer for Glasgow.
Annual reports of the School Medical Officer for Govan.
Annual reports of the School Medical Officer for Huddersfield.
Annual reports of the School Medical Officer for Leeds.

Annual reports of the School Medical Officer for Lincoln.
Annual reports of the School Medical Officer for Mountain Ash.
Annual reports of the School Medical Officer for Nottingham.
Annual reports of the School Medical Officer for Reading.
Annual reports of the School Medical Officer for Rhondda.
Annual reports of the School Medical Officer for Sheffield.
Annual reports of the School Medical Officer for Torquay.
Annual reports of the School Medical Officer for Wakefield.
Annual reports of the School Medical Officer for Warrington.
Armstrong, H. (1905), 'The supposed deterioration and decrease of our population in relation to overcrowding in houses', *Public Health*, 18, 301–10.
Auden, G.A. (1935), 'School medical services', *Medical Officer*, 54, 249.
Auden, G.A. (1936), 'The development of the school medical service', *Medical Officer*, 55, 157.
Badger, W.S. (1913), 'Discontent in the school medical service', *Medical Officer*, 9, 309.
Berry, F.M.D. (1904), 'On the physical examination of 1580 girls from elementary schools in London', *British Medical Journal*, 28/5/04, 1248–9.
Board of Education (1922), *Health of the schoolchild 1921. Annual Report of the Chief Medical Officer of the Board of Education for 1921*, London: HMSO.
Board of Education (1923), *Health of the schoolchild 1922. Annual Report of the Chief Medical Officer of the Board of Education for 1922*, London: HMSO.
Board of Education (1924), *Health of the schoolchild 1923. Annual Report of the Chief Medical Officer of the Board of Education for 1923*, London: HMSO.
Board of Education (1925a), *Health of the schoolchild 1924. Annual Report of the Chief Medical Officer of the Board of Education for 1924*, London: HMSO.
Board of Education (1925b), The Board of Education (Special Services) Regulations 1925 (S.R. & O. 1925 no. 835).
Board of Education (1926), *Health of the schoolchild 1925. Annual Report of the Chief Medical Officer of the Board of Education for 1925*, London: HMSO.
Board of Education (1927), *Health of the schoolchild 1926. Annual Report of the Chief Medical Officer of the Board of Education for 1926*, London: HMSO.
Board of Education (1928), *Health of the schoolchild 1927. Annual Report of the Chief Medical Officer of the Board of Education for 1927*, London: HMSO.
Board of Education (1929), *Health of the schoolchild 1928. Annual Report of the Chief Medical Officer of the Board of Education for 1928*, London: HMSO.
Board of Education (1930), *Health of the schoolchild 1929. Annual Report of the Chief Medical Officer of the Board of Education for 1929*, London: HMSO.
Board of Education (1931), *Health of the schoolchild 1930. Annual Report of the Chief Medical Officer of the Board of Education for 1930*, London: HMSO.
Board of Education (1932), *Health of the schoolchild 1931. Annual Report of the Chief Medical Officer of the Board of Education for 1931*, London: HMSO.
Board of Education (1933), *Health of the schoolchild 1932. Annual Report of the Chief Medical Officer of the Board of Education for 1932*, London: HMSO.
Board of Education (1934), *Health of the schoolchild 1933. Annual Report of the Chief Medical Officer of the Board of Education for 1933*, London: HMSO.
Board of Education (1935), *Health of the schoolchild 1934. Annual Report of the Chief Medical Officer of the Board of Education for 1934*, London: HMSO.
Board of Education (1936), *Health of the schoolchild 1935. Annual Report of the Chief Medical Officer of the Board of Education for 1935*, London: HMSO.
Board of Education (1937), *Health of the schoolchild 1936. Annual Report of the Chief Medical Officer of the Board of Education for 1936*, London: HMSO.
Board of Education (1938), *Health of the schoolchild 1937. Annual Report of the Chief*

Medical Officer of the Board of Education for 1937, London: HMSO.
Board of Education (1939), 'Education of evacuated schoolchildren in time of emergency' (Circular 1469).
Board of Education (1940), *Health of the schoolchild 1938. Annual Report of the Chief Medical Officer of the Board of Education for 1938*, London: HMSO.
Board of Education (1942), 'School medical service' (Circular 1604).
Bowley, A.L. and Hogg, M.H. (1925), *Has poverty diminished?*, London: P.S. King.
Bowley, M. (1945), *Housing and the state 1919–44*, London: George Allen & Unwin.
Bransby, E.R. (1944), 'The wartime growth of schoolchildren', *Monthly Bulletin of the Ministry of Health and the Emergency Public Health Laboratory Service*, 3, 212–15.
Bransby, E.R. (1946a), 'The diets of families with children in 1941', *British Medical Journal*, 1/6/46, 832–5.
Bransby, E.R. (1946b), 'Further note on the wartime growth of schoolchildren', *Monthly Bulletin of the Ministry of Health and the Emergency Public Health Laboratory Service*, 5, 57–60.
Brewer, D. (1927), 'The aims and tendencies of school medicine', *Medical Officer*, 37, 283–4.
British Medical Journal (1871), 'Social Science Association: Annual Meeting held in Leeds, October 1871', *British Medical Journal*, 21/10/1871, 476–83.
British Medical Journal (1874a), 'The spread of infectious diseases in schools', *British Medical Journal*, 2/5/1874, 592.
British Medical Journal (1874b), 'Medical inspection of schools', *British Medical Journal*, 7/11/1874, 593.
British Medical Journal (1876), 'Medical inspection of Board schools', *British Medical Journal*, 5/7/1876, 84.
British Medical Journal (1878a), 'Propagation of infected diseases by schools', *British Medical Journal*, 25/5/1878, 760.
British Medical Journal (1878b), 'Infection in schools', *British Medical Journal*, 29/6/1878, 938.
British Medical Journal (1878c), 'Medical supervision of schools', *British Medical Journal*, 28/12/1878, 971.
British Medical Journal (1882), 'The Education Department and the closing of schools', *British Medical Journal*, 18/3/1882, 395.
British Medical Journal (1883), 'Scarlet fever and the closing of schools', *British Medical Journal*, 10/2/1883, 280–81.
British Medical Journal (1884a), 'International Medical Congress, Eighth Session, held in Copenhagen, August 1884', *British Medical Journal*, 6/9/1884, 468–76.
British Medical Journal (1884b), 'International Congress of Hygiene at the Hague', *British Medical Journal*, 6/9/1884, 484–6.
British Medical Journal (1890), 'Board schools and infectious disease', *British Medical Journal*, 27/12/1890, 1498.
British Medical Journal (1895), 'Public health and Poor Law medical services – measles and school closure', *British Medical Journal*, 6/4/1895, 791.
British Medical Journal (1900), 'The sanitary control of national schools', *British Medical Journal*, 3/3/00, 530–31.
British Medical Journal (1901), 'Medical inspection in American schools', *British Medical Journal*, 14/12/01, 1766.
British Medical Journal (1904a), 'The national physique', *British Medical Journal*, 9/1/04, 104.
British Medical Journal (1904b), 'Medical inspection of schools in Philadelphia', *British Medical Journal*, 19/3/04, 683.

British Medical Journal (1904c), 'Manchester: physiology in education', *British Medical Journal*, 26/3/04, 754.

British Medical Journal (1904d), 'Physical education in elementary schools', *British Medical Journal*, 7/5/04, 1091–2.

British Medical Journal (1904e), 'Physical deterioration', *British Medical Journal*, 30/7/04, 248.

British Medical Journal (1905a), 'Conference on school hygiene: building and equipment of schools', *British Medical Journal*, 18/2/05, 380–82.

British Medical Journal (1905b), 'Sanitation of elementary schools', *British Medical Journal*, 22/4/05, 896.

British Medical Journal (1905c), 'Manchester: physique of Salford schoolchildren', *British Medical Journal*, 27/5/05, 1179.

British Medical Journal (1905d), 'Medical examination of New York schoolchildren', *British Medical Journal*, 26/8/05, 449.

British Medical Journal (1906a), 'School hygiene: the control of measles', *British Medical Journal*, 27/1/06, 216–18.

British Medical Journal (1906b), 'School hygiene', *British Medical Journal*, 7/4/06, 797.

British Medical Journal (1906c), 'The teeth of schoolchildren', *British Medical Journal*, 21/4/06, 919.

British Medical Journal (1906d), 'A discussion on hygiene of the home and state institutions', *British Medical Journal*, 22/9/06, 676.

British Medical Journal (1907a), 'School hygiene: London', *British Medical Journal*, 2/2/07, 272.

British Medical Journal (1907b), 'School hygiene: Leith', *British Medical Journal*, 23/2/07, 445–6.

British Medical Journal (1907c), 'Pulmonary tuberculosis in schoolchildren', *British Medical Journal*, 23/2/07, 459–60.

British Medical Journal (1907d), 'Tasmania: school hygiene', *British Medical Journal*, 2/3/07, 531–2.

British Medical Journal (1907e), 'The inspection of elementary school buildings', *British Medical Journal*, 30/3/07, 779–80.

British Medical Journal (1907f), 'The attitude of the Board of Education to school hygiene', *British Medical Journal*, 21/9/07, 760–61.

British Medical Journal (1907g), 'Medical inspection of schoolchildren', *British Medical Journal*, 30/11/07, 1604–5.

British Medical Journal (1909a), 'Limitation in medical inspection of schoolchildren', *British Medical Journal*, 10/4/09, 924.

British Medical Journal (1909b), 'Medical inspection of schoolchildren in Salford', *British Medical Journal*, 4/6/09, 1387.

British Medical Journal (1910), 'The medical inspection of London schoolchildren', *British Medical Journal*, 30/7/10, 293–4.

British Medical Journal (1927), 'The unification of local health services', *British Medical Journal*, 19/11/27, 924–9.

British Medical Journal (1935), 'Nutrition of schoolchildren', *British Medical Journal*, 28/12/35, 1261.

British Medical Journal (1977a), 'Court report discussed', *British Medical Journal*, 28/5/77, 1424–5.

British Medical Journal (1977b), 'Court report on child health services', *British Medical Journal*, 11/6/77, 1552–3.

British Paediatric Association (1987), *The school health services*, London: British Paediatric Association.

British Paediatric Association (1991), *Towards a combined child health service*, London: British Paediatric Association.

British Paediatric Association (1993), *Health services for school age children: consultative report of the Joint Working Party*, London: British Paediatric Association.

Brockington, C.F. (1938a), 'The influence of the growing family upon the diet in urban and rural districts', *Journal of Hygiene*, 38, 40–61.

Brockington, C.F. (1938b), 'Further observations on the influence of the growing family upon the diet in rural districts in Sussex', *Journal of Hygiene*, 38, 547–57.

Brockington, C.F. (1939), 'Further observations on the relationship between gain in weight and diet in children', *Public Health*, 52, 307–10.

Brown, R.G.S. (1979), *Reorganising the National Health service: a case-study in administrative change*, Oxford: Basil Blackwell and Martin Robertson.

Brunton, L. (1905), 'The Report of the Interdepartmental Committee on Physical Degeneration', *Public Health*, 18, 274–92.

Bryder, L. (1987), 'The First World War: healthy or hungry?', *History Workshop Journal*, 24, 146–65.

Bryder, L. (1988), *Below the magic mountain: a social history of tuberculosis in twentieth century Britain*, Oxford: Clarendon Press.

Buchan, J.J. (1922), 'Coordination of medical services in Bradford', *Public Health*, 35, 101–3.

Burgerstein, L. (1889), *Axel Key's Schulhygienische Untersuchungen . . . in deutscher Bearbeitung, hsrg. von Leo Burgerstein*, Hamburg and Leipzig: L. Voss.

Burnett, J. (1983), *Plenty and want: a social history of diet in England from 1815 to the present day*, London: Methuen.

Burnett, J. (1994), 'The rise and decline of school meals in Britain 1860–1990', in J. Burnett and D. Oddy, eds, *The origins and development of food policies in Europe*, Leicester: Leicester University Press, 55–69.

Cameron, N. (1979), 'The growth of London schoolchildren 1904–66: an analysis of secular trend and intra-county variation', *Annals of Human Biology*, 6, 505–25.

Cantlie, J. (1885), *Degeneration amongst Londoners: the Parkes Museum of Hygiene Lecture for 1885*, London: Field and Tuer.

Central Statistical Office (1948), *Annual Abstract of Statistics no. 84, 1935–46*, London: HMSO.

Central Statistical Office (1949), *Annual Abstract of Statistics, no. 86, 1938–48*, London: HMSO.

Central Statistical Office (1955), *Annual Abstract of Statistics, no. 92, 1955*, London: HMSO.

Central Statistical Office (1956), *Annual Abstract of Statistics, no. 93, 1956*, London: HMSO.

Central Statistical Office (1958), *Annual Abstract of Statistics, no. 95, 1958*, London: HMSO.

Central Statistical Office (1960), *Annual Abstract of Statistics, no. 97, 1960*, London: HMSO.

Central Statistical Office (1965), *Annual Abstract of Statistics, no. 102, 1965*, London: HMSO.

Central Statistical Office (1971), *Annual Abstract of Statistics, no. 108, 1971*, London: HMSO.

Central Statistical Office (1975a), *National income and expenditure 1964–74*, London: HMSO.

Central Statistical Office (1975b), *Annual Abstract of Statistics, no. 112, 1975*, London: HMSO.

Central Statistical Office (1988), *Social Trends 18*, London: HMSO.

Central Statistical Office (1990), *Guide to official statistics, no. 5*, London: HMSO.

City and County of Newcastle upon Tyne (1934), *Investigation into the health and nutrition of certain of the children of Newcastle-upon-Tyne between the ages of one and five years*, Newcastle upon Tyne: Newcastle upon Tyne Cooperative Printing Society.

Clark, F. le G. (1948), *Social history of the school meals service*, London: National Council of Social Service.

Clark, R.V. (1927), 'The amalgamation of child welfare and school medical work: the point of view of the Medical Officer of Health', *Public Health*, 40, 378–81.

Clarke, J.S. (1940), 'London', in R. Padley and M. Cole, eds, *Evacuation survey: a report to the Fabian Society*, London: George Routledge and Sons, 200–09.

Cohn, H. (1867), *Untersuchungen der Augen von 10,000 Schulkindern, nebst Vorschlägen zur Verbesserungen der den Augen nachtheiligen Schuleinrichtungen*, Leipzig, F. Fleischer.

Cohn, H. (1883), 'Des médecins scolaires: conclusions de Monsieur le Professeur H. Cohn, de Breslau', *Quatrième Congrès International d'Hygiène et de Démographie en Genève*, 1882, Geneva: H. Georg.

Cole, M. (1940), 'General effects: billeting' in R. Padley and M. Cole, eds, *Evacuation survey: a report to the Fabian Society*, London: George Routledge and Sons, 69–75.

Coleman, D. and Salt, J. (1992), *The British population: patterns, trends and prospects*, Oxford: Oxford University Press.

Collins, H.B. (1902), 'The child, the doctor and the state', *Public Health*, 15, 600–09.

Collins, H.B. (1904), 'Health and Empire', *Public Health*, 17, 401–13.

Committee on Haemoglobin Surveys (1945), 'Haemoglobin levels in Great Britain in 1943 (with observations upon serum protein levels)', *Medical Research Council Special Report Series*, no. 252.

Court, D. and Alberman, E. (1988), 'Worlds apart', in J.O. Forfar, ed., *Child health in a changing society*, Oxford: Oxford University Press, 1–30.

Crawford, W. and Broadley, H. (1938), *The people's food*, London: Heinemann.

Cripps, L., Greenwood, M. and Newbold, E. (1923), 'A biometric study of the inter-relations of "vital capacity", stature, stem-length and weight in a sample of healthy male adults', *Biometrika*, 14, 317–36.

Cronk, H.L. (1935), 'School medical inspection', *Public Health*, 46, 253–7.

Crosby, T. (1986), *The impact of civilian evacuation in the Second World War*, London: Croom Helm.

Crowley, R.H. (1932), 'Preventive and clinical medicine in relation to the medical care and treatment of children', *British Medical Journal*, 12/11/32, 875–8.

Crowther, M.A. (1988), *British social policy 1914–39*, London: Macmillan.

Cumberland Education Committee (1935), *Annual Report of the School Medical Officer for Cumberland for 1934*, Carlisle: Cumberland Education Committee.

Daglish, N. (1990), 'Robert Morant's hidden agenda? The origins of the medical treatment of schoolchildren', *History of Education*, 19, 139–48.

Danker-Hopfe, H. (1986), 'Menarcheal age in Europe', *Yearbook of Physical Anthropology*, 29, 81–112.

Dawson, W. (1906), *School doctors in Germany* (Board of Education, Educational Pamphlets, no. 4), London: HMSO.

Dearden, W.F. (1905), 'The municipal treatment of physical deterioration', *Public Health*, 18, 237–45.

Department of Education and Science (1964), *Health of the schoolchild 1962–3. Report of the Chief Medical Officer of the Ministry of Education for 1962–3*, London: HMSO.

Department of Education and Science (1965), *The nutritional standard of the school dinner*, London: HMSO.

Department of Education and Science (1966a), Circular 3/66 (26/1/66).

Department of Education and Science (1966b), Circular 23/66 (1/12/66).

Department of Education and Science (1966c), Circular 25/66 (15/12/66).

Department of Education and Science (1966d), *Health of the schoolchild 1964–5. Report of the Chief Medical Officer of the Department of Education and Science for 1964–5*, London: HMSO.

Department of Education and Science (1967), *Statistics of Education 1966. Vol. 1. Schools*, London: HMSO.

Department of Education and Science (1968a), Circular 11/68 (23/4/68).

Department of Education and Science (1968b), Provision of Milk and Meals (Amendment no. 2) Regulations 1968 (S.I. 1968 no. 1251).

Department of Education and Science (1968c), *Psychologists in education services: the report of a Working Party appointed by the Secretary of State for Education and Science: the Summerfield Report*, London: HMSO.

Department of Education and Science (1969a), *Statistics of Education 1968. Vol. 5. Finance and awards*, London: HMSO.

Department of Education and Science (1969b), *Health of the schoolchild 1966–8. Report of the Chief Medical Officer of the Department of Education and Science for 1966–8*, London: HMSO.

Department of Education and Science (1970), *Education and science in 1969, being a Report of the Department of Education and Science*, London: HMSO.

Department of Education and Science (1971), *Education and science in 1970, being a Report of the Department of Education and Science*, London: HMSO.

Department of Education and Science (1972a), *Education and science in 1971: a report of the Department of Education and Science*, London: HMSO.

Department of Education and Science (1972b), *Health of the schoolchild 1969–70. Report of the Chief Medical Officer of the Department of Education and Science for 1969–70*, London: HMSO.

Department of Education and Science (1972c), *Speech therapy services: report of the Committee appointed by the Secretaries of State for Education and Science, for the Social Services, for Scotland and for Wales in July 1969*, London: HMSO.

Department of Education and Science (1973), *Statistics of Education 1972. Vol. 1. Schools*, London: HMSO.

Department of Education and Science (1974a), *Health of the schoolchild 1971–2. Report of the Chief Medical Officer of the Department of Education and Science for 1971–2*, London: HMSO.

Department of Education and Science (1974b), *Education and science in 1973, being a Report of the Department of Education and Science*, London: HMSO.

Department of Education and Science (1974c), Circular 1/74/(4/1/74).

Department of Education and Science (1974d), Circular 3/74 (14/3/74).

Department of Education and Science (1975a), *Education and science in 1974, being a report of the Department of Education and Science*, London: HMSO.

Department of Education and Science (1975b), *Nutrition in schools. Report of the Working Party on the Nutritional Aspects of School Meals*, London: HMSO.

Department of Education and Science (1976), *Statistics of Education 1975. Vol. 5. Finance and Awards*, London: HMSO.

Department of Health (1988), *Health and personal social services statistics for England 1988*, London: HMSO.

Department of Health (1990), *Health and personal social services statistics for England 1990*, London: HMSO.

Department of Health (1991), *Working together under the Children Act: a guide to arrangements for inter-agency cooperation for the protection of children from abuse*, London: HMSO.

Department of Health (1992a), *Child protection: guidance for senior nurses, health visitors and midwives*, London: HMSO.

Department of Health (1992b), *On the state of the public health: Annual Report of the Chief Medical Officer of the Department of Health for 1991*, London: HMSO.

Department of Health and Social Security (1970a), *On the state of the public health: Annual Report of the Chief Medical Officer of the Department of Health and Social Security for 1969*, London: HMSO.

Department of Health and Social Security (1970b), *National Health Service: the future structure of the National Health Service*, London: HMSO.

Department of Health and Social Security (1973a), *Reorganisation of the National Health Service and Local Government in England and Wales: a report from the Working Party on Collaboration between the NHS and Local Government on its activities to the end of 1972*, London: HMSO.

Department of Health and Social Security (1973b), *Reorganisation of the National Health Service and Local Government in England and Wales: a report from the Working Party on Collaboration between the NHS and Local Government on its activities from January to July 1973*, London: HMSO.

Department of Health and Social Security (1974), Circular HRC(74)5 (January 1974).

Department of Health and Social Security (1976), *Priorities for health and personal social services: a consultative document*, London: HMSO.

Department of Health and Social Security (1978a), Circular HC(78)5 (January1978).

Department of Health and Social Security (1978b), *On the state of the public health: Annual Report of the Chief Medical Officer of the Department of Health and Social Security for 1977*, London: HMSO.

Department of Health and Social Security (1978c), *Health and personal social services statistics for England 1978*, London: HMSO.

Department of Health and Social Security (1981), 'Second report by the Sub-committee on Nutritional Surveillance (Committee on Medical Aspects of Food Policy)', *Reports on Health and Social Subjects*, no. 21.

Department of Health and Social Security (1982), *Health and personal social services statistics for England 1982*, London: HMSO.

Department of Health and Social Security (1985), *Health and personal social services statistics for England 1985*, London: HMSO.

Dewey, P. (1988), 'Nutrition and living standards in wartime Britain', in R. Wall and J. Winter, eds, *The upheaval of war: family, work and welfare in Europe 1914–18*, Cambridge: Cambridge University Press, 197–220.

Dreyer, G. (1920), *The assessment of physical fitness by correlation of vital capacity and certain measurements of the body*, London: Cassell.

Drèze, J. and Sen, A. (1989), *Hunger and public action*, Oxford: Clarendon.

Dublin, L.I. and Gebhart, J.C. (1924), *Do height and weight tables identify undernourished children?* New York: New York Association for Improving the Condition of the Poor.

Dwork, D. (1987), *War is good for babies and other young children*, London: Tavistock.

East Sussex Education Committee (1937), *Annual Report of the School Medical Officer for East Sussex for 1936*, Lewes: East Sussex Education Committee.

Education (1977), 'ILEA takes Court to task over GPP proposal', *Education*, 18/11/77, 340.

Education (1980), 'SEO criticise plan to split up area authorities', *Education*, 16/5/80, 424.

Elkington, J. (1908), *Report on the work of the Medical Branch, Education Department, Tasmania*, Hobart: John Vail.

Evans, R. (1991), 'The European family and the Great War', *Social History*, 16, 341–52.

Eveleth, P. and Tanner, J. (1991), *Worldwide variation in human growth*, Cambridge: Cambridge University Press.

Feinstein, C.H. (1972), *Statistical tables of national income, expenditure and output of the United Kingdom 1855–1965*, Cambridge: Cambridge University Press.

Fitzherbert, K. (1982), 'Communication with teachers in the health surveillance of children', *Journal of Maternal and Child Health*, 7, 100–03.

Fitzroy, A.W. (1925a), *Memoirs of Sir Almeric Fitzroy*, London: Hutchinson (2 vols).

Fitzroy, A.W. (1925b), 'Memoirs of the life of Sir Almeric Fitzroy', *British Library Additional Manuscripts*, nos. 48371–80 (10 volumes).

Flack, M. (1920), 'Tests for flying efficiency and flying stress', in Medical Research Council, 'The medical problems of flying', *Special Report Series*, no. 53, London: HMSO.

Floud, R.C., Wachter, K. and Gregory, A. (1985), *The physical state of the British working class: evidence from Army recruits* (National Bureau of Economic Research Working Paper no. 1661), Cambridge, Massachusetts: National Bureau of Economic Research.

Floud, R.C., Wachter, K. and Gregory, A. (1990), *Height, health and history: nutritional status in the United Kingdom 1750–1980*, Cambridge: Cambridge University Press.

Fogarty, M. (1945), *Prospects of the industrial areas of Great Britain*, London: Methuen.

Fogel, R.W. (1986), 'Nutrition and the decline of mortality since 1700: some preliminary findings', in S.L. Engerman and R.E. Gallman, eds, *Long-term factors in American economic growth*, Chicago: University of Chicago Press, 439–555.

Ford, P. (1934), *Work and wealth in a modern port: an economic survey of Southampton*, London: Allen & Unwin.

Forrest, J.A. (1939), 'Epidemiological aspects of A.R.P. evacuation schemes', *Medical Officer*, 61, 201.

Francis, H.W.S. (1973), 'The future of the school health service', *Community Health*, 4, 327–30.

Francis, H.W.S. (1975), 'Education and health: the English tradition', *Public Health*, 89, 129–35, 181–90, 273–7.

Frank, J.P. (1779–1827), *System einer vollständigen medizinischen Polizey*, Mannheim: C.F. Schwan[n] (9 vols).

Fraser, D. (1973), *The evolution of the British welfare state: a history of social policy since the industrial revolution* (1st edn), London: Macmillan.

Fraser, D. (1984), *The evolution of the British welfare state: a history of social policy since the industrial revolution* (2nd edn), London: Macmillan.

Frazer, W.M. (1950), *A history of English public health 1834–1939*, London: Baillière, Tindall and Cox.

Freeman, V. (1934), 'Heights, weights and physical defects in schoolchildren', *Medical Officer*, 52, 65–6.

Garside, W.R. (1990), *British unemployment 1919–39: a study in public policy*, Cambridge: Cambridge University Press.

General Register Office (1944a), *Registrar-General's Statistical Review of England and Wales for the year 1939. New Annual Series, no. 19. Tables. Part I. Medical*, London: HMSO.

General Register Office (1944b), *Registrar-General's Statistical Review of England and Wales for the year 1940. New Annual Series, no. 20. Tables. Part I. Medical*, London: HMSO.

General Register Office (1945), *Registrar-General's Statistical Reivew of England and Wales for the year 1941. New Annual Series, no. 21. Tables. Part I. Medical*, London: HMSO.

General Register Office (1946), *Registrar-General's Statistical Review of England and Wales for the year 1942. New Annual Series, no. 22. Tables. Part I. Medical*, London: HMSO.

General Register Office (1947), *Registrar-General's Statistical Review of England and*

Wales for the year 1945. New Annual Series, no. 25. Tables. Part I. Medical, London: HMSO.

General Register Office (1948), *Registrar-General's Statistical Review of England and Wales for the year 1943. New Annual Series, no. 23. Tables. Part I. Medical,* London: HMSO.

General Register Office (1949), *Registrar-General's Statistical Review of England and Wales for the year 1944. New Annual Series, no. 24. Tables. Part I. Medical,* London: HMSO.

General Register Office (1952), *Registrar-General's Statistical Review of England and Wales for the year 1950. New Annual Series, no. 30. Tables. Part I. Medical,* London: HMSO.

General Register Office (1956), *Registrar-General's Statistical Review of England and Wales for the year 1955. Part I. Tables. Medical,* London: HMSO.

General Register Office (1962), *Registrar-General's Statistical Review of England and Wales for the year 1960. Part I. Tables. Medical,* London: HMSO.

General Register Office (1967), *Registrar-General's Statistical Review of England and Wales for the year 1965. Part I. Tables. Medical,* London: HMSO.

George, R.F. (1937), 'A new calculation of the poverty line', *Journal of the Royal Statistical Society,* 100, part I, 74–95.

Gibb, A. (1983), *Glasgow: the making of a city,* London: Croom Helm.

Gilbert, B. (1965), 'Health and politics: the British Physical Deterioration Report of 1904', *Bulletin of the History of Medicine,* 39, 143–53.

Gilbert, B.B. (1966), *The evolution of national insurance in Great Britain: the origins of the welfare state,* London: Michael Joseph.

Glossop Education Committee (1935), *Annual Report of the School Medical Officer for Glossop for 1934,* Glossop: Glossop Education Committee.

Glover, J.A. (1940), 'Evacuation: some epidemiological observations on the first four months', *Proceedings of the Royal Society of Medicine,* 33, 399–412.

Gosden, P.H.J.H. (1976), *Education in the Second World War,* London: Methuen.

Gosden, P.H.J.H. (1983), *The education system since 1944,* Oxford: Martin Robertson.

Guest H. (1943), 'Work of the school medical service', *Times Educational Supplement,* 21/8/43, 401.

Gulick, L.H. and Ayres, L.P. (1908), *Medical inspection of schools,* New York: Russell Sage Foundation (Charities Publication Committee).

HCTL (1915), 'The school medical service', *Public Health,* 27, 278–9.

HH (1908), 'Medical inspection of schoolchildren', *British Medical Journal,* 8/2/08, 353.

Hall, F. (1941), 'Medical Planning', *Public Health,* 55, 38–9.

Hall, W. (1903a), '"Where men decay" and how', *Yorkshire Post,* 28/3/03, 12b.

Hall, W. (1903b), 'Christian and Jew: a remarkable comparison', *Yorkshire Post,* 2/5/03, 10e.

Hall, W. (1903c), 'Christian and Jew: the case of the girls', *Yorkshire Post* 9/5/03, 9g.

Hall, W. (1903d), 'Gentile and Jew: the care of the children', *Yorkshire Post,* 19/5/03, 8f.

Ham, C. (1992), *Health policy in Britain: the politics and organisation of the National Health Service* (3rd ed), London and Basingstoke: Macmillan.

Hammond, R.J. (1956), *Food. Vol. II. Studies in administration and control,* London: HMSO.

Hannington, W. (1937), *The problem of the distressed areas,* London: Victor Gollancz.

Harris, B. (1988) 'Unemployment, insurance and health in interwar Britain', in B. Eichengreen and T. Hatton, eds, *Interwar unemployment in international perspective,* Dordrecht: Kluwer Academic Publishers, 149–83.

Harris B. (1989), 'Medical inspection and the nutrition of schoolchildren in Britain 1900–50', Ph.D. thesis, University of London.

Harris, B. (1990), 'Voluntary action and unemployment: charity in the South Wales coalfield between the Wars', in E. Aerts and B. Eichengreen, eds, *Unemployment and underemployment in international perspective*, Leuven: Leuven University Press, 101–10.

Harris, B. (1993), 'The demographic impact of the First World War: an anthropometric perspective', *Social History of Medicine*, 6, 343–66.

Harris, B. (1994), 'The height of schoolchildren in Britain 1900–1950', in J. Komlos, ed., *Stature, living standards and economic development: essays in anthropometric history*, Chicago: Chicago University Press, 25–38.

Harris, L. (1936), 'A programme for nutrition surveys', *Lancet*, 25/4/36, 966–8.

Harris, L. (1937), 'The incidence and assessment of malnutrition', *Medical Officer*, 58, 225–9, 237–40, 249–51, 261–5, 273–7.

Harrison, A. and Gretton, J. (1986), 'School health: the invisible service', in A. Harrison and J. Gretton, eds, *Health care UK 1986: an economic, social and policy audit*, London: Policy Journals, 25–32.

Hay, J.R. (1975), *The origins of the Liberal welfare reforms*, (1st edition) London: Macmillan.

Hay, J.R. (1983), *The origins of the Liberal welfare reforms*, (2nd edn), London: Macmillan

Henderson, P. (1957), 'School medical inspection', *Public Health*, 70, 42–8.

Henderson, P. (1975), *The school health service 1908-74. Report of the Chief Medical Officer of the Department of Education and Science and presenting an historical review by Dr Peter Henderson, Principal Medical Officer of the Department of Education and Science from 1951–69*, London: HMSO.

Hendrick, H. (1994), *Child welfare: England 1872–1989*, London: Routledge.

Herd, H. (1935a), 'The school medical service', *Public Health*, 48, 124–9.

Herd. H. (1935b), 'The future of the school medical service', *Journal of the Royal Sanitary Institute*, 56, 103–9.

Hertel, N.T.A. (1885), *Overpressure in high schools in Denmark* (translated by L.G. Sörenson), London: Macmillan and Co.

Hirst, J.D. (1981), 'A failure "without parallel": the school medical service and the London County Council', *Medical History*, 25, 281–300.

Hirst, J.D. (1982), 'Vision testing in London: a rehearsal for the school medical service', *Journal of Educational Administration and History*, 14, 23–9.

Hirst, J.D. (1983), 'The origins and development of the school medical service 1870–1919', Ph.D. thesis, University of Wales (Bangor).

Hirst, J.D. (1989), 'The growth of treatment through the school medical service, 1908–18', *Medical History*, 33, 318–42.

Hirst, J.D. (1991), 'Public health and the public elementary schools, 1870–1907', *History of Education*, 20, 107–118.

HMSO (1932), *Census of Scotland 1931. Vol. 1, part 2. City of Glasgow*, Edinburgh: HMSO.

HMSO (1934), *Census of England and Wales 1931. Occupation tables*, London: HMSO.

Hogarth, A.H. (1907a), 'Medical inspection of schoolchildren', *British Medical Journal*, 21/9/07, 772–3.

Hogarth, A.H. (1907b), 'The Board of Education and medical inspection of schools', *British Medical Journal*, 12/10/07, 1019.

Hogarth, A.H. (1907c), 'The medical inspection of schools', *The Times*, 27/11/07, 18d.

Hogarth, A.H. (1909), *Medical inspection of schools*, London: Oxford University Press/ Hodder and Stoughton.

Hogben, G.H. (1949), 'Opportunities in school medicine', *Public Health*, 62, 83–5.

Holden, O.M. (1935), 'The school medical service: whence and whither?', *Journal of the Royal Sanitary Institute*, 56, 96–102.

Holland, B. (1911), *The life of Spencer Compton, eighth Duke of Devonshire*, London: Longman's, Green & Co. (2 vols).

Horner, J.S. (1977), 'Let the prisoners speak', *Health and Social Service Journal*, 87, 63.
Howarth, W.J. (1921), 'Reflections on certain public health problems', *Public Health*, 35, 33–40.
Hurt, J.S. (1985), 'Feeding the hungry schoolchild in the first half of the twentieth century', in D. Oddy and D. Miller, eds, *Diet and health in modern Britain*, London: Croom Helm, 178–206.
Hutchinson J. (1846), 'On the capacity of the lungs and on the respiratory functions with a view of establishing a precise and easy method of detecting disease by the spirometer', *Transactions of the Royal Medico-Chirurgical Society of London*, 29, 136–252.
Hutt, G.A. (1933), *The condition of the working class in Britain*, London: Martin Lawrence.
Hyamson, A.M. (1951), *A dictionary of universal biography of all ages and of all people*, London: Routledge & Kegan Paul.
Ingram, P. (1972), 'AEC want local control of health services to stay', *Times Educational Supplement*, 21/7/72, 8.
Jepson, A.M. (1982), 'Who is to follow the specialist in community medicine (child health)?', *Community Medicine*, 3, 249–52.
Johnson, S. (1977), 'For and against the Court Report', *Education*, 8/4/77, 248–9 (with a reply by John Tomlinson).
Jolly, H. (1976), 'Time schools were given a dose of new medicine', *The Times*, 11/8/76, 5f-h.
Jolly, R.H.H. (1943), 'The public health service as a career', *Medical Officer*, 70, 109–10.
Jones, D.C. (1934), *The social survey of Merseyside*, London: Hodder & Stoughton (3 vols).
Jones, G.S. (1984), *Outcast London: a study in the relationship between classes in Victorian London*, Harmondsworth: Penguin (1st edn 1971).
Jones, H. (1994), *Health and society in twentieth-century Britain*, London: Longman.
Jones, R.H. (1938), 'Physical indices and clinical assessments of the nutrition of schoolchildren', *Journal of the Royal Statistical Society*, 101, part I, 1–52.
Kelly, F. (1935), 'Fifty years of nutritional science', *Medical Officer*, 53, 65–6.
Kerr, J. (1897), 'School hygiene in its mental, moral and physical aspects', *Journal of the Royal Statistical Society*, 60, 613–80.
Kerr, J. (1905), 'Physical inspection', *Journal of the Royal Sanitary Institute*, 26, 59–63.
Kerr, J. (1926), *The fundamentals of school health*, London: George Allen & Unwin.
Kerr, J. and Wallis, E. eds. (1908), *Second International Congress on School Hygiene, London, 1907: Transactions*, London: Royal Sanitary Institute (3 vols).
Klein R. (1989), *The politics of the National Health Service* (2nd edn), London: Longman.
Komlos, J. (1989), *Nutrition and economic development in the eighteenth-century Habsburg monarchy: an anthropometric history*, Princeton: Princeton University Press.
Kommission for forandret af det høiere skolevæsen (1867), *Forslag til en forandret ordnung af det høiere skolevæsen. Af den ved kgl. resolution af 14de Februar 1865, for af tage under overvielse og afgive forslag til en forandret ordnung af det høiere skolevæsen hedsatte kommission*, Christiania (Oslo): P.T. Mallings bogtrykkeri.
Lancet (1885), 'Reviews and notices of books: *Overpressure in the high schools of Denmark*, by Dr. Hertel', *Lancet*, 15/8/1885, 292–3.
Lancet (1903), 'An impeachment of the national health', *Lancet*, 31/1/03, 315–17.
Lancet (1904a), 'The Education Act and physical fitness', *Lancet*, 9/4/04, 1003–4.
Lancet (1904b), 'Congress of the Royal Institute of Public Health: Section of Child Study and School Hygiene: The physical education of our children', *Lancet*, 30/7/04, 316.

Lancet (1904c), 'The Report of the Privy Council upon Physical Deterioration', *Lancet*, 6/8/04, 390–91.

Lancet (1905), 'The medical control of schools at New York (from our special Sanitary Commissioner)', *Lancet*, 25/3/05, 823–4.

Lancet (1907), 'The Board of Education and the medical inspection of schoolchildren', *Lancet*, 30/11/07, 1547–8.

Lancet (1937), 'An objective test of malnutrition?', *Lancet*, 6/11/37, 1090.

Lancet (1939), 'Town into country', *Lancet*, 9/9/39, 605.

Latham, A. (1982), 'Health appraisal/surveillance by school nurses', *Health Visitor*, 54, 25–7.

Leff, S. and Leff, V. (1959), *The school health service*, London: H.K. Lewis.

Levitt, R, (1976), *The reorganised National Health Service*, London: Croom Helm.

Lewis, J. (1980), *The politics of motherhood: child and maternal welfare in England 1900–39*, London: Croom Helm.

Lewis, J. (1986), *What price community medicine? The philosophy, practice and politics of public health since 1919*, Brighton: Wheatsheaf.

Ling, P.H. (1836), *Reglemente för gymnastik*, Stockholm: Eiméns och Gransbergs.

Lishman, F.J.G. (1944), 'The future of the School Medical Officer', *Public Health*, 58, 35–6.

Liverpool Education Committee (1938), *Annual Report of the School Medical Officer for Liverpool for 1937*, Liverpool: Liverpool Education Committee.

Lloyd, E.M.H. (1936), 'Food supplies and consumption at different income levels', *Journal of Proceedings of the Agricultural Economics Society*, 4, part 2, 89–120.

London County Council (1898), *Diphtheria and elementary schools: Report by the Medical Officer of Health*, London: London County Council.

London County Council (1907), *Report of the Medical Officer (Education) for the year ended 31 March 1907*, London: London County Council.

London County Council (1908), *Education Committee, Day Schools Sub-committee, Agenda, 21/1/08*, London: London County Council.

Lorinser, C.J. (1861), *Zum Schutz der Gesundheit in den Schulen (neuer Abdruck eines Aufsatzes aus der Medizinischen Zeitung, 1836, no. 1)*, Berlin: E.S. Mittler.

Lowe, R. (1978), 'The erosion of state intervention in Britain 1917–24', *Economic History Review*, 2nd series, 31, 270–86.

Lowe, R. (1986), *Adjusting to democracy: the role of the Ministry of Labour in British politics 1916–39*, Oxford: Clarendon Press.

Lowe R. (1993), *The welfare state in Britain since 1945*, London and Basingstoke: Macmillan.

Lucas, S. (1980), 'Some aspects of child health care: contacts between children, general practitioners and school doctors', *Community Medicine*, 2, 209–18.

Lunn, J.E. (1967), 'School health service work in the ordinary day schools', *Public Health*, 87, 303–5.

Lunn, J.E. (1973), 'The periodic medical inspection in school health service work', *Public Health*, 87, 173–8.

McCollum, E. and Simmonds, N. (1929), *The newer knowledge of nutrition*, New York: Macmillan & Co.

Macfarlane, A. and Mitchell, R. (1988), 'Health services for children and their relationship to the educational and social services', in J.O. Forfar, ed., *Child health in a changing society*, Oxford: Oxford University Press, 155–97.

M'Gonigle, G.C.M. (1927), 'The geographical distribution of defects among schoolchildren', *Medical Officer*, 38, 16/7/27, 27.

M'Gonigle, G.C.M. and Kirby J. (1936), *Poverty and public health*, London: Victor Gollancz.

Mackenzie, W.L. assisted by Matthew E. (1904), *The medical inspection of schoolchildren:*

a textbook for Medical Officers of Schools, Medical Officers of Health, school managers and teachers, Edinburgh and Glasgow: William Hodge and Co.

Mackenzie, W.L. (1906), *The health of the schoolchild*, London: Methuen.

McKibbin, R. (1990), 'The social psychology of unemployment in interwar Britain', in R. McKibbin, *Ideologies of class: social relations in Britain 1880–1950*, Oxford: Clarendon Press, 228–58.

Mackintosh, J.M. (1953), *Trends of opinion about the public health 1901–51: the Heath Clark lectures for 1951*, London: Oxford University Press.

Macnicol, J. (1980), *The movement for family allowances 1918–45: a study in social policy development*, London: Heinemann.

Macnicol, J. (1986), 'The effect of the evacuation of schoolchildren on official attitudes to state intervention', in H.L. Smith, ed., *War and social change: British society in the Second World War*, Manchester: Manchester University Press, 3–31.

McPherson, K. and Coleman, D. (1988), 'Health', in A.H. Halsey, ed., *British social trends since 1900: a guide to the changing social structure of Britain*, London: Macmillan, 398–461.

Magee, H.E. (1944), 'War and the nutritional state', *Monthly Bulletin of the Ministry of Health and the Emergency Public Health Laboratory Service*, 3, 146–51.

Magee, H.E. (1946), 'Application of nutrition to public health: some lessons of the war', *British Medical Journal*, 30/3/46, 475–82.

Magee, H.E. (1947), 'Activities in nutrition of the Ministry of Health in England during the war', *Proceedings of the Nutrition Society*, 5, 211–13.

Magee, H.E., Woolham, J.G., Simpson, R.H., Spence, J.C., Hutchison, R., Glover, J.A., Shrubsall, F.C. and Batten, L. (1935), 'Discussion on the assessment of the state of nutrition', *Proceedings of the Royal Society of Medicine*, 28, 713–29.

Maitra, M.K. and Harris, L. (1937), 'Nutrition surveys: vitamin A deficiency among schoolchildren in London and Cambridge' , *Lancet*, 30/10/37, 1009–14.

Manchester Guardian (1904), [no title], *Manchester Guardian*, 29/7/04, 4d.

Manchester Education Committee (1926), *Annual Report of the School Medical Officer for Manchester for 1925*, Manchester: Manchester Education Committee.

Manchester Education Committee (1936), *Annual Report of the School Medical Officer for Manchester for 1935*, Manchester: Manchester Education Committee.

Mann, H.C. (1926), 'Diets for boys during the school age', *Medical Research Council Special Report Series*, no. 105, London: HMSO.

Marrack, J.R. (1935), *Poverty and the child*, London: Labour Research Department.

Marrack, J.R. (1946), 'School meals and milk', *Public Health*, 59, 178–80.

Marrack, J.R. (1947), 'Investigations of human nutrition in the United Kingdom during the war', *Proceedings of the Nutrition Society*, 5, 213–41.

Martin, J.M. (1907), 'Schools and public health', *Public Health*, 21, 116–26.

Maurice. J.F. ('Miles') (1902), 'Where to get men', *Contemporary Review*, 81, 78–86.

Maurice, J.E. (1903), 'National health: a soldier's study', *Contemporary Review*, 83, 41–56.

Mayhew, M. (1988), 'The 1930s nutrition controversy', *Journal of Contemporary History*, 23, 445–64.

Meadowcroft, M. (1980), 'The years of political transition, 1914–39', in D. Fraser, ed., *A history of modern Leeds*, Manchester: Manchester University Press.

Medical Officer (1909), 'Defect averages amongst schoolchildren', *Medical Officer*, 26/6/09, 1050.

Medical Officer (1910a), 'Assessing the nutrition of schoolchildren', *Medical Officer*, 20/9/10, 152.

Medical Officer (1910b), 'National and international standards of nutrition', *Medical Officer*, 12/11/10, 282.

Medical Officer (1911), 'Age-periods for medical inspection of schoolchildren', *Medical Officer*, 19/8/11, 85–6.

Medical Officer (1913), 'Age-periods for inspections', *Medical Officer*, 24/5/13, 250.
Medical Officer (1920), 'School health administration in Scotland', *Medical Officer*, 17/4/20, 157.
Medical Officer (1923), 'The school medical service', *Medical Officer*, 17/11/23, 227.
Medical Officer (1925), 'School medical inspection', *Medical Officer*, 17/10/25, 169.
Medical Officer (1929a), 'Physical effects of prolonged unemployment', *Medical Officer*, 31/8/29, 90.
Medical Officer (1929b), 'The public health service', *Medical Officer*, 7/9/29, 99.
Medical Officer (1932), 'The health of the schoolchildren of Blackburn', *Medical Officer*, 2/7/32, 2–3.
Medical Officer (1933a), 'Notes and comments – Nutrition', *Medical Officer*, 6/5/33, 172–3.
Medical Officer (1933b), 'Unemployment and the young', *Medical Officer*, 8/7/33, 12.
Medical Officer (1934), 'Malnutrition', *Medical Officer*, 11/8/34, 59.
Medical Officer (1935a), 'School medical inspection', *Medical Officer*, 20/4/35, 152.
Medical Officer (1935b), 'Sunderland and economic depression', *Medical Officer*, 25/5/35, 204.
Medical Officer (1936a), 'Tests for the nutrition of schoolchildren', *Medical Officer*, 29/2/36, 83.
Medical Officer (1936b), 'The nutrition of the people', *Medical Officer*, 5/9/36, 94.
Medical Officer (1938), 'An enquiry into malnutrition', *Medical Officer*, 17/12/38, 257.
Medical Officer (1939a), 'Epidemiological aspects of A.R.P. evacuation schemes', *Medical Officer*, 6/5/39, 174.
Medical Officer (1939b), 'School medicine in Birmingham', *Medical Officer*, 27/5/39, 204.
Medical Officer (1940a), 'A study of diets', *Medical Officer*, 6/1/40, 3.
Medical Officer (1940b), 'Appreciation of routine examinations', *Medical Officer*, 20/7/40, 24.
Medical Officer (1943), 'Separation of medical inspection and treatment', *Medical Officer*, 20/11/43, 161.
Medical Officer (1945a), 'The teeth of children', *Medical Officer*, 7/7/45, 3.
Medical Officer (1945b), 'The teeth of schoolchildren of Glasgow', *Medical Officer*, 29/12/45, 215–16.
Medical Officer (1946), 'Delayed health effects of war conditions', *Medical Officer*, 7/9/46, 111.
Medical Press (1887), 'On the importance of certain new biochemical discoveries in relation to voerpressure in shcools', *Medical Press*, 21/12/1887, 595–6.
Medical Research Council (1932), 'Vitamins: a survey of present knowledge', *Special Report Series*, no. 167, London: HMSO.
Medical Research Council (1947), *Medical research in war: Report of the Medical Research Council for the years 1939–45*, London: HMSO.
Mellanby, K. (1941), 'The incidence of head-lice in England', *Medical Officer*, 65, 39–43.
Mellanby, K. (1943), 'The incidence of head-lice in England after four years of war', *Medical Officer*, 70, 205–6.
Mellanby, M. and Mellanby, H. (1948), 'The reduction in dental caries in five-year-old London schoolchildren (1929–47)', *British Medical Journal*, 28/8/48, 409–13.
Milk Nutrition Committee (1939), *Milk and nutrition: new experiments reported to the Milk Nutrition Committee. Part IV. The effects of dietary supplements of pasteurised and raw milk on the growth and health of schoolchildren. Final Report. Summary of all researches carried out by the Committee and practical conclusions*, Reading: National Institute for Research in Dairying.
Miller, H.G. (1938), 'A comparison of physical defects in two groups of Newcastle children', *British Medical Journal*, 1/10/38, 718–19.

Milward, A. (1984), *The economic effects of two world wars on Britain* (2nd edn), London: Macmillan.
Ministry of Education (1945a), The Provision of Milk and Meals Regulations 1945 (S.R. & O. 1945 no. 698).
Ministry of Education (1945b), The Handicapped Pupils and School Health Service Regulations 1945 (S.R. & O. 1945 no. 1076).
Ministry of Education (1946), The Provision of Free Milk Regulations 1946 (S.R. & O. 1946 no. 1293).
Ministry of Education (1947a), *Health of the schoolchild 1939–45: Report of the Chief Medical Officer of the Ministry of Education for 1939–45*, London: HMSO.
Ministry of Education (1947b), Circular 156 (6/11/47).
Ministry of Education (1948a), The Education (Local Education Authorities) Grant Regulations 1948 (S.I. 1948 no. 334).
Ministry of Education (1948b), Circular 179 (4/8/48).
Ministry of Education (1949), *Health of the schoolchild 1946–7. Report of the Chief Medical Officer of the Ministry of Education for 1946–7*, London: HMSO.
Ministry of Education (1952a), *Health of the schoolchild 1948–9. Report of the Chief Medical Officer of the Ministry of Education for 1948–9*, London: HMSO.
Ministry of Education (1952b), *Health of the schoolchild 1950–1. Report of the Chief Medical Officer of the Ministry of Education for 1950–1*, London: HMSO.
Ministry of Education (1953), The School Health Service and Handicapped Pupils Regulations 1953 (S.I. 1953 no. 1156).
Ministry of Education (1954), *Health of the schoolchild 1952–3. Report of the Chief Medical Officer of the Ministry of Education for 1952–3*, London: HMSO.
Ministry of Education (1955), Circular 290 (5/8/55).
Ministry of Education (1956a), *Report of an enquiry into the working of the school meals service (1955–6)*, London: HMSO.
Ministry of Education (1956b), *Health of the schoolchild 1954–5. Report of the Chief Medical Officer of the Ministry of Education for 1954–5*, London: HMSO.
Ministry of Education (1958), *Health of the schoolchild 1956–7. Report of the Chief Medical Officer of the Ministry of Education for 1956–7*, London: HMSO.
Ministry of Education (1959a), The School Health Service Regulations 1959 (S.I. 1959 no. 363).
Ministry of Education (1959b), Circular 352 (24/3/59).
Ministry of Education (1960), *Health of the schoolchild 1958–9. Report of the Chief Medical Officer of the Ministry of Education for 1958–9*, London: HMSO.
Ministry of Education (1962a), Administrative Memorandum 8/62 (22/8/62).
Ministry of Education (1962b), Circular 8/62 (27/8/62).
Ministry of Education (1962c), *Health of the schoolchild 1960–1. Report of the Chief Medical Officer of the Ministry of Education for 1960–1*, London: HMSO.
Ministry of Education (1963a), *Statistics of Education 1962. Part I*, London: HMSO.
Ministry of Education (1963b), Circular 5/63 (5/4/63).
Ministry of Health (1946), *On the state of the public health during six years of war. Annual Report of the Chief Medical Officer of the Ministry of Health 1939–45*, London: HMSO.
Ministry of Health (1967), *Child welfare centres: report of the sub-committee* [of the Standing Medical Advisory Committee], London: HMSO.
Ministry of Health (1968a), *On the state of the public health: Annual Report of the Chief Medical Officer of the Ministry of Health for 1967*, London: HMSO.
Ministry of Health (1968b), *National Health Service: the administrative structure of the medical and related services in England and Wales*, London: HMSO.
Mitchell, M. (1985), 'The effects of unemployment on the social conditions of women and children in the 1930s', *History Workshop Journal*, 19, 105–27.

Morgan, K.O. (1979), *Consensus and disunity: the Lloyd George coalition government 1918–22*, Oxford: Clarendon Press.

Mumford, H. and Young, M, (1923), 'The interrelationships of the physical measurements and the vital capacity', *Biometrika*, 15, 109–33.

Murray, B.K. (1980), *The people's budget 1909/10: Lloyd George and Liberal politics*, Oxford: Clarendon Press.

National Children's Bureau (1987), *Investing in the future: child health ten years after the Court Report: a report of the Policy and Practice Review Group, National Children's Bureau*, London: National Children's Bureau.

Nature (1908), 'Medical inspection of schoolchildren', *Nature*, 5/3/08, 426–7.

Newby, M. and Nicholl, A. (1985), 'Selection of children for school medicals by a pastoral care system in an inner-city junior school', *Public Health*, 99, 331–7.

Newman, G. (1909), 'Medical inspection of schoolchildren', *Public Health*, 22, 160–1.

Newman, G. (1935), 'The health of the people', in H.J. Laski, W.I. Jennings and W.A. Robson, eds, *A century of municipal progress 1835–1935*, London: George Allen & Unwin.

Newman, G. (1939), *The building of a nation's health*, London: Macmillan & Co.

Newman, J.L. (1944), 'Towards a real child health service', *Medical Officer*, 72, 141–3.

Newsholme, A. (1905), 'Alleged physical deterioration in towns', *Public Health*, 18, 293–300.

Newsholme, A. (1907), 'The Children's Charter of Health', *Public Health*, 20, pp. 161–3.

Nicholas, K. (1986), *The social effects of unemployment on Teesside*, Manchester: Manchester University Press.

Oddy, D. (1982), 'The health of the people', in T. Barker and M. Drake, eds, *Population and society in Britain 1850–1980*, London: Batsford Academic and Educational, 121–41.

Office of Population Censuses and Surveys (1972), *Registrar-General's Statistical Review of England and Wales for the year 1965. Part I. Tables.* Medical, London: HMSO.

Office of Population Censuses and Surveys (1976), *Statistics of infectious diseases. Notifications of infectious diseases in England and Wales 1975* (Series MB2, no. 2), London: HMSO.

Office of Population Censuses and Surveys (1977), *Mortality statistics 1974. Review of the Registrar-General on deaths in England and Wales 1974* (Series DHI, no. 1), London: HMSO.

Office of Population Censuses and Surveys (1978), *Mortality statistics. Review of the Registrar-General on deaths in England and Wales 1975* (Series DHI, no. 2), London: HMSO.

One of them (1913), 'The cause of discontent among School Medical Officers', *Medical Officer*, 10, 239–40, 249–50.

Orr, J.B. (1928), 'Milk consumption and the growth of schoolchildren: preliminary report on tests to the Scottish Board of Health', *Lancet*, 28/1/28, 202–3.

Orr, J.B. (1936), *Food, health and income: report on a survey of adequacy of diet in relation to income* (1st edn), London: Macmillan & Co.

Orr, J.B. (1937), *Food, health and income: report on a survey of adequacy of diet in relation to income* (2nd edn), London: Macmillan & Co.

Orr, J.B. and Clark, M. (1930), 'A dietary survey of 607 families in seven cities and towns in Scotland', *Lancet*, 13/9/30, 594–8.

Owen, A.D.K. (1933), *A survey of the standard of living in Sheffield*, Sheffield: Sheffield Social Survey Committee.

Padley, R. (1940), 'The exodus', in R. Padley and M. Cole, eds, *Evacuation survey: a report to the Fabian Society*, London: George Routledge and Sons, 36–55.

Peckham, C., Stark, O. and Moynihan, C. (1985), 'Obesity in schoolchildren: is there a case for screening?', *Public Health*, 99, 3–9.

Peden, G.C. (1983), 'The Treasury as the central department of government, 1919–39', *Public Administration*, 61, 371–85.

Peden, G.C. (1985), *British economic and social policy: Lloyd George to Margaret Thatcher*, Oxford: Philip Allan.

Pelling, M. (1983), 'Medicine since 1500', in P. Corsi and P. Weindling, eds, *Information sources in the history of science and medicine*, London: Butterworth Scientific, 379–407.

Petty, E.C. (1987a), 'Food, poverty and growth: the application of nutrition science', *Bulletin of the Society for the Social History of Medicine*, 40, 37–40.

Petty, E.C. (1987b), 'The impact of the newer knowledge of nutrition: nutrition science and nutrition policy 1900–39', University of London Ph.D. thesis.

Pickstone, J. (1985), *Medicine and industrial society: a history of hospital development in Manchester and its region 1752–1946*, Manchester: Manchester University Press.

Pilgrim Trust (1938), *Men without work*, Cambridge: Cambridge University Press.

Plimmer, R.H.A. (1940), 'The newer knowledge of nutrition in relation to wartime food', *Public Health*, 53, 194–6.

Political and Economic Planning (1937), *Report on the British health services*, London: Political and Economic Planning.

Porter, R. (1985a), 'The patient's view: doing medical history from below', *Theory and Society*, 14, 175–98.

Porter, R. (1985b), 'Introduction', in R. Porter, ed., *Patients and practitioners: lay perceptions of medicine in pre-industrial society*, Cambridge: Cambridge University Press, 1–22.

Price, R. and Bain, G.S. (1988), 'The labour force', in A.H. Halsey, ed., *British social trends since 1900: a guide to the changing social structure of Britain*, London and Basingstoke: Macmillan, 162–201.

Pritchard, D.G. (1963), *Education and the handicapped 1760–1960*, London: Routledge & Kegan Paul.

Public Health (1895), 'School closure for measles', *Public Health*, 7, 263–4.

Public Health (1908a), 'The position of the School Doctor in the Society of Medical Officers of Health', *Public Health*, 21, 173.

Public Health (1908b), 'The medical inspection of schoolchildren', *Public Health*, 21, 185–8.

Public Health (1919a), 'Remuneration of Medical Officers of Health', *Public Health*, 32, 49–50.

Public Health (1919b), 'Ministry of Health Bill 1918: memorandum by Society of Medical Officers of Health', *Public Health*, 32, 51–2.

Public Health (1922), 'The school medical service', *Public Health*, 36, 57–9.

Public Health (1925), 'School health administration', *Public Health*, 38, 217–21.

Public Health (1937), 'Tests of vitamin A deficiency', *Public Health*, 51, 63.

Public Health (1941a), 'Ill-fed families', *Public Health*, 54, 204–5.

Public Health (1941b), 'School meals', *Public Health*, 55, 30.

Public Health (1942), 'The school medical service', *Public Health*, 55, 187.

Public Health (1946), 'Hygiene in the schools and the school health service', *Public Health*, 59, 103–5.

Public Health (1971), 'Cinders no longer?', *Public Health*, 85, 95–8.

Public Health (1972), 'The future of school health', *Public Health*, 86, 105–7.

Public Health (1977), 'Courting disaster', *Public Health*, 91, 64–6.

Richards, H.M. (1902), 'The sanitary control of schools, with special reference to the Education Bill', *Public Health*, 16, 121–36.

Robertson, A.B. (1972a), 'State education and the welfare of schoolchildren: sources for a study of the overpressure controversy 1880–90', *Education Libraries Bulletin*, 15, 20–29.

Robertson, A.B. (1972b), 'Children, teachers and society: the overpressure controversy 1880–86', *British Journal of Educational Studies*, 20, 315–23.

Routh, G. (1980), *Occupation and pay in Great Britain 1906–79*, London and Basingstoke: Macmillan.

Rowntree, B.S. (1902), *Poverty: a study of town life* (2nd edn), London: Macmillan.

Royal College of Physicians (1903), *Annals of the Royal College of Physicians*, 43, 92–4, 119.

Royal Swedish Committee (1907), *Some features of education in Sweden, with special reference to hygienic conditions*, Stockholm: P.A. Norstedt and Sons.

Sayer, E. (1904), 'The deterioration of vision during school age', *British Medical Journal*, 8/5/04: 1418–20.

Searle, G.R. (1971), *The quest for national efficiency: a study in British social and political thought 1899–1914*, Oxford: Blackwell.

Seguin, E. (1846), *Traitement moral, hygiène et éducation des idiots et des autres enfants arrières et idiots*, Paris: Baillière.

Selby-Bigge, L.A. (1927), *The Board of Education*, London and New York: G.P. Putnam's Sons, Ltd.

Sheffield Education Committee (1946), *Annual Report of the School Medical Officer for Sheffield 1945*, Sheffield: Sheffield Education Committee.

Sheffield Education Committee (1969), *Annual Report of the School Medical Officer for Sheffield 1968*, Sheffield: Sheffield Education Committee.

Sigerist, H. (1956), *Landmarks in the history of hygiene: the Heath Clark lectures for 1952*, London: Oxford University Press.

Simon, B. (1965), *Education and the labour movement 1870–1920*, London: Lawrence and Wishart.

Simon, B. (1991), *Education and the social order 1940–90*, London: Lawrence & Wishart.

Smith, C.S. (1977), 'Child health: what of the future?', *Public Health*, 91, 305–11.

Smith, F.B. (1988), *The retreat of tuberculosis 1850–1950*, London: Croom Helm.

Smith, F.B. (1990), *The people's health 1830–1910* (2nd edn), London: Weidenfeld & Nicolson.

Smith, H.L. (1930–35), *The new survey of London life and labour*, London: P.S. King (9 vols).

Smyth, A.W. (1904), *Physical deterioration: its causes and the cure*, London: John Murray.

Soloway, R. (1982), 'Counting the degenerates: the statistics of race deterioration in Edwardian England', *Journal of Contemporary History*, 17, 137–64.

Steedman, C. (1992), 'Bodies, figures and physiology: Margaret Macmillan and the late nineteenth-century remaking of working-class childhood', in R. Cooter, ed., *In the name of the child: health and welfare 1880–1940*, London: Routledge.

Stevenson, J. (1984), *British society 1914–45*, Harmondsworth: Penguin.

Stewart, C.P. (1948), 'The composition of school meals', *British Journal of Nutrition*, 11, 85–7.

Stiebeling, H.K. (1933), *Food budgets for nutrition and production programs*, Washington: United States Department of Agriculture (Miscellaneous Publications, no. 183).

Stocks, P. (1941), 'Diphtheria and scarlet fever incidence during the dispersal of 1939–40', *Journal of the Royal Statistical Society*, 104, 311–45.

Stocks, P. (1942), 'Measles and whooping cough incidence before and during the dispersal of 1939–41', *Journal of the Royal Statistical Society*, 105, 259–91.

Stott, W.B. (1937), 'A nutrition survey', *Medical Officer*, 57, 259–61.

Supplement to the *British Medical Journal* (1907), 'Matters referred to Divisions –

report on the medical inspection of schoolchildren', Supplement to the *British Medical Journal*, 21/12/07, 342.

Supplement to the *British Medical Journal* (1911), 'Medical inspection and treatment of schoolchildren under the London County Council', Supplement to the *British Medical Journal*, 1/7/11, 24–8.

Supplement to the *British Medical Journal* (1940a), 'Medical profession and reserved occupations', Supplement to the *British Medical Journal*, 2/3/40, 25.

Supplement to the *British Medical Journal* (1940b), 'Conscription', Supplement to the *British Medical Journal*, 13/4/40, 47–8.

Supplement to the *British Medical Journal* (1941), 'Medical man-power: allocation between civilian and military services', Supplement to the *British Medical Journal*, 12/4/41, 43–4.

Supplement to the *British Medical Journal* (1942) [no title], Supplement to the *British Medical Journal*, 25/4/42, 66 [column c].

Szreter, S. (1991), 'The General Register Office and the public health movement in Britain 1837–1914', *Social History of Medicine*, 4, 435–64.

Tanner, J.M. (1962), *Growth at adolescence, with a general consideration of the effects of hereditary and environmental factors upon growth and maturation from birth to maturity*, Oxford: Blackwell Scientific Publications.

Tanner, J.M. (1973), 'Trend towards earlier menarche in London, Oslo, Copenhagen, the Netherlands and Hungary', *Nature*, 243, 95–6.

Tanner, J., Whitehouse, R. and Takaishi, M. (1966), 'Height, weight, height velocity, weight velocity: British children, 1965', *Archives of Disease in Childhood*, 41, 454–71, 613–35.

Thane, P. (1982), *The foundations of the welfare state*, London: Longman.

Thom, D. (1992), 'Wishes, anxieties, play and gestures: child guidance in interwar England', in R. Cooter, ed., *In the name of the child: health and welfare 1880–1940*, London: Routledge, 200–19.

Thomas, C.J. (1904), 'School diphtheria in the metropolis', *British Medical Journal*, 27/8/04: 431–3.

Thomas, C.J. (1908), 'The history and practice of school inspection', *Public Health*, 21, 189–93.

Thompson, A.G.G. (1939), 'Epidemiological aspects of A.R.P. evacuation schemes', *Medical Officer*, 61, 192.

Thompson, A.H. (1906), 'Errors of refraction among children attending elementary schools in London', *British Medical Journal*, 28/7/06, 190–93.

Thorne, L.T. (1904), 'The physical development of the London schoolboy: 1890 examinations', *British Medical Journal*, 9/4/04, 829–31.

Thorne, R.T. (1878), 'Remarks on the origin of infection', *Transactions of the Epidemiological Society of London*, 4, 234–46.

Thorne, R.T. (1888), *On the progress of preventive medicine during the Victorian era, being the inaugural address delivered before the Epidemiological Society of London, Session 1887–8*, London: Shaw.

Tibbits, C. (1932), 'A survey and assessment of school medical services', *Medical Officer*, 48, 141–2.

Times (1880), 'Habitual headache and brain exhaustion', *The Times*, 8/4/1880, 7f.

Times (1904), 'Physical deterioration: Report of the Committee', *The Times*, 29/7/04, 12a–d.

Times (1907a), 'The medical inspection of schoolchildren', *The Times*, 18/6/07, 14d.

Times (1907b), 'County Councils Association', *The Times*, 28/11/07, 6a.

Times (1908a), 'Medical inspection of schoolchildren', *The Times*, 12/2/08, 16f.

Times (1908b), 'Medical inspection of children', *The Times*, 18/3/08, 17f.

Times (1908c), 'Deputation to Minister', *The Times*, 20/3/08, 16f.
Times (1921), 'Death of a Major-General', *The Times*, 16/6/21, 13b.
Times (1925a), 'Mr H.M. Lindsell', *The Times*, 31/1/25, 14f.
Times (1925b), 'Sir John Struthers: Organiser of Scottish education', *The Times*, 26/10/25, 16d.
Times (1935), 'Sir Almeric Fitzroy: the Privy Council', *The Times*, 3/6/35, 16b.
Times (1939), 'Evacuation in wartime', *The Times*, 10/1/39, 9b.
Times (1940), 'Mr J.G. Legge', *The Times*, 19/1/40, 10c.
Times (1971a), 'Division on future of pupil health service', *The Times*, 25/1/71, 2d.
Times (1971b), 'Fear for future of school health service', *The Times*, 27/3/71, 2d.
Times Educational Supplement (1917a), 'A statement of policy', *Times Educational Supplement*, 26/4/17, 149–50.
Times Educational Supplement (1917b), 'An education policy', *Times Educational Supplement*, 3/5/17, 162.
Times Educational Supplement (1917c), 'The school medical service', *Times Educational Supplement*, 4/10/17, 383.
Times Educational Supplement (1918), 'The school medical service', *Times Educational Supplement*, 11/7/18: 293.
Titmuss, R. (1938), *Poverty and population: a factual study of contemporary social waste*, London: Macmillan.
Titmuss, R.M. (1950), *Problems of social policy*, London: HMSO.
Torquay Education Committee (1926), *Annual Report of the School Medical Officer for Torquay for 1925*, Torquay: Torquay Education Committee.
Tuxford, A.W. (1917), 'A measure of physical development in schoolchildren', *School Hygiene*, 8, 65–9.
Waites, B. (1987), *A class society at war: England 1914–18*, Leamington Spa: Berg.
Wall, R. (1988), 'English and German families in the First World War 1914–18', in R. Wall and J. Winter, eds, *The upheaval of war: family, work and welfare in Europe 1914–18*, Cambridge: Cambridge University Press, 43–106.
Waller, P.J. (1983), *Town, city and nation: England 1850–1914*, Oxford: Oxford University Press.
Warrington Education Committee (1935), *Annual Report of the School Medical Officer for Warrington for 1934*, Warrington: Warrington Education Committee.
Warrington Education Committee (1936), *Annual Report of the School Medical Officer for Warrington for 1935*, Warrington: Warrington Education Committee.
Watt, M.G. (1948), 'The development of the school meals scheme', *British Journal of Nutrition*, 11, 77–81.
Wear, A.E. (1925), 'Notes on the school medical service', *Public Health*, 38, 109–12.
Weaver, R. (1950), 'Fluorine and wartime diet', *British Dental Journal*, 88, 231–9.
Webb, S. (1909), 'Twentieth century politics: a policy of national efficiency', in S. Webb and the Fabian Society, eds, *The basis and policy of socialism*, London: The Fabian Society.
Webb, S. and Webb, B. (1929), *English Poor Law history. Part II: The last hundred years*, London: Longman's, Green.
Webster, C. (1982), 'Healthy or hungry "thirties?"', *History Workshop Journal*, 13, 110–29.
Webster, C. (1983a), 'The historiography of medicine', in P. Corsi and P. Weindling, eds, *Information sources in the history of science and medicine*, London: Butterworth Scientific, 29–43.
Webster, C. (1983b), 'The health of the schoolchild during the depression', in N. Parry and D. MacNair, eds, *The fitness of the nation: physical and health education in the nineteenth and twentieth centuries: Proceedings of the 1982 Annual Conference of the History

of Education Society of Great Britain, Leicester: History of Education Society of Great Britain, 70–85.

Webster, C. (1985), 'Health, welfare and unemployment during the depression', *Past and Present*, 109, 204–30.

Webster, C. (1988), *The health services since the War. Vol. 1. Problems of health care: the National Health Service before 1957*, London: HMSO.

Webster, C. (1990), 'Conflict and consensus: explaining the British health service', *Twentieth Century British History*, 1, 115–51.

Welsh Office (1976), *Statistics of education in Wales*, no. 1, Cardiff: HMSO.

Welshman, A.J. (1988), 'The school medical service in England and Wales 1907–39', D.Phil. thesis, University of Oxford.

Westminster Gazette (1904), 'Are we deteriorating? Report of the Departmental Committee: Reply to the alarmists', *Westminster Gazette*, 28/7/04, 10a.

White, A. (1899), 'The cult of infirmity', *National Review*, 34, 236–45.

Whiteside, N. (1987a), 'The social consequences of interwar unemployment', in S. Glynn and A. Booth, eds, *The road to full employment*, London: Allen & Unwin, 17–30.

Whiteside, N. (1987b), 'Counting the cost: sickness and disability among working people in an era of industrial depression', *Economic History Review*, 40, 665–82.

Whitmore, K. and Bax, M. (1982), 'School health in the wilderness', *Health Trends*, 14, 52–5.

Who was who (1947a), *Who was who*, vol. 2, London: A. & C. Black.

Who was who (1947b), *Who was who*, vol. 3, London: A. & C. Black.

Who was who (1952), *Who was who*, vol. 4, London: A. & C. Black.

Wilkin, G.C. (1908), 'Medical inspection of schoolchildren', *British Medical Journal*, 22/2/08, 478.

Wilkins, E.H. (1937), 'A nutrition survey', *Medical Officer*, 58, 54.

Wilkins, E.H. (1943), 'War conditions and the schoolchild', *Medical Officer*, 70, 47.

Wilkinson, J. (1905), 'Medical inspection in day schools', *Public Health*, 18, 225–36.

Wilkinson, R. (1989), 'Class mortality differentials, income distribution and trends in poverty', *Journal of Social Policy*, 18, 307–35.

Williams-Freeman, J.P. (1890), *The effect of town-life on the general health, with especial reference to London*, London: W.H. Allen & Co.

Winter, J. (1979), 'Infant mortality, maternal mortality and public health in Britain in the 1930s', *Journal of European Economic History*, 8, 439–62.

Winter, J. (1983), 'Unemployment, nutrition and infant mortality in Britain, 1920–50', in J. Winter, ed., *The working class in modern British history: essays in honour of Henry Pelling*, Cambridge: Cambridge University Press, 232–56.

Winter, J.M. (1986), *The Great War and the British people*, London: Macmillan.

Winter, J. (1988), 'Some paradoxes of the First World War', in R. Wall and J. Winter, eds, *The upheaval of war: family, work and welfare in Europe 1914–18*, Cambridge: Cambridge University Press, 9–42.

Withnell, A. (1957), 'Medical screening in schools', M.D. thesis, University of Manchester.

Withnell, A. (1958), 'The detection of ear defects in schoolchildren', *Medical Officer*, 99, 5–6.

Wohl, A.S. (1983), *Endangered lives: public health in Victorian Britain*, London: Methuen.

Women's Group on Public Welfare (1943), *Our towns: a close-up: a study made during 1939–42* (2nd edn), London: Oxford University Press.

Woodward, J. and Richards, D. (1977), 'Towards a social history of medicine', in J. Woodward and D. Richards, eds, *Health care and popular medicine in nineteenth-century England: essays in the social history of medicine*, London: Croom Helm, 15–55.

Index